THE CHARTERED INSTITUTE OF MARKETING

Chartered Postgraduate Diploma in Marketing

STUDY TEXT

Analysis and Decision

Valid for assessments up to September 2013

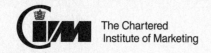

The Chartered
Institute of Marketing

BPP
LEARNING MEDIA

First edition September 2012

ISBN 9781 4453 9150 2

e-ISBN 9781 4453 7623 3

British Library Cataloguing-in-Publication Data
A catalogue record for this book
is available from the British Library

Published by

BPP Learning Media Ltd
Aldine House, Aldine Place
142-144 Uxbridge Road
London W12 8AA

www.bpp.com/learningmedia

Printed in the United Kingdom by Polestar Wheatons

Hennock Road
Marsh Barton Industrial Estate
Exeter, Devon
EX2 8RP

Your learning materials, published by BPP Learning
Media Ltd, are printed on paper obtained from
traceable sustainable sources.

We are grateful to The Chartered Institute of Marketing for
permission to reproduce in this text the unit syllabus.

Lead Author: Adrian Thomas

The Chartered
Institute of Marketing

Contents

1 Studying for The Chartered Institute of Marketing (CIM) qualifications

There are a few key points to remember as you study for your CIM qualification:

(a) You are studying for a **professional** qualification. This means that you are required to use professional language and adopt a business approach in your work.

(b) You are expected to show that you have 'read widely'. Make sure that you read the quality press (and don't skip the business pages), *Marketing*, *The Marketer*, *Research* and *Marketing Week* avidly.

(c) Become aware of the marketing initiatives you come across on a daily basis, for example, when you go shopping look around and think about why the store layout is as it is; consider the messages, channel choice and timings of ads when you are watching TV. It is surprising how much you will learn just by taking an interest in the marketing world around you.

(d) Get to know the way CIM write their exam papers and assignments. They use a specific approach (the Magic Formula) which is to ensure a consistent approach when designing assessment materials. Make sure you are fully aware of this as it will help you interpret what the examiner is looking for (a full description of the Magic Formula appears later).

(e) Learn how to use Harvard referencing. This is explained in detail in our CIM Chartered Postgraduate Diploma Assessment Workbook.

(f) Ensure that you read very carefully all assessment details sent to you from CIM. There are strict deadlines to meet, as well as paperwork to complete for any assignment or project you do. You also need to make sure have your CIM membership card with you at the exam. Failing to meet any assessment entry deadlines or completing written work on time will mean that you will have to wait for the next round of assessment dates and will need to pay the relevant assessment fees again.

2 The Chartered Postgraduate Diploma Syllabus

The Chartered Postgraduate Diploma in Marketing is aimed at Brand Managers, Strategic Marketing Managers, Business Development Managers and middle to senior Marketing Managers. If you are a graduate, you will be expected to have covered a minimum of half your credits in marketing subjects. You are therefore expected at this level of the qualification to demonstrate the ability to manage marketing resources and contribute to business decisions from a marketing perspective and pass the diagnostic entry test to level 7.

The aim of the qualification is to provide the knowledge and skills for you to develop an 'ability to do' in relation to strategic marketing planning and leading its implementation. CIM qualifications concentrate on applied marketing within real work-places.

The complete Chartered Postgraduate qualification is split into two stages. Stage 1 comprises 4 units. Stage 2 is a work-based project that should enable those who pass it, with the relevant experience and continuing professional development, to become Chartered Marketers.

The Stage 1 qualification contains four units:

*   Unit 1 Emerging Themes
*   Unit 2 Analysis and Decision
*   Unit 3 Marketing Leadership and Planning
*   Unit 4 Managing Corporate Reputation

The syllabus, as provided by CIM, can be found below with reference to our coverage within this Study Text.

Unit characteristics – Analysis and Decision

This unit consists of three parts: **Strategic audit**, **Strategic options**, and **Making strategic marketing decisions**. The overall purpose of the unit is to prepare students to undertake a strategic audit of an organisation, assess its capability and capacity to deliver the organisation's business and marketing strategy in a challenging, dynamic and diverse global market place, and to recommend a strategic option, or decision, based on a full critical evaluation of the various options available.

To achieve this aim, students will be expected to carry out the following:

- First they will undertake a sophisticated strategic audit which will help to prioritise the key issues, opportunities and risks facing an organisation in meeting its future objectives. This will be based on a clear and detailed assessment of an organisation and its performance, and the issues and challenges it faces in creating and delivering best value.

- They will use their strategic audit of an organisation to generate strategic options and critically evaluate those options in respect of the key issues faced by the organisation.

- Finally, after exploring the wide range of strategic options available to an organisation to meet its corporate and business strategy, students will need to recommend an option based on, and justified by, a critical evaluation of its suitability in the specific situation.

In doing the above, students should be able to undertake both qualitative and quantitative analysis of the relevant options and be able to make strategic marketing decisions based upon such analysis, justifying decisions and providing reasoned arguments for their recommendations. They will be expected to apply a range of financial and risk models to support their assessments and demonstrate an understanding of how the decisions will support the achievement of the organisation's vision, mission and strategic business and marketing objectives.

Overarching learning outcomes

By the end of this unit students should be able to:

- Undertake a strategic marketing audit, assessing an organisation's competencies, competitive advantage, market performance, customers, competitors, product and service portfolios, positioning, value proposition and market impact

- Assess the impact of external factors on an organisation and its strategic intent and direction

- Utilise the strategic marketing audit to critically evaluate a range of strategic marketing options available to an organisation, including innovation, mergers, acquisitions, partnering, alliances, environmental sustainability and CSR, in order to deliver best value growth and expansion opportunities for the organisation

- Utilise a range of financial and other measurement tools to assess the financial and non-financial benefits of recommended strategic marketing decisions

- Utilise a range of risk assessment tools to critically assess the risk of strategic market decisions and their impact upon an organisation, including financial, corporate and reputational risk.

The Chartered Institute of Marketing

NOTE: All three parts in this unit are of equal weighting. The section weightings within each unit part are shown below.

Part 1 – The strategic audit

SECTION 1 – The strategic marketing audit (weighting 35%)

		Covered in chapter(s)
1.1.1	Utilise a range of techniques, processes and market information to assess the external marketing environment including: • The competitive environment • Customers • Internal politics • Channels (local, international and global) • Market structures	1
1.1.2	Utilise market-based information to critically evaluate an organisation's strategic position within the market place, including consideration of specific positioning issues: • Competitive positioning • Competitive advantage • Value creation • Competitor analysis	1
1.1.3	Utilise a range of tools to critically evaluate an organisation's ability to understand its current customer base and their buying behaviour, in order to be able to develop customer insight and meet their preferences: • Value proposition • Segmental analysis and consumer profiling • Strategic account analysis • Consumer profiling	2
1.1.4	Assess the potential for strategic uncertainty in the external market and the extent to which it involves trends or events, and show how it will impact upon an organisation: • Scenario construction • Market sensing • Forecasting techniques to assess the potential and probability that trends or events will occur • Forecasting techniques utilised to assess timeline for trends and events arising and their impact • Assessing market stability and attractiveness	1

SECTION 2 – The Strategic marketing audit: internal (weighting 35%)

		Covered in chapter(s)
1.2.1	Utilise a range of models and techniques to undertake a strategic audit of the internal environment: ■ Resource and competency audit (physical, human and intangibles) ■ Portfolio analysis ■ Value chain and resource utilisation ■ Innovation audit ■ Cost efficiency ■ Product life-cycle ■ Organisation's vision, mission and values ■ Degree of customer and market orientation ■ Comparative and best practice analysis ■ Core competencies ■ Organisational culture ■ Financial performance	3
1.2.2	Critically evaluate the resource-based view of an organisation and the value of this approach in developing resource and capability to deliver an organisation's vision and mission: ■ Resources, capabilities and competencies ■ The elements of resource-based competitive advantage ■ Knowledge as a resource	4
1.2.3	Critically evaluate the fit between an organisation's culture and its current strategy, and assess its ability to be flexible and agile in a changing marketing environment: ■ Environmental influences on organisational culture ■ Mintzberg's organisational structures ■ Handy's cultural styles	4
1.2.4	Utilise a range of internal information and assessment tools to evaluate an organisation's strengths and weaknesses in order to assess its readiness for development, including an assessment of: ■ Competencies, assets and culture ■ Value chain and value proposition ■ The state of the organisation's financial and non-financial assets	4

SECTION 3 – Developing the organisation's strategic intent and direction (weighting 30%)

		Covered in chapter(s)
1.3.1	Critically evaluate an organisation's current strategic intent, based upon its vision, mission, values and stakeholder expectations: ■ Organisational purpose, mission and values ■ Defining organisational focus ■ Stakeholders analysis ■ Relationship portfolios ■ Organisational configuration ■ CSR and ethics	5
1.3.2	Critically analyse the role of strategic intent in shaping an organisation's strategy development: ■ Strategic intent and strategic vision ■ Strategic intent and leadership ■ Intent and flexibility ■ Strategic opportunism versus strategic drift	5

The Chartered
Institute of Marketing

Part 2 – Strategic options

SECTION 1 – Assessing strategic marketing decisions (weighting 20%)

		Covered in chapter(s)
2.1.1	Critically evaluate the determinants of strategic options and choices: ■ Past and current strategies ■ Organisational capabilities and constraints (financial and non-financial) ■ Financial capabilities and constraints ■ Organisational strengths and weaknesses ■ Product-market opportunities ■ Sources of competitive advantage (Porter) ■ Warfare analogies in strategy (Kotler)	6
2.1.2	Critically evaluate how strategic options can be developed to reflect an organisation's: ■ Value proposition ■ Assets and competencies ■ Business function strategies ■ Functional strategies and programmes ■ Competitive advantage ■ Sustainability	6

SECTION 2 – Strategic options available to a growing organisation (weighting 80%)

		Covered in chapter(s)
2.2.1	Critically evaluate the nature of innovation and new product development (NPD) in marketing and the related factors impacting upon marketing decisions, including ongoing innovation management within an organisation: ■ Importance of innovation ■ Models of innovation ■ Managing innovation	7
2.2.2	Critically evaluate the appropriateness of developing an international marketing strategy for an organisation investing in international markets: ■ Access to low cost materials and labour ■ Economies of scale ■ Avoiding or bypassing trade barriers ■ Access to national/regional incentives eg DFID/Government funding, gateways to strategic markets	8
2.2.3	Critically evaluate a range of issues that impact on an organisation when entering new countries and markets and consider how they may be managed to achieve the organisation's objectives: ■ Extent of global coverage ■ Sequence of countries and timing of entry ■ Value proposition for global markets ■ Standardisation versus customisation	8

		Covered in chapter(s)
2.2.4	Assess the relevance to an organisation of mergers, acquisitions and strategic alliances in growing, expanding and maximising business potential: ■ Motives for strategic alliances ■ Types of strategic alliance ■ Value chain analysis of the competitive potential in alliances, mergers and acquisitions	7
2.2.5	Critically evaluate a range of growth strategies for an organisation: ■ Incremental growth ■ Significant growth ■ The concept of big ideas	7
2.2.6	Critically evaluate the concept of relationship marketing (CRM) as a means of achieving growth and profitability within an organisation: ■ Long term orientation versus transactional marketing ■ Partnering ■ Keeping of promises and developing mutual trust ■ Share of customer's wallet versus market share ■ Customisation ■ Customer loyalty	7
2.2.7	Critically evaluate the development of an organisation's brand and its contribution towards increasing the organisation's value and brand equity: ■ Brand associations ■ Brand identity and image ■ Brand proposition and promise ■ Branding strategies	7
2.2.8	Critically assess the impact of changing an organisation's strategic position within the market place in order to: ■ Reflect the business strategy ■ Resonate with customers ■ Differentiate from competitors ■ Express the values and culture of an organisation in a relevant way ■ Express an organisation's corporate social responsibility (CSR), corporate reputation, sustainability and ethics.	6

The Chartered Institute of Marketing

Part 3 – Making strategic marketing decisions

SECTION 1 – Making and justifying strategic marketing decisions (weighting 20%)

		Covered in chapter(s)
3.1.1	Critically assess strategic alternatives against pre-determined criteria for an organisation, including: ■ Scenario planning – stability versus uncertainty ■ Potential for Return on Investment (ROI) ■ Opportunity to achieve competitive advantage ■ Feasibility, viability and resource ■ Capacity and capability to deliver	4, 6, 9
3.1.2	Assess an organisation's readiness for developing a global strategy including: ■ Strategic importance of the market ■ Position of competitors internationally ■ Cost effectiveness ■ Barriers to trade	8

SECTION 2 – Financial assessment of marketing opportunities (weighting 30%)

		Covered in chapter(s)
3.2.1	Utilising a range of financial tools, assess the financial benefits and risks for an organisation when selecting from its strategic options: ■ Ratios (INITIAL Financial Descriptors), eg Return on Investment (ROI) ■ Investment Appraisal Techniques, eg Payback, Net Present Value (NPV), Discounted Cash Flows (DCF), Internal Rate of Return (IRR) ■ Cost of capital and Weighted Average Cost of Capital (WACC)	9
3.2.2	Critically evaluate the source of funds appropriate to the strategic marketing choice and the long-term sustainability and impact of their utilisation: ■ The concept of the cost of capital ■ Capital Asset Pricing Model (CAPM) ■ Weighted Average Cost of Capital (WACC) ■ Optimal capital structure	9
3.2.3	Assess the impact of the strategic choice upon the shareholder value of organisations in different contexts: ■ The concept of shareholder value-added ■ Cash flow based valuation methods ■ Economic value methods ■ Financial value drivers ■ Timing, sustainability and risk factors in financial valuation	9

		Covered in chapter(s)
3.2.4	Assess the impact on the economic value of an organisation arising from specific decisions on expenditures/cash flows: • The concept of economic value added • Cash flow based valuation methods • Financial value drivers	9

SECTION 3 – Corporate and reputational risk of marketing decisions (weighting 30%)

		Covered in chapter(s)
3.3.1	Utilising a range of risk analysis tools, assess the strategic risks facing an organisation in the selection of strategic alternatives leading to strategic choice: • Risk of strategic uncertainty • Risk of diverting from core business, vision and core competencies • Risk of changing technology and capability • Risk of reputation visibility and vulnerability • Financial risk, including shareholder value, investment, liability and loss	10
3.3.2	Assess the potential for organisational constraints to limit an organisation's success in using any given strategic choice: • Regulation • Structure and competencies • Capital and investment capability • Stakeholder/shareholder engagement and involvement • Competitor activity	10
3.3.3	Assess the risk to an organisation of hostile or declining markets and recommend mitigation strategies, including: • Milk, harvest, divest, liquidate, consolidate • Review margins and develop stronger cost structures • Reduce potential for proliferation of the product and/or brand • Manage share-shifting • Focus on customer	10
3.3.4	Recommend a range of mitigation strategies designed to reduce risks, so as to enhance an organisation's selection of a strategic option: • Scenario planning • Forecasting • Changing approach/direction • Avoidance strategies	10

The Chartered Institute of Marketing

SECTION 4 – Impact analysis of strategic marketing decisions (weighting 20%)

		Covered in chapter(s)
3.4.1	Critically analyse the impact of the priority decisions on an organisation: ■ Strategic vision and direction ■ The organisation's value proposition ■ The key success factors ■ Assets and competencies ■ Positioning, segmentation and targeting ■ Distribution ■ Branding ■ Investment ■ Innovation ■ Manufacturing ■ Increased opportunities and threats	10

3 Assessment

The unit covered by this Study Text (Unit 2 *Analysis and Decision*) is assessed in a three-hour formal examination, with compulsory set tasks which are based upon pre-seen material. This pre-seen material takes the form of a company case study, which will be sent to you prior to the exam. As part of your exam preparation you will need to carry out a detailed analysis of the information contained in the case study.

In order to help you revise and prepare for the exam, we have also written a Chartered Postgraduate Diploma in Marketing Assessment Workbook, which is available either through your usual book retailer or our website: www.bpp.com/learningmedia.

4 The Magic Formula

The Magic Formula is a tool used by CIM to help both examiners write exam and assignment questions, and you, to more easily interpret what you are being asked to write about. It is useful for helping you to check that you are using an appropriate balance between theory and practice for your particular level of qualification.

Contrary to the title, there is nothing mystical about the Magic Formula and simply by knowing it (or even mentioning it in an assessment) will not automatically secure a pass. What it does do, however, is to help you to check that you are presenting your answers in an appropriate format, including enough marketing theory and applying it to a real marketing context or issue.

The Magic Formula for the Chartered Postgraduate Diploma in Marketing is shown below:

Figure A   The Magic Formula for the Chartered Postgraduate Diploma in Marketing

You can see from the pyramid that for the Chartered Postgraduate Diploma marks are awarded in the following proportions:

- Presentation and format – 10%

   You are expected to present your work professionally which means that assignments and projects should **always** be typed. Even in an exam situation attention should be paid to making your work look as visually appealing as possible. CIM will also stipulate the format that you should present your work in. The assessment formats you will be given will be varied and can include things like reports to write, slides to prepare, press releases, discussion documents, briefing papers, agendas and newsletters.

- Concept – 15%

Concept refers to your ability to state, recall and describe marketing theory.

- Application – 30%

Application based marks are given for your ability to apply marketing theories to real life marketing situations. For example, a question may ask you to discuss the definition of marketing and how it is applied within your own organisation. Here you are not only using the definition but are applying it in order to consider the market orientation of the company.

- Evaluation – 45%

Evaluation is the ability to asses the value or worth of something, sometimes through careful consideration of related advantages and disadvantages, or weighing up of alternatives. Results from your evaluation should enable you to discuss the importance of an issue using evidence to justify your opinions.

For example, if you were asked to evaluate whether or not your organisation adopts a marketing approach you should provide reasons and specific examples of why you think they might take this approach, as well as considering why they may not take this approach, before coming to a final conclusion.

5 A guide to the features of the Study Text

Each of the chapter features (see below) will help you to break down the content into manageable chunks and ensure that you are developing the skills required for a professional qualification.

Chapter feature	Relevance and how you should use it
Introduction	Shows why topics need to be studied and is a route guide through the chapter
Syllabus reference	Outlines the syllabus learning outcomes covered in the chapter
Chapter topic list	Study the list, each numbered topic denotes a numbered section in the chapter
Key Term	Highlights the core vocabulary you need to learn
Activity	An application-based activity for you to complete
The Real World	A short case study to illustrate marketing practice
Exam tip/Assessment tip	Key advice based on the assessment
Chapter roundups	Use this to review what you have learnt
Quick quiz	Use this to check your learning
Further reading	Further reading will give you a wider perspective on the subjects you're covering

6 Additional resources

To help you pass Stage 1 of the Chartered Postgraduate Diploma in Marketing we have created a complete study package.

The **Chartered Postgraduate Diploma Assessment Workbook** covers three units of the Chartered Postgraduate Diploma level: Analysis and Decision, Marketing Leadership and Planning and Managing Corporate Reputation. Practice questions and answers and tips on tackling assignments are included to help you succeed in your assessments.

The **Emerging Themes Study Support Text** is a support text written by the CIM Emerging Themes examiner and is designed to guide you through the Emerging Themes unit. It includes guidance on researching themes for different sectors, illustrative examples, publication protocols and best practice on how to present your assessment.

Our A6 set of spiral bound **Passcards** are handy revision cards and are ideal to reinforce key topics for the Analysis and Decision exam.

7 Your personal study plan

Preparing a Study Plan (and sticking to it) is one of the key elements to learning success.

Think about the number of hours you should dedicate to your studies. Guided learning hours will include time spent in lesson, working on fully prepared distance learning materials, formal workshops and work set by your tutor. We also know that to be successful, students should spend **approximately three times** the amount of time spent working through guided learning conducting self study. This means that for the entire qualification with four units you should spend time working in a tutor guided manner and approximately three times that completing recommended reading, working on assignments, and revising for exams. This study text will help you to organise this portion of self study time.

Now think about the exact amount of time you have (don't forget you will still need some leisure time!) and complete the following tables to help you keep to a schedule.

	Date	Duration in weeks
Course start		
Course finish		Total weeks of course:
Examination date	Revision to commence	Total weeks to complete revision:

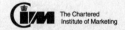 The Chartered Institute of Marketing

Content chapter coverage plan

Chapter	To be completed by	Revised?
1 The external marketing environment		
2 Understanding the customer base		
3 The internal marketing environment		
4 Developing organisational capability		
5 Developing strategy		
6 Assessing strategic marketing options		
7 Growth strategies		
8 International marketing strategy		
9 Financial assessment of marketing opportunities		
10 Corporate and reputational risk		

CHAPTER 1

The external marketing environment

Introduction

This part of the syllabus prepares you for undertaking a strategic audit of an organisation and the assessment of how far the organisation is able to deliver its strategic objectives and create value.

Organisations interact with their environment, and there are many factors in the macro-environment that can affect an organisation and the decisions its managers take. The PEST (or PESTEL) model can be used to help analyse these factors.

Each firm is positioned differently in each particular market and in the industry as a whole, and so will require its own market analysis (section 1). Each industry contains companies aiming to offer similar satisfaction to customers. However, each company has a unique profile compared to its competitors. Market analysis and customer analysis show what companies and industries are competing for.

Identifying who your competitors are is easier said than done, as competition exists outside any particular industry. While competitors are important, only paying customers can determine which firms have competitive advantage with their particular strategic position (section 2).

A wide variety of techniques and tools are available (section 3) to deal with the uncertainty inherent in modern business markets.

Topic list

Assessing the external environment (1)

Evaluating the current strategic position (2)

Strategic uncertainty (3)

1.1.1	Utilise a range of techniques, processes and market information to assess the external marketing environment including:
	▪ The competitive environment
	▪ Customers
	▪ Channels (local, international and global)
	▪ Market structures
1.1.2	Utilise market-based information to critically evaluate an organisation's strategic position within the market place, including consideration of specific positioning issues:
	▪ Competitive positioning
	▪ Competitive advantage
	▪ Value creation
	▪ Competitor analysis
1.1.4	Assess the potential for strategic uncertainty in the external market and the extent to which it involves trends or events, and show how it will impact upon an organisation:
	▪ Scenario construction
	▪ Market sensing
	▪ Forecasting techniques to assess the potential and probability that trends or events will occur
	▪ Forecasting techniques utilised to assess timeline for trends and events arising and their impact
	▪ Assessing market stability and attractiveness

1 Assessing the external environment

A marketing-orientated organisation looks outwards to the environment in which it operates, so that it can take advantage of **opportunities** which arise, and minimise the potential **threats** it faces (Jobber, 2010).

The external environment strongly influences what organisations do, and whether they survive and grow. Therefore, marketers and other strategic decision-makers and planners must take account of potential environmental impacts in order to produce plans that are realistic and achievable.

Where international or even global operations are undertaken, it is particularly important to understand that there may be important differences between the environments present in the various regions and countries involved.

1.1 The macroenvironment

We will begin by examining the marketing environment, and looking at some of the external forces which could affect an organisation's ability to operate effectively in providing goods and services for its customers.

In this respect it is useful to distinguish between the macroenvironment and the microenvironment.

The **macroenvironment** consists of the broad forces which affect not only individual organisations but also the other actors in the microenvironment (Jobber, 2010). These macroenvironmental factors include politics, the economy, society and culture and technological developments, and are often described through 'PEST' analysis.

The **microenvironment** consists of the actors in an organisation's immediate environment which affect its ability to operate effectively in its chosen markets (Jobber, 2010). The key elements of the microenvironment are: customers, competitors, distributors and suppliers.

 The Chartered Institute of Marketing

Figure 1.1 provides an overview of the environmental context in which organisations operate.

Figure 1.1   The external environment

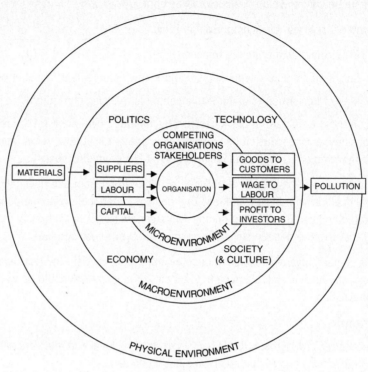

PEST analysis

The mnemonic 'PEST' stands for political, economic, social and technological, and is often used for analysing the macroenvironment, to help an organisation identify the opportunities and threats posed by its environment.

Increasing public concern for the natural environment, corporate social responsibility and sustainability in recent years has led to the inclusion of a second 'E' in the mnemonic; standing for 'environment'. Equally, when legal matters are now given their own heading, the mnemonic becomes expanded to 'PESTEL.'

Figure 1.2   Macro-environmental influences on an organisation

Macro-environmental influences

Political

Government policies affect national economies, and governments are responsible for enforcing and creating a stable framework in which business can be done.

Government policies can be important in providing:

- Physical infrastructure (eg transport).

- Social infrastructure (education, welfare, law enforcement, equal opportunities)

- Market infrastructure (enforceable contracts, policing corruption).

The current global financial crisis has also highlighted how important the relationship between political forces and businesses is, because it has forced governments to support banks financially, and even, in the case of the British government, acquire the failing Northern Rock building society.

Organisations also have to be alert to the potential implications of political change. For example, a change in the political party in office could lead to a change in national economic policies, or the extent to which governments intervene in the economy. More generally, political stability (or instability) in a country can also affect the macro-economic environment in which a business operates.

In this context, organisations need to be aware of political risk: the risk that political factors will invalidate their strategy or could severely damage it. Examples of political risk could be war, civil unrest, corruption or nationalisation.

Economic

The economic environment affects organisations at national and international level, both in the general level of economic activity and in particular variables, such as:

- Inflation and unemployment

- Interest rates

- Exchange rates

- Tax levels

- Business cycles and trends in national income

- International trade

Social and cultural factors

The social and cultural environment features long-term social trends and people's beliefs and attitudes.

Demographics (eg birth and death rates, average age, ethnicity) and **culture** are important for understanding the market, and developing marketing strategies.

Other important social factors include:

- Income distribution

- Attitudes to work and leisure

- Lifestyle choices

Changes in social trends can affect the demand for an organisation's products or services, and can affect the availability and willingness of individuals to work.

The Chartered Institute of Marketing

Technology

Developments in technology can affect all aspects of business, through reducing costs, improving quality and leading to innovation and new product development. Technological developments can result in new:

- Products and services (eg MP3 players; e-readers)

- Methods of providing products and services (eg online shopping)

- Sales channels (e-commerce) and media for communication (eg Internet)

- Way to analyse markets (eg database systems to enable data mining)

- Organisation structures to exploit technology (eg remote working; greater integration across the supply chain)

- According to some reports, 10 million e-Readers were sold in 2010, with market shares at 60% (Kindle) and 35% (Sony). In the summer of 2012, Amazon announced that, for the first time in the UK, digital reading had overtaken demand for the printed versions, with 114 Kindle eBooks sold for every 100 hardback, or paperback, books, something that already happened two years earlier in the US.

Environmental

The physical environment can be important as a source of resources, but organisations also need to consider the impact that their operations have on the physical environment. Environmental protection has become a key aspect of corporate social responsibility, and with businesses coming under increasing pressure to improve their environmental performance. However, while some aspects of the growing desire to protect the environment can be seen as threats (for example, increased taxes being levied on air travel) others can be seen as opportunities (for example, increased demand for environmentally friendly products).

Legal

There are a range of legal factors which can affect organisations:

Table 1.1   **Range of legal factors which can affect organisations**

Factors	Examples
General legal framework	Basic ways of doing business; negligence proceedings; ownership; rights and responsibilities, property
Criminal law	Theft; insider dealing; bribery; deception; industrial espionage
Company law	Directors and their duties; reporting requirements; takeover proceedings; shareholders' rights; insolvency
Employment law	Trade Union recognition; possible minimum wage; unfair dismissal; redundancy; maternity; Equal Opportunities
Health and Safety	Fire precautions; safety procedures (for workers, or in relation to products sold)
Data protection	Use of information about employees and customers
Marketing and sales	Laws to protect consumers (eg refunds and replacement, 'cooling off' period after credit agreements); what is or isn't allowed in advertising
Environment	Pollution control; waste disposal
Tax law	Payment of company and personal taxes
Competition law	Laws relating to acquisitions and mergers to prevent monopolistic profits; prevention of collusion and cartels

> ▶ **Exam tip**
>
> While PEST (or PESTEL) provide a useful checklist for analysing macro-environmental factors, remember that in the real word these factors are often interlinked. Developments and changes in the external environmental can often have implications for more than one factor. In particular, political and economic issues can often be closely linked.
>
> However, it is more important that you recognise the relevant factors which could have an impact on an organisation and its strategies, rather than spending time allocating them to the correct category.
>
> Also, remember that PEST analysis is only concerned with the **external environment**, not the internal strengths and weaknesses, or capabilities, or an organisation.

The Chartered
Institute of Marketing

1.2 The microenvironment

As well as analysing the opportunities and threats presented by the macroenvironment, organisations also need to monitor their more immediate environment (the microenvironment), and the opportunities and threats presented by customers, competitors, distributors and suppliers.

We will look at customers, competitors and distributors in more detail later in this chapter.

1.3 Market analysis

'An organisation has to understand the nature of the relationships within its industry, in order to allow the enterprise to develop strategies to gain advantage of the current relationships.' Drummond *et al* (2008) p26

The following table illustrates how a thorough market analysis will be made up of a range of factors.

Table 1.2   Factors of market analysis

Statistical data	2010	2011	2012 (forecast)
Company/SBU data			
Market name			
Unit sales			
£ sales			
Profitability			
Market data			
Market size			
Market share			
No. of main customers			
No. of dealers/distributors			
Concentration ratio			
Qualitative data	2010	2011	2012 (forecast)
Environmental factors			
Critical success factors			
Growing/stable/declining			
Key competitors and their strategies			
Future competitors			
Segmentation opportunities			
Ease of entry			

We can expand upon some elements of the above checklist.

- **Market size.** This refers to both actual and potential (forecast) size. A company cannot know whether its market share objectives are feasible unless it knows the market's overall size and the position of competitors. Forecasting areas of growth and decline is also important.

- **Customers.** The analysis needs to identify who the customers are, what they need, and their buying behaviour (where, when and how they purchase products or services). This will help to point out opportunities.

  Organisations need to monitor changing customer tastes, lifestyles, behaviours, needs and expectations so that they can continue to meet customer needs effectively, and possibly also seek out new customer needs which have not key been met.

- **Distributors**. The company will need to evaluate its current arrangements for delivering goods or services to the delivering customer. Changes in distribution channels can open up new fields of opportunity (eg the internet).

1.4 Market structures and the competitive environment

In order to trade in a market it is vital to have a detailed knowledge of the market structure and behaviour. Knowledge of the composition, profile and behaviour of the market is fundamental to marketing, whether domestic or internationally based. Typically, information is required on the following points:

- Who are the main **customers**? How, why, where, when and how much do they buy?

- What are the main **channels of distribution** used in such markets? Who are the main distributors, agents etc? Do reciprocal or other possibly limiting trading practices exist that could hamper market entry?

- What **product** attributes, specifications and developments are there in the market?

- Who are the main **suppliers** to the market? What are their relative positions, shares, strengths and weaknesses, strategies and performance?

- Are there significant **geographic variations** in customer requirements, distribution costs, product use, and promotional needs?

- What facilities are there for **promoting** the product into the market? What is the effectiveness of the various forms of promotion and media available?

- What is the **size** of the total market and potential target segments? How durable is the market? For example, is it likely to disappear in adverse economic or political conditions?

In discussing competition, Porter (2004) distinguishes between factors that characterise the nature of competition:

- **In one industry compared with another** (eg in the chemicals industry compared with the clothing retail industry) and make one industry as a whole potentially more profitable than another (ie yielding a bigger return on investment).

- **Within a particular industry**. These relate to the competitive strategies that individual firms might select. For example, do firms seek to differentiate themselves from their competitors on the basis of quality or service, or do they try to produce their products or service at a lower cost than any of their competitors can manage?

▶ **Exam tip**

Five competitive forces influence the state of competition in an industry, which collectively determine the profit (ie long-run return on capital) potential of the industry as a whole. **Learn them**.

1 The threat of new entrants to the industry
2 The threat of substitute products or services
3 The bargaining power of customers
4 The bargaining power of suppliers
5 The rivalry among current competitors in the industry

 The Chartered Institute of Marketing

Aaker & McLoughlin (2010) give examples of each of the factors listed above.

Threat of new entrants

The level of threat depends upon the size and nature of the barriers to entry. Such barriers include required capital investment (eg mobile phone networks), economies of scale (such as Microsoft enjoys), distribution channels (such as Henkel or Danone's access to customers which is not easily duplicated) and product differentiation (Singapore Airlines and Mandarin Oriental hotels have highly differentiated product offerings based on Asian service culture).

Substitutes

Mobile phones have become substitutes for home land lines. Online music availability threatens more traditional music stores. E-mail also presents a threat to some portions of courier companies' express delivery markets.

Customer power

When customers have more power (by size of purchase, or the presence of alternatives) they can force prices down. Wal-Mart has enormous power over its suppliers, meaning it can dictate prices and product specifications. If suppliers resist, Wal-Mart is usually able to find others willing to comply. Approximately 15% of Procter & Gamble sales go through Wal-Mart (and significantly more for some product categories) so even a company as large at P&G is subject to customer bargaining power.

Supplier power

The oil industry is powerful enough to influence profits in its customer industries, because it is either too expensive, or currently impossible, to convert from oil to another energy supply.

Existing competitors

The intensity of competition from existing competitors will depend on several factors including:

- The number of competitors and their size

- How similar competitors' product offerings and strategies are

- The existence of high fixed costs. (Industries with high fixed costs – such as telecommunications or airlines – experience severe price cutting if there is overcapacity and firms are trying to fill capacity.)

- The size of exit barriers (such as specialised assets or long-term contract commitments)

One major factor in the shakeouts which occurred in many industries during and after the financial crisis of 2008/9 was an excessive number of competitors. Easy access to capital and buoyant levels of consumer demand had lowered barriers to entry and attracted competitors into industries, and they were initially able to succeed, even with products with low levels of differentiation. However, consumer demand fell, and they were not able to sustain their positions.

1.5 Customers

Customers are particularly important in any marketing analysis since they are at the centre of the marketing philosophy, and the marketer's task is to satisfy the needs and expectations of customers better than competitors.

However, it is a curious fact that most customers are not worth selling to! The loyal, long-term customer that pays full price and requires little special service attention is the ideal – but very few customers fall into this category. Nevertheless, it is appropriate to target this class of customer specifically rather than simply to aim for a large customer base.

Desirable customers display four important characteristics. They are:

- **Strategic** in that their needs match the company's core capabilities
- **Significant** in terms of their size or potential for growth
- **Profitable**
- **Loyal**

To satisfy customers, organisations need to know how they behave, and why they take the purchasing decisions they do. A number of models and theories exist to explain the dynamics of the 'not always rational' customer's behaviour.

THE REAL WORLD

Capital One's competitive advantage comes from its strength in gathering and using data. 'It is the best data mining shop anywhere in the US', is the assessment of Eric Clemons, Professor of Marketing at Wharton Business School at the University of Pennsylvania.

Capital One's special skill is spotting the patterns that identify 'micro-segments' in the market for consumer credit.

Capital One pioneered fact-based decision making in its lending operations, based on the analysis of large data sets. Previously, credit cards were only issued to customers who had a sound history of repayments, and loans were only offered to borrowers who had collateral to secure the loans.

However, Capital One changed the approach to decision-making, by using data to determine credit worthiness. Its strategy was based on the premise that customers without a credit history could still have the potential to be good borrowers. The most obvious example here is a recent college graduate, with limited capital and a student debt, but with the potential to go on an make a successful business career.

To support its decision-making, Capital One created a huge data warehouse which it uses to conduct tests and experiments to find financially sound offers for different market segments.

1.5.1 What influences customer behaviour?

Customers are subject to a wide range of influences, including their own needs and attitudes; and cultural and social conditioning.

Understanding customer behaviour assists effective marketing management. However, there are many influences on customer behaviour and so the outcome in terms of purchasing decisions can be very difficult to understand from a rational viewpoint. Emotional and rational influences intertwine and lead to purchase outcomes which can seem illogical even to the buyer.

Buyer behaviour models aim to help the marketing manager to understand the buying process, so as to select a marketing strategy which is most applicable to the specific situation. One of these is the Howard-Sheth model.

Figure 1.3   Buyer behaviour (based on Howard-Sheth model)

Source: Adapted from Howard, J. and Sheth, N. (1969) Theory of Buyer Behaviour

Elements in the Howard-Sheth model

■ **Inputs**. Information inputs about the alternative services available include both rational and emotional elements.

■ **Behavioural determinants**. These elements include the existing predispositions of the purchaser which have been influenced by culture, socio-economic group, family and personality factors, amongst others. This element plays a larger role in major or otherwise significant purchase decisions.

■ **Perceptual reaction**. Information from inputs is not accepted at face value but interpreted. For example, an individual is likely to value information more highly if it has been actively sought than if it has been passively received (from TV advertisements for example).

■ **Processing determinants**. These are the factors affecting how the information gathered is evaluated.

■ **Inhibitors**. There are external constraints on actual or potential purchase behaviour.

■ **Outputs**. The outcome of the complex process of interacting elements may be a purchase decision, a decision not to buy or a decision to delay buying.

Eleanor Plantagenet works for Mast, Rick, Tree and Tee, an advertising agency which is beginning to fall on hard times. For example, Bill Mast (the MD) has had to make do with a cheaper company car. There are ominous rumours about making the agency 'leaner and fitter', 'optimising the agency's human resources' and 'delayering'. Eleanor assumes that all this means possible redundancy for people like her, although the managing director has denied all such rumours.

Mortgage payments account for 25% of Eleanor's post-tax monthly salary. Her husband is a freelance financial journalist. His earnings are erratic, but he has recently been commissioned to write a book for the non-specialist reader about the single European currency. They have two children. They invested an inheritance of £15,000 in the Carlowe Bowes saving scheme but the scheme was run by a fraudster, and they lost all their money. Both Eleanor and her husband are hard-working individuals with severe demands on their time. Eleanor earns significantly more than her husband.

One evening, Eleanor's husband tells her of a new financial services product offered by the International Bank of Canonbury. It offers redundancy insurance. This means that Eleanor will be paid £100 per month of unemployment (up to 12 months) for every £5 invested per month, to a maximum monthly benefit of £1,000. No benefit will be paid if Eleanor becomes unemployed within six months of taking out the policy.

Identify the behavioural determinants, inhibitors, inputs, possible perceptual reactions processing determinants and outputs (as in the Howard-Sheth model) in the above situation.

'**Understanding the customer base**' is the subject of Chapter 2, where we also consider the importance of market segmentation and target marketing.

1.6 Distribution and distribution channels

Whilst organisations have to produce products that customers want, and sell them at a price customers are prepared to pay, the products also have to be available in an adequate quantity, at a convenient location and time in order for the customer to buy them. An organisation could have a superior product or service to its competitors, but if it fails to put its product in front of the right customers, it is unlikely to be successful. This highlights the importance of distribution in the marketing process. However, it is also reiterates the importance of organisations knowing their customers: for example, where they buy, and how they prefer to buy.

Different customers in different markets are likely to have different buying habits and expectations. For example, a busy professional consumer will appreciate an online sales channel for grocery shopping. However, an IT manager considering a complex product is likely to require face-to-face contact with a (potential) supplier so that they can discuss technical details and requirements and build a long-term relationship with the seller.

1.6.1 Points in the chain of distribution

In order for a product to be distributed a number of basic functions usually need to be fulfilled.

- The **transport** function may be provided by the supplier, the distributor or may be sub-contracted to a specialist. For some products, such as perishable goods, transport planning is vital.

- For production planning purposes, an uninterrupted flow of production is often essential, so **stocks of finished goods** accumulate and need to be stored, incurring significant costs and risks. For consumer goods, holding stock at the point of sale is very costly; the overheads for city centre retail locations are prohibitive. A good stock control system is essential, designed to avoid stockouts while keeping stockholding costs low.

- As production has tended to become centralised in pursuit of economies of scale, the need to understand **local markets** has grown, particularly when international marketing takes place. The intricacies and idiosyncrasies of local markets constitute key marketing information.

- While major **promotional campaigns** for national products are likely to be carried out by the supplier, the translation of the campaign to local level is usually the responsibility of the local distributor, often as a joint venture.

The Chartered
Institute of Marketing

- **Presentation and display** of the product at the local level is often a function of the local distributor. Specialist help from merchandisers can be bought in but decisions on layout and display need to be taken by local distributors, often following patterns produced centrally.

1.6.2 Points in the chain of distribution

- **Retailers**. These are traders operating outlets which sell directly to households. They may be classified in a number of ways.
    - Type of goods sold (eg hardware, furniture)
    - Type of service (self-service, counter service)
    - Size
    - Location (rural, city-centre, suburban shopping mall, out-of-town shopping centre)
    - Independent retailers (including the local corner shop, although independents are not always as small as this)
    - Multiple chains, some of which are associated with one class of product while others are 'variety' chains, holding a wide range of different stocks
    - Still others are voluntary groups of independents, usually grocers.

- **Wholesalers**. These are intermediaries who stock a range of products from competing manufacturers to sell on to other organisations such as retailers. Many wholesalers specialise in particular products. Most deal in consumer goods, but some specialise in industrial goods, such as steel stockholders and builders' merchants.

- **Distributors and dealers.** These are organisations which contract to buy a manufacturer's goods and sell them to customers. Their function is similar to that of wholesalers, but they usually offer a narrower product range, sometimes (as in the case of most car dealers) the products of a single manufacturer. In addition to selling on the manufacturer's product, distributors often promote the products and provide after-sales service.

- **Agents.** Agents differ from distributors in that distributors buy the manufacturer's goods and re-sell them at a profit, whereas agents do not purchase the manufacturer's goods, but earn a commission on whatever sales they make.

- **Franchisees.** These are independent organisations which, in exchange for an initial fee and (usually) a share of sales revenue, are allowed to trade under the name of a parent organisation. Most fast food outlets are franchises.

- **Multiple stores** (eg supermarkets) buy goods for retailing direct from the producer, many of them under their 'own label' brand name.

1.6.3 Types of distribution channel

> **Key terms**
>
> **Direct distribution** means the product going directly from producer to consumer without the use of a specific intermediary. These methods are often described as active since they typically involve the supplier making the first approach to a potential customer. Direct distribution methods generally fall into two categories: those using media such as the press, leaflets and telephones to invite response and purchase by the consumer and those using a sales force to contact consumers face-to-face.
>
> **Indirect distribution** is a system of distribution, common among manufactured goods, which makes use of intermediaries; wholesalers, retailers or perhaps both. In contrast to direct distribution, these methods are often thought of as being passive in the sense that they rely on consumers to make the first approach by entering the relevant retail outlet.

Choosing distribution channels is important for any organisation, because once a set of channels has been established, subsequent changes are likely to be costly and slow to implement. Distribution channels fall into one of two categories: **direct** and **indirect** channels.

The most fundamental question an organisation needs to ask when choosing their channel strategy is whether they want to sell directly to the ultimate consumer, or whether they want to use **channel intermediaries**, such as retailers and/or wholesalers (Jobber, 2010).

In building up efficient channels of distribution, a manufacturer must consider several factors.

- What are the alternative distribution channels available?

- How many intermediate stages should be used and how many dealers at each stage?

- What support should the manufacturer give to the dealers? It may be necessary to provide an after-sales and repair service, and regular visits to retailers' stores. The manufacturer might need to consider advertising or sales promotion support, including merchandising.

- To what extent does the manufacturer wish to dominate a channel of distribution? A market leader might wish to ensure that its market share is maintained, so that it could, for example, offer exclusive distribution contracts to major retailers.

- To what extent does the manufacturer wish to integrate its marketing effort up to the point of sale with the consumer? Combined promotions with retailers, for example, would only be possible if the manufacturer dealt directly with the retailer (rather than through a wholesaler).

1.6.4 Factors in channel design decisions

Customers

The number of potential customers, their buying habits and their geographical locations are key influences. The use of mail order for those with limited mobility (rural location, illness) is an example of the influence of customers on channel design. Marketing industrial components to the car industry needs to take account of the geographic distribution of the car industry in the UK. The growth of internet trading, both in consumer and business-to-business markets, has been built on the rapid spread of fast internet access.

Product characteristics

Some product characteristics have an important effect on the design of the channel of distribution.

1 **Perishability**

   Fresh fruit and newspapers must be distributed very quickly or they become worthless. Speed of delivery is therefore a key factor.

2 **Customisation**

   Customised products tend to be distributed direct. When a wide range of options is available, sales may be made using demonstration units, with customised delivery to follow.

3 **After-sales service/technical advice**

   Extent and cost must be carefully considered, staff training given and quality control systems set up. Training programmes are often provided for distributors by suppliers.

4 **Franchising**

   Franchising has become a popular means of growth both for suppliers and for franchisees who carry the set-up costs and licence fees. The supplier gains additional outlets quickly and exerts more control than is usual in distribution.

Distributor characteristics

The capability of the distributor to take on the distributive functions' already discussed above' is obviously an important influence on the supplier's choice.

Competitors' channel choice

For many consumer goods, a supplier's brand will sit alongside its competitors' products and there is little the supplier can do about it. For other products, distributors may stock one name brand only (for example, in car distribution) and in return be given an exclusive area. In this case, new suppliers may face difficulties in breaking into a market if all the best distribution outlets have been taken up.

Supplier characteristics

A strong financial base gives the supplier the option of buying and operating their own distribution channel. Boots the Chemist is a prime example. The market position of the supplier is also important: distributors are keen to be associated with the market leader but the third, fourth or fifth brand in a market is likely to find more distribution problems.

1.6.5 Developments in distribution channels

Distribution trends need to be monitored, and digital technologies are having a significant impact on distribution. For example, the Internet has changed the distribution of music and video, and the trend towards downloading music has had a negative impact on music retailers which sells CDs.

Similarly, the growth of internet-based sellers, such as Amazon, has affected bricks-and-mortar bookshops, while the internet is also changing the distribution of newspapers (through making them available online or as mobile applications (apps)).

Other examples of the way digital technologies are changing distribution can be seen in airline booking (with the introduction of e-ticketing), hotel reservations (with online bookings), banking (online banking) and grocery shopping (with the development of home shopping, such as Tesco.com).

THE REAL WORLD

Tesco has operated on in the internet since 1994 and is the UK's largest internet grocery business. In 2000, it formally launched its Tesco.com site, and in 2011 Tesco.com's annual sales had grown to approximately £2.75 billion. In addition to its online grocery business, Tesco has also launched Tesco Direct, its online marketplace for electrical appliances, home furnishings and other non-grocery products.

Financial services. The impact of the Internet is particularly significant in the field of financial services. New intermediaries enable prospective customers to compare the interest rates and prices charged by different organisations for pensions, mortgages, insurance and other financial products. This means that the financial companies are losing control of the marketing of their services, and there is also downward pressure on prices, especially for services which can effectively seen as commodities (eg house and contents insurance).

As a result, Aaker & McLoughlin (2010) point out that when analysis distribution systems, organisations need to consider the following questions:

- What are the trends? What channels are becoming more important? What new channels have emerged or are likely to emerge?

- Who currently has the power in the channel, but how is this likely to change in the light of the trends?

1.6.6 The internet and channel intermediaries

The internet presents a radical challenge to traditional distribution models because allow product/service suppliers to interact directly with their customer, instead of using intermediaries, such as high street retail shops, travel agents or insurance brokers. This change is known as **disintermediation**.

However, as well as disintermediation which has caused the disappearance of some existing intermediaries, the internet has also stimulated the appearance of new intermediaries.

Reintermediation – Reintermediation is the establishment of new intermediary roles for traditional intermediaries that were disintermediated. In some cases, a new intermediary simply replaces a single displaced one, such as Amazon.com replacing retailers. In other cases, a reintermediating entity replaces multiple supply chain elements. These new intermediaries do one of two things:

(a) Provide customers with **new**, **important value-added services** not provided in the new direct customer-supplier relationship. An example is *Kelkoo* which is a shopping/price comparison search engine.

(b) Provide customers with more efficient means of transacting business.

The ever-increasing number of 'hubs', 'portals', 'aggregators', 'clearing houses' and 'exchanges' shows that entirely new ways of doing business are being created. Those organisations (or individuals) clever enough to recognise the opportunities provided by the Web and are reinventing themselves as 'cybermediaries' or 'infomediaries' – intermediaries offering value-added services to consumers and vendors over the Internet.

1.6.7 New types of intermediary

Search engines and directories – search engines, such as *Google* and *Alta Vista* provide search facilities based on data generated by software engines, that search the web. Directories such as *Yahoo* provide a general index of a large variety of different sites.

Portals provide a gateway to the Web and may also offer signposting, selected links and other services to attract users. Examples of Web portals include *Google, MSN* and *Yahoo*.

'E-tailers' or consumer shopping sites such as *Amazon*. While starting as simply a bookshop on the web it has added a variety of products and types of services. By contrast, *Tesco* is an offline retailer which is offering web-based order and delivery services.

Auction sites such as *eBay* support online auctions.

Publisher web sites are traffic generators that offer content of interest to consumers.

Forums, **fan clubs**, and **user groups** can play a large role in facilitating customer-producer feedback and supporting market research.

Financial intermediaries. Any form of e-commerce will require some means of making or authorising payments from buyer to seller. Financial intermediaries such as *PayPal* provide this.

---

2 Evaluating the current strategic position

2.1 Marketing audit

In Section 1 we highlighted the importance of analysing an organisation's environment, and such analysis can be very useful in helping an organisation understand its current strategic position. A marketing audit can also play an important role here.

> ▶ **Key term**
>
> A **marketing audit** is 'a systematic examination of a business's marketing environment, objectives, strategies, and activities, with a view to identifying key strategic issues, problems areas and opportunities.' (Jobber, 2010, p42)

A marketing audit is an important part of marketing planning, and it can provide the basis for future strategies to help improve marketing performance. It also helps answer three key questions in relation to a firm's marketing strategy:

- Where are we now?
- How did we get here?
- Where are we heading?

The answers to these questions depend on an analysis of both the **external** and **internal** environment of a business, invoking models such as PEST analysis and SWOT analysis.

The Chartered
Institute of Marketing

A SWOT analysis is a means of evaluating an organisation's strategic position by identifying its strengths, weaknesses, opportunities and threats. Strengths and weaknesses relate to an organisation's internal resources and capabilities while opportunities and threats relate to external factors.

Importantly though, when evaluating strengths and weaknesses, an organisation should only include those resources and capabilities which would be valued by the customer.

Once a SWOT analysis has been completed, the organisation can then start think how to turn weaknesses into strengths and threats into opportunities. Equally, it should think how it can use its strengths to take advantage of opportunities.

2.1.1 Elements of a marketing audit

Jobber (2010) identifies five aspects of a marketing audit:

1   **Market analysis**. This looks at:

  –   Market size, market growth and trends

  –   **Customer analysis** and buyer behaviour

  –   **Competitor analysis** – competitors' objectives and strategies; market shares and profitabilities; competitors' strengths and weaknesses; barriers to entry

  –   Analysis of different **distribution channels** and their relative strengths and weaknesses

  –   **Supplier analysis** – trends in the supply chain; power of suppliers; strengths and weaknesses of key suppliers

2   **Strategic issues analysis**. This involves considering the suitability of the organisation's marketing objectives in relation to the market place and any changes in the market. Points to consider are likely to include: market segmentation; basis of competitive advantage; core competences; positioning; and product portfolio.

3   **Review of marketing mix effectiveness**: looking at product, price, promotion and distribution

4   **Marketing structure** – including marketing organisation (does the organisation of the marketing department fit with the strategy and the market); marketing training; and intra- and interdepartmental communication (for example, how well does the marketing department communicate with production departments).

5   **Marketing systems**. Three different types of system are considered:

  –   Marketing information systems: What information is provided? Is it sufficient?

  –   Marketing planning systems

  –   Marketing control systems: Can the systems provide an evaluation of marketing campaigns (accurately and on a timely basis)? Do the systems evaluate the key variables affecting company performance?

2.2 Competitive advantage

> ▸ **Key term**
>
> **Competitive advantage**: a business achieves competitive advantage when it earns higher than average profits.

Whatever overall objective is set for a firm – to survive, to create value, to make profit – the key to achieving it lies in the attainment of some form of competitive advantage. Business therefore revolves around the means by which competitive advantage may be attained and sustained. Competitive advantage distinguishes the successful business from the average enabling it to earn an above average level of profit.

There are a number of ways businesses can seek to establish a competitive advantage. For example, Aaker & McLoughin (2007, p233) cite the following examples.

The quality player with the defined product	For example Victorinox Swiss Army knives
The 'value' option	For example Ryanair, Aldi
The innovator	For example Apple
A narrow product focus	For example Ferrari
A target segment focus	For example Hamleys
Being global	For example HSBC

However, overall there are two main kinds of approach to achieving competitive advantage, each encompassing several strands of strategic thinking.

1   **The positioning approach**

The positioning approach to strategy is closely related to the traditional concept of marketing orientation. It starts with an assessment of the commercial environment and positions the business so that it fits with environmental requirements.

2   **The resource-based approach**

The resource-based approach starts with the idea that competitive advantage comes from the possession of distinctive and unique resources.

▶ **Exam tip**

Understand the definition, and the importance, of competitive advantage. Whatever overall objective is set for a firm: to survive, to create value, to make profit; the key to achieving it lies in the attainment of some form of competitive advantage, and all strategic alternatives need to be assessed for their ability to deliver it. Business therefore revolves around the means by which competitive advantage may be attained and sustained. Make no mistake about it: competitive advantage distinguishes the successful business from the average, enabling it to earn an above average level of profit.

2.3 Competitive positioning and target markets

▶ **Key term**

A **target market** is a market or segment selected for special attention by an organisation (possibly served with a distinct marketing mix).

Having analysed the attractiveness of a segment, the firm will choose one or more **target markets**. Marketing policy may be **undifferentiated** (mass), **concentrated** or **differentiated**.

- **Undifferentiated marketing** aims to produce a single product and get as many customers as possible to buy it. Segmentation is ignored.

- **Concentrated marketing** attempts to produce the ideal product for a single segment of the market (eg Rolls Royce cars for the very wealthy).

- **Differentiated marketing** attempts to introduce several versions of a product, each aimed at a different market segment (for example, the manufacture of several different brands of breakfast cereals). The extreme for of differentiated marketing is **micromarketing**.

We will also look at positioning and target markets again in Chapter 2, when we discuss segmentation, targeting and positioning.

2.3.1 Policy options

Having identified distinct market segments, it is necessary to choose which ones to target and how to go about it. Careful consideration must be given to the criteria by which segments will be chosen. **Profitability** is clearly an important consideration but so are **accessibility**, **resources** required and **potential for growth**.

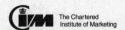

Targeting is a continuing process, since segments change and develop and so do competitors. The company is, to some extent, able to plan and control its own development and it must respond to changes in the market place.

The marketing management of a company may choose one of the following policy options.

Table 1.3   Generic marketing policies

Policy	Comment
Undifferentiated marketing	This policy is to produce a single product and hope to get as many customers as possible to buy it; segmentation is ignored entirely. This is sometimes called **mass marketing**.
Concentrated marketing	The company attempts to produce the ideal product for a single segment of the market (for example, Rolls Royce cars, Mothercare mother and baby shops).
Differentiated marketing	The company attempts to introduce several product versions, each aimed at a different market segment (for example, the manufacture of different styles of the same article of clothing).

Figure 1.4   Marketing policies

The major **disadvantage of differentiated marketing** is the additional costs of marketing and production (more product design and development costs, the loss of economies of scale in production and storage, additional promotion costs and administrative costs and so on). When the costs of differentiation of the market exceed the **benefits** from further segmentation and target marketing, a firm is said to have **over-differentiated**.

The major **disadvantage of concentrated marketing** is the business risk of relying on a single segment of a single market. On the other hand, specialisation in a particular market segment can give a firm a profitable, although perhaps temporary, competitive edge over rival firms.

The choice between undifferentiated, differentiated or concentrated marketing as a marketing strategy will depend on the following factors.

- The extent to which the product and/or the market may be considered **homogeneous**. **Mass marketing** may be sufficient if the market is largely homogeneous (for example, for safety matches).

- The **company's resources** must not be over extended by differentiated marketing. Small firms may succeed better by concentrating on only one segment.

- The product must be sufficiently **advanced in its life cycle** to have attracted a substantial total market; otherwise segmentation and target marketing is unlikely to be profitable, because each segment would be too small in size.

2.3.2 Micromarketing

Segmentation, as part of target marketing, looks certain to play an even more crucial role in the marketing strategies of consumer organisations in the years ahead. The move from traditional mass marketing to **micromarketing** is rapidly gaining ground as marketers explore more cost-effective ways to recruit new customers. This has been brought about by a number of trends.

1. The ability to create large numbers of product variants without the need for corresponding increases in resources is causing markets to become overcrowded.

2. The growth in minority lifestyles is creating opportunities for niche brands aimed at consumers with very distinct purchasing habits.

3. The fragmentation of the media to service ever more specialist and local audiences is denying mass media the ability to assure market dominance for major brand advertisers.

4. The advance in information technology is enabling information about individual customers to be organised in ways that enable highly selective and personal communications.

Such trends have promoted the developments in benefit, lifestyle and geodemographic segmentation techniques outlined. Consumer market segmentation has developed so much in the last few years that the vision of multinational marketers accessing a PC to plan retail distribution and supporting promotional activity in cities across different countries is now a practical reality.

2.3.3 Mass customisation

Micromarketing is made possible by **mass customisation**, which features:

- The huge economies of scale of mass production
- The tailoring of products precisely to the customer's requirements

New manufacturing technology makes this possible. There is less need for a standard product if people's individual preferences can be catered for.

THE REAL WORLD

In 1999, *Levi Jeans* in the US introduced a service whereby customers' measurements were fed through to an automated garment cutting process so, in effect, Levi's had switched from a mass production model to a 'built-for-one' model.

However, this attempt at mass customisation was a failure, and by 2004 Levi's had shut it down. Critics noted that Levi had not managed to turn the customized product into a customized relationship with its customer, such that, for example, re-orders were not easily possible.

Nonetheless, in 2010 Levi came back with a second attempt at mass customization, through a program called Levi's Curve ID. This introduces jeans built around shape, rather than a given size.

Unlike Levi's first experiment with mass customization, users customize their Curve ID online, not in a store. Offering the service via the internet enables Levi to target millions of people instead of the relatively small number who visit selected retail stores.

However, this time Levi isn't engaging completely in mass customization as they are not building the jeans to fit individual measurements. But they are not adopting a one-size-fits-all approach either.

Levi's Vice President of Global Women's Marketing explained: 'Our research showed that 80% of women around the world fall into three distinct body shapes, so one size could never fit all. Our goal is to engage women online with out interactive, custom fit experience that will match them with their perfect Levi's Curve ID fit; whether they are a Slight Curve, Demi Curve or Bold Curve.'

Customers use a 'product configurator' tool to discover their 'Curve ID' so they don't have to try on a number of different pairs of jeans before making a purchase. And the customer's customization settings are saved in their account history so they can easily re-order in future. Levi has realised that allowing for easy repeat purchases is imperative to success in mass customization.

Abridged from blog: '*Levi's second attempt at mass customization*' by treehouselogic, November 4, 2010.

The Chartered Institute of Marketing

2.4 Positioning

Kotler *et al* (2008, p234) highlight that consumers are overloaded with information about products and services. Accordingly, consumers cannot re-evaluate products every time they make a buying decision. 'To simplify the buying process, consumers organise products, services and companies into categories and 'position' them in their minds. A product's position is the complex set of perceptions, impressions and feelings that consumers have for the product compared with competing products.'

However, marketers must also plan positions that will give their products the greatest advantage in selected target markets, and they must design marketing mixes which will create the desired positions.

> ▶ **Key term**
>
> **Positioning** is the act of designing the company's offer and image so that it achieves a distinct and valued place in the target customer's mind.

Positioning can be 'psychological' and 'real'. **Perceptual (or positioning) maps** enable marketers to identify positioning options, by comparing **customers' perceptions** of their products to competing products. The foundation of a **positioning strategy** is to align what the company can do with what customers want. Repositioning is risky and expensive.

2.4.1 Steps in positioning

Step 1   Identify differentiating factors in products or services which provide an organisation with competitive advantage in relation to competitors.

Step 2   Select the most important differences, and select an overall positioning strategy based on them.

Step 3   Communicate, and deliver, the position to the target market.

The value of positioning is that it enables **tactical marketing mix decisions to be made**.

THE REAL WORLD

By 2010, Toyota had established a position as the world's biggest car manufacturer, and the reliability of its vehicles had played a key role in establishing this position.

However, in 2010, Toyota was forced to recall millions of vehicles across the United States, Europe and China because of potential problems with accelerator pedals.

Industry experts warned at the time that the way Toyota handled this recall would determine whether Toyota retained its position, and they pointed out that Toyota had to act openly and rapidly to retain consumers' loyalty and persuade them that reliability and safety is not being sacrificed.

However, analysts also suggested that Toyota's problems indicated potentially bigger problems for the brand. Brand strategic, Simon Middleton, stressed that Toyota must never forget that its appeal is based on reliability. 'Toyota has struggled for a while with that its brand means in the hearts and minds of consumers. And when they [Toyota] hit a problem I'm not convinced the management is sure how to deal with it.... One element of great brands is to be markedly different from your competitors. I haven't been sure for a long time what really made Toyota different, and if it isn't reliability, which is now in question, then what is it?

This point is reinforced by that fact that many of Toyota's cars, with the exception of the eco-friendly Prius, are seen as dull by much of the motoring press. Again, reliability is the main selling point. 'If you take that away' according to the associate editor of Autocar magazine, Hilton Holloway, 'It's unclear why people should buy them.'

Abridged from: '*Recall threatens Toyota's position as top carmaker*', Peter Wilkinson, *CNN*, 10 February 2010

2.4.2 Problems with positioning

How much do people remember about a product or brand?

- Many products are, in fact, very similar, and the key issue is to make them distinct in the customer's mind.

- People remember 'number 1', so the product should be positioned as 'number 1' in relation to a valued attribute.

- Cosmetic changes can have the effect of repositioning the product in the customer's mind. To be effective, however, this psychological positioning has to be reinforced by real positioning.

As **positioning is psychological as well as real**, we can now identify **positioning errors**.

Table 1.4   Problems with positioning

Mistake	Consequence
Under-positioning	The brand does not have a clear identity in the eyes of the customer
Over-positioning	Buyers may have too narrow an image of a brand
Confused positioning	Too many claims might be made for a brand
Doubtful positioning	The positioning may not be credible in the eyes of the buyer

2.4.3 Positioning strategy checklist

Table 1.5   Positioning variables

Positioning variable	Comment
Attributes	Size, for example
Benefit	What benefits we offer
Use/application	Ease of use; accessibility
User	The sort of person the product appeals to
Product category	Consciously differentiated from competition
Quality/price	One should support and validate the other, so that it makes sense to the customer and he understands what he is buying. For example, low quality at a high price is unlikely to sell.

ACTIVITY 1.2

Identify examples of positioning strategies in Table 1.5 above.

2.4.4 Perceptual maps

One simple perceptual map (positioning map) that can be used is to plot brands or competing products in terms of two key characteristics such as price and quality.

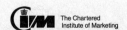
The Chartered
Institute of Marketing

Figure 1.5   Perceptual map showing market positioning (Positioning map)

A perceptual map of market positioning can be used to **identify gaps in the market**. This example might suggest that there could be potential in the market for a low-price high-quality **'bargain brand'**. A company that carries out such an analysis might decide to conduct further research to find out whether there is scope in the market for a new product which would be targeted at a market position where there are few or no rivals.

2.4.5 Mapping positions

We can look at the different competitive positioning strategies an organisation can use by looking at a 3 × 3 matrix of nine different competitive positioning strategies.

Table 1.6   **Price/quality positioning**

Product quality		Product price	
	High price	Medium price	Low price
High	Premium strategy	High-value strategy	Super-value strategy
Medium	Over-charging strategy	Medium-value	Good-value strategy
Low	'Rip off' strategy	Fake company strategy	Economy strategy

The 'natural' combinations of price and quality will be to sell a high quality product at a high price, an average quality product at a medium price, or a low quality product at a cheap price.

However, a company might want to offer a product at a comparatively low price if it is trying to increase its market share (ie, it is pursuing a penetration strategy). For example, a company trying to increase its market share could offer a high quality product at a medium price, or an average quality product at a low price.

By contrast, such a positioning exercise might indicate that some companies are charging a higher price for their products than the quality justifies. Such a strategy is unlikely to be successful in the longer term, so a company in this position will either need to increase the quality of their product, or reduce its price.

Positioning and strategy

Once an organisation has selected what its target segment of a market is, the needs of a targeted segment can be identified, and the marketing mix strategy developed to provide the benefits package needed to satisfy them. Positioning the product offering then becomes a matter of matching and communicating appropriate benefits.

Figure 1.6   Positioning map (sports shoes)

Figure 1.6 indicates that there are a variety of sports shoe products offering distinct positions on the price vs fashion/ functionality spectrum. A firm entering this market could try to establish a unique position, for example, it could offer a high price, ultra-high fashion shoe (at the outer extreme of the top right-hand quadrant.) Possible implications of this might be that the existing product '2' becomes less profitable as fashion-conscious customers switch to the new product; or alternatively, customers may not value the price/fashion mix of the new product, and so sales of product '2' will remain largely unaffected.

2.4.6 Repositioning

Strategic managers must be prepared to deal with under performance and failure. One possible response is repositioning of the market offering.

▶ **Key term**

Repositioning is a competitive strategy aimed at changing position in order to increase market share.

However, this is a difficult and expensive process, since it requires the extensive remoulding of customer perceptions. The danger is that the outcome will be confusion in the mind of the customer and failure to impress the selected new segments.

Table 1.7   Bases for repositioning

Type of position	Comment
Real	Relates to actual product features and design
Psychological	Change the buyer's beliefs about the brand
Competitive	Alter beliefs about competing brands
Change emphasis	The emphasis in the advertising can change over time

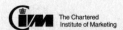
The Chartered Institute of Marketing

2.5 Value creation

One of the crucial points to remember in positioning is that a product's position reflects the value which **customers** perceive it to have.

Ideas of 'value' and 'value creation' lie at the heart of the marketing process. As Kotler *et al* (2008, p53) note:

'Value creation is at the heart of the marketing process. Marketing is the process by which companies create value for customers, and build strong customer relationships in order to capture value from customers in return.'

In this respect, Kotler *et al* (2008) identify that the marketing process involves five steps, of which the first four create value for customers, while the fifth creates value for an organisation. The five steps are as follows:

1 Marketers gain a full understanding of the marketplace and research customer **needs and wants**

2 Marketers design a customer-driven marketing strategy with the goal of **acquiring**, **retaining and growing target customers**. This strategy is base don two key questions: 'What customers will we serve?' and 'How can we best serve them?'

3 Marketers construct a marketing program which delivers superior value. Key elements in this programme will be: **product** and service design (to help build strong brands); **pricing** (to create real value); **distribution** (or **place**; managing distribution channels and supply chains); and **promotion** (communicating the value proposition)

4 Building profitable **customer relationships** and creating customer delight. Customer relationship management is likely to be vital to help build strong relationships with chosen customers.

5 The organisation reaps the rewards of strong customer relationships by **capturing value from customers**: by creating satisfied, loyal customers; and in turn by increasing market share.

2.6 Competitor analysis

'The marketing concept states that, to be successful, an organisation must provide greater customer value and satisfaction than its competitors do' (Kotler & Armstrong, 2012, p92). It is not sufficient for marketers to adapt their products or services to the needs of target customers; in order to gain strategic advantage they have to position their offering more strongly in the minds of consumers than their competitors do.

However, in order to do this, marketers need to analyse their competitors. Competitor analysis helps an organisation understand its competitive advantages/disadvantages compared to its competitors. It can also provide valuable insights into competitors' strategies, which in turn could help an organisation develop its own strategies to achieve (or sustain) competitive advantage over its competitors.

An analysis of individual competitors will cover who they are, their objectives, their strategies, their strengths and weaknesses and how they are likely to respond to an organisation's strategies.

Porter (1980; p47) also highlights the importance of competitor analysis when he argues that 'Competitive strategy involves positioning a business to maximize the value of the capabilities that distinguish it from its competitors. It follows that a central aspect of strategy formulation is perceptive competitor analysis.'

2.6.1 Key questions for competitor analysis

One of the first questions which an organisation needs to ask is: Who are the competitors?

Once it has established this, an organisation then has to establish:

What drives the competitor?

▪ What are its goals or strategic objectives (eg maintaining profitability, building market share, or entering new markets??

- What assumptions does it hold about itself and the industry (eg trends in the market, products and consumers)?

What is the competitor doing and what can it do?

- What strategies is the competitor currently pursuing?

- What are the competitor's strengths and weaknesses? What key resources and capabilities does the competitor have (or not have)?

2.6.2 Customer response profiles

Once an organisation has analysed its competitors' future goals, assumption, current strategies and capabilities, it can begin to ask the crucial questions about how a competitor is likely to respond to any competitive strategy the organisation might pursue. Trying to assess what the competitors' responses are likely to be is a major consideration in making any strategic or tactical decision.

Therefore an organisation needs to ask itself:

- How is the competitor likely to respond to any strategic initiatives which the organisation introduces?

- Will the competitor's response be the same across all products/markets, or might it react more aggressively in some markets than others?

An organisation can build up a competitor response profile to help answer these questions.

Key questions in the **competitor response profile** (Porter, 1980) include:

- Is the competitor satisfied with its current position?
- What strategy shifts or moves is the competitor likely to make?
- Where is the competitor vulnerable?
- What will provoke the greatest and most effective retaliation by the competitor.

Porter (1980) suggests that an organisation could distinguish competitor responses into **offensive moves** (strategic changes initiated by the competitor) and **defensive moves** (responding to other people's strategic changes).

Offensive moves

Key issues which need to be consider here are:

- **Satisfaction with current position** - Based on a comparison of the competitor's goals and its current position, is the competitor likely to try to initiate strategic change?

- **Probable moves** - Based on the competitor's goals, assumptions and capabilities, what are the most likely strategic changes the competitor will make?

- **Strength and seriousness of moves** – Based on analysis of the competitor's goals and capabilities, how significant are the competitor's moves likely to be?

Defensive moves

Similarly, the issues which need to be considered here are:

- **Vulnerability** – Which strategic moves, or other macroeconomic or microeconomic changes would the competitor be most vulnerable to? Which events would have most impact on the competitor's profits?

- **Provocation** – What strategic moves will provoke a retaliation from competitors even if that retaliation is costly for the competitor? In other words, what strategic moves would threaten a competitor's goals or strategic position so fundamentally that it would have to respond, even if it doesn't want to.

- **Effectiveness of retaliation** – Which strategic moves or events would the competitor be least able to react to quickly and effectively given its existing capabilities, strategies and goals?

By analysing these issues an organisation can then consider what its most effective strategy is likely to be, in the context of the competitors' likely response to it.

A key consideration in making any strategic or tactical decision is competitors' response is likely to be. Jobber (2010) points out that a major objective of competitor analysis is to be able to predict competitors responses to market and competitive changes.

How is the competitor likely to respond to any strategic initiatives an organisation introduces?

Will the competitor's response be the same across all products/markets, or might it react more aggressively in some markets than others?

THE REAL WORLD

Southwest Airlines, the largest airline in the US based on domestic passengers carried, is also one of the most profitable. It success is partly due to the way it defined its competition carefully. Most airlines in the US have a 'hub' airport and 'spokes' from it. They collect passengers from 'spokes' cities and fly them to a central 'hub' and then redistribute them other 'spokes.' However, Southwest does not use this arrangement. Most of its flying is non-stop between two points.

That configuration allows Southwest to minimise the time that its planes spend on the ground at crowded, delay-prone hubs, and consequently the average Southwest is in the air for more than an hour longer each day compared to a similar size jet flown by a network carrier.

Southwest defined its main competitor as the motor car – a substitute product – and has designed its marketing mix so as to minimise the time the customer takes travelling. This has meant flying from smaller, less congested airports and speeded-up check-in times.

2.6.3 Who are our competitors?

The danger when identifying competitors is that marketers adopt too narrow a definition of those organisations they are competing against.

For example, an organisation might only consider other organisations offering technically similar products and services as its competitors.

Current competitors

The organisation offering technically similar products and services is, indeed, a competitor. However, this ignores companies which produce substitute products which could perform a similar function, or those which solve a problem in a different way. Therefore, current competitors need to be distinguished into direct competitors and indirect competitors:

Direct competitors are organisations who offer the same (or similar) product or service, to a similar target audience.

Indirect competitors are organisations who offer similar products, or products that offer similar benefits, but target a different audience. The danger is that organisation only monitor their direct competitors, but forget about their indirect competitors. However, they need to remember that they are competing against any alternatives their consumers have. Just because an organisation is currently targeting a different audience, if its product fulfils the same purpose as yours then a customer could potentially buy it from them.

Potential competitors

In addition, as well as existing competitors, organisations need to continue to scan the environment for potential new entrants into the industry, either as direct or indirect competitors.

Again, it is important to be aware that there could be different forms of competitor here: new entrants with products which are technically similar to existing ones; or, those entering the market with new substitute products. For example, Apple's skill in computer electronics enabled it to enter the portable music player market with its iPod brand.

One of the main dangers of companies entering the market with substitute products is that they may be more difficult for marketers to locate than those entering the market with similar products to their own.

2.6.4 What are our competitors' goals or strategic objectives?

Important considerations here are:

- What are the competitors' current goals?
- How well are they achieving them?
- Are their goals likely to change in the future?

Relevant goals and objectives

1 Goals and objectives of the parent company, if the competitor is part of a larger group.

2 The competitors' assessment of risk; a higher risk will require a higher return from a market.

3 The personal goals of key managers. For example, a new chief executive may be brought in to 'turn the company round'. The new chief executive may have made a public commitment to one set of goals and may have invested a lot of prestige in achieving these goals.

4 A company facing cash flow problems may do anything to maximise cash inflow.

5 The competitors' history, position and the underlying assumptions of their management. For example, some firms consider themselves to be 'market leaders'.

6 How dependent the competitor is on the current business? A competitor with one main business will fight much harder to defend it than a competitor exposed to several sectors.

Types of goals

1 Profit
2 Market share
3 Cash flow
4 Technological leadership
5 Service leadership

An important consideration here is whether a company is looking to build, hold or harvest products or strategic business units.

A '**build**' objective will be concerned with increasing sales or market share. A build objective is clearly suitable in markets which are growing, because all the players can achieve higher sales even if some of them are experiencing falling market shares. However, a build objective can also be attractive in mature industries with little (or no) growth, it competitors have weaknesses which can be exploited. In these circumstances, a company can increase its market share by attacking the competitors' weaknesses.

A '**hold**' objective will be concerned with maintaining existing sales or market share. This is primarily a defensive objectives; defending a company's current position again would-be attackers. A 'hold' objective is often appropriate for a market leader in a mature or declining market. However, a 'hold' objective could also be suitable in a growth market, when the costs of attempting to build sales and market share outweigh the benefits; for example, when faced with aggressive rivals who will respond strongly if attacked.

(We will look at 'attacking' and 'defensive' strategies again in Chapter 6.)

A '**harvest**' objective means a company will be looking to maximise short-term cash flow, either through cutting expenditure or raising prices if possible. Even though sales may be falling, the aim is to make the product or business unit extremely profitable and cash positive in the short term. The positive cash flows could be particularly useful to support 'build' objectives elsewhere.

Knowing what type of objective (build, hold or harvest) a competitor is following is important, because it could influence the way they respond to an organisation's strategy. For example, if an organisation decides to reduce the price of its product in order to try to increase market share, a competitor who is also 'building' is likely to follow suit, as is one who is looking to 'hold' the same market share. However, one who is 'harvesting' is unlikely to reduce their prices because they are more concerned with profit margins that unit sales.

2.6.5 Competitors' strategies

There are two key aspects to consider here:

- Are the competitors competing on the basis of **cost** or product **quality**?

- Are they attempting to service the **whole market** or a few segments of a particular **niche**?

Porter (1980) looked at these generic strategies in terms of cost leadership and differentiation.

Cost leadership entails being the lowest cost producer in the industry as a whole.

A **differentiation strategy** involves providing products or services which are perceived to be unique across the industry as a whole.

Instead of looking to compete across the industry as a whole, a firm could also restrict its activities to only part of the market (a segment). This segmentation is indicative of a focus strategy:

- Providing goods and/or services at the lowest cost in a segment (**cost-focus strategy**)

- Providing a differentiated product or service to that segment (**differentiation-focus strategy**)

Cost leadership and differentiation are industry-wide strategies. Focus involves segmentation but involves

2.6.6 Competitors' strengths and weaknesses

Having a good understanding of competitor strengths and weaknesses, and what resources and capabilities they have (or do not have) is an important element in developing competitor strategy. In particular, it can help locate areas of competitor vulnerability, such that an organisation might be able to achieve strategic success if its matches an area of its strength against an area in which a competitor is weak.

Information which could be gathered about competitors' strengths and weaknesses includes:

- Financial performance, including profitability, and profit margins
- Brand strengths, customer loyalty
- Market share
- Quality of management team
- Intellectual property
- Distribution network
- Produce and service quality
- Relative cost structure
- Distinctive competence
    - Technical assistance
    - Customer awareness and customer service
    - Sales staff (and selling ability)
    - Product quality and availability

2.6.7 Analysing competitors' costs

Clearly, the strategic response of competitors can vary significantly on the cost profile of the competitor. Relative costs are more important than absolute costs: It took Western firms too long to understand that

Japanese firms had sustainable cost advantages, and hence were able to compete on price on a sustained basis.

Furthermore, even if the competitor is not competing on price, despite having a lower cost base, the competitor is:

- Under no pressure to raise prices, thus limiting the firm's ability to raise its own
- More profitable, and hence can invest more

2.6.8 Competitor reaction and response

We can identify four types of competitor response.

- **Laid-back**: competitor does not respond, even though it has seen and recognised your move

- **Selective**: competitor only responds to certain types of attack (however, unlike 'Unpredictable' competitors they tend to be consistent in their responses; so, if they respond to price discounting on one occasion they will do so on all occasions)

- **Retaliatory** : competitor reacts and responds aggressively to any attack

- **Unpredictable**: impossible to predict how competitor will react. Sometimes they will react aggressively, other times they will not respond at all.

ACTIVITY 1.3

Why might a competitor be **'laid-back'**?

2.6.9 Good competitors

Monopolies are hard to come by, but some competitors are definitely easier to deal with than others. A good competitor makes life easy for its rivals by:

- Deterring new entrants (assuming you are not a new entrant)
- Sharing similar assumptions about the industry
- Preferring differentiation and focus to competing on price

> ▶ **Key term**
>
> A **strategic group** is a group of firms following the same strategy in a given target market.

2.7 Strategic group analysis

Analysing competitors' strategies can often highlight that groups of companies within an industry have similar business models, or similar strategies. For example, in the restaurant industry, we can clearly distinguish between fast-food restaurants, and fine-dining restaurants. The distinctions between the two can be seen across a range of variables including preparation time, pricing and presentation.

These different groups within an industry which have similar business models or are competing on similar bases are **strategic groups**

Strategic groups are usually identified using two or three sets of characteristics which define the bases of competition within an industry. These characteristics include: product (or service) quality, pricing policy, the extent of product diversity, the extent of geographic coverage, the number of market segments served, distribution channels used, brand loyalty and brand recognition.

By analysing an industry into strategic groups, an organisation can identify who its most direct competitors are, and the basis on which they compete. It might also be able to use strategic group mapping to identify opportunities within an industry; by combining key characteristics in a new, or unique, way. Or alternatively a

The Chartered Institute of Marketing

firm might use strategic group analysis to consider how possible it might be for it (or for competitors) to move from one strategic group to another.

Kotler *et al* (2009) illustrate the idea of strategic groups in relation to the major appliance industry. They show that, by using characteristics of quality and level of vertical integration (organisational integration between the company, its suppliers, and/or distributors and buyers), the industry can be split into four strategic groups.

Figure 1.7   Strategic groups in the appliance industry

Based on Kotler *et al*, (2009)

Kotler *et al* (2009) observe that Group A has three competitors (Miele, SMEG, LG) while Group B has four (BSH, Electrolux, Indesit and Whirlpool). Group C and D are found to have three each, but these are not listed by Kotler *et al*.

One of the important implications of this analysis is that if a company successfully enters a group, the members of that group become its key competitors, in precedence to other players in the appliance industry. For example, Group B companies which produce appliances across the full product range (from washing machines and dryers, to refrigerators, ovens and other appliances will see other Group B companies as their primary competitors rather than, for example, Group A companies which produce a much narrower range of products.

3 Strategic uncertainty

Strategic uncertainty is a key construct in external analysis, because an environmental analysis will typically reveal dozens of uncertainties which could strategic implications for an organisation. However, once they have uncovered these uncertainties, organisations also have to rank them and decide which need in-depth analysis and which only require a more low-key monitoring effort. (Aaker & McLoughlin, 2010)

3.1 The effect of strategic uncertainty

According to Aaker & McLoughlin (2010) the overall impact of strategic uncertainty is related to its impact and its immediacy.

The impact of a strategic uncertainty is related to:

- The extent to which it involves trends or events that will impact the business
- The importance of the business units or products involved to a company
- The number of business units or products potentially affected by the uncertainty

The immediacy of a strategic uncertainty is related to:

- The likelihood of a trend or event occurring – if an event only has a low probability of occurring it may not be worth acting upon than uncertainty
- The timeframe of the trends or events
- The time which will be available in which to react to the event, compared to the time which will be required to develop and implement an appropriate strategy to respond to that event

Figure 1.8   Impact analysis

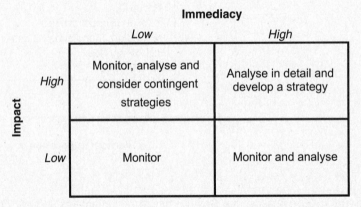

Based on Aaker & McLoughlin, (2010)

3.2 Scenario construction

Because the external environment can be so complex, it is easy to become overwhelmed by the many factors which are at work. Firms, therefore, try to model the future by constructing scenarios to assist them with setting their strategic direction, especially if there is uncertainty, or inherently unpredictable trends at work.

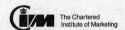

There are two types of scenario analysis:

1   **Strategy developing scenarios** – used to evaluate existing strategies and stimulate new ones
2   **Decision driven scenarios** – a strategy is proposed first, then tested against scenarios that are developed

In either case, there are three general steps to be taken.

1   Create the scenarios
2   Relate them to existing/potential strategies
3   Assess their probability

> **Key term**
>
> A **scenario** is 'an internally consistent view of what the future might turn out to be'.

Scenario analysis accepts that uncertainties are in effect 'certain' to occur, and uses these uncertainties to create descriptions of the future.

3.2.1 Macro scenarios

Macro scenarios use macroeconomic or political factors, creating alternative views of the future environment (taking into account factors such as global economic growth, political changes, interest rates). Macro scenarios developed because the activities of oil and resource companies (which are global and at one time were heavily influenced by political factors) needed techniques to deal with uncertainties.

Steps in scenario planning

Step 1   **Decide on the drivers for change**

■   Environmental analysis helps determine key factors
■   At least a ten-year time horizon is needed, to avoid simply extrapolating from the present
■   Identify and select the important issues and degree of certainty

Step 2   **Bring drivers together into a viable framework**

■   This relies almost on an intuitive ability to make patterns out of 'soft' data, so is the hardest
■   Items identified can be brought together as mini-scenarios
■   There might be many trends, but these can be grouped together

Step 3   **Produce seven to nine mini-scenarios**

Step 4   **Group mini-scenarios into two or three larger scenarios containing all topics**

■   This generates most debate and is likely to highlight fundamental issues
■   More than three scenarios will confuse people
■   The scenarios should be complementary and equally likely
■   The scenarios should be tested to ensure they hang together

Step 5   Write the scenarios

- The scenarios should be written-up in the form most suitable for managers
- Most scenarios are qualitative rather than quantitative in nature

Step 6   Identify issues arising

- Determine the most critical outcomes
- Role play can be used to test what the scenarios mean to key staff involved

3.2.2 Industry scenarios

Porter believes that the most appropriate use for scenario analysis is if it is restricted to an industry. An **industry scenario** is an internally consistent view of an industry's future structure. Different competitive strategies may be appropriate to different scenarios. The entire range, not the most likely 'future', is used to design a competitive strategy.

THE REAL WORLD

Aaker & McLoughlin (2010; p 93) give the example of a publishing company that may be worried about the impact of on-line publishing, lifestyle changes, educational trends, population shifts and printing technology – a wide range of uncertainties!

Importantly, though, any of these issues could in turn involve a host of 'sub-fields' and so could spur further research into the uncertainties involved with them. For example, on-line publishing might involve a variety of issues including the willingness of advertisers to pay for adverts in on-line publications, the likelihood of customers being willing to pay for on-line content, and the impact of free competition on subscription-based on-line content.

Figure 1.9   The process for constructing industry scenarios.

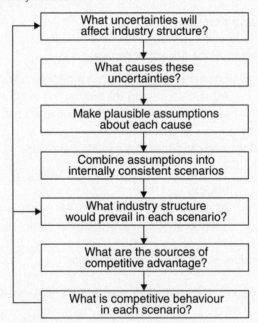

3.2.3 Using scenarios to formulate competitive strategy

- **Assume the most probable**. This choice puts too much faith in the scenario process and guesswork. A less probable scenario may be one which has the worst consequences for the firm.

The Chartered Institute of Marketing

- **Hope for the best**. A firm designs a strategy based on the scenario most attractive to the firm: wishful thinking.

- **Hedge**. The firm chooses the strategy that produces satisfactory results under all scenarios. Hedging, however, is not optimal. The low risk is paid for by a low reward.

- **Flexibility**. A firm taking this approach plays a 'wait and see' game. It is safer, but sacrifices first mover advantages.

- **Influence**. A firm will try and influence the future, for example, by influencing demand for related products in order that its favoured scenario will be realised in events as they unfold, or even by attempting to influence government and regulatory bodies.

3.3 Market sensing

> ▶ Key term
>
> **Market sensing**: 'how those ..... inside the company understand and react to the market place and the way it is changing'. It does not relate to the gathering and processing of information (market research) but how the information is interpreted and understood by decision-makers in the company.   (Piercy, 2008).

Some market signals are hard to pick up, even though they may be of long-term significance. Managers thus need to be skilled in market sensing.

Market sensing does not relate to the gathering and processing of information (market research) but how the information is interpreted and understood by decision-makers in the company.

3.3.1 Process of market sensing

Step 1   Capture information by identifying the environment (eg Porter's five forces), the dimension (eg substitute products), the time frame and the market.

Step 2   'Brainstorm' the events in the environment that are currently developing and assess the probability of their occurrence and their likely effect.

Step 3   Categorise the event on the basis of probability and effect.

- Utopia: likely, desirable
- Dreams: unlikely, desirable
- Danger: likely, undesirable
- Future risks: unlikely, undesirable
- Things to watch: medium likelihood, neutral effect

Probability of event

	High		Low
Effect of event	Utopia		Field of dreams
		Things to watch	
	Danger		Future crises

Step 4   Answer the following questions

- Where are we planning for Utopia?
- Where are we planning for dangers?
- Where are we monitoring the factors in the marketing information system (MkIS)?

It may be quite possible that managers have not made plans to deal with these eventualities or that the information systems do not report on these key issues.

Step 5   Link conclusions from the sensing approach explicitly to marketing plans.

Step 6   Encourage participation across functions and across levels. (Customer service staff have a very different perspective from the board of directors.)

Step 7   Where necessary, change information provision to provide a richer or more relevant picture of the world, while avoiding:

- Information overload
- Confusion as the existing model appears outdated
- Fear of making any decisions at all
- Creating conflict between groups who may have shared a sense of direction

3.4 Forecasting techniques

Conventionally, forecasting techniques can be used to predict demand in the short- to medium-term. However, such techniques depend on the reliability of past data. The uncertainties in using statistical forecasting to predict the future are considerable.

3.4.1 Types of forecast

> ▶ **Key terms**
>
> **Forecasting** is 'the identification of factors and quantifications of their effect on an entity, as a basis for planning'.
>
> A **projection** is 'an expected future trend pattern obtained by extrapolation. It is principally concerned with quantitative factors whereas a forecast includes judgements'.
>
> **Extrapolation** is 'the technique of determining a projection by statistical means'.

Statistical forecasts take past data and endeavour to direct it to the future, by assuming that patterns or relationships which held in the past will continue to do so. Many statistical techniques aim to reduce the uncertainty managers face. In simple/static conditions the past is a relatively good guide to the future.

Judgemental forecasts are used principally for the long-term, covering several decades. However, because of the limitations of short term forecasting they are used for the short-term too. Effectively, they are based on hunches or educated guesses. Sometimes, these prove surprisingly accurate. At other times they are wide of the mark.

3.4.2 Sales potential

Sales potential is an estimate of the part of the market that is within the possible reach of a product.

Factors governing sales potential

- The price of the product
- The amount of money spent on sales promotion
- How essential the product is to consumers
- Whether it is a durable commodity whose purchase can be postponed
- The overall size of the possible market
- Competition

Whether sales potential is worth exploiting will depend on the cost which must be incurred to realise the potential.

Estimating market demand

Estimating market demand is not necessarily as straightforward as you might at first think. Imagine you are the marketing manager of a company producing sports footwear. What is your market demand? Is it the volume of shoes purchased in the UK, or Europe, or the whole world? Should you be considering tennis shoes as well as running shoes? Shoes for children or only adults? And should you be forecasting demand for next year or over the next five years? The permutations seem endless.

A demand function is simply an expression which shows how sales demand for a product is dependent on several factors. These demand variables can be grouped into two broad categories.

1   **Controllable variables** or strategic variables. These are factors over which the firm's management should have some degree of control, and which they can change if they wish.

Controllable variables are essentially the marketing mix.

2   **Uncontrollable variables**. These are factors over which the firm's management has no control.

(a)   Consumer variables depend on decisions by consumers, or the circumstances of consumers (for example, their wealth).

(b)   Competitor variables depend on decisions and actions by other firms, particularly competitors.

(c)   Other variables. These include decisions by other organisations (for example the government) or factors which are outside the control of anyone (for example weather conditions, or the total size of the population).

3.4.3 Time series analysis

Time series analysis data can be used to make forecasts as follows.

Step 1   Plot a trend line: use the line of best fit method or the moving averages method.

Step 2   Extrapolate the trend line. This means extending the trend line outside the range of known data and forecasting future results from historical data.

Step 3   Adjust forecast trends by the applicable average seasonal variation to obtain the actual forecast.

3.5 Market attractiveness

In making a decision as to which market(s) to enter the firm must start by establishing its objectives. Here are some examples.

1   What **proportion of total sales** will be in these markets?

2   What are the **longer-term objectives**?

3   Will it enter one, a few, or many markets? In most cases it is better to start by selling in markets with which there is some familiarity, and then expand into others gradually, as experience is gained. Reasons to **enter fewer markets at first** include the following.

(a)   Market entry and market control costs are high
(b)   Product and market communications modification costs are high
(c)   There is a large market and potential growth in the initial markets chosen
(d)   Dominant competitors can establish high barriers to entry

4   What **types of market** should it enter (in terms of environmental factors, economic development, language used and cultural similarities)? Three major decision criteria are as follows.

(a)   Market attractiveness
(b)   Competitive advantage
(c)   Risk

The matrix which follows can be used to bring together these three major criteria and assist managers in their decisions.

1   **Market attractiveness**. This concerns such indicators as GNP/head and forecast demand, and market accessibility.

2   **Competitive advantage**. This is principally dependent on prior experience in similar markets, language and cultural understanding.

3   **Risk**. This involves an analysis of political stability, the possibility of government intervention and similar external influences.

The best markets to enter are those located at the top left of the diagram. The worst are those in the bottom right corner. Obtaining the information needed to reach this decision requires detailed and often costly marketing research and analysis. Making these decisions is not easy, and a fairly elaborate screening process will be instituted.

Figure 1.10   Evaluating which markets to enter.

Based on Kotler *et al*, (2009)

3.5.1 Market analysis

Aaker & McLoughlin (2010) offer some further questions which could help organisations analyse markets and, in doing so, help them decide which ones to enter:

- **Submarkets** – What submarkets are there within the market; defined by different price points, or niches for example?

- **Size and growth** – What are the size and growth characteristics of the market and submarkets within it? What are the driving forces behind trends in sales? What are the major trends in the market?

- **Profitability** – How profitable is the market and its submarkets now, and how profitable are they likely to be in the future? How intense is the competition between existing firms? How severe are the threats from potential new entrants of substitute products? What is the bargaining power of suppliers and customers?

- **Cost structure** – What are the major cost components for various types of competitor, and how do they add value for customers?

- **Distribution channels** – What distribution channels are currently available? How are they changing?

- **Key success factors** – What are the key success factors, assets and competencies needed to compete successfully? How are these likely to change in the future? Can the organisation neutralise competitors' assets and competencies?

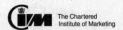

CHAPTER ROUNDUP

- The marketing environment consists of the **macroenvironment** (political, economic, social, technological factors) and the **microenvironment** (customer, competitors, distributors and channels). The external environment shapes the opportunities and threats facing an organisation.

- Marketing is the process by which companies create value for customers, but in order to do this marketers need to have a good understanding of the marketplace and customers' needs and wants. Marketers need to identify which customers to serve, and how they can serve them best.

- To be successful an organisation needs to provide greater customer value and satisfaction than its competitors do. However, in order to be able to do this, the organisation needs to analyse its competitors; to identify their objectives and strategies, their strengths and weaknesses, and how they are likely to respond to the organisation's strategies.

- Organisations need to assess the strategic uncertainties which are present in the environment so that they can plan how to respond to those uncertainties.

FURTHER READING

Johnson, G., Whittington, R. & Scholes, K. (2011) *Exploring Strategy.* (9th edition). Pearson, Harlow. (Chapter 2: 'The Environment'; pp. 48-81.)

Schoemaker, P. (1995) "Scenario Planning: A tool for Strategic Thinking" *Sloan Management Review*, Vol.36, No.2, p.35

REFERENCES

Aaker, D. & McLoughlin, D. (2007) *Strategic Market Management*. John Wiley, Chichester.

Aaker, D. & McLoughlin, D. (2010) *Strategic Market Management: Global Perspectives*. John Wiley, Chichester.

Drummond, G., Ensor, J. & Ashford, R. (2008) *Strategic Marketing Planning and Control*. 3rd edition. Elsevier Ltd, Oxford.

Howard, J. A. & Sheth, N.J. (1969) *Theory of Buyer Behaviour*. John Wiley and Sons, London.

Jobber, D. (2010) *Principles and Practice of Marketing*. 6th edition. McGraw-Hill, Maidenhead.

Kotler, P. & Armstrong, G. (2012), *Principles of Marketing*. 14th edition. Pearson Educational, Harlow.

Kotler, P., Armstrong, G., Wong, V. & Saunders, J. (2008), *Principles of Marketing*. 5th European edition. Pearson Educational, Harlow.

Kotler, P., Keller, K., Brady, M., Goodman, M. & Hansen, T. (2009) *Marketing Management*, Pearson Educational, Harlow.

Piercy, N.F. (2008) *Market-Led Strategic Change – Transforming the Process of Going to Market*. 4th edition. Butterworth-Heinemann, Oxford.

Porter, M.E. (1980), *Competitive Strategy*. Free Press, New York.

Porter, M.E. (2004) *Competitive Advantage*. New edition. Free Press, New York.

Porter, M.E. (2008) *On Competition*. 2nd edition. Harvard Business School Press, Boston.

QUICK QUIZ

1 Give a definition of 'market'

2 What are the five competitive forces?

3 What are the elements of the Howard-Sheth model of buyer behaviour?

4 What is 'indirect' distribution?

5 What is competitive advantage?

6 What are the features of mass customisation?

7 Define 'repositioning'?

8 When undertaking competitor analysis, what are some of the key questions to be asked?

9 What is a strategic group?

10 How should a firm respond to an uncertainty that is of high immediacy and of high impact?

11 What is 'market sensing'?

12 What criteria are brought together when considering market attractiveness?

ACTIVITY DEBRIEFS

Activity 1.1

Behavioural determinants. Eleanor and her husband work in service industries. They are used to the concept of investing (even if unsuccessfully), and have financial interests to protect. The family is perhaps slightly unusual in that the female is the chief breadwinner, and her husband's income is unlikely to be large.

Inputs. Only one product is detailed. As a financial journalist, Eleanor's husband might know of more. He is likely to be interested in the small print, rather than images and feelings.

Inhibitors. If Eleanor feels she is likely to be made redundant within the next six months, she is unlikely to take out the policy as it would not be of much use to her.

Perceptual reaction. Having lost £15,000 in a previous investment, Eleanor and her husband are possibly very risk averse. They will be sensitive to information regarding the status and reputation of the service provider.

Processing determinants. There is a perceived risk that Eleanor will be made redundant, and she is looking for a product which will reduce the financial impact.

Outputs. They will want a benefit which will cover, at least, the mortgage and regular bills.

 The Chartered Institute of Marketing

Activity 1.2

Attributes: Ads for PCs emphasise 'speed', what sort of chip they have.

Benefit: Holidays are advertised as offering relaxation or excitement.

Use/application: 'Easy to use' products (eg hair tints that can be 'washed' in)

User: Reflect user characteristics, to appeal to the target audience and confirm their choice. May use celebrity endorsements.

Product category: The Natural History Museum is fundamentally educational, but is moving towards a 'theme park' image for the schools market.

Quality/price: 'Value for money' advertisements.

Activity 1.3

A 'laid back' competitor may be:

- Unable to respond: lack of capability
- Unwilling to respond owing to differing assumptions about the segment
- Unconcerned about the threat, which it does not take seriously

In this example, it would not be worth spending an extra £5,000 on selling in order to realise an extra sales potential of £10,000, because the net effect would be a loss of £ (5,000 – 4,000) = £1,000.

QUICK QUIZ ANSWERS

1   'Market': a group of actual and potential customers, who can make purchase decisions.

2   (a)   The threat of new entrants to the industry

    (b)   The threat of substitute products or services

    (c)   The bargaining power of customers

    (d)   The bargaining power of suppliers

    (e)   The rivalry among current competitors in the industry

3   Inputs
    Behavioural determinants
    Perceptual reaction
    Processing determinants
    Inhibitors
    Outputs

4   'Indirect' distribution makes use of intermediaries; wholesalers, retailers or perhaps both. They rely on consumers to make the first approach by entering the relevant retail outlet.

5   A business achieves competitive advantage when it earns higher than average profits. Whatever overall objective is set for a firm: to survive, to create value, to make profit; the key to achieving it lies in the attainment of some form of competitive advantage.

6   Mass customisation features economies of scale via mass production;
    The tailoring of products precisely to the customer's requirements.

7   Repositioning is defining a competitive strategy aimed at changing position in order to increase market share.

8   Who are the competitors?
      What are their goals?
      What strategies are they pursuing?
      What are their strengths and weaknesses?
      How are they likely to respond?

9   A strategic group is a group of firms following the same strategy in a given target market.

10   The situation should be analysed in detail, and an appropriate response developed.

11   Market sensing has been defined as 'how those ..... inside the company understand and react to the marketplace and the way it is changing'. It relates to how market information is interpreted and understood by decision-makers in the company.

12   Market attractiveness
      Competitive advantage
      Risk

CHAPTER 2

Understanding the customer base

Introduction

Organisations with a large customer base, a wide range of products, a global market, and several discrete product/brand names may be tempted to treat customers as if they were all alike, all wanting much the same things, all applying similar criteria when judging the product, the service, or the organisation as a whole.

In practice, this is bound to be a misleading assumption. Customer A may want reliability of delivery on an hourly basis; Customer B may want an unusual range of financial options; Customer C may want the highest possible standards of after-sales support; Customer D is only interested in one product.

Research shows that there are differences in customers' expectations which can be exploited, if they are identified and recorded, by offering levels of service which match the needs of particular sectors, possibly withdrawing from some or increasing prices/charges to an economically-justified level.

Understanding the customer base is a critical part of the detailed assessment of an organisation and its performance, and the issues and challenges of providing value to these customers.

This chapter examines the range of tools that can be used to understand customers and their buying behaviour.

Topic list

The value proposition (1)

Market segmentation (2)

Segmental analysis (3)

Strategic account analysis (4)

The importance of consumer profiling and customer intelligence (5)

1.1.3	Utilise a range of tools to critically evaluate an organisation's ability to understand its current customer base and their buying behaviour, in order to be able to develop customer insight and meet their preferences:

- Value proposition
- Segmental analysis and consumer profiling
- Strategic account analysis
- Consumer profiling

1 The value proposition

In Chapter 1 we highlighted the way that marketers can contribute to strategic analysis by helping a firm understand its customers, competitors, markets and environmental forces and trends. However, marketers also play an important strategic role in helping firms develop their business strategies, and the dimension of business strategy most clearly owned by marketing is the customer value proposition – what is the value or benefit that the firm will offer its customers, now and in the future? (Aaker & McLoughlin, 2010)

A firm's value proposition dictates how it will serve its targeted customers – how it will differentiate from its competitors and position itself in the marketplace. Accordingly, a firm's value proposition is the set of benefits or values it promises to deliver to consumers to satisfy their needs. It helps customers answer the question of why they should buy a firm's brand rather than a competitor's (Kotler *et al*, 2008).

Kotler *et al* (2008) offer the following example of a pair of contrasting value propositions: Propel Fitness Water by Gatorade is 'made for bodies in motion.' On the other hand, Red Bull Energy Drink helps customers fight mental and physical fatigue. Red Bull has captured approximately 70% of the energy drinks market by promising that it 'gives you wiiings!'

1.1 What is the value proposition?

> ▶ **Key term**
>
> The **value proposition** has been defined as 'an offering's performance and price promise to potential buyers.' (www.cval.com), or alternatively:
>
> The value proposition is 'The full positioning of a brand – the full mix of benefits on which it is positioned' (Kotler & Armstrong, 2012).
>
> In effect, then, the value proposition is 'what the customer gets for their money'.

A customer can evaluate a company's value proposition on two levels:

1   **Relative performance**: what the customer gets, relative to what he or she would get from a competitor

2   **Price**: payments made to acquire the product or service

The company's marketing and sales efforts offer the value proposition, and its delivery and customer-service processes then fulfil it.

The value proposition is crucial in identifying what differentiates a firm's product from its competitors. In fact, the term 'value proposition' is sometimes used interchangeably with differentiation. It is one of the key factors to consider when determining a marketing strategy. Marketing strategists can check how their value proposition works in the perception of customers, using market research for example.

A value proposition can assist in a firm's marketing strategy, and may guide a business to target a particular market segment. For example: 'Firm Any Co. can provide benefits a, b, and c because of competences x, y, and z.'

Kotler *et al* (2009, p5) give the example of Benetton to highlight the importance of understanding customer needs and making marketing choices to match those needs.

For a number of years, Benetton enjoyed great success with a unique brand of clothing supported by provocative advertising. However, it had to rethink its marketing strategy when new fast-fashion competitors such as Zara and H&M entered the fashion market for teenagers and young adults, and began to capture market share and brand loyalty through their comprehensive marketing strategies.

Zara understood the patterns of consumer behaviour among their target age groups, and recognised that these consumers wanted new styles quickly and cheaply; in effect, they wanted 'disposable clothing.'

Zara studied the elements of the marketing mix and saw that management of its global supply network, service processes, and physical evidence such as store layout and design were more important than traditional marketing expenditure on advertising. Consequently, Zara spent very little on advertising, whereas Benetton was spending millions of Euros on creative advertising.

Zara prospered as a result of its focus on rapid delivery of new lines to the market, while Benetton floundered due to its excessive focus on advertising.

However, following Zara's success, Benetton saw the error its way and began to modernise its global supply chain. Therefore, instead of only being able to deliver new styles to its stores once a month (which was its traditional delivery strategy) it was then able to deliver them once a week.

Benetton had realised that Zara and H&M both had very lean supply chains, capable of replenishing stocks in days rather than months, and this supply chain management was as important as style in the increasingly cut-throat business of mass market apparel.

1.2 The value proposition and competitive advantage

An effective sustainable competitive advantage such as product reliability should enhance the value proposition.

A lot of the benefit from delivering the value proposition is derived from perception. Business reputation for delivering on quality, price (or whatever the value proposition is) is strategically extremely important, as it can give the company valuable breathing space in the event of faltering actual performance, and is hard for competitors to break in to.

Conversely, a solid value proposition may not hold up in the wake of changing perceptions or tastes.

Consumer trust in retail financial services has been severely shaken in the current economic downturn. Many have seen their assets slashed, and are likely to remain cautious even when the recovery arrives.

Opportunities will emerge for innovative companies. Charles Schwab founded his hugely successful brokerage in the wake of the recession of the early 1970s, introducing a new value proposition that resonated with consumers. The current recession has induced a 'deficit of trust', and it is likely that new value propositions will emerge from it in a similar way.

From: Quelch, J & Jocz, K (2009), Keeping a keen eye on consumer behaviour, *Financial Times*, 5 February 2009

2 Market segmentation

The range of products and services available to contemporary consumers, and the variety of needs and expectations which those consumers have, mean that very few products or services can satisfy all the consumers in a market.

Consequently, in order to satisfy customer needs successfully, businesses need to offer different products or services to different customer groups (or market segments).

> ▶ **Exam tip**
>
> In Chapter 1, we introduced the ideas of positioning and target markets.
>
> However, before it can select its target markets, a firm must segment the market.
>
> Once a firm has selected its target market, because the customers in the target should have similar characteristics, the firm can then develop a single marketing mix strategy to meet the customer requirements.
>
> Therefore the process of 'segmentation – target – positioning' is likely to be crucial for a firm when it is developing a marketing strategy.

> ▶ **Key term**
>
> **Market segmentation**: The identification of individuals or organisations with similar characteristics that have significant implications for the determination of marketing strategy.
>
> (Jobber, 2010, p260)

Market segmentation is a technique which marketers use to analyse the diverse nature of markets, and to recognise the diverse needs of potential customers. Customers with different attitudes or needs can be grouped into segments. And segmentation involves the subdivision of a market into distinct and increasingly homogeneous subgroups of customers, in which any subgroup could possibly be selected as a target market to be met with a **distinct marketing mix.**

- Although the total market consists of widely different groups of consumers, each group consists of people (or organisations) with **common needs and preferences**, who perhaps react to 'market stimuli' in much the same way.

- Each market segment can become a **target market** for a firm, and would require a unique marketing mix if the firm is to exploit it successfully.

- The firm can then **position its offer** to account for the roles of each segment.

A target market may occasionally be homogeneous, but this is rare. By contrast, a segmentation approach to marketing is likely to be successful when there are identifiable 'clusters' of customer wants in the market.

The Chartered
Institute of Marketing

An airline cafe-restaurant conducted a segmentation exercise of its customers. It identified a number of possible segments:

- Business travellers
- Groups
- Single tourists
- Airport employees

However, further analysis revealed that running through each of these categories was the same fault line:

- Those 'in a hurry'
- Those with time to spare

For marketing purposes, this latter segmentation exercise was more useful, and the cafe was able to develop an 'express menu' for those in a hurry.

2.1 Benefits of market segmentation

- The organisation may be able to identify **new marketing opportunities**, because it will have a better understanding of customer needs in each segment, with the possibility of spotting further sub groups.

- **Specialists can be used** for each of the organisation's major segments. For example, small business counsellors can be employed by banks to deal effectively with small firms. A computer consultancy can have specialist sales staff for, say, shops, manufacturers, service industries and local government authorities. This builds competencies and establishes effective marketing systems.

- The total marketing budget can be allocated proportionately to each segment and the likely return from each segment. This optimises return on investment.

- The organisation can make small adjustments to the product and service offerings and to the promotional aspects for each segment. This again promotes efficient use of resources.

- The organisation can try to **dominate particular segments**, thus gaining competitive advantage. Advantages accrued function synergistically to promote improved competitive ability; in other words, the overall benefit to an organisation of dominating a number of specific segments is greater than the sum of the individual benefits attained by dominating each segment individually.

- The **product range** can more closely reflect differences in customer needs. We have already identified the importance of a firm's product or service creating value for its customers, and if a firm is able to offer different (or tailored) products for different subgroups in the market it can be more responsive to customer needs than if it tries to meet the needs of the whole market with a single product.

2.2 The bases for market segmentation

There are many different bases for segmentation; one basis will not be appropriate in every market, and sometimes two or more bases might be valid at the same time. One segmentation variable might be 'superior' to another in a hierarchy of variables.

Simple segmentation could be on any of the bases below:

Geographical area	Nationality
Age	Social class
Gender	Personality
Life cycle stage	Lifestyle
Level of income	Benefits sought
Occupation	Purchase occasion
Education	Purchase behaviour
Religion	Usage (eg frequent vs occasional user)
Ethnicity	Perceptions and belief

We will spend a little more time discussing lifestyle segmentation and then behavioural segmentation (which includes benefits sought, purchase occasion, purchase behaviour, usage, and perceptions and belief.)

2.2.1 Lifestyle (psychographic) segmentation

Psychographics – or lifestyle segmentation – seeks to classify people according to their values, opinions, personality, characteristics and interests.

Importantly, lifestyle segmentation deals with the **person** as opposed to the **product or service** being sold, and attempts to discover the particular **lifestyle patterns of customers**, as reflected in their activities, interests and opinions. This offers a richer insight into their preferences for various products and services, and hence their propensity to buy them. For example, in marketing its television channels, Sky has used lifestyle segmentation to target groups with different interests: such as sports enthusiasts (Sky Sports), film buffs (Sky Movies) and these people who want to keep up to date with news and current affairs (Sky News).

Database marketing, which is becoming much more important in identifying and targeting market segments for direct selling, relies heavily on the theories underlying psychographic segmentation.

However, a potential issues which arises with lifestyle segmentation is the extent to which general lifestyle patterns can predict purchasing behaviour in specific markets.

Moreover, while lifestyle analysis may be relevant to advanced western economies it could have little value for analysing markets in emerging economies where the majority of purchases are informed by basic physiological needs.

2.2.2 Geodemographic segmentation

Geodemographics is a segmentation technique which was introduced in the early 1980s, but came into its own in the late 1980s and early 1990s. Basically, it classifies people according to **where they live**, and rests on the idea that **households within a particular neighbourhood exhibit similar purchasing behaviour, outlook and so on**. Two neighbourhoods can be placed in the same category (that is, they can contain similar types of people) even though they are separated geographically.

Geodemographics is able to target people in particular areas who exhibit similar behaviour patterns.

Modern techniques also allow for data to be combined and projected so that knowledge about neighbourhood and age will permit projections about attitudes and behaviour with strong statistical reliability.

2.2.3 Behavioural segmentation

We will look at each of these bases for segmentation in turn (see Table 2.1 below):

> ▶ **Key term**
>
> **Behavioural segmentation** seeks to classify people and their purposes according to the benefits sought, the purchase occasion, purchase behaviour, usage, and perception, beliefs and values.
>
> (Jobber, 2010, p260)

Table 2.1   Bases for behavioural segmentation

Benefits sought	People may seek different benefits from a product. For example, the fruit drink market could be segmented in terms of the following benefits sought: extra energy, vitamins, natural ingredients or low calories.
	More generally, the benefits from purchases could be classified in terms of: pleasure; image; or functionality.
	Markets can also be segmented on the basis of price sensitivity. For example, Tesco has developed its 'Value' range for customers for whom the low price is a benefit, while it has developed its 'Finest' range for customers who are prepared to pay more for a higher quality meal. Similarly, there are two distinct segments in the airline market: low price 'no frills' airlines, as distinct from the higher priced established airlines.
Purchase occasion	Some products may be purchased as a response to an emergency, some may be purchased as gifts, while others may be purchased as routine purchases. Price sensitivity is likely to be greater for routine purchases (eg groceries) than for emergencies (eg replacing a broken window). Similarly, the way gifts are packaged and marketed is likely to be different to the way routine purchases are presented.
Purchase behaviour	Purchase behaviour could relate to the time the purchase is made relative to the launch of a product, or to patterns of purchase.
	If a new product is launched, some people ('innovators') are likely to buy the product soon after launch, but other segments of the market will want more time to assess the benefits from buying the product before doing so.
	Purchase behaviour can also be segmented in terms of brand loyalty. Some buyers remain loyal to a single brand, while others may switch brand in response to special offers (eg money off campaigns, or 'buy one, get one free'), while others show no brand loyalty at all.
	A third illustration of segmenting by purchase behaviour is the way supermarkets use biographics – looking at the actual purchasing behaviour of individuals, and so, in effect, creating a segment of one. Supermarket loyalty cards (for example, Tesco's 'Clubcard') allow supermarkets to gather very precise information about individual customers' purchasing habits, which mean customers can be segmented and targeted very precisely. Analysis of individual customer data also allows supermarkets to stock the products which are most relevant to their customers' lifestyles and expenditures.
Usage	Customers can be distinguished according to whether they are heavy users, light users or non-users of a product.
	The implication of this for marketers is that usage profiles allow the heaviest users of a product group to receive the most marketing attention.
	Segmenting by use also highlights an important issue in market segmentation: the same individual may buy product offerings that would seem to appeal to different people in the market. For example, the same person might buy a business class air ticket and some economy tickets. These purchases are likely to reflect different use occasions: the business class ticket might be for a business trip, whereas the economy fares might be for a family holiday.
	Importantly, the fact that the same individual belongs to different segments does not mean that segmentation is not warranted. In the flight example above, marketing for business-class tickets should still be targeted at business people, and economy flights at leisure travellers, even though on some occasions the same person may overlap both categories.

Perceptions, beliefs and values	Perceptions, beliefs and values are often strongly linked to behaviour.
	Consumers can be grouped by identifying those who view the products in a market in a similar way (perceptual segmentation) and those who hold similar beliefs (belief segmentation). Understanding segments in this way helps marketers understand how customers view the marketplace, and so can help identify opportunities to target specific groups. For example, L'Oreal beauty products (and their tag-line 'Because you're worth it') are targeted at women who believe they are entitled to be pampered.
	Value-based segmentation is based on the assumption that people's values (manifest through attitudes and lifestyles) translate into their behaviours. (Note the similarity between this idea and lifestyle (psychographic segmentation).

2.3 Current developments in segmentation and positioning

Approaches to market segmentation and product positioning change regularly. Here are a few developments in recent years.

Table 2.2 Developments in market segmentation

Development	Comment
There is a growing awareness that consumers should be segmented according to the purpose of the segmentation.	For example, the same customers of a retail bank can be segmented by their account profile, for the purpose of product cross-selling, by their attitudes to risk-taking for the purpose of delivering advertising messages, and by socio-economic type for the purpose of selecting a marketing medium.
There is growing interest in customer database analysis, and the idea of 'letting the data speak for itself'.	Customer information on a database is analysed in order to identify segments or patterns of behaviour. This technique, known as data mining, is likely to increase in significance as internet commerce grows in popularity.
There is growing emphasis on segmentation by 'soft' data.	Consumer attitudes and needs and lifestyles (as distinct from 'hard data' such as age, life style, socio-economic grouping, and so on).
There is a growing use of sub-segmentation or 'hybrid segmentation' methods.	Consumers within a particular segment can be sub-divided into different segments, and each sub-segment is targeted in a different way.
There is a growing use of 'segments of one'	Direct marketing and personalised marketing enable specific marketing messages to be tailored to individual consumers. For example, Amazon makes recommendations for future purchases based on previous purchases.

2.4 Target market selection

Once a firm has identified the different segments in a market (segmentation) it can begin to select its target markets.

▶ **Key term**

A **target market** is a segment of a market that a firm has decided to serve.

Selecting a target market is a three stage process.

1   The requirements and characteristics of the individuals and/or organisations which comprise the whole market are understood

2   On the basis of these requirements and characteristics, customers are grouped into segments . (As we have seen in the previous section, there are a number of different criteria which firms can use to segment a market, so it will need to decide what the most appropriate basis for segmenting the market is.)

3   One or more market segments is chosen for targeting. A marketing mix is then developed for that target market, based on the requirements and characteristics of the target-market customers, and what they value.

The Chartered Institute of Marketing

The benefit of serving specific target markets rather than the whole market it that customers in the target market will have similar characteristics. Therefore a single marketing mix strategy can be developed, and tailored to fit with their requirements. Jobber (2010) observes that the BMW 300 series saloon car which targets middle managers has a completely different design to the BMW X5 4x4 which is targeted at well-off couples with children.

2.4.1 Differentiation

Market segmentation and targeting also allow firms to develop differential marketing strategies. By breaking a market down into its constituent sub-groups a firm can then differentiate its product offerings between segments (if it chooses to target more than one segment). And within each segment it can differentiate its product from the competition, by highlighting the aspects of its product which create the most value for the customers in that segment.

2.4.2 Evaluating market segments

A market segment will only be valid if it is worth designing and developing a unique marketing mix for that specific segment. The following questions are commonly asked to decide whether or not the segment can be used for developing marketing plans.

Table 2.3   Criteria for assessing segment validity

Criteria	Comment
Can the segment be measured?	A market segment might be easy to define but hard to measure. For example, if 'people with a conservative outlook to life' is a segment, how would this be measured?
Is the segment big enough?	There has to be a large enough potential market to be profitable.
Can the segment be reached?	There has to be a way of getting to the potential customers via the organisation's promotion and distribution channels.
Do segments respond differently?	If two or more segments respond in the same way to a marketing mix, the segments are effectively the same. There is no point in distinguishing them from each other.
Can the segment be reached profitably?	Do the identified customer needs cost less to satisfy than the revenue they earn?

2.4.3 Segment attractiveness

A segment might be valid and potentially profitable, but is it potentially **attractive?**

(a)   A segment which has **high barriers to entry** might cost more to enter but will be less **vulnerable to competitors.**

(b)   For firms involved in **relationship marketing**, the segment should be one in which a **viable relationship** between the firm and the customer can be established.

The most attractive segments are those whose needs can be met by building on the company's strengths and where forecasts for **demand**, **sales profitability** and **growth** are favourable.

2.5 Positioning

So far we have looked at market segmentation and target market selection. However, in order to develop an effective marketing strategy a firm then has to decide how to position its product or service in the marketplace.

Positioning strategies are based on the results of two key sets of choices:

- Target markets – **where** a firm wants to compete
- Differential advantage – **how** a firm wants to compete

The objective of positioning is to create and maintain a distinctive place for a company, and/or its products and brands in its chosen markets.

Once the organization has decided which customer groups within which market segments to target, it has to determine how to present the product to this target audience. This allows it to address the needs and requirements of the target groups exactly, with a tangible marketing mix that consists of product characteristics, price, promotional activities and distribution channels.

Dibb & Simkin (2008, p73) summarise the positioning process as follows:

- In each segment, understand customer perceptions of all key brands
- Position the organization's products in the mind of the customers and distributors/dealers in the targeted segment against rivals' products and brands.
- Design an appropriate marking mix which conveys this desired positioning to the targeted customers.

THE REAL WORLD

InterContinental Hotels Group

The Intercontinental Hotels Groups is the world's largest hotel group, with approximately 3,650 hotels in nearly 100 countries. The group has adopted a multi-segment strategy in order to serve a variety a segments. The group's marketers have considered a range of customer characteristics, requirements and behaviours in developing the brands and its respective brand positionings.

Characteristics which the group's marketers have considered include: the duration of stay, hotel location and proximity to other addresses, amenities and services sought or expected, the level of luxury desired, value for money, hotel ambience and 'feel', hotel usage and usage characteristics, size of guest room, and customer profiles (Dibb & Simkin, 2008).

We can illustrate the way the Group has segmented the market by looking at the different target markets of some of its brands:

- InterContinental Hotels and Resorts – are aimed at well-travelled, affluent guests who want to be connected to what's special about a destination.

- Crowne Plaza – The 2011 Annual Report comments that Crowne Plaza's 'core guests are best described as 'Strivers.' These individuals are aspiring business people who choose hotels that understand their ambitions. We are currently repositioning this market more precisely. New products and services are under development to give guests the space and technology they need to be high productive and to feel restored and re-energised for the day ahead.

- Hotel Indigo – Hotel Indigo aims to combine the individuality of a boutique hotel with the reliability of a big brand company. It aims to appeal to the upscale well-travelled guest who has an eye for design and is looking for something different.

- Staybridge Suites – are aimed at upscale business and leisure travellers who want to move in for longer, extended stays and enjoy the best of home and hotel. Guests have their own spacious living areas, fully-equipped kitchens and separate work areas.

- Holiday Inn Express – By contrast to the brands aimed high end customers, Holiday Inn Express is a mid-priced chain with the IHG Group. As an 'express' hotel, its focus is on offering limited services at reasonable prices. Standard amenities lean towards convenience and practicality, to which cater to business travellers and short-term stages.

www.ihgplc.com

 The Chartered Institute of Marketing

Positioning should be used to help a company or brand develop a strong and distinctive image which differentiates it from its competitors, in the minds of its **target customers**. Factors which could be used to help position a product include: price, quality, reliability, supporting services/after-sales service, and value for money. However, because position is ultimately based on customers' perceptions, it is important that marketers focus most on the factors which are most important to the customers. For example, there are a range of product characteristics which car manufacturers could focus on, such as: speed, fuel efficiency, security, luxury interiors, image. The factors which a manufacturer chooses to emphasis should be those which are most important to its target market, such that the positioning image of their car matches the aspirations of its target customers.

However, another consequence of being ultimately based on customers' perceptions, is that it is only partly within marketers' control. External developments could change the way customers think about a product: for example as result of a change in the price of a competitor product, or the launch a new rival product or substitute product, or test results by a consumer magazine or research institution which call into question some of the claims made about a product.

2.6 Customer Profiling

The process of segmenting and targeting also highlights the potential value of customer profiling.

Customer profiling involves grouping people according to their likely similar behaviours and characteristics, in sufficient detail to build a 'profile' of target customers. Then, a firm can tailor its marketing to the specific needs of its customers, based on their profile.

For example, customer profiling is often used by retailers when they are considering where to open a new store. Key questions which the retailer needs to ask are: Who are my customers? What types of people are attracted to my different offerings? What kinds of people live near a given location? What kinds of people live in a given geographic area? Or where do certain kinds of people live?

Questions like this can help the retailer decide where to locate the store, and then can help them know where to target mail-shots and other promotional material once it has opened.

As we saw earlier when we looked at market segmentation, there are a number of different bases which can be used to define groups of people. Again, these bases can be either **demographic** or **behavioural**.

For example, identifying that a core group of customers are married women, with young children, living in exclusive neighbourhoods could help build a profile based on demographic factors.

Equally, identifying a group which visits a firm's website every day could help define a profile based on behavioural characteristics.

The main aim of customer profiling is to help a firm create a portrait of its customers which can then help it make design decisions about its products or services.

In a customer profiling exercise, a firm breaks down its customers into groups sharing similar goals and characteristics. Each group is then given a representative, with a photo, a name, and a description.

A small group of these customer profiles (or 'personas') is then used to help the firm make key decisions. For example, the married woman, with young children, living in an exclusive neighbourhood could become 'Kate' as a persona, allowing the firm to consider which features of a product or service would help Kate achieve her goals most easily.

The internet has spawned a modern phenomenon that marketing was not slow to appreciate. "Viral" advertising campaigns are part of an activity known as "Guerrilla Marketing". Explain what you understand by these terms. Is Guerrilla Marketing an unethical activity, to be avoided? "Going viral" is sometimes seen as a kind of accolade, or reward for a great piece of marketing communications. How can "Viral" be achieved?

3 Segmental analysis

'In a strategic context, segmentation means the identification of customer groups that respond differently from other groups to competitive offerings' Aaker & McLoughlin (2010) p26.

'A segmentation strategy looks to couple the identified segments with a programme to deliver an offering to those segments' (*Ibid*.)

Different segments and different customers offer different levels of profit. As we have already seen, on of the most important tools for market analysis is **segmentation**.

A company can approach this first by examining what market segments it currently markets in, and how big a contribution each segment is making to total turnover and profit. Finally, it should consider whether each market segment is in growth or decline.

A segmental analysis might look like this.

Market segment	Turnover £k	Proportion of total turnover %	Profit £k	Proportion of total profit %
A	500	14	50	9
B	1,000	29	200	36
C	1,500	43	150	27
D	500	14	150	27
	3,500		550	

Market segment	Turnover £k	Profit £k	Profit as a % of turnover %
A	500	50	10
B	1,000	200	20
C	1,500	150	10
D	500	150	30
	3,500	550	

You will note that each segment offers different profit opportunities.

3.1 Evaluating market segments

When evaluating market segments it is necessary to review two issues.

1   **Market attractiveness**, based upon:

- Segment size
- Segment's rate of growth
- Segment's profitability
- Customer price sensitivity

- Stage of industry life cycle
- Predictability
- Demand patterns
- Potential for substitutes
- Five forces analysis
- PEST factors

2   **Ability to address segment needs**

Organisational capability is made up of specific assets and competencies.

3.2 How to calculate profits on a segmental basis

> **▶ Key term**
>
> **Assets** are organisational attributes, tangible or intangible, that can be utilised to gain advantages in the market.

Identifying total turnover is easy. A segment is a collection of customers, and revenue streams from them are fairly easy to identify. Identifying costs is much harder. Here are some different types of cost.

1   **Fixed or variable**

(a)   **Fixed costs** will be incurred however many or however few items are produced or sold. Factory rent is an example. These are also called overheads.

(b)   **Variable costs** relate directly to the number of units produced. For example, a variable cost item in producing books is paper. These are also called direct costs.

2   **Controllable or uncontrollable**

(a)   **Controllable costs** are incurred at management discretion, such as an advertising campaign.

(b)   **Uncontrollable costs** are those which, in the short-run at least, management are committed to.

3   **Avoidable or unavoidable**

(a)   **Avoidable cost**: this cost is affected by a decision.

(b)   **Unavoidable cost**: this cost will not be affected by a decision.

For example, the cost of the managing director's salary will not be affected by a decision not to serve an individual customer.

Table 2.4   Typical marketing costs

Cost	Comment
Direct selling expenses	Personal calls by salesperson
Indirect selling	Sales admin, supervision
Marketing research	Consultancies, primary data collection, analysis
Advertising	Media costs
Sales promotion	Consumer, trade etc
Transport	Carriage costs
Storage	Warehousing
Order processing	Checking, billing, bad debts

These can be allocated, in different ways, to products, customer groups, and sales territories. We are currently interested in segments. The steps involved in segmental analysis are as follows.

Step 1   Identify revenue derived from a segment

Step 2   Identify direct product costs (eg materials)

Step 3   Identify marketing costs

Step 4   Allocate avoidable costs to the segment (ie those costs which would be saved if the segment were not serviced)

4 Strategic account analysis

Another potential benefit of segmenting customers into different groups is that it can help a firm analyse the profitability of serving different customer groups.

In their book '*Killer Customers: Tell the Good from the Bad and Crush Your Competitors*' Selden & Colvin (2003) estimate that the top 20% of an organisation's customers (ranked by profitability) typically generate more than 120% of the organisation's profits. By comparison, the bottom 20% of customers typically generate losses of around 100% of profits, leaving a net 20% for all customer combined. This not only highlights the importance of retaining this top 20% of customers, and improving the profitability of the bottom 20%, but it also highlights the importance of organisations knowing the relative profitability of serving different groups of customers.

By creating a customer database, marketers can segment customers based upon customer profitability and other bases appropriate to their business. Thus marketers can match customers with appropriate levels of investment, with the most profitable customers in the future receiving one set of communications and other groups such as low profit and dormant customers receiving communications appropriate to their status.

4.1 What is a strategic account?

> **Key term**
>
> A **key (strategic) account** is a customer in a B2B market identified by the selling company as being of strategic importance. It often displays the following characteristics (Blythe, 2006):
>
> - It accounts for a significant proportion of sales
> - There is co-operation between channel members rather than conflict
> - There are lengthy negotiations and frequent contact
> - There are often servicing aspects, as well as delivery of physical products

No doubt you are already aware that it is far more expensive to attract a new customer than to do business with an established one. There are several reasons for this.

- Established customers do not qualify for inducements such as introductory offers and discounts.
- There are communications and other marketing costs associated with obtaining new business.

There are other benefits to retaining satisfied customers.

- Established customers do not require as much customer service assistance as new ones.
- Established customers are more likely to generate new business through referrals.
- Established customers tend to purchase more as their relationship with the brand or supplier lengthens.

These advantages mean that customer retention is an important factor in successful trading. Marketers need to be able to monitor such matters as the amount of business that comes from new customers, the number of referrals and the proportion of business that comes from established customers. Of those established customers, some will be defined as 'strategic accounts'.

Many firms – especially in business-to-business markets – sell to a relatively small number of customers. Not all customers are as important as others, and the checklist below can help to identify the most important.

Figure 2.1 Strategic importance evaluation guide

	High	Medium	Low
Fit between customer's needs and our capabilities, at present and potentially			
Ability to serve customer compared with our major competitors, at present and potentially			
'Health' of customer's industry, current and forecast			
'Health' of the customer, current and forecast			
Customer's growth prospects, current and forecast			
What can we learn from this customer?			
Can the customer help us to attract others?			
Relative significance: how important is the customer compared with other customers?			
What is the profitability of serving the customer?			

ACTIVITY 2.2

A firm might wish to identify which customer offer the most profit opportunity. Strategic account analysis calls for six main areas of investigation into customers, as listed below:

- Key customer identity
- Customer history
- Relationship of customer to product
- Relationship of customer to market
- Customer attitudes and behaviour
- Financial performance of the customer

Can you suggest specific topics of investigation under each of these headings?

4.2 Customer profitability

▶ **Key term**

Customer profitability analysis is an analysis of the total sales revenue generated from a customer or customer group, less all the costs that are incurred in servicing that customer group.

An understanding of the different profitability levels that exist within the customer base enables the company to concentrate its efforts on the customers most deserving of them.

The Post Office in the UK is a good example to illustrate how profitability might work. A uniform price is paid for a first class stamp to send a letter anywhere in the UK irrespective of whether it is to be delivered to an address five miles away or five hundred, and therefore irrespective of the significant differences in transport costs. However, the advantages of a uniform price are that there are savings on the costs of administering a wide range of prices, and that people are encouraged to use the postal services.

It is possible to analyse customer profitability over a single period but more useful to look at a longer time frame. Such a multi-period approach fits in with the concept of **relationship marketing**, with its emphasis upon customer retention for the longer-term.

ACTIVITY 2.3

Seth Ltd supplies shoes to Narayan Ltd and Kipling Ltd. Each pair of shoes has a list price of £50 each; as Kipling buys in bulk, Kipling receives a 10% trade discount for every order over 100 shoes. It costs £1,000 to deliver each order. In the year so far, Kipling has made five orders of 100 pairs of shoes each. Narayan Ltd receives a 15% discount irrespective of order size, because Narayan Ltd collects the shoes, thereby saving Seth Ltd any distribution costs. The cost of administering each order is £50. Narayan makes ten orders in the year, totalling 420 pairs of shoes.
Which relationship is most profitable for Seth?

Customer profitability analysis (CPA) focuses upon profits generated by customers and suggests that profit does not automatically increase with sales revenue. CPA can benefit a company in the following ways:

- It enables a company to focus resources on the most profitable areas
- It identifies unexpected differences in profitability between customers
- It helps to quantify the financial impact of proposed changes
- It helps to highlight the cost of obtaining new customers and the benefit of retaining existing ones
- It helps to highlight whether product development or market development is to be preferred
- An appreciation of the costs of servicing clients assists in negotiations with customers

4.3 Cost allocation

It is necessary to focus on the right costs for comparison.

- Costs common to all customers (eg sales director's basic salary) would not be avoided by failing to serve one of them.

- Furthermore, you have to be careful that you choose the 'right' product cost. The 'cost' of a product as revealed by the accounting system might include an amount of marketing overhead, which may not be avoided by ceasing to serve a customer. Therefore only avoidable costs should be taken into account.

The Chartered
Institute of Marketing

The following is a suggested format for a statement of customer or segment profitability. It could be applied equally in a B2B or B2C context.

			£'000
Sales revenue			X
Less: direct product cost			(X)
			X
Customer or segment-specific variable costs	– distribution	X	
	– rebates and discounts	X	
	– promotion etc	X	
			(X)
Other costs	– sales force	X	
	– customer service	X	
	– management cost	X	
			(X)
			X
Financing cost	– credit period	X	
	– customer-specific inventory	X	
			(X)
Customer or segment profitability			X

Such a report can highlight the differences between the cost of servicing different individuals or firms. This information can be used for the following purposes.

- Directing management effort to cutting customer or segment specific costs. Installing an EDI system can save the costs of paperwork, data input and so forth.

- Identifying those customers who are expensive to service, thereby suggesting action to increase profitability.

- Using this as part of a comparison with competitors' costs. A firm which services a customer more cheaply than a competitor can use this cost advantage to offer extra benefits to the customer.

- CPA can indicate cases where profitability might be endangered, for example by servicing customers for whom a firm's core competence is not especially relevant.

CPA might provide answers to the following questions:

1 What **profit/contribution** is the organisation making on sales to the customer, after discounts and selling and delivery costs?

2 What would be the **financial consequences** of losing the customer?

3 Is the customer buying in order sizes that are **unprofitable** to supply?

4 What is the **return on investment** on the plant used?

5 What is the level of **inventory** required to supply these customers?

6 Are there any **specific costs** involved in supplying this customer, eg technical and test facilities, R&D facilities, special design staff?

7 What is the **ratio** of net contribution per customer to total investment?

4.4 The customer life cycle

It has already been mentioned that, in line with the principles of relationship marketing, it is probably appropriate to think in terms of customer revenues and costs over more than one period. We can refine our financial analysis by working in terms of the present value of customer costs and revenues, and by incorporating the concept of the **customer life cycle**. This is less developed than the equivalent product and industry life-cycle models, but it can be useful to consider the following:

1   **Promotional expense** relating to a single customer is likely to be heavily front loaded.

2   It is likely that **sales** to a customer will start at a low level and increase to a higher level as the customer gains confidence, though this is not certain and will vary from industry to industry.

3   A customer who purchases a basic or commodity product initially may move on to **more differentiated products** later.

4   In consumer markets, career progression is likely to provide the individual customer with steadily increasing amounts of **disposable income**, with the family life cycle dictating the likely range of purchases as time passes.

5 The importance of consumer profiling and customer intelligence

Building **accurate and up-to-date profiles** of customers enables a company to:

- Extend **help** to a company's target audience
- **Stimulate further demand**
- **Stay close** to them

Keeping an electronic database of customers and prospects (and of all communications and commercial contacts) helps to improve all future contacts.

5.1 Customer intelligence – why is it so important?

For years the rhetoric of marketing has been that of **warfare**: targets, campaigns, offensives. The approach has been one of trying to beat the 'enemy' into submission and 'win' new customers. Many organisations now realise that there is more to be gained from alternative strategies.

- Investing in activities which seek to **retain existing customers**, based on the argument that it costs more to attract new customers.

- Encouraging existing customers to **spend more**.

Retaining customers is the basis of such relationship marketing techniques. Customers are seen not only in terms of what they are buying today, but also in terms of their **potential for future purchases**.

Although it is clear that **added services** and **quality of service** are the key to retaining customers, this still begs questions: precisely what services to add, for instance?

To be effective at **retention marketing**, the organisation has to have a good database **profiling past, present and prospective customers**, with details of the nature of the relationship; it has to know about their attitudes, their perceptions of the organisation's products and service, and their expectations. Just as importantly, the organisation must know, from systematically-acquired **customer feedback**, precisely what it is doing wrong.

A well-developed customer database will use **postcodes** to overlay specialist **geodemographic data** from **ACORN** or other source, or include **lifestyle information** allowing detailed customer profiles to be developed.

The Chartered
Institute of Marketing

Importantly, market information analysts, have also realized that the growth of the internet and digital media will affect demographic classifications. Consequently, CACI (which developed the ACORN classification) also launched a demographic classification called 'eTypes' to separate the population into different groups to reflect their different internet behaviours, technology use and lifestyle. This type of grouping will allow online marketing campaigns to be targeted as effectively as possible.

▶ **Exam tip**

It is worth emphasising that this unit is about strategy, rather than the design of tactical marketing programmes. Understanding the customer is a huge contributor to that strategy. The list below, covers some of the issues:

- Customers: does the firm take customers seriously and work for customer satisfaction? How do you create a customer-focused organisation?

- How are markets defined and segmented around issues that matter to customers?

- How do we create a value proposition based on our mission and our ability to differentiate from competitors?

CHAPTER ROUNDUP

- A firm's value proposition is the set of benefits or values it promises to deliver to customers to satisfy their needs. The value proposition dictates: how a firm will serve its targeted customers; how the firm will position itself in the marketplace; and how it will seek to differentiate itself from its competitors.

- However, it is unlikely that the customers in the marketplace will all have the same wants or needs, and therefore the firm is unlikely to be able to serve all the customer equally well with a single product. Therefore it needs to segment the market.

- A segment is a group of customers with similar characteristics who can be targeted with the same marketing mix.

- Segmentation bases can include objective classifications (eg age, gender) as well as more subjective approaches such as lifestyles, attitudes and behaviours.

- Segmentation enables firms to differentiate their product or service, in order to meet customer requirements more effectively. Segmentation also enables firms to target particular groups of buyers and establish distinct positions for its product or service.

FURTHER READING

Doole, I., Lancaster, P. & Lowe, R. (2005) *Understanding and Managing Customers*, Pearson, Harlow.

Gronroos, C. (1995), Relationship Marketing: The Strategy Continuum, *Journal of the Academy of Marketing Science*, Vol. 23, No. 4, pp 252-254.

McDonald, M. & Dunbar, .I (2004) *Market Segmentation: How to do it – how to profit from it*, Elsevier, Oxford.

Sheth, J.N. (2002), "The Future of Relationship Marketing", *Journal of Services Marketing*, Vol. 16, No. 7, pp 590-592.

Winer, R.S. (2001), "A Framework for Customer Relationship Management", *California Management Review*, Vol. 43, No. 4, pp 89-105.

REFERENCES

Aaker, D. & McLoughlin, D. (2007) *Strategic Market Management*. John Wiley, Chichester.

Aaker, D. & McLoughlin, D. (2010) *Strategic Market Management: Global Perspectives*. John Wiley, Chichester.

Blythe, J. (2006), *Principles and Practice of Marketing*. Thomson Learning, London.

Dibb, S & Simkin, L. (2008) *Marketing Planning: A Workbook for Marketing Managers*, Cengage Learning, London

Jobber, D. (2010) *Principles and Practice of Marketing*, 6th edition. McGraw-Hill, Maidenhead.

Kotler, P. & Armstrong, G. (2012) *Principles of Marketing*. 14th edition. Pearson, Harlow.

The Chartered Institute of Marketing

Kotler, P., Armstrong, G., Wong, V. & Saunders, J. (2008) *Principles of Marketing*. 5th European edition, Pearson, Harlow.

Kotler, P., Keller, K., Brady, M., Goodman, T. & Hansen, T. (2009) *Marketing Management*. Pearson, Harlow.

Selden, L. & Colvin, G. (2003) *Killer Customers: Tell the Good from the Bad and Crush your Competitors*, Penguin, London.

QUICK QUIZ

1   Define 'value proposition'

2   How does the customer evaluate a company's value proposition?

3   Give an example of a value proposition

4   What is segmentation?

5   What are two issues to consider when evaluating market segments?

6   Give an example of a fixed cost, and explain why it is regarded as such

7   Present two organisational benefits from retaining satisfied customers

8   What is customer profitability analysis?

9   Why might a company want to build profiles of its customers?

10 'Customers are seen not only in terms of what they are buying ...., but also in terms of their .... purchases' (Fill in the blanks)

ACTIVITY DEBRIEFS

Activity 2.1

"Guerrilla marketing" began as a fringe movement and was first identified as a concept by **Jay** Conrad Levinson in the 1980s. Levinson built up a whole movement around those activities that, put simply, comprise non-conventional ways of getting a commercial message across. People like to talk about their involvement with products and services for a variety of reasons. Viral marketing has emerged as the electronic form of Word of Mouth (WoM) and, just as people you meet recount episodes of their lives, or humorous, or dramatic stories they have heard about, people will actively participate in passing on film clips, jokes or other material to people they know. If the commercial message is composed in a suitable way, with sufficient content that grabs attention or tells a story, then the effect can be like the spreading ripples from a stone thrown in a pool. A good example is the Lynx commercial *"Even angels will fall"*, or the one that shows a female athlete pole-vaulting into a young fellow's bedroom. If people wish to pass on these "sketches", no harm is done and the ethical question is not invoked.

Activity 2.2

Area	Detail
Key customer identity	Name of each key customer
	Location
	Status in market
	Products they make and sell
	Size of firm (revenue, number of employees, capital employed)
Customer history	First purchase date
	Who makes the buying decision in the organisation?
	What is the average order size, by product?
	What is the regularity of the order, by product?
	What is the trend in the size of orders?
	What is the motive in purchasing?
	What does the customer know about the firm's and competitors' products?
	On what basis does the customer re-order?
	How is the useful life of the product judged?
	Were there any lost or cancelled orders? For what reason?
Relationship of customer to product	What does the customer use the product for?
	Do the products form part of the customer's own service/product?
Relationship of customer to potential market	What is the size of the customer in relation to the total end-market?
	Is the customer likely to expand, or not? Diversify or integrate?
Customer attitudes and behaviour	What interpersonal factors exist which could affect sales by the firm and by competitors?
	Does the customer also buy competitor products?
	To what extent may purchases be postponed?
The financial performance of the customer	How successful is the customer?

Activity 2.3

You can see below that the profit earned by Seth in servicing Narayan is greater, despite the increased discount.

	Kipling	Narayan
Number of shoes	500	420
	£	£
Revenue after discount	22,500	17,850
Transport	(5,000)	
Administration	(250)	(500)
Net profit	17,250	17,350

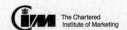

1   Value proposition can be said to be 'what the customer gets for his money'.

2   Performance, relative to competitors; price.

3   Product quality, price, delivery times, product reliability (these are just a few!)

4   Segmentation is the identification of customer groups that respond differently from other groups to competitive offerings.

5   Market attractiveness, and the overall ability to address segment needs.

6   Rent is a fixed cost, because it remains the same regardless of how many units of a product are produced.

7   (a)   Established customers do not require as much customer service assistance as new ones.

         (b)   Established customers are more likely to generate new business through referrals.

8   Customer profitability analysis is an analysis of the total sales revenue generated from a customer or customer group, less all the costs that are incurred in servicing that customer group.

9   Building accurate and up-to-date profiles of customers enables a company to:

- Extend help to a company's target audience
- Stimulate further demand
- Stay close to them

10   Today; future

CHAPTER 3

The internal marketing environment

Introduction

A look at the internal environment of an organisation is a way of identifying strengths and weaknesses. It therefore covers all aspects of the organisation. This is because the other functions of the organisation effectively act as constraints over what marketing personnel can achieve.

A company needs to evaluate its ability to compete and satisfy customer needs. The firm's resources, once identified, must be harnessed to a market orientation to ensure that those resources are directed at satisfying those needs.

There are a number of approaches to be taken with regard to corporate capability. In this chapter we conduct an overview of resources in the context of organisational effectiveness. The key issues are what resources the organisation has and how they are deployed.

An analysis of corporate/marketing resources (section 1) covers three main areas:

1   What the organisation currently has or owns.

2   What the organisation has access to, even if it currently does not own the resources.

3   How effectively it deploys its resources.

The culture (section 2) of an organisation is strategically important. Culture is to some extent formed by past strategic success, and influences the development of strategy for the future. An awareness and understanding of the interaction between culture and strategy is therefore an important part of internal strategic assessment.

Topic list

Products and resources   ①

Organisational culture and performance   ②

1.2.1	Utilise a range of models and techniques to undertake a strategic audit of the internal environment:
	• Resource and competency audit (physical, human and intangibles)
	• Portfolio analysis
	• Value chain and resource utilisation
	• Innovation audit
	• Cost efficiency
	• Product life-cycle
	• Organisation's vision, mission and values
	• Degree of customer and market orientation
	• Comparative and best practice analysis
	• Core competencies
	• Organisational culture
	• Financial performance

1 Products and resources

In Chapter 1, we looked at the external environment, which presents opportunities and threats to a firm. However, successful strategies are also dependent on a firm having the internal strategic capability required for success. In this Chapter we are going to look at the internal environment of a firm.

'There would be no point in having state-of-the-art equipment if it were not used effectively. The efficiency and effectiveness of physical or financial resources, or the people in an organisation, depend, not just on their existence, but on the systems and processes by which they are managed, the relationships and cooperation between people, their adaptability, their innovatory capacity, the relationship with customers and suppliers and the experience and learning about works well and what does not.' (Johnson, Whittington & Scholes, 2012, p51)

1.1 Resources and competences

> ▶ **Key terms**
>
> The **resource audit** covers technical resources, financial resources, managerial skills, the organisation and its information system. It is a review of assets of all kinds which are available to the organisation.
>
> Resources are deployed as **competences** which support a competitive position. A distinctive competence is hard to imitate.

1   **Technical resources**

    (a)   Technical ability

    (b)   Processes for NPD

    (c)   Ability to convert new technology into new marketing products

2   **Financial standing**. Firms with a good financial standing find it easier to raise money.

3   **Managerial skills**. An effective management is a key organisation resource in planning activities, controlling the organisation and motivating staff.

4   **Organisation**. Organisation structure can be a resource for marketers, for example, product divisionalisation or brand management control at brand level. The organisation structure should facilitate communication and decision-making.

5   **Information systems**. Information systems have a strategic role.

Resources are of no value unless they are organised into systems, and so a **resource audit** should go on to consider how well or how badly resources have been utilised, and whether the organisation's systems are **effective** and **efficient** in meeting customer needs profitably.

1.2 The value chain

In Chapter 1, we identified the importance of marketing a process by which companies create value for their customers. Here we will look in more detail at the ways in which companies create value.

1.2.1 The value chain

The **value chain** models how an organisation creates value through managing value activities and the linkages between them. These can be deployed to give distinct customer benefits.

The **value chain** model of corporate activities, developed by Michael Porter (1985), offers a bird's eye view of the firm and what it does. Competitive advantage, says Porter, arises out of the way an organisation uses its inputs and transforms them into the outputs that customers pay for. The processes involved in this transformation are called **value activities**.

▶ **Exam tip**

The value chain is a very useful model and a favourite with examiners. It is an excellent checklist of the things in a business that you might need to discuss in almost any question.

1.2.2 Activities

▶ **Key term**

Value activities are the means by which a firm creates value in its products.

Activities incur costs, and, in combination with other activities, provide a product or service that earns revenue. 'Firms create value for their buyers by performing these activities.'

Example

Let us explain this point by using the example of a **restaurant**. A restaurant's activities can be divided into buying food, cooking it, and serving it (to customers). There is no reason, in theory, why the customers should not do all these things themselves, at home. The customer, however, is not only prepared to **pay for someone else** to do all this but also **pays more than the cost of** the resources. The ultimate value a firm creates is measured by the amount customers are willing to pay for its products or services above the cost of carrying out value activities. A firm is profitable if the realised value to customers exceeds the collective cost of performing the activities.

- Customers **purchase value**, which they measure by comparing a firm's products and services with similar offerings by competitors.

- The business **creates value** by carrying out its activities either more efficiently than other businesses, or combining them in such a way as to provide a unique product or service.

ACTIVITY 3.1

Outline different ways in which the restaurant can create value.

Figure 3.1   The value chain (Porter))

Based on Porter, Competitive Strategy (1985)

The **margin** is the excess the customer is prepared to **pay** over the **cost** to the firm of obtaining resource inputs and providing value activities.

Primary activities are directly related to production, sales, marketing, delivery and service.

Table 3.1   Primary activities

Activity	Comment
Inbound logistics	Receiving, handling and storing inputs to the production system: warehousing, transport, stock control.
Operations	Convert resource inputs into a final product. Resource inputs are not only materials. People are a resource especially in service industries.
Outbound logistics	Storing the product and its distribution to customers: packaging, warehousing, testing.
Marketing and sales	Informing customers about the product, persuading them to buy it, and enabling them to do so: advertising, promotion.
After-sales service	Installing products, repairing them, upgrading them, providing spare parts and so forth.

Support activities provide purchased inputs, human resources, technology and infrastructural functions to support the primary activities.

Table 3.2   Support activities

Activity	Comment
Procurement	Acquire the resource inputs to the primary activities (eg purchase of materials, subcomponents equipment).
Technology development	Product design, improving processes and/or resource utilisation.
Human resource management	Recruiting, training, developing and rewarding people.
Management planning	Planning, finance, quality control: Porter believes they are crucially important to an organisation's strategic capability in all primary activities.

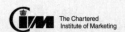

Linkages connect the activities of the value chain.

(a) **Activities in the value chain affect one another**. For example, more costly product design or better quality production might reduce the need for after-sales service.

(b) **Linkages require co-ordination**. For example, just-in-time requires smooth functioning of operations, outbound logistics and service activities such as installation.

1.2.3 Value system

Value is also created by the links between one value chain and the next: together, they make up a **value system**.

Activities that add value do not stop at the organisation's **boundaries**. For example, when a restaurant serves a meal, the quality of the ingredients – although they are chosen by the cook – is determined by the grower. The grower has added value, and the grower's success in growing produce of good quality is as important to the customer's ultimate satisfaction as the skills of the chef. A firm's value chain is connected to what Porter calls a **value system**.

Figure 3.2   A value system

Based on Porter, Competitive Strategy (1985)

1.2.4 Using the value chain

The value chain can be used to understand the strategic position of an organisation in three ways (Johnson, Whittington & Scholes, 2012):

1. By providing a general description of the organisation's activities it can help managers understand if there is a cluster of activities which provide benefit to customers within particular areas of the chain. For example, a firm could be particularly good at outbound logistics, linked to its marketing and sales operation, and supported by its technology department. However its inbound logistics and operations functions might be less good.

2. By analysing the competitive position of the organisation, by helping to identify:

    - Which value-creating activities are especially significant for meeting customer needs

    - Whether the factors which create value for an organisation are rare or unique, or whether its competitors will also have them

- How easy it will be for competitors to imitate the activities which create value for the organisation, or whether they are embedded within the organisation

- Whether any aspects of the value chain are vulnerable to substitution

3. By analysing the cost and value of activities within the organisation. For example:

- How dos the cost of different activities relate to the amount of value they add to the final product or service?

- How does the cost of different activities (and the value created by them) compare with similar activities in competitors?

- Where, and how, can costs be reduced? For example, could some activities be outsourced, or could cost-savings be made by changing the way activities are structured; for example, through combining fragmented purchasing activities into a central procurement system.

Overall, the value chain highlights that a firm can secure competitive advantage by:

- Inventing new or better ways to do activities
- Combining activities in new or better ways
- Managing the linkages in its own value chain
- Managing the linkages in the value system

THE REAL WORLD

Toyota

In November 2007, on the eve of its 70th year, Toyota unveiled its Global Vision 2020.

The 'Global Vision' was an investment plan which revealed Toyota's intention to invest heavily in cutting-edge technologies and to continue its policy of making its value chain ever more effective and efficient.

Toyota has become an iconic manage of the modern keiretsu – a network of mutually supportive companies. Toyota's keiretsu, which comprises group companies, several large component manufacturers and a large number of smaller suppliers, sustains a relationship which would be hard to replicate elsewhere. The keiretsu corporate family creates an environment of trust which acts as a dynamic driver for constantly improving the value chain.

(Based on example in Kotler *et al*, 2009)

ACTIVITY 3.2

Sana Sounds is a small record company. Representatives from Sana Sounds scour music clubs for new bands to promote. Once a band has signed a contract (with Sana Sounds) it makes a recording. The recording process is subcontracted to one of a number of recording studio firms which Sana Sounds uses regularly. (At the moment Sana Sounds is not large enough to invest in its own equipment and studios.) Sana Sounds also subcontracts the production of records and CDs to a number of manufacturing companies. Sana Sounds then distributes the disks to selected stores, and engages in any promotional activities required.

What would you say were the activities in Sana Sounds' value chain?

The example value chains which follow are based on two supermarket chains, one concentrating on low prices, the other differentiated on quality and service. See if you can tell which is which.

The Chartered
Institute of Marketing

Figure 3.3   Contrasting value chains from two supermarkets

1

	INBOUND LOGISTICS	OPERATIONS	OUTBOUND LOGISTICS	MARKETING & SALES	SERVICE
Firm infrastructure	Central control of operations and credit control				
Human resource management	Recruitment of mature staff	Client care training	Flexible staff to help with packing		
Technology development		Recipe research	Electronic point of sale	Consumer research & tests	Itemised bills
Procurement	Own label products	Prime retail positions		Adverts in quality magazines & poster sites	
	Dedicated refrigerated transport	In-store food halls Modern store design Open front refrigerators Tight control of sell-by dates	Collect by car service	No price discounts on food past sell-by dates	No quibble refunds

2

	INBOUND LOGISTICS	OPERATIONS	OUTBOUND LOGISTICS	MARKETING & SALES	SERVICE
Firm infrastructure	Minimum corporate HQ				
Human resource management		De-skilled store-ops	Dismissal for checkout error		
Technology development	Computerised warehousing		Checkouts simple		
Procurement	Branded only purchases big discounts	Low cost sites			Use of concessions
	Bulk warehousing	Limited range Price points Basic store design		Low price promotion Local focus	Nil

The two supermarkets represented are based on the following.

(a)   The value chain in (1) is based on a firm which seeks to differentiate on quality and service. Hence the 'no quibble' refunds, the use of prime retail sites, and customer care training.

(b)   The value chain in (2) is similar to that of a 'discount' supermarket chain which differentiates on price, pursuing a cost leadership, or perhaps more accurately, a cost-focus strategy. This can be seen in the limited product range and its low-cost sites.

1.2.5 IT and the value chain

IT can be used at each stage in the value chain.

Operations

IT can be used to **automate and improve physical tasks** in the operating core. It also **provides information** about operational processes.

Inbound and outbound logistics

- **Warehousing**. A number of companies now use IT systems to monitor and control exactly where their goods or orders are at any time. (Many also allow customers to track the progress of their orders; for example, so that the customers can see when an order has been packed for delivery, or when it has been shipped from the warehouse).

- Create **virtual warehouses** of stock actually held at **suppliers**. For example an organisation with several outlets might have each connected to a system which indicates the total amount of stock available at different sites.

- Planning procedures to schedule production, such as in MRPII (manufacturing resource planning) software.

Sales and marketing

- **Internet websites** can be used as an advertising medium and to gather information about customers.

- **Customer databases** enable firms to monitor consumers' buying habits and to identify new segments.

- Supermarkets use **EPOS** systems to give them a precise hour-by-hour idea of how products are selling to enable speedy ordering and replenishments.

Services

IT can be used **to plan and schedule after-sales service**, and to support service staff on the ground.

1.3 Portfolio analysis

▶ **Key terms**

Portfolio: A collection of products/SBUs reporting to one entity. Each product or SBU can be separately identified for decision-making and performance measurement.

Portfolio analysis compares the marketing and financial performance of a firm's products and/or SBUs with a view to decision-making.

Portfolio planning analyses the current position of an organisation's products or SBUs in their markets, and the state of growth or decline in each of those markets. Several matrices have been developed to analyse market share, market growth and market position.

1.3.1 Market share, market growth and cash generation: the Boston classification

The **BCG matrix**, Figure 3.4, classifies products (or business units) in terms of potential cash generation, on the basis of their **market share relative to that of their competitors** and the **rate of growth in the market** as a whole. The split on the horizontal axis is based on market share relative to the market leader, while the location of the split on the vertical axis will depend on the rate of growth in the market. (Note that the measure here is based on market growth, not the growth rate of an individual business).

Figure 3.4   The BCG matrix

Boston Consulting Group (1970)

You should note that BCG analysis can also be applied to:

- Individual products
- Strategic business units (SBUs)

On the basis of this classification, each product (or, working at a higher level, each strategic business unit) will then fall into one of four broad categories.

(1)   A **question mark** has a small relative market share in a high growth industry. The generic product is clearly popular, but customer support for the company brand is limited. A small market share implies that competitors are in a strong position and that if the product is to be successful it will **require substantial funds**, and a new marketing mix. If the market looks good and the product is viable, then the company should consider a **build** strategy to increase market share. This would require the commitment of funds to permit more active marketing. If the future looks less promising then the company should consider the possibility of withdrawing the product.

(2)   A **star** is a product with a high relative market share in a high growth industry. By implication, **the star has potential for generating significant earnings** currently and in the future. However, at this stage it may still require substantial marketing expenditures to maintain this position, but would probably be regarded as a **good investment for the future**.

(3)   A **cash cow** has a high relative market share but in a mature slow growth market. Typically, it is a well established product with a high degree of consumer loyalty. Product development costs are low and the marketing campaign is well established. The cash cow will normally make a **substantial contribution to overall profitability**. The appropriate strategy will vary according to its precise position. If market growth is reasonably strong then a **hold** strategy will be appropriate, but if growth or share are weakening, then a **harvest** strategy may be more sensible, cutting back on marketing expenditure and maximise short-term cash flow.

(4)   A **dog** is a product characterised by low relative market share and low growth. Also, typically a well established product, it is apparently losing consumer support and may have cost disadvantages. The usual strategy would be to consider **divestment** unless cash flow position is strong, in which case the product would be **harvested** in the short-term prior to deletion from the product range.

Implicit in the matrix is the notion that **markets are dynamic**. The typical new product is likely to appear in the 'question mark' category to begin with; if it looks promising and is given effective marketing, it might be expected to become a star, then, as markets mature, a cash cow and finally a dog. The suggestion that most products will move through these stages does not weaken the role played by marketing. On the contrary, it strengthens it, since poor marketing may mean that a product moves from being a problem child to a dog without making any substantial contribution to profitability. Equally, of course, good marketing may enable the firm to **prolong** the star and cash cow phases, thus maximising **cash flow** from the product.

The framework provided by the matrix can offer guidance in terms of developing **appropriate strategies** for products and in maintaining a **balanced product portfolio**, ensuring that there are enough cash generating products to match the cash-using products.

An industrial equipment company has five products with the following sales and market characteristics.

Product	Sales £m	£m sales Top 3 firms			Market growth rate %	Relative share
A	0.5	0.7	0.7	0.5*	15%	0.71
B	1.6	1.6	1.6*	1.0	18%	1.0
C	1.8	1.8*	1.2	1.0	7%	1.5
D	3.2	3.2*	0.8	0.7	4%	4.0
E	0.5	2.5	1.8	1.7	4%	0.2

The circles indicate the contribution the product makes to overall turnover. The centre of circles indicates their position on the matrix:

What can you deduce about the company's product portfolio from this diagram?

Huawei smartphones

Sales of smartphones are booming, though very few phone makers have been rejoicing. In the three months to July 2012, Nokia made losses of £1.1 billion as it has battled to remain in a smartphone market dominated by Apple and Samsung, which between them have over 50% of the global market.

Nokia was once the world's leading mobile phone maker, but in the second quarter of 2012 it sold 4 million Windows phones, which is only a fraction of Apple's expected sales of 30 million iPhones or Samsung's 50 million smartphones.

However, one other big winner has emerged in the smartphone market: Huawei Technologies. Although they were only the seventh largest smartphone maker in 2011, it is thought that they may have passed Nokia in the second quarter of 2012 to become the third-largest smartphone maker.

Huawei was founded in 1987, and quickly became a high-tech success story in China by selling telecom products to phone companies, routinely beating rivals such as Alcatel-Lucent Ericsson, and Cisco Systems with good-enough products and great prices. Only in the mid-2000s did it start making mobile phones. However, the Shenzhen-based company's inexpensive, often unbranded models gained market share in China, the Middle East, and Africa.

Huawei kept this low-cost approach as it got serious about smartphones, in 2009. It didn't try to build its own software operating system like Apple, or Microsoft; but it used Android instead. And unlike Samsung, or Motorola, it didn't try to differentiate Google's mobile software with its own tweaks. It simply installed Android on its hardware and then began to distribute it.

In 2012, Huawei expects to triple its smartphone sales to 60 million units, in part by taking a bigger chunk of the U.S. market. Until now, it's sold handsets costing less than US $200 to carriers such as MetroPCS and Cricket that offer pay-as-you-go plans, mostly to lower-income consumers.

In November 2011, it landed a deal with a top-tier U.S. carrier when AT&T started selling Huawei's Impulse phone for $29. And in July 2012, T-Mobile announced that Huawei would be building two models in the carrier's MyTouch line of handsets.

"We essentially made the market for affordable smartphones," says William Plummer, Huawei's U.S. vice president for external affairs. "We're in a good position because we've established ourselves as a trusted partner to carriers."

However, succeeding in smartphones is vital for Huawei if it wants to remain a fast-growing company. Its US$23 billion-a-year telecom equipment business grew only 3.5 percent in 2011, before tumbling due to the slowdown in China's economy this year. The company reorganised in 2011 to create a separate Huawei Devices unit to drive what executives say is the company's best growth opportunity. The division also makes laptop modems and other functional devices.

Huawei's growth rate may even make it a plausible challenger to Samsung in smartphone sales, believes Horace Dediu, of equity research firm Asymco. Dediu argues that Samsung has prospered largely because of vertical integration; it makes many of the chips and screens that go into its devices. Yet he doubts Samsung has built up enough brand loyalty to withstand a much cheaper alternative; not least because Samsung itself was only the fourth or fifth largest supplier only a few years ago.

So, as smartphones evolve from novelty technology into just another gadget, Huawei will be well positioned to benefit. Although their phones may not be as sophisticated as some competitors, they are inexpensive and as one research analyst commented 'Their devices don't have to have jet packs to do 90 percent of what most people need.'

Based on: Burrows, P. 'The New Smartphone Powerhouse: Huawei', July 19, 2012, www.businessweek.com

Latham, C, 'Nokia loses £1.1 bn as rivals steal limelight', July 20, 2012, *Metro*.

ACTIVITY 3.4

The marketing manager of Juicy Drinks Ltd has invited you in for a chat. Juicy Drinks Ltd provides fruit juices to a number of supermarket chains, which sell them under their own label. 'We've got a large number of products, of course. Our freshly squeezed orange juice is doing fine – it sells in huge quantities. Although margins are low, we have sufficient economies of scale to do very nicely in this market. We've got advanced production and bottling equipment and long-term contracts with some major growers. No problems there. We also sell freshly squeezed pomegranate juice: customers loved it in the tests, but producing the stuff at the right price is a major hassle: all the seeds get in the way. We hope it will be a winner, once we get the production right and start converting customers to it. After all the market for exotic fruit juices generally is expanding fast.

What sort of products, according to the Boston classification, are described here?

The BCG portfolio analysis is useful because it provides a framework for planners to consider and forecast potential market growth and to evaluate the competitive dimension through an evaluation of market share and the likely changes in cash flow.

Shortcomings of BCG

- Factors besides market share and sales growth affect cash flow and profit.

- Many firms still use return on investment when assessing the attractiveness of a business opportunity, despite the opportunity it gives for accounting manipulation and the fact that it ignores the time value of money.

- The model provides no real insight into how to compare one opportunity with another when considering which opportunity should be allocated investment resources, eg how does a star in one segment compare with a question mark in another?

- As we have seen, in the right conditions a firm can profit from a low share of a low-growth market.

- The techniques do not tell you how to generate new businesses.

- Defining the market or segment is difficult.

- Market share appears to be a significant advantage in high technology industries, where the learning effect is most apparent, but may bring diseconomies of scale in service industries.

1.3.2 Competitiveness of products

The **GE Business Screen** is a more complex analytical model using similar but more complex criteria: market attractiveness and business strength. It examines a company's competences in market sectors, without reference to individual products.

1   **Determinants of industry/market attractiveness**

- Market factors (eg size, growth)
- Competitors
- Investment factors
- Price elasticity
- Technological change
- Other PEST factors
- Growth rate
- Bargaining power of buyers

2   **Determinants of business strength**

- Product quality and range
- Distribution
- Brand reputation
- Proprietary technology
- Production capacity
- Management skill
- Market share
- Perceived differentiation

These factors can then be scored and weighted. For example, a market with a low size and intense competition based on price might receive a lower weighting than a market with high growth and limited competition.

Figure 3.5   **GE Business Screen**

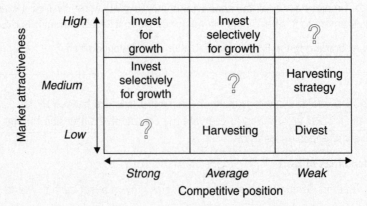

Mckinsey, for General Electric (1970) Each 'cell' requires a different management approach.

The Chartered
Institute of Marketing

- Each SBU can be plotted in one of the cells and the appropriate management approach adopted.

- It is possible that SBUs might move around the matrix. Changes in PEST (political, economic, social, technological) factors may change an industry/market's attractiveness.

- The matrix ignores the possibility of **knowledge generation** and **competence** sharing between SBUs.

Applications in one SBU may be of value elsewhere.

1.3.3 Shell Directional Policy Matrix

Another example is the **Shell Directional Policy Matrix**, which is based on prospects for sector profitability and the enterprise's competitive capabilities.

Figure 3.6   Shell Directional Policy Matrix

Prospects for sector profitability

	Unattractive	Average	Attractive
Weak	Disinvest	Phased withdrawal	Double or quit
Average	Phased withdrawal	Custodial Growth	Try harder
Strong	Cash generation	Growth Leader	Leader

Enterprise's competitive capabilities (vertical axis label)

Adapted from the BCG matrix by Shell in the 1970s

1.3.4 The advantages and disadvantages of portfolio planning

Portfolio planning provides an excellent framework for analysis, and a starting point for developing a product-market mix strategy.

Drawbacks

- Portfolio models are simple: they do not reflect the uncertainties of decision-making.

- BCG analysis, in particular, does not take risk into account.

- They ignore opportunities for creative segmentation or identifying new niches.

- They assume a market is given rather than something that can be created and nurtured. After all, markets may be unattractive because customer needs have not been analysed sufficiently.

- A lot of complicated analysis is needed to come up with relevant data. How do you decide whether an industry is attractive or not?

- The complexity of the assessment process means that management consensus will tend to focus upon medium categories that everyone can agree on.

1.4 Innovation audit

> ▸ **Key term**
>
> An **innovation audit** identifies a firm's record of innovation and how it can be enhanced. It covers the organisation climate and culture, the value to the customer, policies to encourage innovation and the management team.

The chief object of being innovative is to ensure organisational success in a changing world. It can also have the following advantages.

- Improvements in quality of **products** and **service.**

- A **leaner structure** – layers of management or administration may be removed.

- Prompt and imaginative **solutions to problems.**

- **Less formality** in structure and style, leading to better communication.

- **Greater confidence** inside and outside the organisation in its ability to cope with change. Innovation and new product development (NPD) is essential for many firms to survive and prosper. It is an increasingly important area.

A firm needs to assess how well it is able to deliver the level and type of innovation necessary to continue to meet customer needs and expectations. Drummond & Ensor (1999) identify **four key areas** for the innovation audit.

- The current organisational climate.
- Measures of the organisation's **current performance** with regard to innovation.
- Review of **policies and practices** supporting innovation and facilitating it.
- The balance of **styles** of the management team.

1.4.1 Organisational climate

Barriers to innovation in marketing

1   **Resistance to change**: Any new method of management thinking can experience some resistance from established managers. This resistance may be due to concern to protect the *status quo*, or because managers are ignorant of the new thinking. Integrating marketing communications seems so obvious that it may be overlooked or seen as a superficial approach.

2   **Old planning systems**: have sometimes downgraded marketing decisions to the tactical level. Advertising expenditure is decided on the basis of what the company can afford rather than what is strategically required. Promotion is seen as a series of short-term actions rather than as a long-term investment.

3   **Old structures/functional specialists**: Complementing traditional planning systems are traditional organisation structures. These structures freeze out new thinking on integrated marketing strategy. Individuals have limited specific responsibilities – just for advertising, say, or just for public relations – and this inhibits new thinking on integration.

4   **Centralised control**: If the chief executive keeps tight control of the organisation and of its planning and is unconvinced of the benefits of innovation then it will not happen.

5   **Cost considerations**: Innovation usually requires investment.

THE REAL WORLD

Fostering innovation and creativity

Pixar

When Disney bought Pixar in 2006, a number of commentators highlighted the differences in culture between the two organisations. In particularly, they highlight the contrast between Disney's formalized, big-business culture which was perceived to encourage inefficiency and stifle creativity, and Pixar's more relaxed approach in which staff were given more freedom and encouraged to develop ideas.

In an article in the Harvard Business Review in 2008, the president of Pixar and Disney Animation Studies, Ed Catmull notes that in filmmaking, as in many other kinds of complex product development, creativity involves a large number of people from different disciplines working effectively together to solve a number of inherently unforeseeable problems.

Catmull also highlights three elements which he argued were crucial to fostering collective creativity: (i) Place the creative authority for product development in the hands of the project leaders and not corporate executives; (ii) build a culture and

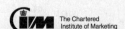
The Chartered Institute of Marketing

processes that encourage people to share their work-in-progress and support one another; and (iii) dismantle the barriers that divide disciplines.

Schiphol Airport

The facilities managers at Schiphol Airport had become fed up at the male passengers inability to 'hit the target' when using the urinals in the public toilets. Therefore they decided to tackle the problem, and asked an advertising agency to help them.

The traditional (and most obvious) response would be to create a poster that asks men not to pee on the floor. And the likely outcome of such a campaign would be men reading the poster while peeing on the floor.

However, at Schiphol they etched the image of a house-fly on to the base of the urinal. In turn the fly gave users something to aim at, and 'accuracy' increased by around 80%.

However, many advertising agencies, and firms more generally, are not employing, or even talking to the 'fly-in-the-urinal guy.' But they should be, because this will help them acquire a wider set of skills and expertise. Collaboration is what they need.

Collaboration provides the opportunity to bring together areas of expertise that make things possible which otherwise wouldn't be possible. And by bringing together ideas from different disciplines, new and unexpected things happen – as illustrated, perhaps most successfully by Google, which combined technology and psychology.

So one way in which organisations can continue to innovate and develop new ideas is by finding new ways to bring people with different areas of expertise together.

Based on: Catmull, E. (2008) How Pixar Fosters Collective Creativity, *Harvard Business Review*, September 2008.

Themistocleous, P. (2012) How a fly in a urinal made an airport a cleaner place, *Metro*, May 29, 2012.

Methods of overcoming these barriers

1 **Top management commitment:** The most effective way of overcoming these barriers to change is through the commitment of top management. The chief executive in particular needs to be convinced of the appropriateness of the new thinking and be enthusiastic about its implementation throughout the organisation.

2 **Training and development:** It is one thing to change attitudes. It is another thing to be in a position to know exactly what to do. It needs the services of individuals trained in strategic thinking. The individuals chosen to implement any new programme must be enthusiasts capable of overcoming resistance to change.

3 **Marketing as a competitive advantage:** Those with responsibility for implementing an integrated marketing programme must do so with the objective of developing it as a sustainable, long-term competitive advantage.

4 **Producing the results:** Nothing succeeds like success. Producing the business results as a consequence of effective marketing communications will boost confidence and gain management converts to the new thinking on an integrated approach.

1.4.2 Stages of an innovation audit

If asked to describe the innovation **audit**, here is a possible approach.

Step 1 **Benchmark with leading competitors.** For example, many motor firms regard the rate and speed of NPD as something they must emulate.

Step 2 **Assess reactivity: identify performance indicators** for innovation and compare with previous years

- Rate of NPD
- Number of innovations
- Success rate (more important than quantity)
- Percentage of revenue derived from innovations (3M has a target)

- Incremental sales resulting from innovation
- Average annual sales per new product/service
- Customer satisfaction ratings
- Staff turnover, if this affects climate of innovation

Note that if a higher percentage of revenue comes from **innovation** a **incremental** products, it looks as if innovatory products are **cannibalising** existing sales.

Step 3   Identify obstacles to innovation which typically reside in the corporate cultural structure.

Step 4   Recommend innovation objectives.

1.5 Product life cycle

> ▶ **Key term**
>
> The **product life cycle** assumes that the marketing and financial characteristics of a product change over time, in relation to the market and in relation to other products. It is an attempt to recognise distinct stages in a product's sales history.

Many firms make a number of different products or services. Each product or service has its own **financial, marketing and risk characteristics**. The combination of products or services influences the profitability of the firm.

Marketing managers distinguish between product class, form and brand.

1. **Product class**: this is a broad category of product, such as cars, washing machines, newspapers, also referred to as the generic product.

2. **Product form**: within a product class there are different forms that the product can take, for example five-door hatchback cars or two-seater sports cars, twin tub or front-loading automatic washing machines, national daily newspapers or weekly local papers etc.

3. **Brand**: the particular type of the product form (for example Ford Fiesta, Vauxhall Astra; *Financial Times, Daily Mail, Sun*).

The product life cycle applies in differing degrees to each of the three cases. A **product class** (eg cars) may have a long maturity stage, but a particular make or brand within the class might have an erratic life cycle. **Product forms**, however, tend to conform to the classic life cycle pattern, which is illustrated by Figure 3.7 below.

Figure 3.7   Product life cycle

Theodore Levitt (1965)

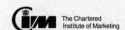
The Chartered Institute of Marketing

Introduction

- A new product takes time to find acceptance by would-be purchasers and there is a slow growth in sales. Unit costs are high because of low output and expensive sales promotion.

- There may be early teething troubles with production technology.

- The product for the time being is a loss-maker.

Growth

- If the new product gains market acceptance, sales will eventually rise more sharply and the product will start to make profits.

- Competitors are attracted. As sales and production rise, unit costs fall.

Maturity. The rate of sales growth slows down and the product reaches a period of maturity which is probably the longest period of a successful product's life. Most products on the market will be at the mature stage of their life. Profits are good.

Decline. Some products reach a stage of decline, which may be slow or fast. Eventually, sales will begin to decline so that there is over-capacity of production in the industry. Severe competition occurs, profits fall and some producers leave the market. The remaining producers seek means of prolonging the product life by modifying it and searching for new market segments. Many producers are reluctant to leave the market, although some inevitably do because of falling profits.

The product life cycle concept has implications for many aspects of business, including all of the four Ps in the basic marketing mix, as is shown in Table 3.3 below.

Table 3.3   Marketing issues and the product life cycle

	Phase			
	Introduction	**Growth**	**Maturity**	**Decline**
Products	Initially, poor quality. Product design and development are a key to success. No standard product and frequent design changes (eg microcomputers in the early 1980s).	Competitors' products have marked quality technical differences. Quality improves. Product reliability may be important.	Products become more standardised and differences between competing products less distinct.	Products even less differentiated. Quality becomes more variable.
Customers	Initial customers willing to pay high prices. Customers need to be convinced about buying.	Customers increase in number.	Mass market. Market saturation. Repeat-buying of products becomes significant. Brand image also important.	Customers are 'sophisticated' buyers of a product they understand well.
Promotion	High advertising and sales promotion costs.	High advertising costs still, but as a % of sales, costs are falling.	Markets become segmented. Segmentation and extending the maturity phase of the life cycle can be key strategies.	Less money spent on advertising and sales promotion.

	Phase			
	Introduction	**Growth**	**Maturity**	**Decline**
Competition	Few or no competitors.	More competitors enter the market. Barriers to entry can be important.	Competition at its keenest: due to high sales volume. Higher prices in some market segments.	Competitors gradually exit from the market. Exit barriers can be important.
Prices and costs	High prices but losses due to high fixed costs.	High prices. High contribution margins, and increasing profit margins. High P/E ratios for quoted companies in the growth market.	Falling prices but good profit margins due to high sales volume. Higher prices in some market segments.	Still low prices but falling profits as sales volume falls, since total contribution falls towards the level of fixed costs. Some increase in prices may occur in late decline stage.
Manufacturing	Over-capacity. High production costs.	Under-capacity. Move towards mass production and less reliance on skilled labour.	Optimum capacity. Low labour skills.	Over-capacity because mass production techniques are still used.
Place	Few distribution channels.	Distribution channels flourish and getting adequate distribution channels is a key to marketing success.	Distribution channels fully developed, but less successful channels might be cut.	Distribution channels dwindling.

In reviewing outputs, planners should assess the following.

- The **stage of its life cycle** that any product has reached.

- The **product's remaining life**, ie how much longer the product will be able to contribute significantly to profits.

- How **urgent is the need to innovate**, to develop new and improved products in time?

1.5.1 Difficulties of the product life cycle concept

The product life cycle has been extensively criticised.

- **Recognition**. How can managers recognise where a product stands in its life cycle?

- **Not always true**. The traditional curve of a product life cycle does not always occur in practice.

- Some products have no maturity phase, and go straight from growth to decline. Some never decline if they are marketed competitively (eg certain brands of breakfast cereals).

- **Changeable**. Strategic decisions can change or extend a product's life cycle.

- **Competition varies** in different industries. The financial markets are an example of markets where there is a tendency for competitors to copy the leader very quickly, so that competition has built up well **ahead** of demand.

Also, the concept has been denounced as promoting a product orientation at the expense of a market orientation.

The Chartered Institute of Marketing

1   **Introduction and launch**

   (a)   Does the firm lead in NPD or copy competitors?

   (b)   Penetration or skimming: should the firm seek to get as much market share as early as possible or should it seek to recoup as much profit as possible?

2   **Growth stage**

   (a)   What competitive strategy is most appropriate in the market place? Will the firm have to differentiate its offer?

   (b)   How long should the firm continue the intense marketing support needed at this stage to build a market?

3   **Maturity**. Higher profits can be achieved by segmenting the market and modifying the product. Market share objectives and distribution are strategically important. Should you rejuvenate a mature product or finish it off? If so, what strategies can you use for rejuvenation: product enhancement, segmentation and so on?

4   **Decline** is probably the hardest to negotiate.

   (a)   Manage decline. Sales will be falling, so costs should be cut to maintain dealer loyalty. Decline needs to be managed slowly and smoothly, so that the firm can redirect its resources elsewhere.

   (b)   Rejuvenation involves 'fining new needs or uses for the product and fitting the product to them to produce new sales.' This involves modifying the mix, producing new versions of the product or positioning the product for another group. For example Campbell's condensed soups have been additionally positioned as ingredients for cooking sauces.

5   As a general rule, any answer about the PLC should cover its drawbacks as well as its merits.

1.5.2 The PLC and cash generation

It is essential that firms plan their portfolio of products to **ensure that new products are generating positive cash flow** before existing 'earners' enter the decline stage.

The **product life cycle** concept can be added to a market share/market growth classification of products, as illustrated in Figure 3.8 below.

Figure 3.8 **Classification of products over their life cycles**

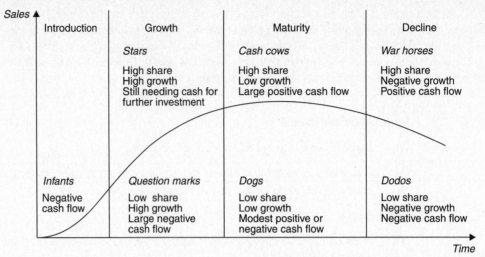

The product life cycle concept probably has more value as a **control tool** than as a method of **forecasting** a product's life. Control can be applied to speeding up the growth phase, extending the maturity phase and recognising when to cease making a product altogether.

The management of a product should fit its prevailing life cycle stage, as each stage has different financial characteristics.

1   **Development**. Money will be spent on market research and product development. Cash flows are negative and there is a high business risk.

2   **Launches** require expensive promotion campaigns.

3   **Growth**. The market grows, as does the demand for the product. Risks are competitor action.

    (a)   The market price mix might turn out to be inappropriate for the product (eg the price is set too high).

    (b)   Competitors will enter, thereby reducing the profits that can be earned.

4   **Maturity**. Few new competitors will enter the market. Risk is low, so the concentration is on profit.

Table 3.4

	Launch	Growth	Maturity	Decline
Characteristics	High business risk. Negative net cash flow. DCF evaluation for overall investment.	High business risk. Neutral net cash flow.	Medium business risk. Positive cash flow.	Low risk. Neutral-positive cash flow.
Critical success factors	Time to launch.	Market share growth. Sustaining competitive advantage.	Contribution per unit of scarce resource. Customer retention.	Timely exit.
Information needs	Market research into size and demand.	Market growth, share. Diminishing returns. Competitor marketing strategies.	Comparative competitor costs. Limiting factors.	Rate of decline; best time to leave; reliable sale values of assets.

	Launch	Growth	Maturity	Decline
Financial and other controls	Strategic 'milestones'. Physical evaluation. Mainly non-financial measures owing to volatility (eg rate of take up by consumers).	Discounted cash flow. Market share. Marketing objectives.	ROI. Profit margin. Maintaining market share.	Free cash flow (for investment elsewhere).

2 Organisational culture and performance

Four key organisational components are structure, systems, people and culture. For an organisation to be successful, it must be internally congruent and its components and must be aligned with the business strategy. (Aaker & McLoughlin, 2010).

2.1 Vision, mission and values

Strategic analysis is concerned with understanding the strategic position of the organisation via the following tools:

1   **Environmental analysis** (external appraisal) is the scanning of the business's environment for factors relevant to the organisation's current and future activities.

2   **Position or situation audit**. The current state of the business in respect of resources, brands, markets etc.

3   **Mission**

   (a)   The firm's long-term approach to business
   (b)   The organisation's value system

   An organisation's mission relates to its goals and refers to the overriding purpose of the organisation. It is sometimes described in terms of 'apparently simple but challenging question: 'What business are we in?' The mission statement should make this clear in terms of long-term purpose. Two linked questions managers might ask are: 'What would be lost if the organisation did not exist?' and 'How do we make a difference?' (Johnson, Whittington, & Scholes, 2012, p79.)

   A firm might decide upon its mission *after* assessing the needs of the organisation and its environmental situation.

4   **Goals** interpret the mission to the needs of different stakeholders (eg customers, employees, shareholders).

5   **Objectives** should embody mission and goals. They should be more precise than mission or goals, and should ideally be **quantifiable** measures of the organisation's goals, against which actual performance can be assessed.

6   **Corporate appraisal**. A critical assessment of strengths, weaknesses, opportunities and threats (SWOT) existing in the internal and environmental factors affecting an organisation.

7   **Gap analysis**. A projection of current activities into the future to identify if there is a difference between the firm's objectives and the results from the continuation of current activities.

Organisational culture is considered in more detail in Chapter 4. Organisational vision, mission and values are also covered in Chapter 5 in the context of strategic management and strategic direction.

2.2 Customer and market orientation

John Lewis

The UK department store, John Lewis, has an unusual ownership structure, under which the staff own John Lewis, its food retailing arm, Waitrose, and its financial services business Greenbee. Staff receive an annual bonus based on the profits of the business. So, the more effort they put in, they more they can get back.

And despite the recession, and tough trading conditions in the UK, John Lewis has continued to perform well.

One of the reasons for this, according to Andy Street, the managing director of John Lewis, is that its ownership structure enables the business to pay slightly more than competitors do, and the business uses that to recruit people who take more of a pride in their work. This helps the chain deliver strong customer service. Equally, customers are attracted by the chain's long-held promise to be 'never knowingly undersold' by its rivals.

Mr Street feels that these factors have become increasingly important in the economic downturn, because they have enabled John Lewis to retain customers' trust. Customers knew that the business was not compromising on product quality, on price, or on service. As a result, customers continued to want to shop with John Lewis.

However, while John Lewis continues to focus primarily on the middle to premium market, it has introduce a value range of homewares such as cutlery and electrical appliances, in recognition of the challenging economic conditions and outlook in the UK. Similarly in 2009, Waitrose also launched its value range – essential Waitrose – which centred around the tagline 'Quality you'd expect at prices you wouldn't.'

Commenting in October 2011, Waitrose Marketing Director, Rupert Thomas, said that Waitrose had had a mammoth response to the range, and since its launch 'essential Waitrose has been extended to new products and categories. 'Our customers are telling us that value is now more important than ever – and they want it with no sacrifice on quality, innovation or service.'

Based on Case Study in Hooley et al (2012), and press release from www.waitrose.presscentre.com

The marketing concept of business is to put the customer at the heart of the organisation's activities.

Customer focus should be present in all departments and functions. The organisation is thus **market-led**.

2.2.1 Marketing-led and market-led orientation

> **Key terms**
>
> A **market** is a customer or a group of customers.
>
> A **market-led firm** is a company in which everyone puts the customer at the centre of decision-making. The customer is not owned by the marketing department.
>
> **Market orientation** is an organisational culture which focuses on meeting the needs of customers in order to create superior value for them and, as a result, superior value for the organisation.

In a company with a market orientation, the aim of **providing superior customer value** dominates all thinking:

- What the business is
- Which markets to serve
- Investments and acquisitions
- Which people to employ and how to promote them

In **market-led** organisations, the marketing department is not in a world of its own. Customer value is designed and created by **multi-function** product teams supporting **all the business functions**.

Hooley *et al* identify the following components of a market orientation.

- **Customers**: know them well enough to give superior value.
- **Competition**: what are their short- and long-term capabilities?
- **Inter-functional**: mobilise the entire company to create superior customer value.
- **Culture**: employee behaviour should be managed to ensure customer satisfaction.
- **Long-term profit focus**: have a strategic but realistic vision.

The Chartered Institute of Marketing

Tata Motors

The Tata Indica is a range of hatchback cars manufactured by Tata Motors, and is considered to be India's first indigenously developed passenger car. When Tata (previously a lorry-manufacturing company) decided to enter the car market, in the 1990s it developed the Indica from nothing in three years and at a cost only one-third as great as a European or US equivalent project.

However, when the Indica was launched there were immediate problems with the suspension and air conditioning and most of all with after-sales service. The initial, corporate-culture conditioned response was 'we haven't done anything wrong'. However, the CEO insisted that the customer had to be put first. Five hundred engineers were sent out into the marketplace to talk to buyers. Customers were invited into the factory to describe their experiences.

The next generation Indica was ready three years later and quickly became a big seller in the small car segment. Version 3 was launched in early 2008 and offered three versions each with four sub-models. The Indica is now an established and popular product.

www.tatamotors.com

The type, or model, of marketing practiced in any organisation depends on a number of factors, not least of which are the nature of the business context and the organisation's dominant orientation. Marketing activities in organisations can be grouped broadly into four models:

1 **Sales support** – The emphasis in this model is essentially reactive: marketing supports the direct sales force. It may include activities such as telesales or telemarketing, responding to enquiries, co-ordinating diaries, customer database management, organising exhibitions or other sales promotions, and administering agents. These activities usually come under a sales and marketing director or manager. This form of marketing is common in SMEs and some organisations operating in a B2B context.

2 **Marketing communications** – The emphasis in this model is more proactive: marketing promotes the organisation and its product/service at a tactical level, either to customers (pull) or to channel members (push). It typically includes activities such as providing brochures and catalogues to support the sales force. Some B2C organisations may use marketing to perform the 'selling' role using direct marketing techniques and to manage campaigns based on a mix of media to raise awareness, generate leads and even take orders. In B2B markets, larger organisations may have marketing communications departments and specialists to make efficient use of marketing expenditures and to co-ordinate communications between business units.

3 **Operational marketing** – The emphasis in this model is for marketing to support the organisation with a co-ordinated range of marketing activities including market research, brand management, product development and management, corporate and marketing communications, and customer relationship management. Given this breadth of activities, planning is also a function usually performed in this role but at an operational or functional level. Typically part of FMCG or B2C organisations, the operational marketing role is increasingly used in B2B organisations.

4 **Strategic marketing** – The emphasis in this model is for marketing to contribute to the creation of value and competitive customer strategy. As such, it is practised in customer focused and larger organisations. In a large or diversified organisation, it may also be responsible for the co-ordination of marketing departments or activities in separate business units. Strategic marketing decisions, when not made by professional marketers, are taken by business leaders.

2.3 Comparative and best practice analysis

2.3.1 Benchmarking and the market environment

Benchmarks can be set on a variety of key performance indicators as an objective form of control. Marketing research and competitor intelligence would be needed to establish benchmarks and to monitor progress.

The practice of benchmarking is becoming increasingly popular. **Competitor benchmarking** focuses on the performance and relative strengths of direct competitors using information from customer and supplier interviews and published data from any source available. A firm tries to be as good as its competitors.

2.3.2 Monitoring competitor performance

When an organisation operates in a competitive environment, it should try to obtain information about the financial performance of competitors, to make a comparison with the organisation's own results. It might not be possible to obtain reliable competitor information, but if the competitor is a public company it will publish an annual report and accounts.

Financial information that might be obtainable about a competitor

- Total profits, sales and capital employed.

- ROCE, profit/sales ratio, cost/sales ratios and asset turnover ratios.

- The increase in profits and sales over the course of the past twelve months (and prospects for the future, which will probably be mentioned in the chairman's statement in the report and accounts).

- Sales and profits in each major business segment that the competitor operates in.

- Dividend per share and earnings per share.

- Gearing and interest rates on debt.

- Share price, and P/E ratio (stock exchange information).

2.4 Cost efficiency and financial performance

There is a relationship between the quantity of products produced and the cost per unit. There are many routes to cost advantage. They include:

- Economies of scale
- The experience curve
- Product design innovations
- Using the newest and most efficient production technologies
- The use of 'no-frills' offerings
- Minimising overheads

A publisher contracts with a printer to print Study Texts.

Quantity printed	Cost £	Cost per book £
100	500	5.00
1,000	2,500	2.50
2,000	4,720	2.36

There are the same **fixed costs** incurred (for example, in setting-up the press) no matter how many or few books are printed.

The quantity produced affects the cost per unit. For example, if customers are unwilling to pay more than £3 for their books, and the publisher wants to make £0.50p profit on top of print cost, then the publisher has to sell **at least** 1,000 books.

How is this relevant to considerations of market share?

2.4.1 Experience curves

The **experience curve** takes it further. The more units **over time** that a firm produces, the cheaper each unit will be to produce. Why?

- **Economies of scale**, as identified above.

- **Learning**: the more people do a task, the more efficient they become (up to a point), and it takes them less time.

- **Technological** improvements: firms can improve their production operations and make better use of equipment.

- **Simplifying products can cut costs**. For example, car manufacturers are cutting costs by ensuring that the same components can be used in different marquees.

Japanese firms pioneered target costing in the 1960s. They identified a customer need and specified a product to satisfy that need.

The production department and its accountants then worked out:

- How the product could be built
- The volume needed to reach the market price
- How quickly costs could be driven down

▶ **Key terms**

Market share is 'one entity's sales of a product or service in a specified market expressed as a percentage of total sales by all entities offering that product or service'. Thus, a company may have a 30% share of a total market, meaning that 30% of all sales in the market are made by that company.

Relative market share is the share of the market relative to that of the manufacturer's largest competitor.

2.4.2 Market share performance

An evaluation of market shares helps to identify **who the true competitor really is**, and avoids trying to outdo the wrong competitor.

Such an approach serves as a basis for marketing strategy, with a firm seeking as a target to build up an x% share of a particular market.

When a market manager is given responsibility for a product or a market segment, the product or market segment will be a profit centre, and measures of performance for the centre will include profits and cost variances etc. However, another useful measure of performance would be the **market share** obtained by the organisation's product in the market. A market share performance report should draw attention to:

- The link between **cost and profit** and market performance in both the short and the long term.
- The performance of the **product or market segment** in the context of the product life cycle.
- Whether or not the product is gaining or losing ground, as its market share rises or falls.

Changes in market share have to be considered against the change in the **market as a whole**, since the product might be increasing its share simply when the market is declining, but the competition is losing sales even more quickly. (The reverse may also be true. The market could be expanding, and a declining market share might not represent a decline in absolute sales volume, but a failure to grab more of the growing market.)

THE REAL WORLD

Athletic footwear and 'toning' shoes

Although Nike held on to its position as the market leader in the US women's athletic footwear market in the first quarter of 2010, its share slipped about 7 percentage points, to 31 % in the face of gains by adidas's Reebok unit, and Skechers.

The main reason for this was the popularity of Reebok and Skechers' 'toning' shoes. However, although Nike was watching its rivals developing their shoes, it did nothing about it, and the results showed it was paying the price of a missed opportunity.

Toning shoes re designed to simulate the feeling of walking on sand, and make wearers stabilize their steps, leading to stronger leg, buttock, back and abdominal muscles, according to Skechers. And women's toners (with prices of $100-plus) were some of the most lucrative footwear in the US.

The growth of the market was extremely rapid. Toning-shoe sales in the US in 2008 totaled just $17 million. By 2009 (when Reebok and Skechers first introduced their models) this had risen to $145 million, and in the first four months of 2010 sales had sky-rocketed even further – to $252 million.

After Reebok increased its advertising for toning shoes in the third quarter of 2009, retailer Foot Locker couldn't keep up with demand for the shoes. Foot Locker's CEO Ken Hicks said 'The American consumer is always looking for an easy way to lose weight, and this proves it.'

Abridged from: Townsend, M. (2010) 'Toning' shoes gain traction, _www.businessweek.com_, 3 June 2010.

2.4.3 Profit impact of market strategies (PIMS)

PIMS analysis attempts to establish the profitability (ie return on capital) of various marketing strategies, and identifies a link between the size of **return on capital** and **market share** so that companies in a strong competitive position in the markets for their base products would be earning high returns.

In general, profits increase in line with market share.

Three possible reasons have been put forward for this correlation.

1 **Economies of scale** and experience curve effects enable a market leader to produce at lower unit costs than competitors, and so make bigger profits. A company with the highest market share, especially if this company is also the innovator with the longest experience, will enjoy a considerable competitive advantage. This is referred to as the experience curve.

2 **Bargaining power**. A strong position in the market gives a firm greater strength in its dealings with both buyers and suppliers.

3 **Quality of management**. Market leaders often seem to be run by managers of a high calibre.

CHAPTER ROUNDUP

- A firm needs to use its resources and competences to help it create a competitive advantage in relation to its rivals. A useful way of identifying resources and competences which create value is value chain analysis.

- The value chain categorizes the value-creating activities in a firm, and divides them into primary activities (inbound logistics, operations, outbound logistics (distribution), marketing and service) and support activities (procurement, technology, HRM and infrastructure).

- The products and services which a firm has to offer can also affect its position in the market. The product life cycle highlights that sales from existing products will not continue at their current level indefinitely, and so a firm needs to develop a balanced set of products.

- The BCG matrix and product portfolio planning reinforces this idea of having a balanced portfolio, with the cash generated from cash cows being used to support question marks and stars.

- Another point which the product life highlights is the need for new product development and innovation. Creating and nurturing an innovative culture within an organisation could be an important aspect of being able to sustain its competitive advantage.

FURTHER READING

Lynch, R. (2012) *Strategic Management*, 6th edition, Pearson, Harlow. (Chapter 4: Analysing resources and capabilities.)

See also:

Channon, D. (2005) Value chain analysis, in McGee, J. & Channon, D. (eds) *Encyclopaedic Dictionary of Management*, 2nd edition, Blackwell, Oxford.

REFERENCES

Aaker, D. & McLoughlin, D. (2010) *Strategic Market Management: Global perspectives*. John Wiley, Chichester.

Drummond, G. Ensor, J. & Ashford, R. (2008) *Strategic Marketing Planning and Control*. 3rd edition. Elsevier, Oxford.

Drummond, G. & Ensor, J. (1999) *Strategic Marketing – Planning and Control*. Butterworth-Heinemann, Oxford.

Hooley, G., Piercy, N. & Nicoulaud, B. (2012) *Marketing Strategy and Competitive Positioning*. 5th edition. Pearson, Harlow.

Johnson, G., Whittington, R. & Scholes, K. (2012) *Fundamentals of Strategy*, Pearson, Harlow.

Kotler, P., Keller, K., Brady, M., Goodman, M. & Hansen, T. (2009) *Marketing Management*, Pearson, Harlow.

Piercy, N. F. (2008) *Market-Led Strategic Change – Transforming the Process of Going to Market*. 4th edition. Butterworth-Heinemann, Oxford.

The Chartered Institute of Marketing

Porter, M.E (1985) *Competitive Advantage*. Free Press, New York.

QUICK QUIZ

1   What is covered by the resource audit?

2   In the context of the value chain, what is 'margin'?

3   What are the criteria used by the General Electric Business Screen?

4   What is covered by an innovation audit?

5   Distinguish between product class, form and brand

6   What are the four broad groupings of marketing activity in organisations?

7   What is benchmarking?

8   Why might economies of scale promote a cost advantage against competitors?

9   'In general, profits increase in line with ....' Fill in the blank.

10 How is the product life cycle related to marketing orientation?

ACTIVITY DEBRIEFS

Activity 3.1

Here are some ideas:

1   It can become more efficient, by automating the production of food, as in a fast food chain.

2   The chef can develop commercial relationships with growers, so he or she can obtain the best quality fresh produce.

3   The chef can specialise in a particular type of cuisine (eg Nepalese, Korean).

4   The restaurant can be sumptuously decorated for those customers who value atmosphere and a sense of occasion, in addition to a restaurant's purely gastronomic pleasures.

5   The restaurant can serve a particular type of customer (eg celebrities).

Each of these options is a way of organising the activities of buying, cooking and serving food in a way that customers or chosen customers will value.

Activity 3.2

Sana Sounds is involved in the record industry from start to finish. Although recording and CD manufacture are contracted out to external suppliers, this makes no difference to the fact that these activities are part of Sana Sounds' own value chain. Sana Sounds earns its money by managing the whole set of activities. If the company grows then perhaps it will acquire its own recording studios. A value chain of activities is not the same as an organisation's business functions.

Activity 3.3

The evaluation and resulting strategic considerations for the company illustrated are that:

(a)   There are two 'cash cows', thus the company should be in a cash-positive state.

BPP
LEARNING MEDIA

(b)   New products will be required to follow on from A.

(c)   A is doing well (15%) but needs to gain market share to move from position 3 in the market – continued funding is essential. Similar for B.

(d)   C is a market leader in a maturing market – strategy of consolidation is required.

(e)   D is the major product which dominates its market; cash funds should be generated from this product.

(f)   E is very small. Is it profitable? Funding to maintain the position or selling-off are appropriate strategies.

Activity 3.4

(a)   Orange juice is a cash cow.

(b)   Pomegranate juice is a question mark, which the company wants to turn into a star.

Activity 3.5

It shows that high market share can, by spreading fixed costs over many units of production, be more profitable.

Higher sales volumes can mean lower costs per unit, hence higher profits. The Boston Consulting Group estimated that as production volume doubles, cost per unit falls by up to 20%.

High market share therefore gives cost advantages.

QUICK QUIZ ANSWERS

1   The resource audit covers technical resources, financial resources, managerial skills, the organisation and its information system.

2   Margin is the excess the customer is prepared to pay over the cost to the firm of obtaining resource inputs and providing value activities.

3   Market attractiveness and business strength

4   Innovation audit covers the organisation climate and culture, the value to the customer, policies to encourage innovation and the management team

5   'Class' is a broad category; form is an example within a class; brand is the offering (or group of offerings) from a particular supplier.

6   Sales support; marketing communications; operational marketing and strategic marketing.

7   Benchmarking is an external target of performance, against which a firm measures its activities. Benchmarks can be set on a variety of key performance indicators as a form of control.

8   Economies of scale enable a market leader to produce at lower unit costs than competitors, and so make larger profits.

9   Market share

10   It may be that over-attention to the PLC actually produces a product orientation.

The Chartered
Institute of Marketing

CHAPTER 4

Developing organisational capability

Introduction

The central theme of strategic planning is how a firm can create and sustain competitive advantage, and thereby enable itself to maintain a higher level of profit than its competitors.

There are two main approaches to achieving competitive advantage, each encompassing several strands of strategic thinking.

1   **The positioning approach**

   The positioning approach to strategy is closely related to the traditional concept of marketing orientation. It starts with an assessment of the commercial environment and positions the business so that it fits with environmental requirements.

2   **The resource-based approach**

   The resource-based approach starts with the idea that competitive advantage comes from the possession of distinctive and unique resources, or 'organisational capability'.

   This chapter focuses on the resource-based approach to strategy development, in which an organisation analyses its own internal resources and competences and then adopts a strategy which helps it exploit them.

Topic list

1.2.2	Critically evaluate the resource-based view of an organisation and the value of this approach in developing resource and capability to deliver an organisation's vision and mission:
	▪ Resources, capabilities and competencies
	▪ The elements of resource-based competitive advantage
	▪ Knowledge as a resource
1.2.3	Critically evaluate the fit between an organisation's culture and its current strategy, and assess its ability to be flexible and agile in a changing marketing environment:
	▪ Environmental influences on organisational culture
	▪ Mintzberg's organisational structures
	▪ Handy's cultural styles
1.2.4	Utilise a range of internal information and assessment tools to evaluate an organisation's strengths and weaknesses in order to assess its readiness for development, including an assessment of:
	▪ Competences, assets and culture
	▪ Value chain and value proposition
	▪ The state of the organisation's financial and non-financial assets
3.1.1	Critically assess strategic alternatives against pre-determined criteria for an organisation, including:
	▪ Scenario planning – stability versus uncertainty
	▪ Potential for Return on Investment (ROI)
	▪ Opportunity to achieve competitive advantage
	▪ Feasibility, viability and resource
	▪ Capacity and capability to deliver

1 The resource-based view of strategy

Strategies capabilities are 'the capabilities of an organisation that contribute to its long-term survival or competitive advantage…There are two components of strategic capability: resources and competences. Resources and the assets that organisations have or can call upon (e.g. from partners or suppliers); competences are the ways those assets are used or deployed effectively. A shorthand way of thinking about this is that resources are 'what we *have*' and competences are 'what we *do well*.'' (Johnson, Whittington & Scholes, 2012, p51)

1.1 Resources, capabilities and competences

The resource-based approach to strategy begins from a consideration of strengths and weaknesses and, in particular, of **distinctive competences**. It was developed in response to two issues:

▪ Many environments are **too complex and dynamic** to permit continuing effective analysis and response.

▪ Once an opportunity is discerned and an offering made, it is very easy for **competitors to make similar offerings**, thus rapidly eroding competitive advantage.

The resource-based view is that sustainable competitive advantage is only attained as a result of the **possession of distinctive resources**. These may be physical resources, such as the effective monopolisation of diamonds by De Beers, or, more typically in today's service economies, they may be **core competences**. Core competences critically underpin an organisation's competitive advantage.

Sometimes, often in what are exceptional circumstances, a strength may disappear, signaling trouble ahead if an alternative is hard to find.

BA's big strength has always been the Heathrow hub and its dominance of the lucrative business traffic across the Atlantic. In 2007/08, the final year of the financial-services boom, BA posted a record result. Corporate Lawyers. merchant bankers and other masters of the universe thought nothing paying £4,000 and more for a return trip to America, and the cash rolled in.

BA's profit in 2007/08 was £922 million, and it achieved an operating margin of 10% (something that had eluded BA managers for the previous two decades). BA even paid a dividend to shareholders for the first time since 2001.

However, a year later, the position had changed dramatically. As the Chief Financial Officer's report in the 2008/09 Annual Report & Accounts notes: 'Last year we said that record profitability has put us in a good position to weather economic slowdown. This has been invaluable as we face the sharpest downturn in our Company's history.' The credit crunch and recession revealed the reliance on Heathrow and Atlantic business traffic to be not a strength but a weakness. Business traffic dried up with companies, and in particular the big banks, slashing their travel budgets.

BA's results for the 2008/09 financial year showed how hard and fast the downturn had hit. The airline recorded a £401 million pre-tax loss – £331 million of which came in the final quarter of the year alone – scrapped the dividend.

BA's lifeblood 'premium traffic' – first and business class – fell 17% in April 2008 and by the same amount in May. Business class fares across Atlantic have dropped sharply. Figures from IATA showed that premium traffic across the industry as a whole declined by around 19% in the first three months of 2009.

BA said it would reduce capacity in the winter of 2009 by a further 4%, having reduced its schedule by 3% in the same period in 2008, by grounding 16 planes including eight jumbo 747s.

However, BA noted despite a number of carriers going out of business or being forced into rushed mergers, competition remained fierce, particularly at Heathrow and on important transatlantic routes. This meant the need to deliver world-leading customer service and operational performance remained, if anything, more important than ever before. This was emphasised in the key goals which BA published; one of which was to 'Deliver an outstanding service for customers at every touch point.'

www.britishairways.com

ACTIVITY 4.1

What could BA do to respond to these tough conditions?

1.1.1 Competences

Competences essentially represent what a business does well. They can develop in a variety of ways:

- **Experience** in making and marketing a product or service
- The talents and potential of **individuals** in the organisation
- The **quality of co-ordination**

Johnson, Scholes & Whittington (2011) divide competences into two types.

1   An organisation must achieve at least a **threshold level** of competence in **everything** it does.
2   Its **core competences** are those where it **outperforms competitors** and that are **difficult to imitate**.

Hamel and Prahalad (1996) suggest that an important aspect of strategic management is the determining of the competences the company will require **in the future** in order to be able to provide new benefits to customers. They say a **core competence** must have three qualities.

- It must make a **disproportionate** contribution to the **value** the customer perceives.

- It must be '**competitively unique**', which means one of three things: actually unique; superior to competitors; or capable of dramatic improvement.

- It must be **extendable**, in that it must allow for the development of an array of new products and services.

Bear in mind that **relying on a competence is no substitute for a strategy**. However, a core competence can form **a basis for a strategy**. Here it is important to reiterate that a core competence must be **difficult to imitate** if it is to confer lasting competitive advantage. In particular, skills that can be bought-in are unlikely to form the basis of core competences, since competitors would also be able to buy them in just as easily. Core competences are more about what the organisation *is* than about what it *does*. So it is possible to regard a strong **brand** as a kind of core competence: it is a unique resource that confers a distinct competitive advantage.

1.1.2 Capabilities

In addition to looking at resources and competences as a basis for their strategies, organisations should also consider their capabilities. Again, these can be distinguished into two levels:

Figure 4.1   Levels of capability

	Resources	Comptetences
Threshold capabilities Basic requirements to be able to compete in a market	Threshold resources	Threshold competences
Distinctive capabilities Provide basis of competitive advantage	Distinctive resources	Distinctive competences

Based on Johnson, Scholes & Whittington (2011)

The matrix in Figure 4.1 highlights that, whilst organisations need a certain level of capabilities in order to compete in market (threshold capabilities) it is the higher level of capabilities (distinctive capabilities) which enable the organisation to achieve competitive advantage over its rivals.

1.1.3 Dynamic capabilities

So far, when looking at resources and competences, we have tended to view them as long-term phenomena; since, for example, resources will be more valuable if they can be counted upon to take for a long time, or because it might take an organisation a long time to develop its core competences.

However, in the context of a dynamic and rapidly changing environment, firms may find it harder to create a long-term competitive advantage over their competitors.

Therefore, we could suggest that the traditional resource-based view (of resources and competences) needs to be extended to acknowledge that, in order to sustain competitive advantage, firms may need to renew – or upgrade - their competences in line with the changing business environment (Wang & Ahmed, 2007). Teece *et*

 The Chartered Institute of Marketing

al, (1997) refer to this ability to achieve new forms of competitive advantage, by developing and changing competences to meet the needs of rapidly changing environments as **dynamic capability**.

The term 'dynamic' refers to the 'capacity to renew competences so as to achieve congruence with the changing business environment'; the term 'capability' emphasises 'the key role of strategic management in appropriately adapting, integrating, and reconfiguring internal and external organisational skills, resources, and functional competences to match the requirements of a changing environment.' (Teece *et al*, 1997; 514)

Wang & Ahmed (2007) suggest that the distinction between resources, and capabilities is important because it enables us to develop a hierarchical order which we can use to analyse a firm's ability to create and sustain competitive advantage.

Resources form the base of the hierarchy, the 'zero-order' element. They are the foundation of the firm, and need to be in place before a firm can develop any higher capabilities. However, by themselves resources cannot be a source of sustainable competitive advantage.

Capabilities are the 'first-order' and represent the ability to deploy resources to attain a desired goal. In this way, capabilities are likely to result in improved performance; however, this improved performance will be manifest at an operational level – for example through the performance of business processes – rather than at a strategic level.

Core capabilities (in effect, the 'distinctive capabilities' in Figure 4.1) are 'second-order', and are a bundle of a firm's resources and capabilities that are strategically important to its competitive advantage at a certain point. However, these core capabilities might still not necessarily confer sustainable competitive advantage if (or when) the environment changes. Depending on the nature and extent of the change, capabilities might either become irrelevant or might even become 'core rigidities.' (That is, a potential down side of core capabilities is that they inhibit innovation, because managers prefer instead to concentrate on using resources in the current way, rather than combining them in different ways or extending them for new use, such as producing new product lines.)

Therefore 'third-order' dynamic capabilities emphasize a firm's constant pursuit of the renewal, reconfiguration and re-creation of resources, capabilities and core capabilities to address the changing environment. This ability to adapt to changes in markets or the environment sooner and more astutely than competitors is at the heart of dynamic capabilities, and is also a source of sustained competitive advantage.

THE REAL WORLD

Apps make the world go round

It is hard to identify the drivers of the current Smartphone boom. Is it from the enhanced features that the latest models of the iPhone, BlackBerry, Samsung Galaxy, Windows Phone, iPad and other tablets possess? Or is it the question of the extraordinary proliferation of wonderfully creative Apps (application software), essential to the whole experience?

Probably both, in an extraordinary display of synergy that fuels the whole digital revolution that has already taken off, but with miles to go yet.

As far as the technology of the actual smartphone or tablet is concerned, latest developments include: Siri technology that allows a number of operations by voice command, the incredible clarity of the Retina display of the iPad 3 and TellMe, the voice recognition function coming from Nokia's collaboration with Microsoft on the Phone 7. Perhaps, one of the most significant advances is the interoperability between Windows Phone and the desktop version of Windows Office. At the time of writing, September 2012, the new Windows Phone 8 is about to be launched, timed to eclipse the new Apple iPhone.

All this contributes to an amazing experience and a promising future for smartphone applications. In truth, no-one quite knows where all this will end up.

But certainly, the availability at low cost of the thousands of Apps has made the whole thing into a Consumer phenomenon. The Apple Apps Store opened in July 2008 and, as of January, 2011, reported over 10 billion downloads. There is something like half a million third-party Apps available to 200 million iOS users.

1.1.4 Marketing and resource-based strategy

To some extent, the resource-based approach is diametrically opposed to the marketing concept since, instead of approaching strategy on the basis of giving customers what they want, it concentrates on exploiting what the business already has to offer. In fact, this distinction is largely theoretical, but it leads to some important ideas.

- Where the marketing concept is adopted, it will still be necessary to deploy threshold capabilities in all critical areas and the possession of unique resources and core competences will enhance the market offering.

- Conversely, where strategy is built on unique resources and core competences, marketing activities must be carried out with at least threshold competence if the customer is to be satisfied.

1.1.5 Organisational capability

Organisational capabilities and culture will have great influence on success and failure. An important variable is **organisational structure**. In the days of mass marketing, a vertically organised hierarchical form was appropriate for achieving economies of scale and expertise. Companies now seeking to cut overheads, achieve fast response to changing markets and competition and exploit the advantages of a mass customisation approach need something better. Increasingly, advances in IT are producing organisations based on **networks**.

- **Internal networks** take the form of horizontally-oriented, cross-functional teams with responsibility for processes that deliver customer satisfaction. Communication flows freely, making the best use of resources whatever their functional label. This style of working reduces costs, speeds response and improves motivation.

- **External networks** are created when companies withdraw from activities that are not fundamental to their specific value-creating strategy and **concentrate on their core competences**. They buy-in the services they no longer perform for themselves, using the core competences of other companies to support their own. This type of organisation arises under the pressure of new technologies, new markets and new processes that make it difficult for any organisation to do everything well.

The **McKinsey 7S model**, Figure 4.2, was designed to show how the various aspects of a business relate to one another. It is a useful example of the way culture fits into an organisation. In particular, it shows the links between the organisation's behaviour and the behaviour of individuals within it.

Figure 4.2   The McKinsey 7S framework

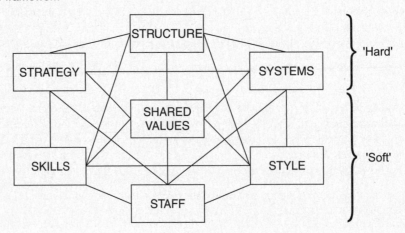

Based on a framework developed by Waterman & Peters (1982)

Three of the elements were originally considered 'hard', but in today's context they are becoming more flexible.

- **Structure**. The organisation structure determines division of tasks in the organisation and the hierarchy of authority from the most senior to junior. Today's company is likely to be made up of flat, empowered networks.

- **Strategy**. Strategy is the way in which the organisation plans to outperform its competitors; it will be market-led.

- **Systems**. Systems include the technical systems of accounting, personnel, management information and so on, with particular emphasis on how market-related information is distributed and used.

The McKinsey model suggests that the 'soft' elements are equally important.

- **Shared values** lie at the heart of the organisation and are the guiding principles for the people in it. They are vital for developing the motivation to drive the organisation to achieve.

- **Staff** are the people in the organisation. They have their own complex concerns and priorities. The successful organisation will recruit the right staff and develop their motivation to pursue the right goals.

- **Style** is another aspect of the **corporate culture**, and includes the shared assumptions, ways of working and attitudes of senior management.

- **Skills** are the core competences that enable the company to create value in a particular way.

1.1.6 Marketing contexts

It is worth remembering at this point that organisations operate in a variety of contexts using different marketing activities, and this has a large impact on structure and capabilities. There is no 'one size fits all' approach.

Organisations and their marketers have to select and use techniques appropriate to their specific context. Typical marketing contexts are summarised as:

- **FMCG**: Used in organisations with a strong market orientation, the 'standard' model of marketing is based on identification of customers' needs and techniques of segmentation, targeting and positioning supported by branding and customer communications.

- **B2B**: The model of marketing adopted depends on factors such as the importance of face-to-face selling, the dominant orientation and power of buyers. Markets are often less information-rich than FMCG markets, which constrains marketing decisions.

- **Capital projects**: A variant of the B2B model where opportunities for positioning are few and the value of any single order constitutes a significant proportion of turnover in a period

- **Not-for-profit**: The organisation is not driven by shareholder value and competition may not be a significant factor in strategy

- **SMEs**: Operating in any of the above sectors, SMEs are characterised by their limited marketing resources and the limited use of marketing techniques.

ACTIVITY 4.2

What would the effects be of introducing a marketing approach to a charity?

1.2 Knowledge as a resource

Knowledge management entails identifying knowledge and using a variety of organisational and technological means to ensure that it is **shared**.

A **knowledge-based economy** is an economy based on application of knowledge. Organisations' capabilities and efficiency in using their knowledge override other, more traditional, economic factors such as land and capital. We are living in an age in which the competitiveness of organisations depends on the accumulation of knowledge and its rapid mobilisation to produce goods and services.

- Producing unique products or services or producing products or services at a lower cost than competitors is based on superior knowledge.

- Knowledge is especially valuable as it may be used to create new ideas, insights and interpretations and for decision-making.

- Knowledge, like information, is of no value unless it is applied.

As the importance of knowledge increases, the success of an organisation becomes increasingly dependent on its ability to gather, produce, hold and disseminate knowledge.

1.2.1 Where does knowledge reside?

There are various actions that can be taken to try to determine the prevalence of knowledge in an organisation. One is the identification and development of informal networks and communities of practice within organisations. These self-organising groups share common work interests, usually cutting across a company's functions and processes. People exchange what they know and develop a shared language that allows knowledge to flow more efficiently.

Another means of establishing the prevalence of knowledge is to look at knowledge-related business outcomes. One example is product development and service innovation. While the knowledge embedded within these innovations is invisible, the products themselves are tangible.

1.2.2 Knowledge management

Knowledge management is a relatively new concept in business theory. It is connected with the theory of the learning organisation and founded on the idea that knowledge is a major source of competitive advantage in business. The aim of knowledge management is to exploit existing knowledge and to create new knowledge so that it may be exploited in turn. This is not easy. All organisations possess a great deal of data, but it tends to be unorganised and inaccessible. It is often locked up inside the memories of people who do not realise the value of what they know. Even when it is recorded in some way it may be difficult and time consuming to access, as is the case with most paper archives.

In a knowledge-based economy, knowledge, therefore, has to be actively managed. Knowledge includes tacit knowledge in employees' heads as well as formally recorded facts (known as codified knowledge) and transactions.

Knowledge management programmes are attempts at:

- Designing and installing techniques and processes to create, protect and use **explicit knowledge** (codified knowledge that the company knows that it has). Explicit knowledge includes facts, transactions and events that can be clearly stated and stored in management information systems.

- Designing and creating environments and activities to discover and release **tacit knowledge** ..

Tacit knowledge is expertise held by people within the organisation that has not been formally documented.

- Tacit knowledge is a difficult thing to manage because it is **invisible** and **intangible**. We do not know what knowledge exists within a person's brain, and whether he or she chooses to share it is a matter of choice.

- The **motivation to share** hard-won experience is sometimes low; the individual is 'giving away' their value and may be very reluctant to lose a position of influence and respect by making it available to everyone.

For these two reasons an organisation may never fully know what knowledge it possesses and could exploit. Knowledge management is an attempt to address this problem. It attempts to turn all relevant knowledge, including personal knowledge, into corporate **knowledge assets** that can be easily and widely shared throughout an organisation and appropriately applied.

Table 4.1   Examples of tacit and explicit knowledge in a company

Tacit knowledge	Explicit knowledge
Practical and unwritten procedures.	Costing procedures codified in company accounting manuals.
Informal networks and procedures for sales order processing.	New product development through formal company review procedures.
Multifunctional team working on new projects that rely on informal contacts.	Company patents and legal contracts.
Experience of what has worked in practice in branding development over a number of years.	A company's written history of its past events and experience, successes and failures – often very limited.
Specific company treatment of some detailed aspects of management accounting.	Training schemes and apprenticeship programmes that develop and teach best practice.

Knowledge management covers a variety of aspects.

- **Creation**   How is knowledge created?
- **Capture**   How is knowledge obtained by the system?
- **Storage**   How is knowledge stored?
- **Availability**   How is knowledge made available?
- **Utilisation**   How is knowledge used?

The purpose of the process is to build on what is already known, and extend further the knowledge available to the organisation.

Knowledge is now commonly viewed as another source of **competitive advantage**. Producing unique products or services or producing products or services at a lower cost than competitors is based on **superior knowledge**. As the importance of knowledge increases, the success of an organisation becomes increasingly dependent on its ability to gather, produce, hold and disseminate knowledge. This is vastly facilitated by information technology.

1.2.3 Customer knowledge within the organisation

Many business functions deal with customers, including marketing, sales, service, logistics and financial functions. Each function will have its own reasons for being interested in customer information, and may have its own way of recording what it learns and even its own customer information system. The diverse interests of different departments make it difficult to pull together customer knowledge in one common format and place and the problem is magnified because all have some political reason to keep control of what they know about customers.

Organisational means of encouraging sharing include emphasising it in the corporate culture, evaluating people on the basis of their knowledge behaviour and rewarding those who display good knowledge-sharing practice.

On a more practical level, information and communications technology can be of great assistance too.

The more information that a firm can obtain about competitors and customers, the more it should be able to adapt its product/service offerings to meet the needs of the market place through strategies such as differentiation. For example, mail order companies that are able to store data about customer buying habits can exploit this data by recognising patterns of buying behaviour, and offering products at likely buying times that are in line with the customer's profile.

Good information systems may alter the way business is done and may provide organisations with new opportunities. The very term 'information' has strong links with IT, and the role of IT in helping marketers to make decisions is ever growing.

Marketers often face 'information overload' where they have too much information thrown at them from multiple sources. IT systems can help alleviate this by helping to store and structure the information to hand. The key point to remember, however, is that technology alone does not help to cut through the sheer amount of information. Marketers need to understand the decisions that have to be made, define them well and then clearly identify the information that is then required. No IT system to date has been able to do that: human intervention and planning is always required.

2 Organisational culture

'If the fundamental principles of marketing are not accepted by the organisation, any move towards being market-led and customer orientated could be dismissed as 'not the way we do it'.' Drummond *et al* (2008) p248

2.1 Environmental influences on organisational culture

> ▶ **Key term**
>
> **Organisation culture** may be defined as:
>
> - 'The collection of traditions, values, policies, beliefs and attitudes that constitute a pervasive context for everything we do and think in an organisation' (Mullins, 2007)
> - 'The way we do things around here'

Culture is the collective programming of the mind, which distinguishes the members of one group of people from another (Hofstede, 1984). It can be identified as ways of behaving, and ways of understanding, that are shared by a group of people.

Schein (2004) defines organisational culture as 'the set of shared, taken-for-granted implicit assumptions that a group holds and that determines how it perceives, thinks about and reacts to its environment'. He also suggests that the culture of an organisation is grounded in the founder's basic beliefs, values and assumptions, and embedded in the organisation over time – what Schein calls 'the residue of success'.

Culture may therefore be identified as ways of behaving, and ways of understanding, that are shared by a group of people. Referring to it as: 'The way we do things round here', Schein says that organisational culture matters because cultural elements determine strategy, goals and modes of operating.

The Chartered Institute of Marketing

Table 4.2   Examples of organisation culture.

Item	Example
Beliefs and values, which are often unquestioned	'The customer is always right'.
Behaviour	In the City of London, standard business dress is still generally taken for granted and even 'dress down Fridays' have their rules.
Artefacts	Microsoft encourages communication between employees by setting aside spaces for the purpose.
Rituals	In some firms, sales people compete with each other, and there is a reward, given at a ceremony, for the salesperson who does best in any period.
Symbols	Corporate logos are an example of symbols, but they are directed outwards. Within the organisation, symbols can represent power: dress, make and model of car, office size and equipment and access to facilities can all be important symbols.

Manifestations of culture in an organisation may thus include:

- How formal the organisation structure is
- Communication: are senior managers approachable?
- Office layout
- The type of people employed
- Symbols, legends, corporate myths
- Management style
- Freedom for subordinates to show initiative
- Attitudes to quality
- Attitudes to risk
- Attitudes to the customer
- Attitudes to technology

Influences on organisational culture include:

1 The organisation's **founder**. A strong set of values and assumptions is set up by the organisation's founder, and even after he or she has retired, these values have their own momentum. Or, to put it another way, an organisation might find it hard to shake off its original culture.

2 The organisation's **history**.

   (a) Culture reflects the era when the organisation was founded.

   (b) The effect of history can be determined by stories, rituals and symbolic behaviour. They legitimise behaviour and promote priorities.

3 **Leadership and management style**. An organisation with a strong culture recruits and develops managers who naturally conform to it, who perpetuate the culture.

4 The **organisation's environment**. As we have seen, nations, regions, occupations and business types have their own distinctive cultures, and these will affect the organisation's style.

Cultural values can be used to guide organisational processes without the need for tight control. They can also be used to motivate employees, by emphasising the heroic dimension of the task. Culture can also be used to drive change, although – since values are difficult to change – it can also be a powerful force for preserving the *status quo*.

2.2 Mintzberg's organisational structures

Mintzberg (1979) believes that all organisations can be analysed into five components, according to how they relate to the work of the organisation, and how they prefer to co-ordinate.

Figure 4.3   Mintzberg's organisational structures

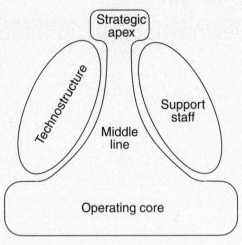

Mintzberg (1979)

Table 4.3   Characteristics of Mintzberg's organisational structures

Component	Job	Preferred means of co-ordination
Strategic apex	Ensures the organisation follows its mission. Manages the organisation's relationship with the environment.	Direct supervision (especially in small businesses).
Operating core	People **directly** involved in the process of obtaining inputs, and converting them into outputs.	Mutual adjustment; standardisation of skills.
Middle line	Converts the desires of the strategic apex into the work done by the operating core.	Standardisation of outputs (results).
Technostructure	■ Analysers determine the best way of doing a job. ■ Planners determine outputs (eg goods must achieve a specified level of quality). ■ Personnel analysts standardise skills (eg training programmes).	Standardisation of work processes or outputs.
Support staff	Ancillary services such as public relations, legal counsel, the cafeteria. Support staff do not plan or standardise production. They function independently of the operating core.	Mutual adjustment

These **components are linked** in five ways.

1   **Organisation hierarchy** and formal authority.

2   **Flow of regulated activity**. Inputs are processed into outputs.

3   **Informal communications** supplement or bypass the formal communication system and formal hierarchy.

4   **System of work constellations**. Groups of people work together on distinct tasks.

    (a)   For example, in producing a set of annual financial statements, people from the finance department (for the numbers), the sales department (for detailed statistics) and public relations (for presentation) need to be involved.

    (b)   On a more on-going basis, the members of the accounts department work together to produce financial information.

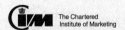 The Chartered Institute of Marketing

5   *Ad hoc* **decision processes**. A decision process involves recognising a problem, diagnosing its causes, finding a solution and implementing it. For any one decision, these activities occur in a number of different places in the organisation.

In most organisations, tasks and people are grouped together in some rational way: on the basis of specialisation, say, or shared technology or customer base. This is known as **departmentation**. Different patterns of departmentation are possible, and the pattern selected will depend on the individual circumstances of the organisation.

Organisations can be **departmentalised** on a **functional** basis (with separate departments for production, marketing, finance etc), a **geographical** basis (by region, or country), a **product** basis (eg worldwide divisions for product X, Y etc), a **brand** basis, or a **matrix** basis (eg someone selling product X in country A would report to both a product X manager and a country A manager). Organisation structures often feature a variety of these types, as **hybrid** structures.

2.3 Handy's cultural styles

In his book '*Gods of Management*', Charles Handy (2009) wrote about organisational classification under four types, differentiated by their structures, processes and management methods. The differences are so significant as to create **distinctive cultures**, to each of which Handy gives the name of a Greek God.

- Power culture (Zeus) is shaped by one individual.
- Role culture (Apollo) is a bureaucratic culture shaped by rationality, rules and procedures.
- Task culture (Athena) is shaped by a focus on outputs and results.
- Existential/person culture (Dionysus) is shaped by the interests of individuals.

Zeus: Power culture	**Apollo: Role culture**
The organisation is controlled by a key central figure, owner or founder. Power is direct, personal, informal. Suits small organisations where people get on well.	Classical, rational organisation: bureaucracy. Stable, slow-changing, formalised, impersonal. Authority based on position and function.

Athena: Task culture	**Dionysus: Person culture**
Management is directed at outputs: problems solved, projects completed. Team-based, horizontally-structured, flexible, valuing expertise – to get the job done.	The purpose of the organisation is to serve the interests of the individuals who make it up: management is directed at facilitating, administering.

2.3.1 Power culture

Zeus is the god representing the **power culture** or **club culture**. Zeus is a dynamic entrepreneur who rules with snap decisions. Power and influence stem from a central source, perhaps the owner-directors or the founder of the business. The degree of formalisation is limited, and there are few rules and procedures. Such a firm is likely to be organised on a functional basis.

- The organisation is capable of adapting quickly to meet change.

- Personal influence decreases as the size of an organisation gets bigger. The power culture is therefore best suited to smaller entrepreneurial organisations, where the leaders have direct communication with all employees.

- Personnel have to get on well with each other for this culture to work. These organisations are clubs of 'like-minded people introduced by the like-minded people, working on empathetic initiative with personal contact rather than formal liaison.'

2.3.2 Role culture

Apollo is the god of the **role culture** or **bureaucracy**. There is a presumption of logic and rationality.

- These organisations have a formal structure, and operate by well-established rules and procedures.

- Individuals are required to perform their job to the full, but not to overstep the boundaries of their authority. Individuals who work for such organisations tend to learn an expertise without experiencing risk; many do their job adequately, but are not over-ambitious.

- The bureaucratic style, as we have seen, can be very efficient in a stable environment, when the organisation is large and when the work is predictable.

2.3.3 Task culture

Athena is the goddess of the **task culture**. Management is seen as completing a succession of projects or solving problems.

- The task culture is reflected in project teams and task forces. In such organisations, there is no dominant or clear leader. The principal concern in a task culture is to get the job done. Therefore the individuals who are important are the experts with the ability to accomplish a particular aspect of the task.

- Performance is judged by results.

- Task cultures are expensive, as experts demand a market price.

- Task cultures also depend on variety, and to tap creativity requires a tolerance of perhaps costly mistakes.

2.3.4 Person culture

Dionysus is the god of the **existential** or **person culture**. In the three other cultures, the individual is subordinate to the organisation or task. An existential culture is found in an organisation whose purpose is to serve the interests of the individuals within it. These organisations are rare, although an example might be a partnership of a few individuals who do all the work of the organisation themselves (with perhaps a little secretarial or clerical assistance): for example, barristers (in the UK) work through chambers.

Management positions in these organisations are often lower in status than the professionals and are labelled secretaries, administrators, bursars, registrars or clerks.

The organisation depends on the talent of the individuals; management is derived from the consent of the managed, rather than the delegated authority of the owners.

| THE REAL WORLD |

Handy (2009) cites a pharmaceutical company which at one time had all its manufacturing subcontracted, until the turnover and cost considerations justified a factory of its own. The company hired nine talented individuals to design and run the factory. The results were as follows:

- The design team ran on a task culture, with a democratic/consultative leadership style, using project teams for certain problems. This was successful while the factory was being built.

- After its opening, the factory, staffed by 400, was run on similar lines. There were numerous problems. Every problem was treated as a project, and the workforce resented being asked to help sort out 'management' problems. In the end, the factory was run in a slightly more autocratic way. Handy states that this is a classic case of a task culture (to set something up) being superseded by a role culture (to run it). Different cultures suit different businesses.

Handy (2009) also matched appropriate cultural models to Anthony's (1965) classification of managerial activity.

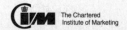
The Chartered
Institute of Marketing

- **Strategic management** (carried out by senior management) is concerned with direction-setting, policy-making and crisis handling. It therefore suits a **power culture**.

- **Tactical management** (carried out by middle management) is concerned with establishing means to the corporate ends, mobilising resources and innovating (finding new ways of achieving goals). It therefore suits a **task culture**.

- **Operational management** (carried out by supervisors and operatives) is concerned with routine activities to carry out tactical plans. It therefore suits a **role culture**.

ACTIVITY 4.3

Review the following statements. Ascribe each of them to one of Handy's four corporate cultures.

People are controlled and influenced by:

(a) The personal exercise of rewards, punishments or charisma.

(b) Impersonal exercise of economic and political power to enforce procedures and standards of performance.

(c) Communication and discussion of task requirements leading to appropriate action motivated by personal commitment to goal achievement.

(d) Intrinsic interest and enjoyment in the activities to be done, and/or concern and caring for the needs of the other people involved.

'If the [chosen] strategy goes against the dominant culture it is likely to fail unless a major effort is made to develop and maintain support. This could be achieved through staff training, appraisal and restructuring.' Drummond *et al* (2008, p260)

3 Assets

> ▶ **Key term**
>
> '**Assets** are organisational attributes, tangible or intangible, that can be utilised to gain advantages in the market.' Drummond *et al, 2008,* p260

'The organisation's current and potential capabilities have to be identified and this can be achieved by evaluating the assets and competencies that make up the company's resources.' Drummond *et al, (op.cit.,* p89)

Specifically, a **marketing asset** is something that a firm can use to advantage in the marketplace.

Examples of assets that create competitive advantage include:

- Scale advantages (market share, leverage, global presence, specialist skills)
- Production processes (flexibility, innovation, capacity, uniqueness)
- Customer franchises (relationships, patents, brands)
- Working capital (access, amount, location)
- Distribution networks (coverage, relationships, size)
- Relationships (suppliers, banks, JVs)
- Property (type, location, quality)

3.1 The asset-based approach

An **asset-based approach** identifies the types of assets the marketer will use: customer; distribution and internal assets. It matches 'marketing assets' with customer requirements. There are four types of marketing assets (Hooley *et al*, 2007).

1   **Customer-based** assets
2   **Distribution-based** assets

3 **Internal** assets

4 **Alliance-based** assets

3.1.1 Customer-based assets

These exist in the customer's mind.

- Corporate **image and reputation** can be an asset or a liability, depending on the received wisdom.
- A **brand** is an asset.
- **Market domination**. High market share is an asset because of the economies of scale it brings.
- **Better products/services** as perceived by the customer.

3.1.2 Distribution-based assets

- **Distribution network**. This covers sites and access to customers. For many years banks regarded their branch networks as an asset, but branches are costly to maintain. In the UK in recent years, hundreds of branches have been closed as banks reduce their networks to cut costs (a move which has been assisted by the greater access which customers have to their accounts through the development of telephone and internet banking.)

- **Distribution control**. Control of distribution constitutes a barrier to entry to other competitors.

- **Pockets of strength**. Where a company cannot serve a wide market, it can build strength in specific regions or through selected distribution outlets.

- **Uniqueness**. A unique or hard-to-copy distribution channel is an asset.

3.1.3 Internal assets

- **Low costs** give a firm the flexibility to choose low prices or to benefit from better margins.

- **Information systems and market intelligence**. Customer databases are built up over time and can enable offers to be targeted.

- The **existing customer base**. Satisfied customers are more likely to be repeat customers.

- Other assets include **technological skills** which can support marketing activities, production **expertise**, **intellectual property**, partnerships and corporate culture.

3.1.4 Alliance based assets

Many firms are expanding through alliances. For example, airlines have code sharing arrangements. Such assets include:

- Market access
- Management skills
- Shared technology or competences
- Shared knowledge and expertise
- Exclusivity (eg shutting out competitors)

However, it is important to be aware of the limitations of strategic alliances. In particular the risk that there may be disputes over control of strategic assets leading to a breakdown of trust and co-operation between the alliance partners.

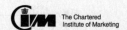
The Chartered
Institute of Marketing

Many airlines have alliances in which they 'share' passengers for flights on certain legs. For example, a passenger flying BA might, on certain journeys, be transferred to a Qantas flight.

In theory this can be an asset to both companies, provided that customer expectations are met (ie that BA and Qantas offer similar standards of service quality).

Alliances such as 'oneworld' (*) also have benefits for customers, for example making transfers easier and faster for passengers and their luggage. Wherever possible, oneworld airlines will issue boarding passes for all connecting oneworld flights, and will check-in bags from the initial departure point to the final destination.

At selected connecting airports, oneworld airlines also work together to monitor connecting flights and to assist passengers when their connections are in jeopardy. Wherever possible, oneworld customer representatives will meet connecting passengers upon arrival and issue them with 'Express Connections' documents which allow them to use dedicated fast lanes through customs, immigration and security to expedite the connecting process. Oneworld's baggage teams will also be engaged to transfer passengers' bags to that they make it on time to the final destination.

www.oneworld.com

(*): The 'oneworld' alliance currently (2012) contains 11 airlines: airberlin; American Airlines; British Airways; Cathay Pacific; Finnair; Iberia; Japan Airlines; LAN; Qantas; Royal Jordanian; S7 Airlines.

▸ **Exam tip**

To some extent, the resource-based approach is diametrically opposed to the marketing concept since, instead of approaching strategy on the basis of giving customers what they want, it concentrates on exploiting what the business already has to offer.

In fact, this distinction is largely theoretical, but it leads to some important ideas that you could use in the exam.

1   When the marketing concept is adopted, it will still be necessary to deploy threshold capabilities in all critical areas and the possession of unique resources and core competences will enhance the market offering.

2   Conversely, where strategy is built on unique resources and core competences, marketing activities must be carried out with at least threshold competence if the customer is to be satisfied.

A case study scenario in a past exam focused on low cost airlines. Low cost airlines are giving the customers what they want (low cost air travel, opening up air travel to people who may not have thought they could afford to fly overseas) and they are able to do this by exploiting their assets through their particular business model:

- Modern fleets
- Single class cabins
- Point-to-point routes (reduce complexity)
- Few frills, with 'extras' charged for
- Direct sales (online, with no use of travel agents)
- Good fleet utilisation
- Use of secondary airports
- Simple ground facilities
- Short haul only
- Performance-based compensation for employees

CHAPTER ROUNDUP

- The resource-based view suggests that, when managers develop strategies, they need to focus less on products and market, and the external environment, and more on the organisation's resources, competences and capabilities.

- The resource-based approach to strategy starts from a consideration of an organisation's strengths and weaknesses, and highlights the importance of developing core competences as a basis of competitive advantage.

- Where markets and products are rapidly changing, a company needs to consider its capability to anticipate these changes and to meet them. The notion of 'dynamic capabilities' can help explain how firms can achieve and sustain competitive advantage in situations of rapid and unpredictable change.

- Knowledge management aims to exploit existing knowledge within an organisation and create new knowledge which can then also be exploited.

- An asset-based approach to strategy aims to identify the assets (customer; distribution and internal assets) which marketers can use to contribute to a firm's competitive advantage in the market place. The strategy then aims to match these 'marketing assets' with customer requirements.

- It is also important to understand organisational culture , because cultural elements can determine strategy, goals and modes of operating. It is also important that the activities and processes within an organisation are linked effectively in order to create value for its customers.

FURTHER READING

Belbin, R. M. (2011). *Belbin Team Roles*. Retrieved August 1, 2012 from http://www.belbin.com/rte.asp?id=8

Handy, C. (1989). *The Age of Unreason*. Harvard Business School Press. Boston MA.

Narver, J., Slater, S. (1990). The effect of a market orientation on business profitability. *Journal of Marketing*, Vol 54 (4), 20-35.

Zeidan, H. (2009). "The Blake Mouton Managerial Grid". *The Certified Accountant*, Vol 39 (3), 82-85.

REFERENCES

Anthony, R.N. (1965) *Planning and Control Systems*. Harvard Business, Boston.

Drummond, G. Ensor, J. & Ashford, R. (2008) *Strategic Marketing Planning and Control*. 3rd edition. Elsevier Ltd, Oxford.

Hamel, G. & Prahalad, C.K. (1996) *Competing for the Future*. Harvard Business School Press, Boston.

Handy, C. (2009) *Gods of Management: The Changing Work of Organisations*. Souvenir Press Ltd, London.

Hofstede, G. (1984) *Culture's Consequences: International Differences in Work-Related Values*. (abridged edition). Sage Publications Inc, Thousand Oaks California.

Hooley, G. Saunders, J. Piercy, N. & Nicoulaud, B. (2007) *Marketing Strategy and Competitive Positioning*. 4th edition. FT Prentice Hall, Harlow.

Johnson, G., Scholes, K. & Whittington, R. (2011) *Exploring Strategy*, 9th edition, Pearson, Harlow.

Johnson, G., Whittington, R. & Scholes, K. (2012) *Fundamentals of Strategy*, Pearson, Harlow.

Mintzberg, H. (1979) *The Structuring of Organisations*. US edition. FT Prentice Hall, Harlow.

Mullins, L.J. (2007) *Management and Organisational Behaviour.* 8th edition. FT Prentice Hall, Harlow.

Schein, E. (2004) *Organisational Culture and Leadership*. 3rd edition. Jossey Bass, San Francisco.

Teece, D., Pisano, G. & Shuen, A. (1997) Dynamic Capabilities and Strategic Management, *Strategic Management Journal*, Vol. 18, No. 7 (August), pp. 509-533.

Wang, C. & Ahmed, P. (2007) Dynamic capabilities: A review and research agenda, *International Journal of Management Reviews*, Vol. 9, No. 1, pp. 31 – 51.

Waterman, R. & Peters, T. (1982) *In search of excellence*, Harper & Row, London. [Reprinted in 2004, by Profile Books, London.]

QUICK QUIZ

1   How do Johnson, Scholes & Whittington categorise competences?

2   What qualities are required of a core competence by Hamel & Prahalad?

3   The resource-based view of strategy is that sustainable .... is only attained as a result of the possession of .... Fill in the blanks.

4   Give the seven elements of the McKinsey 7S model.

5   Effective knowledge management requires a range of aspects. What are they?

6   Define 'organisational culture'.

7   What are Mintzberg's five organisational components?

8   How did Anthony categorise the hierarchy of management activity?

9   What are the four types of marketing asset defined by Hooley *et al*?

10   What is a marketing asset?

ACTIVITY DEBRIEFS

Activity 4.1

An obvious option is to embark upon a round of cost cutting. This is clearly the logic behind BA's decision to cut capacity and ground some of its planes. BA also cut a number of jobs, while others were asked to take reduced hours or to work some of their hours for free (in effect, taking a pay cut.) BA's Chief Executive summarised the issues when he said that the companies survival depends on everyone across the organisation contributing to changes that permanently remove costs from all parts of the business.

However, alongside measures to control costs, BA could also look at its pricing strategy. And this is something it did too. It found that a strategy of keeping ticket prices high was not compensating for the loss of passengers it was suffering. Therefore, it could concentrate on trying to drive up passenger numbers and capacity on its flights – which is a key part of the strategy adopted by low cost airlines such as Easyjet or Ryanair. (However, BA should not aim to compete directly on price with the low cost airlines, because its business strategy is based on differentiation (for example, through high quality customer service) rather than through cost leadership.)

Activity 4.2

1   The reasons for the organisation's existence should be expressed in terms of the consumer or client.

2   Marketing research should be used to find out:

(a)   Who needs help, and in what ways, and how satisfactory is the current help provided.

(b)   Where funds should be raised, and what the best approaches should be.

(c)   Which political figures are susceptible to lobbying and how such lobbying should best be conducted.

3   Target markets would be identified for charitable acts, fund-raising and influencing.

4   The charity might also wish to promote an image to the public, perhaps by means of public relations work.

5   The management of the charity will be aware that they are in competition for funds with other charities, and in competition with other ways of spending money in trying to obtain funds from the public. It should organise its 'sales and marketing' systems to raise funds in the most effective way.

(a)   Many charities now engage in telemarketing.

(b)   Many charities have acquired logos – even some NHS hospitals.

Activity 4.3

(a)   Zeus/power culture
(b)   Apollo/role culture
(c)   Athena/task culture
(d)   Dionysus/person culture

QUICK QUIZ ANSWERS

1   Johnson, Scholes & Whittington divide competences into two types:

(a)   An organisation must achieve at least a **threshold** level of competence in everything it does.
(b)   Its **core** competences are those where it outperforms competitors and that are difficult to imitate.

2   It must make a disproportionate contribution to the value the customer perceives.

It must be 'competitively unique'.

It must be extendable, in that it must allow for development of new products.

3   Competitive advantage; distinctive resources

4   Structure; Strategy; Systems; Shared values; Staff; Style; Skills.

5   Creation; capture; storage; availability; utilisation.

6   Organisational culture may be identified as ways of behaving, and ways of understanding, that are shared by the group of people working for an organisation.

7   Strategic apex; operating core; middle line; technostructure; support staff.

8   **Strategic management**: concerned with direction-setting, policy-making and crisis handling.

Tactical management: concerned with establishing means to the corporate ends, mobilising resources and innovating.

Operational management: concerned with routine activities to carry out tactical plans.

9   Customer-based assets
Distribution-based assets
Internal assets
Alliance-based assets

10   A marketing asset is something that a firm can use to advantage in the marketplace.

CHAPTER 5

Developing strategy

Introduction

This chapter develops the wide subject of the development of corporate strategy. In your Analysis & Decision studies, it is important that you appreciate the way that 'strategy' and 'marketing' relate to one another and also that you recognise the importance of coordinating the often disparate functions of an organisation to help it achieve its chosen strategies.

The Analysis & Decision syllabus requires you to have a good grasp of the evolving nature of strategic processes. In this chapter we discuss ways in which strategy is made in organisations. There are many approaches, each with something to offer, but the important this is to have a consistent framework to make sure that all influences can be taken account of.

We review the **rational model**. This is the classic approach; it has its weaknesses, but its great strength is that it is thorough. As a result, this method actually forms a good checklist of the things that strategists should consider, if only brief.

There are other approaches to strategy. These are, generally speaking, **descriptive** rather than **prescriptive**; that is to say, they are based on observation of what real world organisations actually do when making their strategies.

It is important to be aware that the terminology commonly used in this area of study is rather imprecise: 'strategy', 'corporate strategy', 'business strategy', 'marketing' and 'marketing strategy' are terms that are often used as if they were interchangeable.

Topic list

Evaluating the current direction   (1)

Models of strategic management   (2)

1.3.1	Critically evaluate an organisation's current strategic intent, based upon its vision, mission, values and stakeholder expectations:
	• Organisational purpose, mission and values
	• Defining organisational focus
	• Stakeholders analysis
	• Relationship portfolios
	• Organisational configuration
	• CSR and ethics
1.3.2	Critically analyse the role of strategic intent in shaping an organisation's strategy development:
	• Strategic intent and strategic vision
	• Strategic intent and leadership
	• Intent and flexibility
	• Strategic opportunism versus strategic drift

1 Evaluating the current direction

Organisations should be able to summarise their strategy with a strategy statement. 'Strategy statements should have three main themes: (i) the fundamental *goals* that the organisation seeks, which typically draw on the organisation's mission; vision and objectives (ii) the *scope* or domain of the organisation's activities; and (iii) the particular advantages or capabilities it has to deliver all of these.' (Collis & Rukstad, cited in Johnson, Scholes & Whittington, 2011.)

1.1 Organisational mission

The terminology of strategic management is not universally defined. There is a number of words that are used almost interchangeably: mission, purpose, values, objectives, aims, targets, goals, policies.

An organisation's **mission** refers to the overriding purpose of the organisation, and should reflect the organisation's long-term approach to business. As we noted in Chapter 3, Johnson, Scholes & Whittington's (2011) suggest that an organisation's mission can be described in terms of the questions 'What business are we in?'

An organisation's **values** relate to its goals, and refer to the desired future state of the organisation. So a vision statement should answer the question 'What do we want to achieve?' (Johnson, Scholes & Whittington, 2011)

Goals interpret the mission to the needs of different stakeholders (eg customers, employees, shareholders), and **objectives** should embody mission and goals! However, objectives should be more precise statements of the organisation's goals over a given period of time, and they should ideally be quantifiable. In effect, they should be used to ask 'What do we have to achieve in the coming period?' (*Op Cit.*)

▶ **Key terms**

Strategic analysis is concerned with understanding the strategic position of the organisation.

Mission denotes values, the business's rationale for existing

Vision refers to where the organisation intends to be in the future.

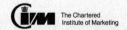

The Chartered Institute of Marketing

Customers and the mission statement

In the increasingly competitive service sector, it is no longer enough to promise customer satisfaction. Today, customer 'delight' is the stated aim for companies battling to retain and increase market share.

Amazon

We seek to be the Earth's most customer-centric company for four primary customer sets: consumers, sellers, enterprises and content creators.   www.amazon.com

Subway

The US sandwich restaurant chain, Subway, has the following mission statement in the US:

'Delight every customer so they want to tell their friends – with great value through fresh, delicious, made-to-order sandwiches, and an exceptional experience.

Subway also has a larger vision, which underlies its international restaurant operations (franchises):

'Be the Number 1 Quick Service Restaurant franchise in the world, while delivering fresh, delicious sandwiches and an exceptional experience.'

McDonald's

McDonald's brand mission is 'to be our customers favourite place and way to eat.'

The mission statement is more clearly defined through the 'McDonald's Values' which reflect the experience that customers can expect when walking into a McDonald's restaurant no matter where it is located.

McDonald's Values:

'We place the customer experience at the core of all we do.' Customers are the reason for McDonald's existence, and so its goals is to provide quality, service, cleanliness and value for each and every customer, every time they visit.

'We are committed to our people.' McDonald's aims to provide opportunities for its staff so that it nurtures talent (through training), develops leaders and rewards achievement.

'We believe in the McDonald's System.' The McDonald's business model highlights the importance of franchise owners, suppliers and company employees, and aims to balance the interests of the three groups.

'We operate our business ethically.' Sound ethics is perceived as good business, so this highlights the need for high standards of fairness, honesty, integrity, accountability and collective responsibility.

'We give back to our communities.' This value highlights the importance of corporate social responsibility; helping communities and supporting the Ronald McDonald House Charities.

'We grow our business profitably.' McDonald's is a publicly traded company and so it has to generate sustainable profitable growth for its shareholders. This requires a continuous focus on customers and the workings of its business model.

'We strive continually to improve.' McDonald's recognises that it needs to anticipate and respond to changing customer, employee and system needs, and it strives to do this through constant evolution and innovation.   www.aboutmcdonalds.com

What the organisation wishes to achieve – its mission – is fundamental to any focused control of its activities. One aspect of this control is analysis of those groups with an interest in what the organisation does. The organisation needs to satisfy the agendas of these various groups. As mentioned in the syllabus guidance notes, the 'best' strategy (measured using accepted business criteria) may not be acceptable to them, or may not fit with the current direction.

1.2 Stakeholder analysis and relationships

Mendelow (1985) classifies stakeholders on a matrix whose axes are 'power held' and 'likelihood of showing an interest' in the organisation's activities. These factors will help define the type of relationship the organisation should seek with its stakeholders.

Figure 5.1   Mendelow's stakeholder matrix

Mendelow (1985)

How should a company treat stakeholders in the various segments?

Stakeholder analysis identifies the interest groups in an enterprise. Different stakeholders will have their own views as to strategy. As some stakeholders have negative power, in other words power to impede or disrupt the decision, their likely response might be considered. An analysis of stakeholder risk has two elements.

- The risk that any particular strategic option poses to the interests of the different stakeholders.

- The risk that stakeholders might respond in such a way as to make a proposed strategy less attractive.

Table 5.1

Stakeholder	Interests at stake	Response risk
Management	Pay, status, power, promotion	Subtle sabotage, procrastination, internal politics
Employees	Pay, security, expertise	Strike action, resignation
Shareholders	Return on investment	Sell shares, or refuse to invest more
Bankers	Loan security; profits	Refusal to continue lending arrangements
Customers	Product	Switch to another supplier
Suppliers	Business	Will fail to deliver
Government	Public interest; election; taxes	Will regulate or tax

The firm can make strategic gains from managing stakeholder relationships. Studies have revealed:

- Correlation between employee retention and customer loyalty (eg, low staff turnover in service firms generally results in more repeat business).

- Continuity and stability in relationships with employees, customers and suppliers is important in enabling organisations to respond to certain types of change.

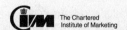

These soft issues are particularly pertinent for industries where creativity is important and for service businesses. Knowledge-based and service industries are likely to be the growth industries of the future.

1.3 Organisational configuration

The importance of organisational structure was discussed in Chapter 4. The way that an organisation is structured has a significant influence upon its strategic direction.

As we saw in Chapter 4, the **McKinsey 7S model** shows how the various aspects of a business relate to one another. It is a useful illustration of the influences upon an organisation's behaviour. To recap:

Figure 5.2   **The** McKinsey 7S framework

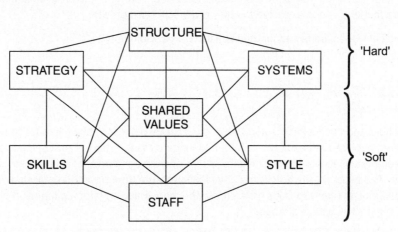

Based on a framework developed by Waterman & Peters (1982)

The organisation structure determines division of tasks in the organisation and the hierarchy of authority from the most senior to junior.

1.4 Ethics

The conduct of an organisation, its management and employees will be measured against ethical standards by the customers, suppliers and other members of the public with whom they deal. Types of ethical problem a manager may meet with in practice are:

- **Production practices**. Attempts to increase profitability by cutting costs may lead to dangerous working conditions, inadequate safety standards in products or reprehensible practices (eg child labour). This is a problem for firms which outsource production to low cost factories overseas.

- **Gifts**. There is a fine line to be drawn between gifts, accepted as part of a way of doing business, and bribes.

- **Social responsibility**. Companies are being held to account for their influences upon such matters as pollution levels and human rights issues.

- **Competitive behaviour**. There is a distinction between competing aggressively and competing unethically and illegally.

An organisation's mission, as discussed at the beginning of this chapter, should incorporate recognition of the ethical dimension.

ACTIVITY 5.2

The Heritage Carpet Company is a London-based retailer which imports carpets from Turkey, Iran and India. The company was founded by two Europeans who travelled independently through these countries in the 1970s. The company is the sole customer for carpets made in a number of villages in each of the source countries. The carpets are hand woven. Indeed, they are so finely woven that the process requires that children be used to do the weaving, thanks to their small fingers. The company believes that it is preserving a 'craft', and the directors believe that this is a justifiable social objective. Recently, a UK television company has reported unfavourably on child exploitation in the carpet weaving industry. There were reports of children working twelve-hour shifts in poorly lit sheds and cramped conditions, with consequent deterioration in eyesight, muscular disorders and a complete absence of education. The examples cited bear no relation to the Heritage Carpet Company's suppliers although children are used in the labour force, but there has been a spate of media attention. The regions in which the Heritage Carpet Company's supplier villages are found are soon expected to enjoy rapid economic growth.

What social and ethical issues are raised for the Heritage Carpet Company?

▶ **Exam tip**

It is important to understand that if ethics is applicable to corporate behaviour at all, it must be a fundamental aspect of mission, since everything the organisation does flows from that. Managers responsible for strategic decision-making cannot avoid responsibility for their organisation's ethical standing. Ethics and environmental considerations can conflict with business objectives, however. For example, the airline industry faces pressure from environmentalists and governments to cut carbon emissions, and some environmental groups have suggested that scrapping airport expansion plans would be one way government could help tackle climate change.

THE REAL WORLD

Apple, and Foxconn employees in China

While Apple's iPhones and iPads are becoming 'must-have' consumer items in Western countries, an investigation by two non-governmental organisations (NGOs) into the conditions of Chinese workers has revealed the shocking human cost of producing these items.

The investigation revealed disturbing allegations of excessive working hours and draconian workplace rules at two major plants in southern China. It has also uncovered an "anti-suicide" pledge that workers at the two plants have been urged to sign, after a series of employee deaths in 2010.

The investigation gives a detailed picture of life for the 500,000 workers at the Shenzhen and Chengdu factories owned by Foxconn, which produces millions of Apple products each year. The report accuses Foxconn of treating workers "inhumanely, like machines".

Among the allegations made by workers interviewed by the NGOs – the Centre for Research on Multinational Corporations and Students & Scholars Against Corporate Misbehaviour (Sacom) – are claims that:

■ Excessive overtime is routine, despite a legal limit of 36 hours overtime per month. One payslip indicated that the worker had performed 98 hours of overtime in a month.

■ Workers attempting to meet the huge demand for iPads were sometimes pressured to take only one day off in 13.

■ In some factories, workers who were deemed to be 'performing badly' were required to be publicly humiliated in front of colleagues.

■ In the wake of a spate of suicides at Foxconn factories in the summer of 2010, workers were asked to sign a statement promising not to kill themselves and pledging to "treasure their lives".

Foxconn produced its first iPad at Chengdu in November 2010 and expects to produce 100 million a year by 2013. In 2010, Apple sold more than 15 million iPads worldwide, and sold close to five million in the first quarter of 2011.

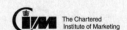
The Chartered Institute of Marketing

When the allegations uncovered by the NGOs were put to Foxconn, Foxconn manager Louis Woo confirmed that workers sometimes worked more than the statutory overtime limit to meet demand from western consumers, but claimed that all the extra hours were voluntary. Workers claimed that, if they turn down excessive demands for overtime, they will be forced to rely on their basic wages. Workers in Chengdu are only paid 1,350 yuan (£125) a month for a basic 48-hour week, equivalent to about 65p an hour.

Asked about the suicides that have led to anti-suicide netting being fitted beneath the windows of workers' dormitories, Woo said: "Suicides were not connected to bad working conditions. There was a copy effect. If one worker commits suicide, then others will follow."

In a statement, Apple said: "Apple is committed to ensuring the highest standards of social responsibility throughout our supply base. Apple requires suppliers to commit to our comprehensive supplier code of conduct as a condition of their contracts with us. We drive compliance with the code through a rigorous monitoring programme, including factory audits, corrective action plans and verification measures."

In April 2012, Apple was finally granted access to the Chinese factories, after it ordered the Foxconn City plant be opened to independent inspectors. The Washington-based Fair Labour Association has been appointed to interview Foxconn employees and observe their working conditions before continuing inspections at Apple's other Chinese manufacturers.

Based on: Chamberlain, G (2011) Apple's Chinese workers treated 'inhumanely, like machines' The Guardian, 30 April,
www.guardian.co.uk

1.4.1 The scope of corporate ethics

Corporate ethics may be considered in three contexts.

1 The organisation's interaction with national and international society
2 The effects of the organisation's routine operations
3 The behaviour of individual members of staff

1 **Influencing society**. Businesses operate within, and interact with, the political, economic and social framework of wider society. It is both inevitable and proper that they will both influence and be influenced by that wider framework. Governments, individual politicians and pressure groups will all make demands on such matters as employment prospects and executive pay. Conversely, businesses themselves will find that they need to make their own representations on such matters as monetary policy and the burden of regulation.

International variation in such matters and in the framework of corporate governance will affect organisations that operate in more than one country. It is appropriate that the organisation develops and promotes its own policy on such matters.

2 **Corporate behaviour**. The organisation should establish corporate policies for those issues over which it has direct control. Examples of matters that should be covered by policy include health, safety, labelling, equal opportunities, environmental effects, political activity, bribery and support for cultural activities.

3 **Individual behaviour**. Policies to guide the behaviour of individuals are likely to flow from the corporate stance on the matters discussed above. The organisation must decide on the extent to which it considers it appropriate to attempt to influence individual behaviour. Some aspects of such behaviour may be of strategic importance, especially when managers can be seen as representing or embodying the organisation's standards. Matters of financial rectitude and equal treatment of minorities are good examples here.

Business ethics are also relevant to competitive behaviour. This is because a market can only be free if competition is, in some basic respects, fair. There is a distinction between competing aggressively and competing unethically.

1.4.2 Ethics and marketing

> ▶ **Key term**
>
> The **societal marketing concept** is a management orientation that holds that the key task of the organisation is to determine the needs and wants of target markets and to adapt the organisation to delivering the desired satisfactions more effectively and efficiently than its competitors in a way that preserves or enhances the consumer's and society's well-being.

The marketing function has its own specific areas of ethical responsibility, as acknowledged by the 'societal marketing concept' and the CIM's own Code of Professional Standards.

Application of ethical considerations to the marketing mix

1   **Product/service**

   (a)   Failure to inform customers about risks associated with the use of the product: dishonesty. Currently, there are lawsuits in the US in which people are suggesting that the tobacco companies, despite their denials, have known for some time that nicotine is addictive.

   (b)   Using materials of a poorer quality in a bid to cut costs.

   (c)   Does manufacture involve an unacceptable environmental cost?

2   **Pricing**.

   In economic terms, price is a matter of supply and demand and, in the pursuit of profit, prices are what the market will bear. Ethics come into the discussion when:

   (a)   Cartels attempt to fix prices by rigging the market.
   (b)   Consumers are sometimes charged extras, not officially disclosed.

3   **Promotion**

   (a)   Advertising: honest, legal, decent and truthful.
   (b)   Tastefulness of imagery (eg violence, sexual stereotyping).

4   **Place**.

   Ethical concerns regarding relationships with intermediaries can involve the use of power, or delays in payment.

THE REAL WORLD

London 2012 Olympics

An Olympics watchdog for the London 2012 Olympics, appointed by the mayor of London, resigned in January 2012 in protest at a £7 million deal with a controversial chemical company.

Ethics commissioner, Meredith Alexander, told the Boris Johnson (London mayor) that she could play no further part in plans for the Games. She was angry that Dow Chemical – which has links to the deadly gas leak at the Bhopal plant in India in 1984 – was sponsoring the fabric 'wrap' which surrounds the Olympic stadium in east London.

Critics say that Dow, which bought the Bhopal plant's owners, Union Carbide, in 1999, has not done enough to compensate casualties or clear the contaminated site.

3,500 people died within days of the leak in 1984, and more than 15,000 have subsequently died as a result of it according to the Indian government. Campaigners say that the effects of the gas are still continuing now.

Ms Alexander said she could no longer endorse the Dow link up, or the ethic' commission apparent approval of it. She said that while she was really excited about the Olympic games, 'they shouldn't have the toxic legacy of Dow on their consciences. The Games organisers have given Dow an opportunity to whitewash their past and reputation.'

The Chartered Institute of Marketing

There was also anger in India when the deal with Dow was announced in August 2011, and there were even some suggestions that Indian athlete's could boycott the games. Dow agreed to withdraw branding from stadium panels, but denied this was to placate protesters. Dow argued that it should no longer be judged on the 'awful legacies' of the past.

Based on Radnedge, A. (2012) 'Olympics ethics boss quits over sponsor's Bhopal Link' *Metro*, 26 January, 2012.

1.4.3 Corporate Social Responsibility (CSR)

The behaviour of organisations may also be considered in the light of notions of corporate social responsibility. This is a rather poorly defined concept. However, there does now seem to be widespread acceptance that commercial organisations should devote some of their resources to the promotion of wider social aims that are not necessarily mandated by either law or the rules of ethics.

There is a fundamental split of views about the nature of corporate responsibility.

- The stakeholder view that a range of goals should be pursued
- The view that the business organisation is a purely economic force, subject to law

Businesses, particularly large ones, are subject to increasing expectations that they will exercise social responsibility. This is an ill-defined concept, but appears to focus on the provision of specific benefits to society in general, such as charitable donations, the creation or preservation of employment, and spending on environmental improvement or maintenance. A great deal of the pressure is created by the activity of minority action groups and is aimed at businesses because they are perceived to possess extensive resources. The momentum of such arguments is now so great that the notion of social responsibility has become almost inextricably confused with the matter of ethics. It is important to remember the distinction. Social responsibility and ethical behaviour are not the same thing.

In this context, you should remember that a business managed with the sole objective of maximising shareholder wealth can be run in just as ethical a fashion as one in which far wider stakeholder responsibility is assumed. On the other hand, there is no doubt that many large businesses have behaved irresponsibly in the past and some continue to do so.

2 Models of strategic management

Strategic market management is often frustrating because the environment is difficult to understand and predict. The communication and choices required within the organisation can create strain and internal resistance. The most valuable organisational resource, management time, is absorbed. The alternative of simply waiting for and reacting to exceptional opportunities often seems efficient and adequate.

Despite these costs and problems, strategic market management still has the potential to be very useful for organisations.

Strategic market management is intended to:

- Precipitate the consideration of strategic choices (eg What events are creating opportunities and threats for an organisation? What strategic options should be considered?)
- Help a business cope with change
- Force a long-range view
- Make visible the resource allocation decision (eg how are resources allocated between a small but promising business, and a larger business which could absorb an excessive amount of resources)
- Aid strategic analysis and decision-making (by encouraging the business to collect and analyse information)

- Provide a strategic management and control system. (The focus on the assets and competencies, and the development of objectives can provide the basis for managing a business strategically.)

- Provide both horizontal and vertical communication and coordination systems

(Aaker & McLoughlin, 2010)

Importantly, as Aaker & McLoughlin (2010) highlight, the alternative to strategic market management is usually to drift strategically, becoming absorbed in day-to-day problems and issues rather than maintaining a strategic focus.

2.1 Strategic marketing

The primary role of strategic marketing is to identify and create value for the business through strongly differentiated positioning. It achieves this by influencing the strategy and culture of the organisation in order to ensure that both have a strong customer focus.

In organisations where strategic marketing does not exist as a function, the process or decisions are still undertaken by senior managers or business leaders. Where it is an explicit function, the strategic marketing role will usually be performed by a marketing function in a business unit and by a corporate level marketing function, which may also have a responsibility for co-ordinating the activities of marketing departments in business units.

When this role is carried out by a marketing specialist, it is called 'marketing director' or 'strategic marketing manager', sometimes based in a department called 'marketing' rather than 'strategic marketing'. Strategic marketers should champion the customer experience and exert a strong influence on the organisation to adopt a customer orientation, contribute together with other directors and senior managers to its competitive strategy, align the organisation's activities to the customer, and manage the organisation's marketing activities.

During strategy formulation, strategic marketing is about choices that customer-focused organisations make on where and how to compete and with what assets. It is also about developing a specific competitive position using tools from the marketing armoury including brands, innovation, customer relationships and service, alliance, channels and communications, and increasingly, price. Strategic marketing does not own the business strategy but, like other departments and functions, should contribute to it and control the operational levers that make a strategy effective. However, marketing has an exceptional contribution to make in identifying opportunities and determining ways to create value for customers and shareholders.

During implementation, strategic marketing is the 'glue' that connects many aspects of the business. It will often manage one or a portfolio of brands. Increasingly, it works with HR to ensure that the culture and values in the organisation are consistent with the brand and to ensure that marketing competences are part of the overall framework for staff development across the business. Strategic marketing also has responsibility for directing the implementation of marketing activities needed to execute the organisation's strategy. Other key tasks of strategic marketing in today's organisations are:

- **Contributing to strategic initiatives** being undertaken by the organisation, for example marketing input to a 'due diligence' evaluation of a prospective merger or acquisition. In some cases, strategic marketers will be managing multi-disciplinary teams.

- **Co-ordinating and managing customer information** across the organisation within the data protection and privacy legislation. This involves close relationships with the IT function.

- **Advising on competitive positioning**: that is, determining target market segments and how they will be approached. This will include developing and driving the business case for investment in brands, new products and services.

- **Championing and developing innovation** and entrepreneurship within the organisation.

- Ensuring that the marketing function is appropriately skilled and resourced.

The Chartered Institute of Marketing

■ Providing input with finance on the valuation of brands for reporting and disclosure.

This concept of strategic marketing draws heavily on theory and practice of strategic management, not just of marketing. This is an important distinction since strategic marketing is as much a part of directing how the organisation competes as it is a part of marketing itself. Professional marketers engage in relationships with most functions within the organisation and are 'business people' rather than 'technical marketers'. This is particularly so at the strategic level. It requires participants at this level to embrace a wider range of management theory and practice than has been the case in the past.

In addition to traditional marketing theory, strategic marketing also embraces:

■ Business and corporate strategy
■ Investment decisions
■ Culture and change management
■ Quality management
■ Programme and project management

Marketers still have an essential role to play in contributing their specialist marketing skills to the formulation, implementation and control of strategy.

▶ **Exam tip**

It goes without saying that strategic marketing operates in a global context. Nonetheless, strategic management issues could be equally important for an organisation pursuing a domestic strategy or entering its first foreign market. Even if an organisation is not operating across borders, it is likely to be working in a market in which competitors based in other countries are operating – in other words, a global context.

2.1.1 The role of marketing in market-led strategic management

Ohmae (1991) summarises business strategy as a triangular relationship involving the three Cs: the corporation, the customers and the competition. The corporation and its competitors will seek to provide value to customers and incur costs in doing so.

Marketing plays a vital role in the management of this strategic triangle via the creation of an advantageous marketing mix. Such a mix will match the needs of the customer with the strength of the corporation and effectively differentiate the resulting value offered from those of the competitors. Marketing expertise and personnel are important drivers in taking a firm to the customer and making the organisation '**market-led**' (focusing on the customer).

In short, the pursuit of **customer satisfaction** is at the heart of the market-led company, but there are issues arising from this (Piercy, 2008):

New customers	– **Rising expectations**: customers exposed to world class service will expect it everywhere
	– **Sophistication**: customers can see through marketing-speak, and want transparency
	– Increased **cynicism** about marketing
New competitors	– From **overseas**
	– **Reinventing** the business (eg Direct Line Insurance)

New type of organisation	– **Outsourcing** arrangements – **Collaboration** arrangements – **Alliances** (eg airlines) – **Stakeholder** influences
New ways of doing business	– **Customer-specific** marketing – **Databases** are used to develop profiles of individual customers to entice them into a **relationship** – **Internet marketing**: buyers and sellers can conduct a dialogue as the Internet is interactive – **Customer co-operatives**: Internet newsgroups and chatrooms enable customers to get together perhaps to negotiate discounts or to share experience of a brand

2.2 Strategic intent, vision and leadership

▶ **Key terms**

Strategy: a course of action including the specification of resources required to meet a specific objective.

Corporate strategy is concerned with the overall purpose and scope of the organisation and how value will be added to the different parts (business units) of the organisation.

Tactics: the deployment of resources to execute an agreed strategy.

Policy: a general statement providing guidelines for management of decision-making.

Strategic management: the development, implementation and control of agreed strategies. There is more to strategy than merely deciding what you want to achieve and how you are to achieve it.

Synergistic planning is a rational process of determining further action based on realistic consideration of the current situation and desired outcome.

Any level of the organisation can have objectives and devise strategies to achieve them. The strategic management process is multi-layered, as illustrated in Figure 5.3:

Figure 5.3   Levels of strategy

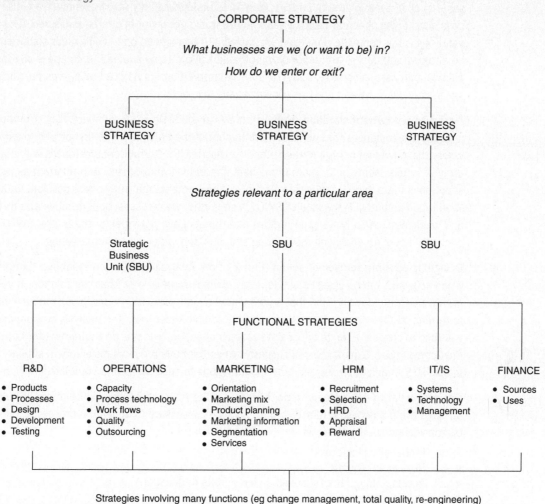

Figure 5.3 Levels of strategy

CORPORATE STRATEGY

What businesses are we (or want to be) in?

How do we enter or exit?

| BUSINESS STRATEGY | BUSINESS STRATEGY | BUSINESS STRATEGY |

Strategies relevant to a particular area

Strategic Business Unit (SBU)   SBU   SBU

FUNCTIONAL STRATEGIES

R&D	OPERATIONS	MARKETING	HRM	IT/IS	FINANCE
• Products	• Capacity	• Orientation	• Recruitment	• Systems	• Sources
• Processes	• Process technology	• Marketing mix	• Selection	• Technology	• Uses
• Design	• Work flows	• Product planning	• HRD	• Management	
• Development	• Quality	• Marketing information	• Appraisal		
• Testing	• Outsourcing	• Segmentation	• Reward		
		• Services			

Strategies involving many functions (eg change management, total quality, re-engineering)

Corporate decisions relate to the scope of a firm's activities, the long-term direction of the organisation, and allocation of resources. The 'planning' model of strategy formation suggest a logical sequence which involves:

- Analysing the current situation
- Generating choices (relating to competitors, products and markets)
- Implementing the chosen strategies

It is important to recognise the hierarchical level of planning and control decisions, because decision-makers can only make plans or take control action within the sphere of the authority that has been delegated to them. Synergistic planning, introduced above, has been described in several ways. We will discuss it under four main headings.

1   Determining the desired outcome
2   Analysing the current situation
3   Designing possible courses of action
4   Deciding what to do and how to do it

2.2.1 The synergistic planning process

1   **Determining the desired outcome**. Any process of planning must start with a clear definition of what is to be achieved. This process of objective setting is frequently undertaken in a very superficial manner in the real world and sometimes hardly performed at all. There may be an assumption that 'everybody

knows what we are trying to achieve' or reference back to long-established objectives that have lost some or all of their relevance under current circumstances. Only when objectives are clearly defined can possible courses of action be assessed and eventual success or failure be measured. The process of definition is not complete until everyone concerned has agreed on a single clear statement of what is to be attained. Vagueness and imprecision of language are to be avoided, but appear all too often for political purposes, since they allow different interpretations to be used by parties pursuing different agendas. Vagueness and ambiguity hamper affective action.

2   **Analysing the current situation** (Part 1 of the Analysis & Decision syllabus). Any plan must take into account circumstances that will affect attainment of the objective. The first step is to establish just where the individual or organisation stands to begin with. Current circumstances will include a vast array of factors, some of far more immediate importance than others. An important aspect of the current situation is the potential that exists for future developments that may affect possible future action. You should be familiar with the idea of SWOT – strengths, weaknesses, opportunities and threats. Strengths and weaknesses exist now; opportunities and threats have potential for the future. SWOT is a very common model for analysing the existing situation and widely used in marketing.

3   **Designing possible courses of action** (Part 2 of the Analysis & Decision syllabus). Simple problems, when analysed, often suggest a single, fairly obvious route to a satisfactory solution. If you come home from a skiing holiday and find that a cold snap has left you with a burst pipe, you have little alternative to turning off the water at the main and trying to find a plumber. The analysis of more complex problems will tend to suggest a range of possible courses of action. There is a requirement for both experience and imagination here. Experience will suggest routes that have proved satisfactory in similar circumstances in the past. Imagination suggest both modifications to such plans and completely new ones.

4   **Deciding what to do and how to do it** (Part 3 of the Analysis & Decision syllabus). When a range of possible plans has been outlined, it then becomes necessary to undergo a process of selection, normally by considering such matters as:

- Probability of success
- Resources required
- Acceptability of the proposed action and its implications
- Potential obstacles

The process of planning is not complete when a course of action has been chosen. It is then necessary to prepare detailed plans for all the groups and individuals involved. These must be integrated in such a way that all action undertaken supports the attainment of the overall objective. Performance measures and control mechanisms must also be established so that effort is not wasted and obstacles can be overcome.

2.2.2 Levels of strategy

We have already identified three levels of strategy in a large organisation.

- **Corporate strategies**. Corporate strategy might involve diversifying into a new line of business or closing a business down. It might mean global expansion or contraction.

- **Business strategies**. Business strategy is about individual business units should compete in their particular markets. For example, it might include decision about how the business should respond to competitors' moves.

- **Operational and functional strategies**, eg:

  - Segment the market and specialise in particularly profitable areas
  - Compete by offering a wider range of products
  - Offer a differentiated product

Some large, diversified firms have separate strategic business units dealing with particular areas. Functional/operational strategies deal with specialised areas of activity.

The Chartered
Institute of Marketing

Ikea's vision, business idea and market positioning statement provide a framework for all Ikea's marketing communication worldwide.

Ikea's Vision: 'To create a better everyday life for the many people.'

Ikea's business ideas is: 'To offer a wide range of well designed, functional home furnishing products at prices so low that as many people as possible will be able to afford them.'

Ikea's market positioning statement is: 'Your partner in better living. We do our part, you do yours. Together we save money.'

Nine key messages are then used within Ikea's marketing communications to build on the relationship with the customer, and to illustrate how Ikea can fulfil its customers' needs.

(i)   The Ikea concept is based on the market positioning statement. 'We do our part' focuses on Ikea's commitment to product design, consumer value and clever solution. By using inexpensive materials in a novel way, and minimising production, distribution and retail costs, customers benefit from low prices.

(ii)   The Ikea product range has been developed to be extensive enough to have something that appeals to everyone and to cover all the functions in the home The products are modern yet not too trendy, so they remain practical enough for everyday use.

(iii)   Ikea is the home furnishing specialist. Ikea products and functional yet appealing, so they enable many people to improve their home life, by providing practical solutions to everyday problems.

(iv)   Low price is not appealing unless it represents good value for money. Ikea is committed to having a good relationship with its suppliers, which enables it to purchase good quality, economically produced designs, bought in bulk to keep costs down. By making all its furniture flat packed, Ikea cuts down on transportation and assembly costs.

(v)   Function. Ikea products are based on a functional approach to design. They are practical and easy to use, and are made of the most suitable materials for their purpose. But they don't have unnecessary features, and expensive features are not included if a less expensive alternative can do just as good a job.

(vi)   Quality. The quality of a product must be appropriate for its intended use. Ikea products are subjected to rigorous texts to ensure they meet all appropriate standards.

(vii)   Convenient shopping. Ikea stores offer 'everything under one roof' with most stock available for immediate take-away. Ikea offers service where customers need it, but allows customers to make most of the decisions themselves. This means that it needs to be easy for customers to choose the right products – by ensuring they are displayed correctly and described accurately. And there is a simple returns policy should customers need it.

(viii) A day out for the family. Ikea aims to look after its customers by planning for their needs. It offers inspiration and ideas, but also encourages customer to touch, fell and use the products on display to see how they would fit into their own homes. But it also offers seasonal themes, play areas for children, and a family restaurant.

(iv)   Swedish roots. The key Ikea messages all have their roots in the Swedish origin of Ikea. Swedish furniture is light and fresh, yet unpretentious. And the warm, welcoming Swedish style has become a model of simplicity, practicality and informality. However, while thrift is also a strong characteristic of the region of Smaland (where Ikea is based).

www.ikea.com

2.2.3 A corporate strategic planning model

A model of the **corporate strategic planning process** is outlined below. There are three stages:

1   **Strategic analysis**

Strategic analysis is concerned with understanding the strategic position of the organisation.

- **Environmental analysis** (external appraisal) is the scanning of the business's environment for factors relevant to the organisation's current and future activities.

- **Position or situation audit**. The current state of the business in respect of resources, brands, markets etc.

- **Mission**

  - The firm's long-term approach to business
  - The organisation's value system

- **Goals** interpret the mission to the needs of different stakeholders (eg customers, employees, shareholders).

- **Objectives** should embody mission and goals. Generally, they are quantitative measures, against which actual performance can be assessed.

- **Corporate appraisal**. A critical assessment of strengths, weaknesses, opportunities and threats (SWOT) existing in the internal and environmental factors affecting an organisation.

- **Gap analysis**. A projection of current activities into the future to identify if there is a difference between the firm's objectives and the results from the continuation of current activities.

Note that you might decide the mission after assessing the needs of the organisation and its environmental situation.

2   Strategic choice

Strategic choice is based on strategic analysis.

- **Strategic options generation**. Here are some examples.

  - Increase market share
  - International growth
  - Concentration on core competences
  - Acquisition

- **Strategic options evaluation**. Alternative strategies are developed and each is then examined on its merits.

  - Acceptability to the organisation's stakeholders
  - Suitability
  - Feasibility

- Strategy selection

  - Competitive strategy is the generic strategy determining how you compete.
  - Product-market strategy determines where you compete.
  - Institutional strategies determine the method of growth.

3   Strategic implementation

The implementation of the strategy has to be planned. This is the conversion of the strategy into detailed plans or objectives for operating units.

- Some plans detail specifications as to how the activities should be carried out.

- Others will specify targets which managers are expected to reach on their own initiative.

- The planning of implementation has several aspects.

  - Resource planning (ie finance, Human Resources (HR). This involves assessing the key tasks, and the resources to be allocated to them.

  - Systems. Systems are necessary to provide the necessary strategic information, as well as essential operational procedures. Control systems are used to assess performance.

  - Organisation structure.

The Chartered Institute of Marketing

Ganymede Ltd is a company selling widgets. The finance director says 'We plan to issue more shares to raise money for new plant capacity – which will enable us to enter the vital and growing widget markets of Latin America. After all, we've promised the shareholders 5% profit growth this year, and trading is tough'.

Identify the corporate, business and functional strategies in the above statement.

Figure 5.4   The rational strategic planning model

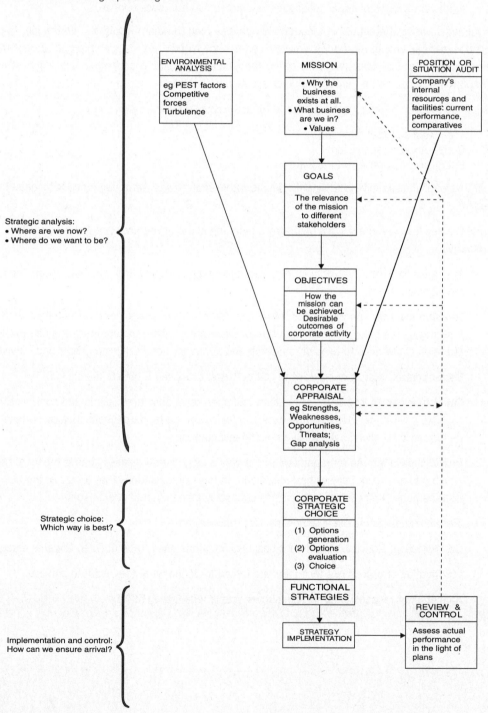

2.2.4 Strategic planning and leadership

> **▸ Key term**
>
> **Leadership** is the process of influencing others to work willingly towards a goal, and to the best of their capabilities. 'The essence of leadership is followership. In other words it is the willingness of people to follow that makes a person a leader'
>
> Koontz, O'Donnell, Weihrich (1988)

Leadership comes about in a number of different ways.

- A manager is **appointed** to a position of authority within the organisation. Leadership of subordinates is a function of the position.

- Some leaders are **elected**.

- Other leaders **emerge** by popular choice or through their personal drive. The personal, physical or expert power of leaders is more important than position power alone. Within teams and groups of equal colleagues leadership can and does change.

If a manager has indifferent or poor leadership qualities then the team would still do the job, but not efficiently. A good leader can ensure more than simply a compliance with orders. Leadership and management are different but linked activities; two sides of the same coin. Managing is concerned with logic, structure, analysis and control. If done well, it produces predictable results on time.

Leadership requires a different mind set and the leader has different tasks.

- Creating a sense of direction
- Communicating the vision
- Energising, inspiring and motivating

All of these activities involve dealing with people rather than things. A manager needs leadership skills to be effective.

One of the key features of a system of strategic planning is that it requires leadership. Specifically, it encourages:

1. **Managers to think**. Strategic planning can encourage creativity and initiative by tapping the ideas of the management team.

2. **Decision-making**. Companies cannot remain static – they have to cope with changes in the environment. A strategic plan helps to chart the future possible areas where the company may be involved and draws attention to the need to keep on changing and adapting, not just to 'stand still' and survive.

3. **Better control**. Management control can be better exercised if targets are explicit.

4. **Consistency at all levels**. Long, medium and short-term objectives, plans and controls should be made consistent with one another. Otherwise, strategies can be rendered ineffective by budgeting systems with performance measures which have no strategic content.

5. **Public knowledge**. An entrepreneur who builds a long-lasting business has 'a theory of the business' which informs his or her business decisions. In large organisations that theory of the business has to become public knowledge, as decisions cannot be taken by only one person.

6. **Time horizons**. Some plans are needed for the long term.

7. **Co-ordination**. Activities of different business functions need to be directed towards a common goal.

8. **Clarification of objectives**. Managers are forced to define what they want to achieve.

9. **Allocation of responsibility**. A plan shows people where they fit in.

2.3 Strategic intent and flexibility: taking account of other influences

▶ Key terms

Emergent strategies are those that develop out of patterns of behaviour. The task of strategic management is to control and shape these emergent strategies as they develop.

Johnson, Scholes & Whittington (2011) anchor plans in the behaviour of the organisation and the people in it. They suggest an approach which follows a similar outline to the rational model, but which recognises the need for some flexibility in taking account of, among other influences, the political and cultural influences on managers.

2.3.1 Culture's influence on strategy

Johnson, Scholes & Whittington (2011, p 174) quote George Davis (the founder of clothing retailer Next, and the man who established the Per Una brand in Marks &Spencer) who sees culture as central to strategic management: 'Culture is the thing that makes us do things and stops us doing things.

In effect, then, culture becomes and unintended driver of strategy.

For example, if managers are faced with a changing business environment, they are more likely to attempt to deal with the situation by searching for solutions they can understand in terms of the existing culture, or which are linked to similar solution they have used in the past.

Such a situation could be an example of what Johnson, Scholes & Whittington refer to as 'strategy as experience.'

Managers who have this kind of perspective on strategy view strategy as an **adaptation and extension of what has worked in the past**. Their view is likely to be based on the experience and assumptions of influential figures in an organisation, and the ways of doing things that **fit with the organisation's culture**.

The 'strategy as experience' view appreciates that managers tend to **simplify the complexity** they face in order to be able to deal with it, selecting and using the elements of their knowledge and understanding that seem most relevant or important.

However, this simplification may pose a risk to the organisation. For example, if an organisation has identified a key competitor, this competitor may come to represent competition in general. The problem is that this may blind managers to the actions of emerging competitors that have the potential to disrupt the existing market structure.

Where there are choices or disputes about strategic choices, these are resolved by negotiation and bargaining. The result is decisions that **satisfice rather than optimise**, and strategies that develop in an incremental and adaptive way.

2.3.2 Paradigm and politics

The word **paradigm** may be used to signify the basic assumptions and beliefs that an organisation's decision-makers hold in common. Note that this is a slightly different concept from culture. The paradigm represents collective experience and is used to make sense of a given situation; it is thus essentially conservative and inhibiting to innovation, while an innovative culture is entirely feasible.

The **politics** of the organisation may also influence strategy. 'The political view of strategy development is that strategies develop as the outcome of processes of bargaining and negotiation among powerful internal or external interest groups (or stakeholders).'

Johnson, Scholes & Whittington (2011) describe the processes by which paradigm and politics influence the process of strategy development.

Step 1   **Issue awareness**

- Internal results, customer responses or environmental changes can make individuals aware of a problem.

- A trigger alerts the formal information system to the problem, so that organisational activity takes over from the individual's consideration of the problem.

Step 2   **Issue formulation**

Managers try to analyse and get to the root of the problem. Information may be used to rationalise, rather than challenge, management's existing view of the situation. Formal analysis, in practice, plays a small role.

Step 3   **Solution development**

Some possible solutions are developed and one is selected.

- Memory search: solutions which worked in the past
- Passive search: wait for a solution to suggest itself

Solutions begin with a vague idea, which is further refined and explored by internal discussion.

Step 4   **Solution selection**

- Eliminate unacceptable plans. This screening process involves bargaining, diplomacy and judgement rather than formal evaluation according to the business case. ('Unacceptable' might mean unacceptable in terms of organisational politics, rather than in terms of business sense.)

- Endorsements. Many strategic decisions originate from management subsystems, which senior managers authorise. Junior managers might filter strategic information, or ignore certain options, to protect themselves.

2.3.3 Criticisms of formal strategic planning

Criticisms of the strategic planning model concern how it has worked in practice and more fundamental problems of theory. They can be summed up as a recognition of the need to be flexible when making strategic plans and decisions.

Table 5.2   Criticisms of strategic planning in practice

Criticism	Comment
Practical failure	Empirical studies have not proved that formal planning processes (the delineation of steps, the application of checklists and techniques) contribute to success.
Routine and regular	Strategic planning occurs often in an annual cycle. But a firm cannot allow itself to wait every year for the appointed month to address its problems. It may need to 'do something' straight away.
Reduces creative initiative	Formal planning discourages strategic thinking. Once a plan is locked in place, people are unwilling to question it.
Internal politics	The assumption of objectivity in evaluation ignores political battles between different managers and departments.
Exaggerates power	Managers are not all-knowing, and there are limits to the extent to which they can control the behaviour of the organisation.

The Chartered Institute of Marketing

Table 5.3   Criticism of the rational model in theory

Criticism	Comment
Formalisation	We have no evidence that any of the strategic planning systems – no matter how elaborate – succeed in capturing (let alone improving on) the messy informal processes by which strategies really do get developed.
Detachment: divorcing planning from operations	Managers manage by remote control. Senior managers at the top 'think great thoughts' while others scurry beneath them. This implies that managers do not really need day-to-day knowledge of the product or market.
Formulation precedes: Implementation	A strategy is planned – then it is implemented. But defining strengths and weaknesses is actually very difficult in advance of testing them.
Formulation precedes: Predetermination	Planning assumes that the environment can be forecast, and that its future behaviours can be controlled, by a strategy planned in advanced and delivered on schedule. This is only true of stable environments.

THE REAL WORLD

This is a classic example of what can go unexpectedly right.

Honda is now one of the leading manufacturers of motorbikes. The company is credited with identifying and targeting an untapped market for small 50cc bikes in the US, which enabled it to expand, trounce European competition and severely damage indigenous US bike manufacturers. By 1965, Honda had 63% of the US market. But this occurred by accident.

On entering the US market, Honda had wanted to compete with the larger European and US bikes of 250ccs and over. These bikes had a defined market, and were sold through dedicated motorbike dealerships. Disaster struck when Honda's larger machines developed faults – they had not been designed for the hard wear and tear imposed by US motorcyclists. Honda had to recall the larger machines.

Honda had made little effort to sell its small 50cc motorbikes – its staff rode them on errands around Los Angeles. Sports goods shops, ordinary bicycle and department stores had expressed an interest, but Honda did not want to confuse its image in its 'target' market of men who bought the larger bikes.

The faults in Honda's larger machines meant that, reluctantly, Honda had to sell the small 50cc bikes just to raise money. They proved very popular with people who would never have bought motorbikes before.

Eventually the company adopted this new market with enthusiasm with the slogan: 'You meet the nicest people on a Honda'. The strategy had emerged, against managers' conscious intentions, but they eventually responded to the new situation.

2.4 Alternatives to planning

2.4.1 No strategic planning: 'freewheeling opportunism'

▶ **Key term**

Intended strategies are plans. Those plans or aspects of plans which are actually realised are called deliberate strategies.

The **freewheeling opportunism approach** suggests firms should not bother with strategic plans and should exploit **opportunities** as they arise, judged on their individual merits and not within the rigid structure of an overall corporate strategy.

Advantages

- Opportunities can be seized when they arise, whereas a rigid planning framework might impose restrictions so that the opportunities are lost.

- It might encourage a more flexible, creative attitude among lower-level managers.

Disadvantages

- **No co-ordinating framework** for the organisation as a whole.

- The firm ends up **reacting** all the time rather than acting purposively.

2.4.2 Strategic 'drift'

Figure 5.5   Vision versus opportunism

Figure 5.5 demonstrates the risks associated with the different types of strategic focus. With a focus on the future, a company can be said to have 'strategic vision', but there is the risk that this becomes a kind of stubbornness and misguided determination to forge ahead with a strategy that may not be justified by events or business circumstances. On the other hand, a concentration on the present , exploiting opportunities as they arise, can lead to what is known as 'strategic drift'.

Under conditions of strategic drift, decisions are made incrementally (see below) rather than as the result of being directed by some unifying and overarching 'vision'. Short lived opportunities may be mistaken for ones that truly merit long-term strategic investment. Expected synergies may fail to materialise. New business areas will have been put in place without any sustainable business advantage.

2.4.3 No strategic planning: incrementalism

Herbert Simon (1970) suggested that managers do not optimise (ie, get the best possible solution), but instead they satisfice. Managers are limited by time, by the information they have and by their own skills, habits and reflexes. They do not in practice evaluate all the possible options open to them in a given situation, but choose between relatively few alternatives. This is called bounded rationality.

- Strategy-making tends to involve **small scale extensions of past policy** – **incrementalism** – rather than radical shifts following a comprehensive rational 'search' and evaluation of the alternatives.

- In marketing terms, small scale adjustments of current marketing programmes *may* not be enough either to:

    - **Move** with existing customers and their needs

    - **Identify** new markets or sets of customers

On the other hand, an incremental approach may be both safe and satisfactory.

The Chartered
Institute of Marketing

Tesco.com and Webvan

Tesco.com, the online shopping operation set up by the UK supermarket giant is an excellent example of successful incrementalism.

In 1996, Tesco decided to test the potential for online grocery shopping with a website based on a single store at Osterley in West London. Over the next two years the business model was refined and the crucial decision to impose a delivery charge was made. This had the beneficial effect of leading customers to place fewer, larger orders so as to derive the greatest benefit from the flat-rate charge. Tesco.com has grown successfully each year since its launch, partly because costs have been held down by making deliveries from existing stores. By 2007, Tesco.com had 850,000 customers, and completed more than 250,000 online orders each week.

By 2010, over 15,000 products were available online. As well as offering an online grocery shopping service, Tesco.com also offers a wide range of other products, including electronic goods, entertainment and books, clothing, and homewares. In 2011, Tesco.com's annual sales were approximately £2.75 billion.

Tesco's approach was markedly different from that of Webvan, which set out to completely remodel the US grocery retailing industry in 1997. It aimed to create a chain of highly automated warehouses in order to increase worker productivity and offered free delivery regardless of customers' location. Unfortunately, Webvan was never really in control of its costs and it was estimated that the company lost US$130 on every order. By July 2001, the company was declared insolvent after losing US$1.2 billion.

2.4.4 Emergent strategies

Some strategies do not arise out of **conscious** strategic planning, but result from a number of **ad hoc choices**, perhaps made lower down the hierarchy, which may not be recognised at the time as being of strategic importance. These are called **emergent** strategies. They develop out of **patterns of behaviour** which become clear over time, in contrast to planned strategies which are imposed from above.

An emergent strategy is one whose final objective is **unclear at the outset**, and whose elements develop during its life as the strategy proceeds.

Aldebaran Ltd is a public relations agency founded by an entrepreneur, Estella Grande, who has employed various talented individuals from other agencies to set up in business. Estella Grande wants Aldebaran Ltd to become the largest public relations agency in North London. Management consultants, in a planning document, have suggested 'growth by acquisition'. In other words, Aldebaran should buy up the other public relations agencies in the area. These would be retained as semi-independent business units, as the Aldebaran Ltd group could benefit from the goodwill of the newly acquired agencies.

When Estella presents these ideas to the Board there is general consensus with one significant exception. Livia Strange, the marketing director, is horrified. 'How am I going to sell this to my staff? Ever since we've been in business, we've won business by undercutting and slagging off the competition. My team have a whole culture based on it. I give them champagne if they pinch a high value client. Why acquire these new businesses – why not stick to pinching their clients instead?'

What is the source of the conflict?

Mintzberg uses the metaphor of **crafting strategy** to help understand the idea. Emergent strategies can be shaped by managers. Strategies are shaped as they develop, with managers giving help and guidance, devoting more resources to some, exploiting new opportunities and responding to developments. For example, Honda's management reacted to the emergent strategy, eventually, and shaped its development.

Separating 'thinking' and 'doing' has the following result.

- A purely deliberate strategy hampers rapid learning from experience.

- A purely emergent strategy defies control. It may in fact be a bad strategy, dysfunctional for the organisation's future health.

Deliberate strategies introduce strategic change as a sort of quantum leap in some organisations. In this case, a firm undergoes only a few strategic changes in a short period, but these are very dramatic.

However, managers cannot simply let emerging strategies take over. Why?

- **Direction**. The emergent strategy may be inappropriate for the long-term direction of the organisation and may have to be corrected. An insistence on carrying it through is the 'strategic stubbornness' we saw earlier.

- **Resources**. It may have future implications for resource use elsewhere: in most organisations, different parts of the business compete for resources. Managers might wish to build on the strategy by actively devoting more resources to it.

No realised strategy will be wholly deliberate or wholly emergent. The line between deliberate and emergent elements within each strategy will be in part influenced by organisation structure and culture. The environment is uncertain and there are limits on what managers can achieve. Small steps may be a more practical way to move forward than to attempt to follow a grand plan: as already mentioned this is known as 'incrementalism' and is characterised by small scale extensions of past practice.

2.4.5 Deliberate and emergent strategies

Figure 5.6 below helps explain the material in this section.

Figure 5.6   Deliberate and emergent strategies

The diagram above also highlights the important distinction between **realised** and **unrealised** strategies.

Realised strategies are what the organisation is actually doing in practice. This may be a result of the intended strategy, but it may also be the outcome of emergent strategy process. In practice, it will often be a combination of the two:

Unrealised strategies are aspects of the intended strategy which do not come about in practice. There could be many reasons for this: for example, the environment might change so managers decide the planned strategy should not be put into practice. Equally, plans may be unworkable for a variety of reasons: resources may be inadequate, important stakeholders may oppose them, and so on.

You have probably encountered examples in everyday life where an intended strategy is not realised. For example, how many times have organisations promised you 'excellent customer service' or 'first rate service'? Has the service you have actually received matched those promises? The intended plan may have been to offer 'excellent customer service', but what is realised often falls short of what is intended.

> **Exam tip**
>
> The great thing about the rational model is that it is comprehensive. Even if it is unrealistic to think of a given organisation moving with stately deliberation through an annual planning cycle, the rational model does give us a checklist that can be used to identify areas in which a company's strategy-making may be capable of improvement. You may well find it a useful source of ideas.

ACTIVITY 5.5

How do you see the current "state of the art", regarding the rise of Mobile Marketing?

CHAPTER ROUNDUP

- An organisation's mission guides its strategic decisions, and provides an overall direction for the organisation. Mission statements can play an important role in the strategic planning process, but they have also be criticised for being over-generalised, which leads to them effectively being ignored in practice.

- An organisation's goals and objectives should derive from its mission, and, in turn, should support the mission.

- Organisations need strategies to establish their direction and scope in the long term, and to determine the resources and competences needed to achieve a desire course of action.

- The rational model describes a highly structured approach to strategic planning. An organisation identifies its objectives, analyses its current position, developments its strategic options, and then selects which strategies it is going to implement in order to try to achieve its objectives.

- However, a basic distinction can be made between prescriptive (rational model) and emergent approaches to strategy. An emergent approach does not identify final strategic objectives in advance, and so is more adaptable than a prescriptive approach.

- Business success is increasingly linked to maintaining high standards of business and ethical conduct. Ethical issues have an impact on all aspects of the marketing mix.

- Corporate social responsibility highlights an organisation's commitment to behave ethically and to recognise the impact its behaviour and activities can have on society and the environment.

- Organisations have many stakeholders, and different stakeholder groups could have conflicting interests. Organisations must try to manage their stakeholders in order to create productive and long-lasting relationships with their key stakeholders.

FURTHER READING

Kotler, P. and Keller, K. L. (2012) *A framework for marketing management.* 5th edition. Pearson, Harlow. (Chapter 2: Developing marketing strategies and plans).

Lynch, R. (2012) Strategic Management. 6th edition. Pearson, Harlow. (Part 3: Developing the Strategy.)

REFERENCES

Aaker, D. & McLoughlin, D. (2007) *Strategic Market Management.* John Wiley, Chichester.

Johnson, G., Scholes, K. & Whittington, R. (2011) *Exploring Strategy.* 9th edition. Pearson, Harlow.

Koontz, H. O'Donnell, C. & Weihrich, H. (1988) *Management.* Revised edition. McGraw-Hill Education, Maidenhead.

Mendelow, A. (1985) 'Stakeholder analysis for strategic planning and implementation' in *Strategic Planning & Management Handbook*, King & Cleland (eds). Van Nostrand Reinhold, NY.

Mintzberg, H. (2000) *The Rise and Fall of Strategic Planning.* FT Prentice Hall, Harlow.

Ohmae, K. (1991) *The Mind Of The Strategist: The Art of Japanese Business.* McGraw-Hill Professional, London.

The Chartered Institute of Marketing

Piercy, N.F (2008) *Market-Led Strategic Change – Transforming the Process of Going to Market*. 4ᵗʰ edition. Butterworth-Heinemann, Oxford.

Simon, H. (1970) *Sciences of the Artificial*. MIT Press, New York.

Waterman, R. & Peters, T. (1982) *In search of excellence*, Harper & Row, London. [Reprinted in 2004, by Profile Books, London.]

QUICK QUIZ

1   What do you understand by the term 'strategic analysis'?

2   What are the two elements of stakeholder risk?

3   What is the 'societal marketing' concept?

4   What is 'strategic marketing'?

5   List Ohmae's three 'Cs'.

6   What are the three layers of strategy?

7   List the three stages of strategic planning.

8   Contrast intended and emergent strategies.

9   What is 'strategic drift'?

10 What are some of the practical criticisms of strategic planning?

ACTIVITY DEBRIEFS

Activity 5.1

(a)   Key players are found in segment D: strategy must be acceptable to them, at least. An example would be a major customer.

(b)   Stakeholders in segment C must be treated with care. While often passive, they are capable of moving to segment D. They should, therefore, be kept satisfied. Large institutional shareholders might fall into segment C.

(c)   Stakeholders in segment B do not have great ability to influence strategy, but their views can be important in influencing more powerful stakeholders, perhaps by lobbying. They should therefore be kept informed. Community representatives and charities might fall into segment B.

(d)   Minimal effort is expended on segment A.

Activity 5.2

Many. This is a case partly about boundary management and partly about enlightened self-interest and business ethics. The adverse publicity, although not about the Heritage Carpet Company's own suppliers, could rebound badly. Potential customers might be put off. Economic growth in the area may also mean that parents will prefer to send their children to school. The Heritage Carpet Company as well as promoting itself as preserving a craft could reinvest some of its profits in the villages (eg by funding a school), by enforcing limits on the hours children worked. It could also pay a decent wage. It could advertise this in a 'code of ethics' so that customers are reassured that the children are not simply being exploited. Alternatively, it could decide not to import child-made carpets at all. (This policy, however, would be unlikely to help communities in which child labour is an economic necessity.)

Activity 5.3

The corporate objective is profit growth. The corporate strategy is the decision that this will be achieved by entering new markets, rather than producing new products. The business strategy suggests that those markets include Latin America. The functional strategy involves the decision to invest in new plant (the production function) which is to be financed by shares rather than loans (the finance function).

Activity 5.4

Livia Strange's department has generated its own pattern of competitive behaviour. It is an emergent strategy. It conflicts directly with the planned strategy proposed by the consultants. This little case history also makes the additional point that strategies are not only about numbers, targets and grand plans, but about the organisational cultures influencing people's behaviour.

Activity 5.5

With over 6,500 different types of web-capable devices, and over 25 per cent of all mobile phone owners using smartphones, most brands now need to have a very strong mobile strategy.
Mobile matters to Consumers and therefore to marketers. Not only for the one thousand and one Apps that can make life easier, more pleasant and more entertaining, but for the reading experience too. In fact, a greater number of users are registered on all three types of reading platforms: computers, tablets, and smartphones. Despite the current resistance to digital reading –mostly among older people- the newspaper and magazine reader of tomorrow will choose to read (and purchase) their magazines on the device most easily accessible at key points through the day. While reading and watching videos and live feeds on mobile digital devices our "Tomorrow Consumer" will also be impacted by advertising and will make purchases.

QUICK QUIZ ANSWERS

1   Strategic analysis is concerned with understanding the strategic position of the organisation.

2   The risk that any particular strategic option poses to the interests of different stakeholders. The risk that stakeholders might respond in such a way as to make a proposed strategy less attractive.

3   The societal marketing concept holds that the key task of the organisation is to determine the needs of target markets and to deliver them more effectively and efficiently than its competitors, in a way that promotes the consumer's and society's well-being.

4   The primary role of strategic marketing is to identify and create value for the business through strongly differentiated positioning. It achieves this by influencing the strategy and culture of the organisation in order to ensure that both have a strong customer focus.

5   Company; customers; competition.

6   Corporate; business; tactical/operational.

7   Strategic analysis; strategic choice; strategic implementation.

8   Intended strategies are plans. Those plans or aspects of plans which are actually realised are called deliberate strategies. Emergent strategies are those that develop out of patterns of behaviour.

9   Too much concentration on the present, exploiting opportunities as they arise, can lead to what is known as 'strategic drift'. Under conditions of strategic drift, decisions are made incrementally rather than as the result of direction from a unifying and overarching 'vision'.

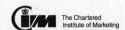

10   Practical failure: Empirical studies have not proved that formal planning contribute to success.

Routine and regular: A firm cannot allow itself to wait every year for the appointed month to address its problems.

Reduces creative initiative: Formal planning discourages strategic thinking.

Internal politics: The assumption of objectivity ignores internal political battles.

Exaggerates power: Managers are not all-knowing.

CHAPTER 6

Assessing strategic marketing options

Introduction

Any plan must take into account circumstances that will affect attainment of its objectives. As we have already seen, the first step is to establish just where the individual or organisation stands to begin with, and an important aspect of the current situation is the potential that exists for future developments. Strategic choice is based on strategic analysis, and has three aspects:

1   **Strategic options generation**. Here are some examples.

   - Increase market share
   - International growth
   - Concentration on core competences
   - Acquisition

2   **Strategic options evaluation and development**. Alternative strategies are developed and each is then examined on its merits. A useful way to assess the appropriateness of different options is by analysing their suitability; acceptability and feasibility.

3   **Strategy selection**

   - Competitive strategy is the generic strategy determining *how* you compete.
   - Product-market strategy determines *where* you compete.
   - Institutional strategies determine the *method* of growth.

To be successful, strategic options should contain both real and perceived value propositions and be relevant, sustainable and feasible.

This chapter looks at the different approaches to generating and evaluating strategic options.

Topic list

2.1.1	Critically evaluate the determinants of strategic options and choices:
	■ Past and current strategies
	■ Organisational capabilities and constraints (financial and non-financial)
	■ Financial capabilities and constraints
	■ Organisàtional strengths and weaknesses
	■ Product-market opportunities
	■ Sources of competitive advantage (Porter)
	■ Warfare analogies in strategy (Kotler)
2.1.2	Critically evaluate how strategic options can be developed to reflect an organisation's:
	■ Value proposition
	■ Assets and competencies
	■ Business function strategies
	■ Functional strategies and programmes
	■ Competitive advantage
	■ Sustainability
2.2.8	Critically assess the impact of changing an organisation's strategic position within the market place in order to:
	■ Reflect the business strategy
	■ Resonate with customers
	■ Differentiate from competitors
	■ Express the values and culture of an organisation in a relevant way
	■ Express an organisation's corporate social responsibility (CSR), corporate reputation, sustainability and ethics.
3.1.1	Critically assess strategic alternatives against pre-determined criteria for an organisation, including:
	■ Scenario planning – stability versus uncertainty
	■ Potential for Return on Investment (ROI)
	■ Opportunity to achieve competitive advantage
	■ Feasibility, viability and resource
	■ Capacity and capability to deliver

1 Determinants of strategic options

'What characteristics of a business make some options unfeasible without a major organisational change? What characteristics will be pivotal in choosing among strategic options?' Aaker & McLoughlin (2007, p119)

After looking at the context in which strategic planning decisions are made, and the internal and external factors which affect strategic decisions, we will now look at the range of strategic options which organisations can choose from, and the factors which make some options more appropriate for an organisation than others.

1.1 Past and current strategies

It is important to make an accurate profile of past and current strategies. Strategy is a pattern of senior management decisions, arising out of the general management process whereby senior managers direct and control the business. This general management process generates consistent decisions. For example, a firm's managers may prefer certain types of market opportunities (eg low risk) than others. Sometimes, however, a strategy evolves into something very different from what was planned.

Strategic opportunities must be related to the firm's resources. A strategic approach involves identifying a firm's competences.

As we have already seen, the distinctive competence of an organisation is what it does well, uniquely, or better than rivals. For a relatively undifferentiated product such as cement, the ability of a maker to run a truck fleet more effectively than its competitors will give it competitive strengths (if, for example, it can satisfy orders quickly). These competences may come about in a variety of ways.

- Experience in making and marketing a product or service
- The talents and potential of individuals in the organisation
- The quality of co-ordination

1.2 Organisational capabilities and constraints

Organisations are successful when they intentionally achieve internal harmony and external adaptation to their environment. Managers should use analytical techniques to identify the relationship between the organisation's internal capability and competences, and the external outputs. In very basic terms, the need for the fit is identified by the SWOT analysis and strategies are undertaken to secure the fit.

Arguably, the choice of strategy should follow a strategic logic.

- It must be consistently related to the objectives of the organisation.

- It must match the organisation's capability (including its structure, control systems and culture) to its environment.

The idea is that all the pieces of the strategic puzzle should fit together in a predetermined manner.

A business needs to identify those business processes that have the greatest impact on customer satisfaction, such as quality and employee skills.

- Companies should also attempt to identify and measure their distinctive competences and the critical technologies they need to ensure continued leadership. Which processes should they excel at?

- To achieve these goals, performance measures must relate to employee behaviour, to tie in the strategic direction with employee action.

- An information system is necessary to enable executives to measure performance. An executive information system enables managers to drill down into lower level information.

While these perspectives identify the current parameters for competitive success, the company needs to learn and to innovate to satisfy future needs. This might be one of the hardest items to measure.

- How long does it take to develop new products?

- How quickly does the firm climb the experience curve to manufacture new products?

- What percentage of revenue comes from new products?

- How many suggestions are made by staff and are acted upon?

- What are staff attitudes? Some firms believe that employee motivation and successful communication are necessary for organisational learning.

- Depending on circumstances, the company can identify measures for training and long-term investment.

1.3 Financial capabilities and constraints

A growth strategy, even if it simply involves growth within the existing product market (ie, market penetration) usually requires working capital and other assets, so an organisation needs to have funds available to facilitate the growth strategy.

Financial performance indicators indicate whether the company's strategies, implementation, and execution are contributing to bottom-line management and the generation of investment resources. A realistic appraisal of the resources (probable, actual and potential) that are required by the business can make strategy development itself more realistic.

Financial issues do not take care of themselves.

- Money is a resource, and financial measures will ultimately effect a firm's ability to obtain that resource (eg by raising the firm's cost of capital, if shareholders perceive greater risk).

- Well-designed financial control systems can actually assist in performance management programmes (eg by identifying variances).

Moreover, financial control techniques are vital to successful strategy, and apply to both the planning and implementation phases of strategies. Drummond *et al* (2008) highlight the importance of ratio analysis, budgeting and variance analysis, and argue that all business activities are ultimately measured in financial terms. (We will look at financial controls and tools in Chapter 9 of this Study Text.)

1.4 Organisational strengths and weaknesses

We have already seen that the competitive advantage of an organisation is likely to be based on the strategic capabilities it has that are valuable to customers, and which its rivals do not have or cannot obtain.

In this context, strategic options can be seen as a way of establishing value propositions for specific products and/or markets by taking advantage of an organisation's strategic capabilities.

In effect, then a strategic option is a particular value proposition for a specific product market, supported by assets and competencies, and by functional strategies and programmes.

We discussed value propositions in Chapter 1, but as a recap value propositions are often based on:

- Quality
- Customer relationships
- Value
- Innovation
- Focus
- Being global
- Brand equity

You should also be familiar with the idea of **SWOT** – strengths, weaknesses, opportunities and threats. Strengths and weaknesses exist now; opportunities and threats have potential for the future. SWOT is a very common model for analysing the existing situation and widely used in marketing. And a key issue it so try to identify the extent to which an organisation's strengths and weaknesses are relevant to, or are capable of dealing with, the changes which are taking place in the business environment (Johnson, Scholes & Whittington, 2011).

1.4.1 Corporate appraisal

SWOT analysis is a useful technique for organising information about an organisation's strengths and weaknesses (**internal** appraisal) and the opportunities and threats (**external** appraisal) which it encounters. SWOT can be enhanced by **ranking** items in order of significance, and it is always important not to confuse the level at which the analysis is conducted (eg corporate SWOT and marketing SWOT). The SWOT can be used to identify possible **strategies**.

The purpose of **corporate appraisal**, is to **combine** the assessment of the environment and the analysis of the organisation's internal resources and capabilities.

A **strengths and weaknesses** analysis expresses which areas of the business have:

- Strengths that should be exploited.
- Weaknesses which should be improved.

A SWOT analysis therefore covers the results of the position audit.

Opportunities

- What opportunities exist in the business environment?
- Their inherent profit-making potential.
- The organisation's ability to exploit the worthwhile opportunities.

Threats

- What threats might arise?
- How will competitors be affected?
- How will the company be affected?

The opportunities and threats could be analysed through PEST analysis or Porter's five forces model. However, it is also important to remember that a SWOT is not absolute, but should be relative. In other words, SWOT analysis is most useful when it is comparative – examining an organisation's strengths, weaknesses, opportunities and threats in relation to its competitors. (Johnson, Scholes & Whittington, 2011).

ACTIVITY 6.1

Assess the company which is the subject of the following SWOT:

Strengths	Weaknesses
£10 million of capital available	Heavy reliance on a small number of customers
Production expertise and appropriate marketing skills	Limited product range, with no new products and expected market decline. Small marketing organisation.

Threats	Opportunities
A major competitor has already entered the new market	Government tax incentives for new investment
	Growing demand in a new market, although customers so far relatively small in number

Effective SWOT analysis does not simply require a categorisation of information, it also requires some **evaluation of the relative importance** of the various factors under consideration.

- These features are only of relevance if they are **perceived to exist by the customers**. Listing corporate features that internal personnel regard as strengths/weaknesses is of little relevance if customers do not perceive them as such.

- In the same vein, threats and opportunities are conditions presented by the external environment and they should be independent of the firm.

The SWOT can now be used to guide strategy formulation. The two major options are **matching** and **conversion**.

Figure 6.1   SWOT and strategic options

Matching

This entails finding, where possible, a match between the strengths of the organisation and the opportunities presented by the market. Strengths which do not match any available opportunity are of limited use while opportunities which do not have any matching strengths are of little immediate value.

Conversion

This requires the development of strategies which will convert weaknesses into strengths in order to take advantage of some particular opportunity, or converting threats into opportunities which can then be matched by existing strengths.

ACTIVITY 6.2

Hall Faull Downes Ltd has been in business for 25 years, during which time profits have risen by an average of 3% per annum, although there have been peaks and troughs in profitability due to the ups and downs of trade in the customers' industry. The increase in profits, until five years ago, was the result of increasing sales in a buoyant market, but more recently, the total market has become somewhat smaller and Hall Faull Downes has only increased sales and profits as a result of improving its market share.

The company produces components for manufacturers in the engineering industry.

In recent years, the company has developed many new products and currently has 40 items in its range compared to 24 only five years ago. Over the same five-year period, the number of customers has fallen from 20 to nine, two of whom together account for 60% of the company's sales.

Give your appraisal of the company's future, and suggest what it is probably doing wrong.

> ▶ **Exam tip**
>
> In practice (and for the purposes of analysing the pre-screen case study material) it helps if you rank the items of the SWOT in order of **importance** and **urgency**. Concentrate your resources on the essentials.

1.4.3 Weihrich's TOWS matrix

Weihrich, one of the earliest writers on corporate appraisal, originally spoke in terms of a TOWS matrix (Weihrich, 1982) in order to emphasise the importance of threats and opportunities.

Note that this is therefore an inherently **positioning** approach to strategy. A further important element of Weihrich's discussion was his categorisation of strategic options.

- SO strategies employ strengths to seize opportunities.
- ST strategies employ strengths to counter or avoid threats.
- WO strategies address weaknesses so as to be able to exploit opportunities.
- WT strategies are defensive, aiming to avoid threats and the impact of weaknesses.

One useful impact of this analysis is that the four groups of strategies tend to relate well to different time horizons. SO strategies may be expected to produce good short-term results, while WO strategies are likely to take much longer to show results. ST and WT strategies are more probably relevant to the medium-term.

This consideration of time horizon may be linked to the overall resource picture: SO strategies can be profitable in the short-term, generating the cash needed for investment in WT strategies, improving current areas of weakness so that further opportunities may be seized. ST and WT strategies are likely to be more or less resource-neutral, but care must be taken to achieve an overall balance.

1.4.4 Other approaches

Both the basic SWOT approach and Weihrich's more sophisticated method require careful thought.

- Apparently distinct factors may be linked.
- A single factor may seem to fit into more than one category.
- It is important to prioritise the various factors.

Less prescriptive frameworks may assist the process of synthesis and may even be satisfactory in themselves in simple circumstances.

- **Issue analysis** avoids problems of classification by simply examining issues in depth.

- **The 6 Cs framework** can be used to give structure to the rather open-ended issue analysis approach.

  - Customers
  - Competitive position
  - Core competences
  - Chance and opportunity
  - Critical success factors
  - Constraints

1.5 SPACE analysis

Another framework which can be used to help **develop** a company's strategy is the **S**trategic **P**osition and **Ac**tion **E**valuation matrix (or SPACE analysis matrix.) SPACE analysis can also be used for **evaluating** the strategic options generated by a tool such as Ansoff's matrix (which we look at later in this chapter.)

The SPACE analysis matrix (Rowe *et al*, 1989) looks at four dimensions which should determine the general theme of a company's strategy. Two of these are external (industry attractiveness; environmental stability) and two of these are internal (financial strengths; competitive advantage).

Ratings are awarded for each dimension, and by combining these on the matrix diagram, SPACE analysis can guide a company's strategic agenda, based on a choice of four strategic postures: competitive, aggressive, conservative, or defensive.

Table 6.1   Factors to consider in SPACE analysis

External (industry) dimensions	Internal (company) dimensions
Factors determining industry attractiveness	Factors determining Financial Strength
Growth potential	Return on investment
Profit potential	Leverage (debt to equity)
Financial stability (within the sector)	Liquidity (cash held)
Technological know how (required for the sector)	Capital required / capital available
Resource utilisation	Cash flow
Capital intensity (required to operate in sector)	Ease of exit from the market
Ease of entry into sector	Risk involved in the business
Level of productivity and capacity utilisation	Other relevant factors
Other relevant factors	
Average =	Average – 6 =
Factors determining environmental stability	Factors determining Competitive Advantage
Technological changes	Market share
Rate of inflation	Product / service quality (compared to competitors)
Variability of demand	Product life cycle stage (for range of products)
Price range of competing products	Product/service replacement cycle
Barriers to entry into the market	Customer loyalty
Competitive pressure	Utilisation of capacity by competitors
Price elasticity of demand	Technological knowledge and competence
Other relevant factors	Degree of vertical integration
	Other relevant factors
Average =	Average – 6 =

Each factor is rated, with a score from 0 to 6 where '0' is low, poor (or otherwise unfavourable), and '6' is high, good (or otherwise favourable).

An average score for the factors in each quadrant is then calculated. (So, for example, the total score for 8 factors relating to industry attractiveness was 40, then the average for industry attractiveness is 5.)

The logic of the matrix is that financial strength (FS) and industry attractiveness (IA) are 'strengths' while competitive advantage (CA) and environmental stability (ES) could be potential weaknesses, and so could be negative. Therefore, while the results for FS and IA are simple averages, the results for CA and ES are the averages, minus 6, in each case.

The values for CA and IA are plotted on the horizontal axis, while the values for FS and ES are plotted on the vertical axis. (The logic behind this combination of dimensions is that financial strength is needed to compensate for environmental instability; while industry attractiveness and competitive advantage are potentially alternative sources of sustainable profits.)

Figure 6.2   SPACE analysis matrix map

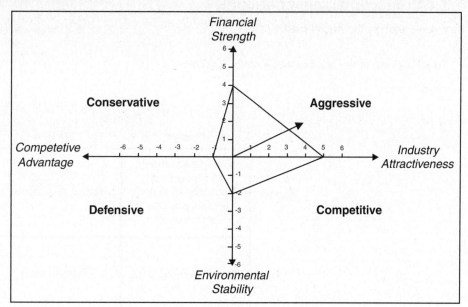

In our example figure above, the scores for each factor are IA = 5, CA = -1; FS = 4; ES = -2.

In turn, this means the net SPACE score for the horizontal dimension (IA + CA) is 4; and the net SPACE score for the vertical dimension (FS + ES) is 2. The arrow indicating the strategy which the company should pursue can then be drawn using this result.

In our example, the arrow indicates that the company should pursue an aggressive strategy.

Aggressive strategy – Firms that find themselves in the aggressive quadrant are likely to enjoy significant advantages yet are likely to face threats from new competitors. The implicit strategy is for the firm to try to grow its business, raising the stakes for all the competitors. The chief danger is complacency, which could prevent firms from strengthening their market because by developing products with a competitive edge. However, the firms financial strength could make it attractive for them to seek acquisitions.

Competitive posture – This suggests a firm has established a competitive advantage in an attractive industry. However, the firm does not have sufficient financial strength to overcome the environmental instability it faces. Such firms need more financial resources to maintain their competitive position. In the longer term this could be achieved by improving efficiency and productivity, but their position suggests they are also likely to need to raise capital or merge with a cash-rich company.

Conservative strategy – This is typical of financially strong companies in mature markets, where the lack of need for investment has generated financial surpluses. The lack of investment could mean that the companies compete at a disadvantage while the lack of opportunities in their existing markets could make them vulnerable in the longer term. Therefore such companies need to defend their existing positions while looking for new opportunities in more attractive markets.

Defensive strategy – A company in this position has scored poorly in all respects and so is clearly vulnerable, and could be heading for failure unless the external environment becomes more favourable. Because it has little residual strength, it should retreat from all but its strongest segments and then concentrate its limited resources on defending its position there. However, it could still only be a matter of time before the firm succumbs to its competitors.

1.6 Product-market opportunities

Models such as the **Ansoff matrix** (1957, 1988) can also be applied to strategy selection.

To remind you of the matrix, see Figure 6.3 below.

Figure 6.3   Ansoff matrix

Product

	Present	New
Present	Market penetration: (for growth) or consolidation (to maintain position or withdrawal)	Product development
New	Market development	Diversification

(Market on vertical axis)

Ansoff (1957)

Market penetration – A firm seeks to increases the sales of an existing product or to increase its share of its current markets; for example, through advertising campaigns or sales promotions. Alternatively, a firm could look to increase usage by existing customers (for example, through the use of loyalty cards).

In addition, another way of gaining market penetration is to buy competitors. For example, in the UK, in 2004 the supermarket chain Morrisons acquired Safeway, a competitor, in order to increase its sales volume and market share.

Market development – Under a market development strategy, a firm seeks to sell its existing products to new markets or new market segments.

There are a number of ways a firm could seek to do this:

- Expanding into new geographical areas and export markets
- Selling to new demographic segments (for example, different age groups)
- Using new distribution channels to attract new customers.

In this context, the development of the internet and e-commerce could be particularly useful to an organisation, in allowing it to expand sales internationally. One of the characteristics of e-marketing which differentiates it from traditional marketing is the way it enables global communications, and thereby enables firms to access markets which they couldn't reach before. For example, customers can buy products through a firm's website regardless of their physical location in relation to the firm.

Online revenues

In July 2012, a leap in profits at BSkyB and ITV heralded deeper moves into the online market for both companies.

BSkyB reported a 14% jump in profits to £1.2 billion, and will invest £30 million into its internet TV service, Now TV. At a cost of £15 per month, Now TV will compete with online services such as Netflix and LoveFilm. It will start by offering films, and will then add Sky's sports and entertainment package over the newt year.

BskyB chief executive Jeremy Darroch said 'We continue to transform out financial performance through discipline on costs, combined with strong revenue growth from 3 million product additions and over 300,000 new Sky households during the year.

Meanwhile, Euro 2012 and Britain's Got Talent helped boost revenues at ITV by 15% to £235 million for the year to June 2012, and it announced it hoped to launch its online pay-per-view service by the autumn of 2012. ITV is also considering whether to offer content which is currently free to view for up to 30 days as a paid-for service.

ITV's Chief Executive Adam Crozier also highlighted that online viewers are increasing looking to watch their favourite ITV shows on mobile platforms, which meant that ITV's revenues from online, pay and interactive increased by 24% to£47 million in the first half of 2012. At the same time, ITV has also amassed 4 million viewer email addresses.

Based on: Latham, C. (2012) Profit boost secures online TV surge for BSkyB and ITV, *Metro*, 27 July 2012.

Spanier, G. (2012) ITV boosted by rush to watch its programmes on mobile, *The Independent*, 27 July 2012; www.independent.co.uk

Product development – A firm seeks to develop new products for sale in its existing markets. For example, Nintendo is scheduled to launch its 'Wii U' in 2012. The new products is intended to be a new and improved version of the best-selling 'Wii' games console, featuring a new touch-screen controller, HD gaming and a revamped look.

Similarly, following the success of the original 'iPod', Apple launched the iPod nano, shuffle and touch; thereby providing its target market (of relatively young music lovers) with greater choice in terms of size, capacity and price of the 'iPod' systems they used for listening to their music.

Diversification – A diversification strategy involves selling new products to new markets. Diversification is a higher risk strategy than the other options, because a firm is unfamiliar with both the product and the target market. However, diversification also have the potential to produce higher rewards that other strategies for the same reason – it is generating revenues from selling a new product to a new market. For example, Apple's launch of the iPod music player could be seen as a diversification strategy, because Apple's core competences prior to this had been in computer electronics (with the Macintosh (Mac) product range.)

One of the key questions an organisation has to consider is how far it should diversity in terms of products and markets. Diversification involves increasing the range of products and market served by an organisation, but diversification can be sub-divided in related and unrelated diversification.

Related diversification involved diversifying into products or services which are linked to an organisation's existing business. By contrast, **unrelated** (or **conglomerate**) **diversification** involves diversifying into products or services with no relationships to the existing business.

Lucozade

Energy drinks

The energy drink Lucozade was first manufactured in 1927 as a source of energy for people who were suffering from illnesses such as the common cold or influenza.

However, in 1983 the advertising agency Ogilvy & Mather began rebranding Lucozade and shifting the brand's associations away from 'illness' and towards 'empowerment.' The brand's slogan was changes from 'Lucozade aids recovery' to 'Lucozade replaces lost energy' alongside an advertising campaign featuring the Olympic champion decathlete Daley Thompson.

The promotional message behind Lucozade energy drinks now is that they are designed to give you an energy boost to keep you active and alert.

Sports drinks

Lucozade's shift away towards being a sports and energy brand was highlighted further when 'Lucozade Sport' was launched as an isotonic sports drink in 1990. The ingredients of the drink were designed to replace salts and minerals lost through sweating during exercise, and in turn to play an important role in maintaining fluid balance and performance. The ingredients are designed to enable 'athletes and other active people to obtain energy before, during and after exercise.' This clearly identifies the target market for the drink as being 'athletes and other active people.'

However, Lucozade has continued to evolve its products to suit the changing lifestyles and needs of its customers. In 2010, it released Lucozade Sport Lite a low calorie sports drink which continues to provide the rehydration benefits of Lucozade Sport but which is designed to benefit people who exercise less intensively.

Revive

Then in March 2012, Lucozade launched Revive, a low-calorie sparkling energy drink, made with natural flavours (lemongrass with ginger; orange with acai; and cranberry with acai). All three flavour varieties contain 'B' vitamins, which help fight tiredness, and help with everyday energy release, but only contain 50 calories per 380 millilitre bottle.

The range is seen as a response to consumer demand for healthier options, but unlike Lucozade Sports Lite, it is designed to offer something relevant to customers who don't currently drink energy (or sports) drinks.

www.lucozade.com

1.6.1 International product-market opportunities

When looking at market development we have already identified that one market development strategy might be to expand into new countries.

However, it is worth considering how Ansoff's ideas could be applied to international marketing strategy. Unfortunately this may not be easy, as the categories may shift.

1   It is obviously easy to suggest what the **new market** might be: another country.

2   What, however, do we mean by '**new product**'? Is the product new to the company? Has it only been developed? Is the company still on a learning curve in its domestic market? In this case there might be a choice.

    (a)   Introduce the new product **simultaneously** in domestic and overseas markets.

    (b)   Have a continuing rolling programme.

        Year 1: the domestic market is dealt with first
        Year 2: existing overseas markets are serviced
        Year 3: genuinely new overseas markets are addressed

The Chartered
Institute of Marketing

By year 3, the decision to introduce new products into new markets has effectively become one of market development, on the grounds that product has already been on sale at home and in existing overseas markets.

3   It would appear **unlikely** that a company would set up abroad in a completely unfamiliar market with a completely new product, when there are easy opportunities to minimise the risk.

Other strategic models such as the BCG matrix may also be applied to global operations.

> ▶ **Exam tip**
>
> The Ansoff matrix, above, can be applied equally to a company looking for new international development or to an established global player. Many strategic developments are concerned with building on where the organisation currently sits in the global market, via current products and competences and stretching them to improve competitive position. There are a number of options for expanding or contracting operations.

1.7 Market segmentation and repositioning

In Chapter 2, we discussed the idea of market segmentation as a means of subdividing a market into distinct subsets of customers, such that each subset could be selected as a target market. In turn a firm will then try to position its products in the mind of the customers and distributors n the target segment more favourable than its' rivals products and brands. It will try to do this by designing an appropriate marketing mix which conveys its desired positioning to its targeted customers. (Dibb & Simkin, 2008).

However, a product's position will not always remain the same. And in the same way that Ansoff's matrix suggests four growth strategies (market penetration, market development, product development and diversification) we can also identify four repositioning strategies based around the same combination of products and markets.

Figure 6.4   Repositioning strategies

	Product	
	Present	*Different*
Present	Image repositioning	Product repositioning
Different	Intangible repositioning	Tangible repositioning

(Left axis label: **Target market/ market segment**)

Based on Jobber (2010)

Image repositioning – The product and the target remain the same, but the image of product needs changing. The product may already be acceptable in functional terms, but it is currently not proving popular to customers because it lacks the required image to make it desirable to them.

Product repositioning – Here, the product is changed, but the target market remains the same. For example, following the sale of its PC division to Lenovo IBM has repositioned itself from a computer manufacturer to a provider of software and services, to essentially the same type of business customers.

Intangible repositioning – In this strategy the product remains essentially the same but it is targeted at a different market segment. For example, as we saw in Lucozade case study, the original Lucozade energy drink was targeted at sick children. However, Lucozade's energy-giving attributes have subsequently been used to appeal to young adults as a sports drink, with the repositioning supported by advertisements featuring well-known athletes and footballers.

Tangible repositioning – Here, both product and target market are change. For example, a company may decide to move up- or down-market, by introducing a new range of products to meet the needs of target customers in the new market segment it wants to appeal to. For example, Samsung Electronics originally manufactured cheap, undifferentiated televisions and microwaves, but Samsung now makes premium-priced flat screen televisions and smartphones, focusing on higher-end customers.

1.8 Sources of competitive advantage

The key to superior performance is for an organisation to gain, and the sustain a **competitive advantage** over its rivals. This competitive advantage can come from better products, customer perceptions, costs, competences, assets, economies of scale, attitudes and relationships, offensive and defensive. However, competitive advantage:

- Only really exists in the customer's mind.
- Can be easily lost as a result of market changes or new ways of doing business.

Competitive advantage will be lost, gradually or rapidly, if the organisation's chosen strategy loses its relevance, customers' needs are no longer met and market share declines.

1.8.1 Different types of advantage

Table 6.2   Sources of competitive advantage

Competitive advantage	Example/comment
Better product in some way	Renault –'safest car in its class'
Perceived advantage or psychic benefit	Exclusivity (eg Harrods)
Global skills	BA; HSBC
Low costs, via high productivity or focus	Discount retailers or supermarkets such as Lidl or Aldi
Better competences	Some firms are 'better' at marketing or aligning technologies to markets than others
Superior assets	Property, cash or brands
Economies of scale	Size can be a source of competitive advantage
Attitude	This is partly related to culture and management abilities
Superior **relationships**	Companies can exploit business alliances and develop personal relationships

The most important competitive advantages depend on the market and existing competitors.

The Chartered
Institute of Marketing

TK Maxx

The first TK Maxx store opened in Bristol in 1994, and despite recording the fourth lowest score for customer satisfaction in a 2006 'Which?' survey, by October 2011 TK Maxx's estate had grown to 261 stores across the UK and Ireland.

The TK Maxx strategy is to sell genuine branded goods at deep discounts of up to 60% less than the recommended retail price. Consequently it has become increasingly widely recognised by shoppers as a top destination for fashions and brand labels at affordable prices.

TK Maxx is a cost conscious business, but more importantly its strategy depends on a core competence of opportunistic buying from both suppliers and retailers who have excess stock. TK Maxx has a pool of buyers sourcing stock from all vendors over the world, enabling them to take advantage of a huge number of opportunities as soon as they arise. They buying teams scan for the biggest labels and names with a 'buzz' around them. And when they see something they like, they negotiate the best price possible for the products in question.

Once the buyers have agreed a deal, the distribution team swing into action. They process the products and make sure they head to the rights stores at the right time. A typical TK Maxx store has over 50,000 items in stock and receives 10,000 new items every week. This means that customers will find new items every time they visit.

www.tkmaxx.com

1.9 Warfare analogies

Firms can choose a variety of strategies to **attack or defend** their position. Different strategies are appropriate to challengers, followers, leaders and nichers.

The broad generic strategies outlined above have some flaws, as we have seen. We suggested a number of approaches to price and value. In this section we describe how marketing activities can be used against **competitors**.

Considering strategic options from a competitor rather than customer orientation is referred to as **competitive marketing strategy**.

1.9.1 Offensive warfare strategies

Offensive strategies can be used by all companies. In order to ensure success, a company must be able to gain an advantage over the competition in the segment or area of attack. Kotler (2001) describes the following **attack strategies**.

Table 6.3   Attack strategies

Strategy	Comment
Frontal attack	This is the direct, head-on attack meeting competitors with the **same product line**, **price**, **promotion and so on**. Because the aggressor is attacking the enemy's strengths rather than weaknesses, it is generally considered the riskiest and least advised of strategies.
Flanking attack	The aim is to engage competitors in those product markets where they are weak or have no presence at all. Its overreaching goal is to build a position from which to launch an attack on the major battlefield later without waking 'sleeping giants'.

Strategy	Comment
Encirclement attack	Multi-pronged attack aimed at diluting the defender's ability to retaliate in strength. The attacker stands ready to block the competitor no matter which way he turns in the product market. ■ An attacker can encircle by **product proliferation** as Seiko did in the watch market, supplying 400 watch types in the UK out of 2,300 models worldwide. ■ **Market encirclement** consists of expanding the products into all segments and distribution channels.
Bypass attack	This is the most indirect form of competitive strategy as it **avoids confrontation** by moving into new and as yet uncontested fields. Three types of bypass are possible; develop **new products**, diversify into **unrelated products** or diversify into **new geographical markets**.
Guerrilla warfare	Less ambitious in scope, this involves making small attacks in different locations while remaining mobile. Such attacks take several forms: law suits, poaching personnel, interfering with supply networks and so on. The overriding aim is to **destabilise** by prods rather than blows.

Based on: Kotler *et al* (2009)

1.9.2 Defensive warfare strategies

It is generally agreed that **only a market leader** should play defence in an attempt to hold on to its existing markets in the face of competitive attack.

Table 6.4   Defensive strategies

Strategy	Comment
Position defence	Static defence of a current position, retaining current product-markets by consolidating resources within existing areas. **Exclusive reliance** on a position defence effectively means that a business is a **sitting target** for competition.
Mobile defence	A high degree of **mobility prevents the attacker's chances of localising defence** and accumulating its forces for a decisive battle. A business should seek market development, product development and diversification to create a stronger base.
Pre-emptive defence	**Attack is the best form of defence**. Pre-emptive defence is launched in a segment where an attack is **anticipated** instead of a move into related or new segments.
Flank position defence	This is used to occupy a position of **potential** future importance in order to deny that position to the opponent. Leaders need to develop and hold secondary markets to prevent competitors using them as a spring board into the primary market. (For example, Japanese manufacturers used the upper–end executive and coupe market to break into the volume car sector in the US.)
Counter-offensive defence	This is attacking where one is being attacked. This requires **immediate response** to any competitor entering a segment or initiating new moves. Examples are price wars, where firms try to undercut each other.
Strategic withdrawal	May be a last resort, but 'cutting your losses' can be the best option in the long run. Management resistance to what is seen as a drastic step is likely to be the biggest barrier.

Based on: Kotler *et al* (2009)

The five attacking strategies for challenging market leaders and the six defensive strategies used to fight off challenges are not mutually exclusive. As contingent factors change, a successful company will reconsider and revise its core strategies.

The Chartered
Institute of Marketing

Hester Bateman plc (HB plc) is a manufacturing cutler: that is, the company makes knives, forks and spoons. HB is based in Sheffield in the United Kingdom which has been the centre of the UK cutlery industry for at least 100 years. When the industry was first established, it was very fragmented and there were many small entrepreneurial businesses making cutlery. Often, these businesses were organised around a family and they usually employed between six and ten people. Hester Bateman was one such entrepreneur. The industry began to consolidate, in the late nineteenth century and early twentieth century, as a series of mergers were effected.

HB plc was constituted in its present form in the 1920s when it obtained its market listing on the Stock Exchange. It now consists of a large factory which employs 500 people and a Head Office employing 200 people. These are both in Sheffield.

In 1990 HB plc made a rights issue to finance a modernisation programme in its factory. At that time the Board reviewed the company's objectives. A statement was issued by the Board which said:

'HB plc is a UK manufacturing cutler based in Sheffield, the home of the cutlery industry. Our success is due to harnessing local skills in production and design and using these to deliver the finest quality product to our customers across the world. They know that the finest cutlery in the world is stamped "Made in Sheffield". We intend to continue with our fine traditions.'

HB plc has always made all its cutlery in Sheffield and attaches great importance to the fact that it can, therefore, be marked 'Made in Sheffield'.

HB plc usually spends approximately £150,000 a year on research and development. Five per cent of this spending is on new designs for the export market and the remainder is evenly split on designs for the home market and on improvements in production systems.

BQ plc

There is another UK manufacturing cutler of a similar size to HB plc, BQ plc, which is based in Birmingham.

Since 1991 BQ plc has followed a different production policy to HB plc. Approximately half of its cutlery is made in Korea and imported to the UK and marketed under BQ plc's brand names.

Markets

From the date of its formation until the late 1980s HB plc did very good business with countries across the world.

Since 1990 HB plc has experienced increasing competition from countries of the Pacific Rim – Korea, Taiwan, Hong Kong and Singapore. This competition has been conducted on the basis of cost. This has been possible because the production technology involved in making cutlery is a mature one. It is also comparatively cheap and readily available. Further, for many users cutlery has become a generic product.

Generics are unbranded, plainly packaged, less-expensive versions of products, purchased in supermarkets, such as spaghetti, paper towels and canned peaches.

HB plc has experienced a growing loss of market share in the UK to imports from the Pacific Rim. HB plc's export markets have largely disappeared. The only export business which it does is an annual sale of about £200,000 of very high quality cutlery to a department store in New York. HB plc makes a gross margin of 45% on this business.

Estimated market data at December 2010:

UK market share by:	Quantity %	Value %
HB plc	35	45
BQ plc*	30	35
Imports	35	20

* These percentages include all cutlery sold by BQ plc whether made in the UK or in Korea.

Financial performance

The increasingly competitive environment has had a marked effect on HB plc's profitability and stock market performance. After the publication of its latest annual results the following comment was made in an influential UK financial newspaper:

'HB plc's latest results which show a profit after tax of £2.25 million look deceptively good. However, these are flattered by the fact that HB plc has not made any major investments since the 1980s.

Its ROCE is about 4% and this could be beaten by any fixed return risk-free deposit investment. There seems to be little prospect of growth in any direction. These shares are really only a HOLD for the sentimental; otherwise SELL.'

Required

1   How can Porter's classification of generic strategies be used by HB plc to analyse its current competitive position?

2   Discuss the extent to which you believe that the statement of objectives made in 1990 is still applicable today.

3   Recommend possible marketing strategies for HB plc. Discuss the advantages and disadvantages of your recommendations.

We can apply these warfare strategies to firms with different positions in the market.

- Pioneers
- Followers
- Challengers
- Nichers

1.9.3 Strategies for pioneers

Pioneers' strategies will be required to protect their market positions from new entrants and challengers. Therefore, they will need to be defensive strategies:

- Position defence
- Mobile defence
- Flank position defence
- Contraction defence (withdrawal)
- Pre-emptive defence
- Counter-offensive defence

1.9.4 Strategies for challengers

Challengers can either attack lenders, accept the *status quo*, or try and win market share from other smaller companies in the market.

- Frontal attack
- Flanking attack
- Encirclement attack
- Bypass attack
- Guerrilla attack

Flanking attacks

The growth in ethical consumption has provided opportunities for ethically based brands to issue a flanking attack on traditional suppliers. For example, companies such as Green & Black's (organic chocolate), Cafedirect (fair trade coffee), innocent (smoothie drinks based on natural ingredients) and Ben & Jerry's (an ethically orientated ice cream company) have all been highly successful in growing sales and profits.

A **flanking defence** is characterized by the defence of a previously unprotected market segment. One of the risks of flanking defences is that they are half-hearted as the segment being 'defended' is not central to its main business.

When a flanking defence is required against successful but smaller attackers, acquisition may be an attractive option. For example, many large companies have responded to the attacks by ethically minded rivals by acquiring them. Cadbury acquired Green & Black's (in 2005) ; and Unilever purchased Ben & Jerry's (in 2000).

Another example of a flanking attack in the ice cream industry was when Mars attacked Unilever's Walls ice cream subsidiary in Europe in the 19802 by launching a range of premium brands such as its ice cream Mars bar and a series of ice cream versions of its chocolate brands, such as Snickers, Galaxy and Bounty.

Unilever regarded this flanking attack as a major threat to its ice cream business. Its response was to launch a range of premium brands of its own, including Magnum and Gino Ginelli, and also to defend vigorously its shop exclusivity deals (which prevent competitors from selling their products in shops that sell Walls ice cream) and freezer exclusivity deals (which prohibit competitors from placing their ice cream in freezer cabinet supplied by Unilever.

Frontal attack?

Now, in 2012, Unilever has ice cream sales of about $13 billion across all its brands, and is the world's biggest ice cream maker. It accounts for around 20% of the $85 billion global ice cream market.

However, it has not managed to crack the US ice cream market. The US market is very different to Europe in that the majority of its total sales come from packaged tubs (sold in supermarkets and eaten at home) whereas in Europe more ice cream consumption takes place outside the home in single-serve portions (which are more profitable).

So Unilever has taken the European model to the US and are increasingly shifting their focus to single-serve portions, on sticks or in cones. (Single serve portions currently only make up about 21% of the US market (2012), but analysts have suggested this area of the market does have the potential to grow).

However, to get to the top of the US market, Unilever has to unseat Nestle's 'Skinny Cow' the best selling novelty treat in the US. Interestingly, though, sales of Skinny Cow (which is a low-fat product) have decreased slightly since a peak in 2010 as consumers appear to be gravitating back towards full-fat items and fuller taste.

This could provide an opportunity for Unilever's Magnum brand. Magnums (whose flavours include Double Caramel, and Mochaccino) typically contain higher levels of calories and fat than Skinny Cow products, but they did so well in US market tests in 2010 that Magnum's US launch was brought forward from 2012 to 2011m and was supported by a marketing budget of about $15 million.

Unilever's attack appears to have been successful as well. Sales topped $100 million in the first year (50% more than Unilever forecast) and Americans bought so many Magnum bars that suppliers ran low and Unilever had to send additional stocks over from Italian factories to meet demand.

Based on example in Jobber (2010); and article: Boyle, M. (2012), Fat is back as Unilever Magnum bites Skinny Cow, *Bloomberg News*, 5 August 2012, www.businessweek.com

1.9.5 Strategies for followers

Many firms succeed by imitating the leaders. This is common in financial services markets where the basic functionality of a product is similar. Given that there are controls over monopoly status, most markets will have at least two players. Followers can follow:

- **Closely**, by imitating the marketing mix, and targeting similar segments
- **At a distance**, with more differentiating factors
- **Selectively** to avoid direct competition

Kotler (2001) makes the important point that 'followership' is not the same as being passive or a carbon copy of the leader. The follower has to define a path that does not invite competitive retaliation. He identifies three broad followership strategies.

1 **Cloner**. This is a parasite that lives off the investment made by the leader in the marketing mix (such as in products or distribution). The **counterfeiter** is an extreme version of the cloner, who produces fakes of the original (eg fake Rolex watches for sale in the Far East).

2 **Imitator**. This strategy copies some elements but differentiates on others (such as packaging).

3 **Adapter**. This involves taking the leader's products and adapting or even improving them. The adapter may grow to challenge the leader.

1.9.6 Market nichers

This is associated with a **focus** strategy and relies partly on segmentation, and partly on specialising. There are several specialist roles open to market nichers.

- **End-user specialist**, specialising in one type of customer
- **Vertical level specialist**, specialising at one particular point of the production/ distribution chain
- **Specific customer specialist**, limiting selling to one or just a few customers
- **Geographic specialist** selling to one locality
- **Product or service specialist**, offering specialised services not available from other firms
- **Quality/price specialist** operating at the low or high end of the market
- **Channel specialist**, concentrating on just one channel of distribution

---

2 Assessing strategic options

Which strategic option or set of options should form the basis for a business strategy? To answer this question, each option 'should be challenged with respect to whether it contains a real and perceived value proposition and whether it is feasible, relevant and sustainable.' Aaker & McLoughlin, (2010, p154)

Strategies are evaluated according to their **suitability** to the firm's situation; their **feasibility** in terms of resources and competences; and their **acceptability** to key stakeholder groups, particularly shareholders and customers.

2.1 Suitability and sustainability

Suitability relates to the strategic logic of the strategy. The strategy should fit the situation of the firm over the longer term.

It should satisfy a range of requirements.

- Exploit strengths: that is, unique resources , core competences and points of difference over time
- Rectify company weaknesses
- Neutralise or deflect environmental threats
- Help the firm to seize opportunities
- Satisfy the goals of the organisation
- Fill the gap identified by gap analysis
- Generate/maintain competitive advantage
- Involve an acceptable level of risk
- Suit the politics and corporate culture

The Chartered
Institute of Marketing

2.2 Feasibility

Feasibility asks whether the strategy can be implemented and, in particular, if the organisation has adequate resources.

- Enough money
- The ability to deliver the goods/services specified in the strategy
- The ability to deal with the likely responses that competitors will make
- Access to technology, materials and resources
- Enough time to implement the strategy

Strategies that do not make use of existing competences, and, therefore, call for new competences to be acquired, might not be feasible, since gaining competences takes time and can be costly.

Two important financial approaches to assessing the feasibility of particular strategies are **funds flow analysis** and **breakeven analysis**. Funds flow analysis examines the way money flows into the business and out of it; where it comes from, where it goes, what it is committed to and how much of it is available. Breakeven analysis is the study of the level of activity that has to be sustained if the firm is not to lose money.

Resource deployment analysis makes a wider assessment of feasibility in terms of resources and competences. The resources and competences required for each potential strategy are assessed and compared with those of the firm. A two-stage approach may be followed.

1   Does the firm have the necessary resources and competences to achieve the threshold requirements for each strategy?

2   Does the firm have the core competences and unique resources to maintain competitive advantage?

2.2.1 Elements of a feasibility study

1   **Corporate audit**

(a)   Objectives, five-year plan
(b)   Key criteria for project appraisal/evaluation

2   **The scenario or project**

3   **Assumptions**

4   **Feasibility research**

(a)   Experimental/technical research: design studies, performance specification, timings, costs.

(b)   Market research: demand analysis, competition, buying motives, pricing etc.

(c)   Commercial potential (to include analysis of the feasibility research in terms of timing, cost, human resource needs). Outline income and expenditure analysis.

- Venture capital required
- Cost of capital at current interest rate
- Working capital
- Short-term loans/overdraft requirements
- Cash flow projections – funding periods
- Contingencies
- Payback periods and net gains

2.3 Acceptability and relevance

The acceptability of a strategy depends on the views of **stakeholders**.

Strategies will be primarily evaluated by considering how far they contribute to meeting the dominant objective of increasing shareholder value. A wide range of measures is available to help assess financial viability.

- Return on investment
- Profits
- Growth
- EPS
- Cash flow
- Price/Earnings
- Market capitalisation
- Cost-benefit analysis

Specific projects and ventures can be assessed using a variety of financial techniques. The most satisfactory is the net present value (NPV) approach, which is explained in Chapter 9.

There are several important stakeholder groups.

1   The **workforce** constitutes an important stakeholder group that typically has an interest in the financial implications of strategy because of its links to job security. Successful strategies that enhance shareholder value tend to reduce or put on hold the search for economies in head count. However, the success of some strategies may derive from cost reductions achieved partly by reducing the need for labour.

2   **Customers** may object to a strategy if it alters the perceived value they receive. Such an approach is likely to be followed rapidly by failure of the strategy in the targeted market segment.

3   **Banks** are interested in the implications for cash resources, debt levels and so on.

4   **Government**. A strategy involving a takeover may be prohibited under competition legislation.

5   **The public**. The environmental impact may cause key stakeholders to protest. For example, out of town superstores are now frowned upon by national and local government in the UK.

6   **Risk**. Different shareholders have different attitudes to risk. A strategy which changed the risk/return profile, for whatever reason, may not be acceptable.

How stakeholders relate to the management of the company depends very much on what type of stakeholder they are – internal, connected or external – and on the level in the management hierarchy at which they are able to apply pressure. Clearly a company's management will respond differently to the demands of, say, its shareholders and the community at large.

2.4 Levels of strategy

As we saw in the previous chapter, any level of the organisation can have objectives and devise strategies to achieve them. The strategic management process is multi-layered.

2.4.1 Corporate strategies

> ▶ **Key term**
>
> **Corporate strategy** is concerned with the overall scope of an organisation and how value is added to the constituent businesses of the organisational whole.
>
> Johnson, Scholes and Whittington (2011, p7)

Corporate-level strategic issues include the geographical scope of the markets in which a company wants to compete; the diversity of products or services it offers; the acquisition of new businesses (or the divestment of existing businesses) and how resources are allocated between the different business units in an organisation (Johnson, Scholes & Whittington, 2011).

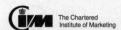

Table 6.5   Defining aspects of corporate strategy

Characteristic	Comment
Scope of activities	Strategy and strategic management impact upon the whole organisation: all parts of the business operation should support and further the strategic plan.
Environment	The organisation counters threats and exploits opportunities in the environment (customers, clients, competitors).
Resources	Strategy involves choices about allocating or obtaining corporate resources now and in future.
Values	The value systems of people with power in the organisation influence its strategy.
Timescale	Corporate strategy has a long-term impact.
Complexity	Corporate strategy involves uncertainty about the future, integrating the operations of the organisation and change.

2.4.2 Business strategy

> ▶ **Key term**
>
> **Business strategy** is about individual businesses or business units should compete in their particular markets.
>
> Johnson, Scholes and Whittington (2011, p7)

Business strategy can involve decisions such as whether to segment the market and specialise in particularly profitable areas, or to compete by offering a wider range of products. For this reason, business-level strategy can often be called 'competitive strategy' (Johnson, Scholes & Whittington, 2011).

THE REAL WORLD

Smartphones

It appears that the battle to become market leader in the smartphone market is going to be between Apple and Android. As smartphone usage increase, and players like Sony, RIM and Nokia decline, we will be left with a struggle between Apple and Google (which owns Android).

Most estimates in the US give Android a market share of about 40% of smartphone operating systems, with Apple having about 30% (March 2012). In the UK, about half of the smartphone market uses Android compared to Apple's share of about 20%.

However, behind the headline figures, Apple's position may not be as favourable as it may seem.

Although there are relatively few reliable surveys of the demographic and lifestyle differences between Apple and Android users, those that are point to the same significant differences, and in particular that Apple users are more likely to be over 35 while a typical Android skews heavily in the 18- 34 age group.

There is a perception that the iPhone is a 'parent's phone' rather than a young person's person; and this could be a problem for Apple in the longer term. In the short term, it is good news for Apple, because parents are a high spending market segment, and so Apple's smaller market share is going to be worth relatively more than Android's. But over time the picture is not so good.

Over time, the 'youthful' Android phone owner will grow up, earn a higher salary and become more valuable. And because of Apple's image relative to Android's the consumers are unlikely to migrate to Apple as they get older.

In other words, although Apple has played the 'cool brand' in its battles with Microsoft, it appears that on this occasion it could be on the receiving end of segmentation dynamics.

And if this is, indeed, the case, the key question will be what Apple can do about it. Apple's current strategy is wholly based on a premium pricing model, which could make it very difficult for Apple to drop its prices in an attempt to lure younger consumers to buy iPHones. And because Apple uses an endorses brand architecture across all its products, this reduces its scope to launch a new brand aimed directly at the younger demographic segment in the smartphone market.

Based on Ritson, M. (2012) Apple stands on the edge of a parent trap, *Marketing Week*, 22 March 2012, www.marketingweek.co.uk

Some large, diversified firms have separate **strategic business units** (SBUs) dealing with particular areas. Business strategy for such large organisations is strategy at the SBU level.

2.4.3 Functional and operational strategies

In most businesses, the success of the business strategy depends on the decisions which are taken, and the activities which occur, at the operational level. Therefore operational strategies are vital to successful strategy implementation (Johnson, Scholes & Whittington, 2011).

Individual operational strategies are often the concern of business functions, so they are also known as functional strategies. Here are some examples.

Table 6.6   **Functional strategies**

Functional area	Comment
Marketing	Devising products and services, pricing, promoting and distributing them, in order to satisfy customer needs at a profit. Marketing and corporate strategies are interrelated.
Production	Factory location, manufacturing techniques, outsourcing and so on.
Finance	Ensuring that the firm has enough financial resources to fund its other strategies by identifying sources of finance and using them effectively.
Human resources management	Secure personnel of the right skills in the right quantity at the right time, and ensure that they have the right skills and values to promote the firm's overall goals.
Information systems	A firm's information systems are becoming increasingly important, as an item of expenditure, as administrative support and as a tool for competitive strength. Not all information technology applications are strategic, and the strategic value of IT will vary from case to case.
R&D	New products and techniques.

▶ **Exam tip**

The syllabus also mentions the importance of understanding the effects of *changing* strategic direction. The company might change its strategic position in the marketplace for a number of reasons:

1   To reflect a new business strategy (eg, producing cheaper products to appeal to customers with less to spend.)

2   To resonate with customers (eg, advertising of 'no frills' brands in a tougher economic climate)

3   To differentiate from competitors (eg through innovation and new product development)

4   To express organisational values and culture (eg Innocent Drinks selling orange juice to attract a new set of customers)

5   To express CSR, reputation, sustainability and ethics (eg EasyJet welcoming the EU emissions trading scheme, when other airlines are resisting)

It is important to understand the implications for the organisation of any decision to work outside its previously agreed strategy – namely in terms of compatibility, the resources required to fulfil the new approach and the organisation's capacity and capability to deliver.

The Chartered
Institute of Marketing

GE Healthcare

GE Healthcare (part of the US conglomerate, General Electric) is threatening the control which western multinational pharmaceutical companies' currently have over drug and vaccine production in emerging companies, with a new venture to provide low-cost 'disposable' factories.

In December 2011, GE Healthcare said that it was finalising its contracts to build two biopharmaceutical plants in Latin America, and one in the Middle East, through an alliance with an engineering consultancy.

The projects reflect growing demand from developing countries to produce their own vaccines, insulin and other generic biological drugs domestically, in order to undercut the higher priced versions currently produced by international companies.

If domestic producers can produce lower-cost goods which comply with regulatory standards for their own use (and possibly also for export) this could significantly weaken the barriers which currently shield the large market-leading drug companies from more generic competition.

GE's aim is that its turnkey factories in the new countries should be able to halve the cost and time taken to construct of a factory, and should also have the cost of the products being produced, as a result of the lower capital expenditure and lower labour costs.

Another significant cost saving can be made by using disposable plastic containers inside the fermenters which are used to produce the drugs. Using plastic containers will allow a quicker – and safer - switch between products than is traditionally available with glass containers.

The general manager of GE's healthcare life sciences division noted that it would be possible to improve utilisation by up to 15-20% with disposable production, because the biggest heartache for the industry is currently cleaning, which leads to down time and to the risk of contamination.

Summarised from: Jack, A. (2011) GE Healthcare in 'low-cost' factories tie-up, *Financial Times*, 14 December 2011.

CHAPTER ROUNDUP

- A firm has to make strategic choices about how to compete (based on its generic strategy) and where to compete (based on its product and market choices)

- Critically evaluate the determinants of strategic options and choices

- Critically evaluate how strategic options can be developed

- Critically assess the impact of changing an organisation's strategic position within the market place

- Critically assess strategic alternatives against pre-determined criteria for an organisation

FURTHER READING

Doyle, P. and Stern, P. (2006) *Marketing management and strategy.* 4th Edition. Pearson, Harlow.

Yankelovich, D & Meer, D, 2006, Rediscovering Market Segmentation, *Harvard Business Review,* Vol 84 (2), pp 122-131.

REFERENCES

Aaker, D. & McLoughlin, D. (2007) *Strategic Market Management.* John Wiley, Chichester.

Aaker, D. & McLoughlin, D. (2010) *Strategic Market Management: Global Perspectives.* John Wiley, Chichester.

Ansoff, I. (1957) Strategies for Diversification, *Harvard Businesss Review*, Vol. 35 (5), pp 113-124.

Ansoff, H. I. (1988) *Corporate Strategy.* 2nd edition. Penguin Books, London.

Dibb, S & Simkin, L. (2008) *Marketing Planning: A Workbook for Marketing Managers*, Cengage Learning, London

Drummond, G. Ensor, J. & Ashford, R. (2008) *Strategic Marketing Planning and Control.* 3rd edition. Elsevier Ltd, Oxford.

Jobber, D. (2010), *Principles and Practice of Marketing*, 6th edition, McGraw-Hill, Maidenhead.

Johnson, G. Scholes, K. & Whittington, R. (2011) *Exploring Strategy.* 9th edition. Pearson, London.

Kotler, P. (2001) *Kotler on Marketing.* Free Press, London.

Kotler, P., Keller, K., Brady, M., Goodman, M. & Hansen, T. (2009) *Marketing Management*, Pearson, Harlow.

Rowe, A., Mason, R., Dickel, K. & Synder, N (1989) *Strategic Management: A methodological approach.* 3rd edition. Prentice Hall, Wokingham.

Weihrich, H. (1982) The TOWS Matrix – A Tool for Situational Analysis. *Long Range Planning*, Vol 15 (2), pp 52 – 64.

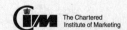

The Chartered
Institute of Marketing

1   Identify three categories of strategic choice.

2   Give some examples of means of obtaining competitive advantage.

3   Identify possible strategies which challengers can use to try to win market share from market leaders.

4   Identify strategies for market followers.

5   Identify possible approaches to market development.

6   Why are past and current strategies a useful guide in strategy development?

7   What measures might be used to assess financial viability?

8   Describe Weihrich's categorisation of strategic options.

ACTIVITY DEBRIEFS

Activity 6.1

The company is in imminent danger of losing its existing markets and must diversify its products and/or markets. The new market opportunity exists to be exploited, and since the number of customers is currently small, the relatively small size of the existing marketing force would not be an immediate hindrance. A strategic plan could be developed to buy new equipment and use existing production and marketing to enter the new market, with a view to rapid expansion. Careful planning of manpower, equipment, facilities, research and development would be required and there would be an objective to meet the threat of competition so as to obtain a substantial share of a growing market. The cost of entry at this early stage of market development should not be unacceptably high.

Activity 6.2

A general interpretation of the facts as given might be sketched as follows.

1   **Objectives.** The company has no declared objectives. Profits have risen by 3% per annum in the past, which has failed to keep pace with inflation but may have been a satisfactory rate of increase in the current conditions of the industry. Even so, stronger growth is indicated in the future.

2   Many new products developed

Marketing success in increasing market share

Possible decline in the end-product

Smaller end-product market will restrict future sales prospects for Hall Faull Downes.

Products may be reaching the end of their life and entering decline.

New product life cycles may be shorter.

Reduction in customers.

Excessive reliance on a few customers.

Doubtful whether profit record is satisfactory

None identified.

3   **Strengths.** The growth in company sales in the last five years has been as a result of increasing the market share in a declining market. This success may be the result of the following.

(a)   Research and development spending

(b)   Good product development programmes

(c)   Extending the product range to suit changing customer needs

(d)   Marketing skills

(e)   Long-term supply contracts with customers

(f)   Cheap pricing policy

(g)   Product quality and reliable service

4   **Weaknesses**

(a)   The products may be custom-made for customers so that they provide little or no opportunity for market development.

(b)   Products might have a shorter life cycle than in the past, in view of the declining total market demand.

(c)   Excessive reliance on two major customers leaves the company exposed to the dangers of losing their custom.

5   **Threats**. There may be a decline in the end-market for the customers' product so that the customer demands for the company's own products will also fall.

6   **Opportunities**. No opportunities have been identified, but in view of the situation as described, new strategies for the longer term would appear to be essential.

7   **Conclusions**. The company does not appear to be planning beyond the short term, or is reacting to the business environment in a piecemeal fashion. A strategic planning programme should be introduced.

8   **Recommendations**. The company must look for new opportunities in the longer term.

(a)   In the short term, current strengths must be exploited to continue to increase market share in existing markets and product development programmes should also continue.

(b)   In the longer term, the company must diversify into new markets or into new products and new markets. Diversification opportunities should be sought with a view to exploiting any competitive advantage or synergy that might be achievable.

(c)   The company should use its strengths (whether in R & D, production skills or marketing expertise) in exploiting any identifiable opportunities.

(d)   Objectives need to be quantified in order to assess the extent to which new long-term strategies are required.

Activity 6.3

1   In Hester Bateman's (HB's) case, the issues are not particularly clear cut. The size of the market is changing. From being strictly demarcated on national lines, the market has become global. This trend is certain to continue. In this new global market, what strategies can HB pursue?

(a)   Cost leadership would seem out of the question, in the short term at least. This is because cutlery making technology can be easily imitated by countries in the Pacific. At the moment, their labour costs are much lower; how long this will remain is a different question.

(b)   Differentiation. HB could differentiate the product on a global basis, on the basis of quality (by using special alloys) or by designing products that are attractive to users, or by introducing a range of new designs.

(c)   Focus. HB could decide to serve the UK or European market only, but it will still be vulnerable to cheaper competition. On the other hand it could position itself as a luxury brand to serve wealthier consumers.

Clearly, differentiation or focus are the way forward, as HB will always be vulnerable to lower cost competition, from Pacific Rim countries first of all, and then from other countries as they industrialise.

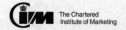 The Chartered Institute of Marketing

2 **Statement of objectives**

The statement of objectives contains remarkably few of them! Nothing has been quantified. As a mission statement it addresses the past not the future, on the assumption that past traditions can be preserved as a guarantee for future success.

To some extent, having survived the recessions of the early 1980s and 1990s, HB is in a strong position, having obviously taken steps to maintain its competitiveness. It is still able to trade on its quality image, as it has 45% of the market by value, as opposed to only 35% by volume. This is still significantly more than its competitors from overseas, suggesting that they are fighting over a niche that is relatively unprofitable for UK companies. Concentrating on the higher end of the market, rather than battling over market share for cheap generic items has been a sound strategy.

However, can this strategy be continued? It is possible that competitors will do their best to raise quality and HB's premium position will no longer be secure. Furthermore, the lack of investment will begin to tell. Finally, although the firm has maintained its market position in the short term, it has lost the confidence of investors in its ability to deliver long-term improvements.

HB therefore needs to update its objectives with a proper mission statement to satisfy the needs of its various stakeholders.

- To what extent can it continue to trade on its quality image?
- What customers is it looking to satisfy?
- What does it intend to do to address the concerns of its investors?

Clearly, the survival of the firm itself as an independent entity is in doubt. Investors are being advised to sell, yet the firm is still profitable and has a large share of the UK market. An argument perhaps is that it has failed to capitalise on the competitive strengths it has. If it is exporting to a New York department store, it is clear that there might be further export opportunities, which are not being satisfied, in the luxury goods market.

HB's position is therefore confused. On the one hand, it has survived two recessions, no mean feat. It has a commanding position in the British market, and its designs satisfy choosy US customers. Investors however have another viewpoint. The firm seems vulnerable to a take-over.

3 **Marketing strategies**

HB must first of all decide which generic strategy it is to pursue. We have suggested that cost leadership is out of the question, and so either differentiation or focus should be pursued. Once this is decided, a suitable marketing mix must devised. We can suggest a focus strategy, exploiting product differentiation (ie a differentiation-focus strategy). HB already produces cutlery of a different quality (eg the highest quality is exported to the US). In order to improve profits, HB first of all needs to identify which product markets are the most profitable, and deal with them in a suitable way. Different strategies might be suggested for different market niches to ensure profit streams.

Furthermore, the firm needs to undertake a programme of market research to find out what its customers (both retailers such as the New York department store, and the end-consumer or user) think about HB, and how it can better satisfy their needs.

Product

'Made in Sheffield' goods enable the firm to charge a premium price. The firm should concentrate on exploiting the international luxury market for high quality 'designer' goods. For example, scotch whisky is exported to Japan, and HB can channel its R and D towards producing a variety of innovative designs that can combine premium prices at the high end of the market.

At the same time it needs to enhance the profits earned from the UK market where it is facing cheap generic competition. It has little scope for cutting prices, and so it might be a good idea to maintain its position but at a lower price. It could set up, therefore, a brand of cheap imported cutlery, to compete with BQ and the other importers. This would release resources to concentrate on higher quality premium-priced products which could still have the Made in Sheffield tag. HB can therefore set up two brands. There are obviously profits to be earned from the generic end of the market, and HB still has the opportunity to deliver.

Many firms sell low and high-quality versions of a product under different brand names. It is not so much the company that has to be positioned appropriately in the market, as its brands.

The firm could also use its expertise in quality metal work to expand its product range (using Ansoff's product development strategy) into the same market. Suggestions might include:

- Related products such as silver (soup tureens, trays, silver goblets)
- Less plausibly, perhaps, ornaments, jewellery, even cufflinks

Price

The price element of the mix is implicit in the product. To increase its profitability, HB is to manufacture premium products at premium prices. This is in order to increase the ROCE: the New York business earns a gross margin of 45%.

Under a different brand name, HB is to import cheap generic products from Pacific Rim or cheaper countries, and use its existing networks to take on the competition. This will hopefully generate more profits, or at least cover costs, as the expensive manufacturing capability will be directed elsewhere. HB will be able to compete more effectively.

Place

The distribution system is an important element of the marketing mix. HB has obviously no problem in the UK, but perhaps it needs to consider whether it is as effective and efficient as it could be. We are told little about HB's existing distribution and logistics systems.

However, the twin pronged strategy does require some new expertise.

(a) If the company is importing its generic products from overseas, it will need to have suitable warehousing and storage facilities, and to have systems which can predict likely demand, so customers do not have to wait too long.

(b) It is hoped that many of the premium priced products will be exported. The US department store is a model for strategies that can be adopted in other countries in the EU and over the world. HB will need assistance, perhaps from one of the UK government's export advisory services, to find distributors for its product. The distributors will inevitably have a significant say in how the goods are to be positioned and sold. In a market such as Japan, HB will need a suitable partner to negotiate the thickets of the distribution system; in a country that uses chopsticks, demand for cutlery will be limited, but it can be sold as a luxury item.

However, the main markets would be the US where further expansion is obviously possible and the EU.

The company might consider offering an enhanced service to customers, for example a just-in-time delivery system.

Promotion

Promotional strategies will be an essential feature of HB's repositioning itself as a premium priced quality product. This means finding a suitable advertising agency, and researching the communications messages the company wishes to pursue. It might mean advertising in media it has not used before (eg magazines promoting luxury goods, or lifestyle magazines such as The World of Interiors).

Finally, the firm needs to promote itself to another audience: investors, who have to be convinced that the new strategy will work. At the moment they are critical, and will sell to a bidder. To keep their jobs,

The Chartered Institute of Marketing

the existing managers must work to convince investors that the company's existing and potential strengths can be better exploited in future.

QUICK QUIZ ANSWERS

1   How to compete; direction of growth; method of growth.

2   Better product; perceived advantage; global skills; low costs; better competencies; superior assets; economies of scale; attitude; superior relations.

3   Frontal; flanking; encirclement and bypass attacks and guerrilla warfare.

4   Cloning, adaptation and imitations.

5   New geographical areas; different package sizes; new distribution channels; differential pricing.

6   Strategy is a pattern of senior management, and the process tends to generate consistent decisions. For example, a firm's managers may prefer certain types of market opportunities (eg low risk) than others. Such factors can be an important guide in evaluating the acceptability of potential future strategies.

7   Return on investment
    Profits
    Growth
    EPS
    Cash flow
    Price/Earnings
    Market capitalisation
    Cost-benefit analysis

8   SO strategies employ strengths to seize opportunities.
    ST strategies employ strengths to counter or avoid threats.
    WO strategies address weaknesses so as to be able to exploit opportunities.
    WT strategies are defensive, aiming to avoid threats and the impact of weaknesses.

Analysis and Decision

CHAPTER 7

Growth strategies

Introduction

Organisations often seek to extend their reach without increasing their size by forming strategic alliances (closer working relationships) with other organisations. This involves partnerships and joint ventures as well as contracting out services to outside suppliers.

It results in improved access to information and technology, and quicker responses. However, alliances are vulnerable to management failures and so must be carefully selected; in addition they involve genuine moves away from bureaucracy and hierarchy.

You already know that the strategic choices available to an organisation can be classified and analysed using Ansoff's matrix. For example:

- Market penetration – increase market share; increase product usage (frequency, quantity, revitalise, new applications)
- Product development – line extensions; expand the product scope; develop new products
- Market development – expand geographically; target new segments
- Diversification – related and unrelated
- Vertical integration strategies – forward and backward

This chapter examines some areas where growth strategies can be pursued.

Topic list

2.2.1	Critically evaluate the nature of innovation and new product development (NPD) in marketing and the related factors impacting upon marketing decisions, including ongoing innovation management within an organisation:
	▪ Importance of innovation
	▪ Models of innovation
	▪ Managing innovation
2.2.4	Assess the relevance to an organisation of mergers, acquisitions and strategic alliances in growing, expanding and maximising business potential:
	▪ Motives for strategic alliances
	▪ Types of strategic alliance
	▪ Value chain analysis of the competitive potential in alliances, mergers and acquisitions
2.2.5	Critically evaluate a range of growth strategies for an organisation:
	▪ Incremental growth
	▪ Significant growth
	▪ The concept of big ideas
2.2.6	Critically evaluate the concept of relationship marketing (CRM) as a means of achieving growth and profitability within an organisation:
	▪ Long term orientation versus transactional marketing
	▪ Partnering
	▪ Keeping of promises and developing mutual trust
	▪ Share of customer's wallet versus market share
	▪ Customisation
	▪ Customer loyalty
2.2.7	Critically evaluate the development of an organisation's brand and its contribution towards increasing the organisation's value and brand equity:
	▪ Brand associations
	▪ Brand identity and image
	▪ Brand proposition and promise
	▪ Branding strategies

1 Mergers, acquisitions and strategic alliances

'Strategic alliances play an important role in global strategies because it is common for a firm to lack a key success factor for a market. It may be distribution, a brand name, a sales organisation, technology, R & D capability or manufacturing capability.' (Aaker & McLoughlin (2007) p218)

'Given the frequent failures of acquisitions and alliances, the fundamental issues is when to acquire, when to ally or when is it better to 'do it yourself'? (Johnson, Scholes & Whittington, 2011 p 287)

The Chartered
Institute of Marketing

1.1 Motives for strategic alliances

Strategic alliances allow the alliance partners to create value for their customers and shareholders which could not otherwise be created by individual firms.

Alliances can take a number of forms.

- Agreements to co-operate on various issues
- Shared research and development
- Joint ventures, in which the partners create a separate business unit
- Supply chain rationalisation
- Licensing and franchising
- Purchase of minority stakes

Strategic alliances speed up market penetration, normally by providing extra distribution effort. Many firms are expanding through alliances. For example, airlines have code sharing arrangements, which give them access to a larger base of assets. Such assets include:

- Market access
- Management skills
- Shared technology
- Exclusivity (eg shutting out competitors)

Strategic alliances can be motivated by the potential for:

- Generating scale economies
- Gaining access to strategic markets
- Overcoming trade barriers

Or it may be needed (as hinted at in the opening quote) to compensate for a weakness:

- Filling out a product line (eg car manufacturers)

- Gaining access to technology

- Using excess capacity, such as spare or idle plant

- Gaining access to low cost manufacturing (eg consumer electronics)

- Access a particular customer relationship (eg via Japanese firms who prefer to do business with Japanese suppliers)

Hooley *et al* (2011) give an overview of some of the environmental factors that are stimulating the need for alliances:

- Scarce resources
- Increased competition
- Higher customer expectations
- Pressures from strong distributors
- Internationalisation of markets
- Changing markets and technologies
- Turbulent and unpredictable markets

In this context, Hooley et al (2011; p. 418) highlight that two factors have been particularly important in transforming business structures in many industries:

- The age of mass production is over, and customers are now demanding unique value. In this respect, value is shifting from products to 'solutions' and 'experiences' in such a way that relationship are taking over as the central element of exchange.

- As a consequence, it increasingly becomes the case that no single business is likely to be big enough to cope with the complexity and diversity of customer demands which is emerging. This underlines the importance of alliances and networks in delivering customer values – collaborative networks of suppliers which can be configured in different ways as required to meet different customer needs.

Alliances have also become a popular model for global expansion. Writers such as Ohmae (1999) claim that globalisation has made them essential for successful strategies. According to Aaker & McLoughlin (2010) the top 500 global companies have an average of 60 major alliances each; but these alliances need to be actively managed. The participants tend to be competing firms from different countries, seeking to enhance their competences by combining resources, but without sacrificing autonomy. The strategic alliance is usually concerned with gaining market entry, remaining globally competitive and attaining economies of scale.

According to Jeannet & Hennessey (2004), they can be categorised as:

- **Production-based alliances** – improving manufacturing and production efficiency
- **Distribution-based alliances** – sharing distribution networks
- **Technology-based alliances** – pooling R & D costs

THE REAL WORLD

The future of Mobile Marketing

A recent study by CIM's Head of Research, Mark Blayney Stuart: *It's not a phone: a future of mobile marketing* was published in the form of a white paper, available at http://library.cim.co.uk/ (look for "all papers"). In it, Stuart points out that the mobile device is unlikely to supersede the TV, the computer or newspapers but will eventually become the preferred medium for almost every activity currently using other forms. The reason for this is the smartphone's ubiquity: it is always on, always handy and knows where you are. It remains to be seen how the fight between the smartphone and the tablet will pan out. After all, the tablet is, in essence, just a larger version of the same thing. However, for many, the small size of the smartphone's screen is its biggest drawback, so perhaps tablets, becoming thinner and lighter (and for years, people have been talking of "roll-up" screens and the like) will eventually take the lead.

Marketers cannot lag behind this trend. Mark Blayney Stuart says that, in 3 or 4 years, the smartphone will be **the** default communication tool for everyone. But, of course, the old way of doing things is dead. This is the age of advertising on demand, of permission marketing. Advertisers have to explore new, exceptionally creative ways of getting their message across, via influencing Consumer Generated Content (CGC), via Search Engine Optimisation (SEO), via Pay Per Click (PPC) and by any other means.

1.2   Alliances and networks

Many firms are growing by **alliances** with other firms, short of a full scale merger or acquisition. These are supposed to offer synergies and mutual benefits.

Growth can involve:

1   **Building up new businesses** from scratch and developing them (sometimes called organic growth).

2   **Acquiring** already existing businesses from their current owners via the purchase of a controlling interest in another company.

3   A **merger** is the joining of two or more separate companies to form a single company.

4   Spreading the costs and risks (**joint ventures, alliances** or other forms of **co-operation**).

1.3 Acquisitions

The purpose of acquisitions

1   **Marketing advantages**

- Buy in a new product range

The Chartered Institute of Marketing

- Buy a market presence (especially true if acquiring a company with overseas offices and contacts that can be utilised by the parent company). For example, when Kraft acquired Cadbury in 2010, this enabled it to benefit from Cadbury's market share and distribution networks in India. At the time of the acquisition a network of about 1.2 million shops across India sold Cadbury's products.

- Unify sales departments or to rationalise distribution and advertising

- Eliminate competition or to protect an existing market

2   **Production advantages**

- Gain a higher utilisation of production facilities and reap economies of scale by larger machine runs

- 'Buy in' technology and skills

- Obtain greater production capacity

- Safeguard future supplies of raw materials

- Improve purchasing by buying in bulk

3   **Finance and management**

- Buy a high quality management team, which exists in the acquired company
- Obtain cash resources where the acquired company is very liquid
- Gain undervalued assets or surplus assets that can be sold off ('asset stripping')
- Obtain tax advantages (eg purchase of a tax loss company)

4   **Risk-spreading**

5   **Independence**. A company threatened by a take-over might acquire another company, just to make itself bigger and so a more expensive 'target' for the predator company.

6   **Overcome barriers to entry**

1.4 Organic growth

Organic growth (sometimes referred to as **internal development**) is the primary method of growth for many organisations, for a number of reasons. Organic growth is achieved through the development of internal resources.

1.4.1 Reasons for pursuing organic growth

- **Learning**. The process of developing a new product gives the firm the best understanding of the market and the product.

- **Innovation**. It might be the only sensible way to pursue genuine technological innovations, and exploit them.

- There is **no suitable target for acquisition**.

- Organic growth can be **planned more meticulously** and offers little disruption.

- It is often **more convenient** for managers, as organic growth can be financed easily from the company's current cash flows, without having to raise extra money on the stock market (eg to fund an acquisition).

- The **same style of management and corporate culture** can be maintained.

- **Hidden or unforeseen losses are less likely** with organic growth than with acquisitions.

- **Economies of scale** can be achieved from more **efficient use of central head office functions** such as finance, purchasing, personnel, management services and so on.

1.4.2 Problems with organic growth

- **Time** – sometimes it takes a long time to climb a **learning curve**.

- **Barriers to entry** (eg distribution networks) are harder to overcome: for example, a brand image may be built-up from scratch.

- The firm will have to **acquire the resources independently**.

- Organic growth may be **too slow for the dynamics of the market**.

The Chartered Institute of Marketing

1.5 Alliances and synergy

1.5.1 Obtaining synergy from alliances

1. **Marketing synergy**: use of common marketing facilities such as distribution channels, sales staff and administration, and warehousing. Petrol stations can double as burger outlets.

2. **Operating synergy**: arises from the better use of operational facilities and personnel, bulk purchasing, a greater spread of fixed costs whereby the firm's competence can be transferred to making new products.

3. **Investment synergy**: the joint use of plant, common raw material stocks, transfer of research and development from one product to another – ie from the wider use of a common investment in fixed assets, working capital or research.

4. **Management synergy**: the advantage to be gained where management skills concerning current operations are easily transferred to new operations because of the similarity of problems in the two industries.

1.5.2 Successful alliances

'The results of the collaboration should have strategic value and contribute to a viable venture that can withstand competitive attack and environmental change.' Aaker & McLoughlin (2007) p219

Factors for success:

- Choose partners with complementary skills, products, markets
- Understand the 'strategic intent' of the partnership
- Adopt the most appropriate partnership structure
- Resolve the leadership issue at the outset
- Define the benefits expected from the partnership
- Communicate the purpose and intent of the partnership internally
- Keep communicating with your partner and anticipate problems
- Define an exit strategy for failure at the outset
- Monitor the benefits the partnership delivers
- Recognise a company may need multiple partnerships in a global business market

1.5.3 Consortia

Consortia: organisations co-operate on specific business prospects.

THE REAL WORLD

In July 2012, Saudi Arabia gave an early nod to four consortia to build a new metro system in Riyadh to ease congestion on the capital's streets. Saudi Arabia currently only has limited public transport facilities and Riyadh suffers from gridlock for much of the day and into the evenings.

The Saudi state news agency, SPA, said that the pre-qualified consortia were made up from 33 companies from 15 different countries, and included some of the largest train manufacturers in the world.

One consortium is led by France's largest listed construction and concessions firm, Vinci, and also includes the German firm Siemens.

A second consortium is led by the Canadian firm, Bombardier, and includes Turkey's Yapi Merkezi, Spain's Obrascon Huarte, Korea's GS Engineering and Construction Corporation, and Britain's Serco.

A third consortium is led by Spain's FS Engineering and Construction, and includes Alstom Transport (from France) and Samsung C&T Corporation from Korea.

1.6 Joint ventures

Two firms (or more) join forces for manufacturing, financial and marketing purposes and each has a share in both the equity and the management of the business. A joint venture is a separate business unit set up for the reasons outlined below.

1   **Share funding**. As the capital outlay is shared, joint ventures are especially attractive to smaller or risk-averse firms, or where very expensive new technologies are being researched and developed (such is the civil aerospace industry).

2   **Cut risk**. A joint venture can reduce the risk of government intervention if a local firm is involved (eg Club Mediterranée pays much attention to this factor).

3   Participating enterprises **benefit from all sources of profit**.

4   **Close control** over marketing and other operations.

5   Overseas, a joint venture with an indigenous firm provides **local knowledge, quickly**.

6   **Synergies**. One firm's production expertise can be supplemented by the other's marketing and distribution facility.

7   **Learning** can also be a 'learning' exercise in which each partner tries to learn as much as possible from the other.

8   **Technology**. New technology offers many uncertainties and many opportunities. Such alliances provide funds for expensive research projects, spreading risk.

9   **The joint venture itself can generate innovations**.

10 The alliance can involve **'testing' the firm's core competence** in different conditions, which can suggest ways to improve it.

1.6.1 Disadvantages of joint ventures

- Conflicts of interest between the different parties.

- Disagreements may arise over profit shares, amounts invested, the management of the joint venture and the marketing strategy.

- One partner may wish to withdraw from the arrangement.

1.7 Licensing

A **licensing agreement** is a commercial contract whereby the licenser gives something of value to the licensee in exchange for certain performances and payments. The licenser may provide, in return for a royalty:

- Rights to produce a patented product or use a patented production process
- Manufacturing know-how (unpatented)
- Technical advice and assistance
- Marketing advice and assistance
- Rights to use a trademark, brand and so on

Subcontracting is also a type of alliance. Co-operative arrangements also feature in supply chain management, JIT and quality programmes.

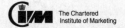

1.8 Franchising

Franchising is a method of expanding the business on less capital than would otherwise be possible. For suitable businesses, it is an **alternative business strategy to raising extra capital** for growth. Franchisers include Budget Rent-a-car, Dyno-rod, Holiday Inn, Kall-Kwik Printing, KFC, Prontaprint, Sketchley Cleaners, Subway and even McDonald's.

- The **franchiser** offers its:

    - Name, and any goodwill associated with it
    - Systems and business methods
    - Support services, such as advertising, training, help with site decoration etc

- The franchisee:

    - Provides capital, personal involvement and local market knowledge
    - Pays the franchiser for being granted these rights and services
    - Has responsibility for the running and profitability of his franchise

1.9 The virtual firm

An extreme example of an alliance is the so-called **virtual firm**. A virtual firm is created out of a **network of alliances** and subcontracting arrangements: it is as if most of the activities in a particular value chain are conducted by different firms, even though the process is loosely co-ordinated by one of them. It is outsourcing taken to its greatest extent.

For example, assume you manufacture small toys. You could in theory **outsource**:

- The design to a consultancy
- Manufacturing to a subcontractor in a low-cost country
- Delivery arrangements to a specialist logistics firm
- Debt collection to a bank (factoring)
- Filing, tax returns, bookkeeping to an accountancy firm

Virtual corporations effectively put market forces in all linkages of the value chain – this has the advantage of creating **incentives** for suppliers, perhaps to take risks to produce a better product, but can lead to a loss of control.

ACTIVITY 7.1

Summarise some of the features of strategic alliances

---

2 Innovation and new product development

'While many firms strive for innovation, not all achieve it. Success requires a true commitment to innovation that survives pressure for short term results. This commitment must be well-managed so that the right people are given the right environment. Further, the organisation must be competent at turning innovation ... into commercial products and must be willing to take chances and be wrong.' Aaker & McLoughlin, 2007, p197

2.1 The importance of innovation

▶ **Key term**
Innovation 'is about changing established products, processes and practices.'

Innovation is a major responsibility of modern management, particularly in commercial organisations.

This is because both technology and society are developing extremely rapidly; new products must be matched with new market opportunities if businesses are to survive and prosper. Innovation in marketing is particularly important, since marketing provides much of the interface between the organisation and its rapidly changing environment.

Since innovation is likely to be a major requirement for success in most commercial organisations, it will be an important part of the marketing manager's job: recognising innovative ideas when they appear and developing and managing the conditions and processes that support innovation.

It is important to remember that the need for innovation does not just relate to products and services: internal business processes are likely to be fertile ground for innovation and improvement. Innovation responses to the demands made of the marketing function will also be required and may prove to be particularly rewarding.

Tidd & Bessant (2009) identify four elements of innovation:

Product innovation – changing the product being offered; for example, Windows Vista replaced XP and improved on the existing software; Toyota Prius introduced a new concept - the hybrid engine.

Process innovation – changing how firms create and deliver a product offering; for example, through the development of telephone banking and online banking; or through offering an improved range of banking services in a bank branch.

Position innovation – changing the way a product offering is targeted; for example, through the introduction of low cost airlines.

Paradigm innovation – changing the way organisations 'frame' what they do. For example, IBM has changed from being a computer manufacturer into a consultancy and service company.

THE REAL WORLD

The Internet is having a significant impact on the entertainment business, and particularly the music business.

At one level, it has provided new 'e-tailing' channels where customer can purchase the music they want from Amazon or a range of the websites.

But there has also been a more fundamental shift in the ways in which music is created and distributed. This, in turn, is changing the business model on which the music industry has been based.

Traditionally, songwriters and artists depended on A&R (artists and repertoire) staff from the record labels to select what would be recorded.

The labels' production staff would then record albums in complex and expensive studios, before other production staff would oversee the manufacture of physical discs (CDs), and marketing and distribution staff would ensure the product was publicised and then distributed to retailers.

However, the internet now provides the potential for creating, storing and distributing music online, for example as MP3 downloads. This means that aspiring musicians could now record and distribute their music themselves rather than relying on the record companies to record and produce physical CDs for them. And the emergence of social networks and chatrooms means that musicians could also publicise their music themselves rather than relying on the record labels to promote it for them.

The Chartered
Institute of Marketing

2.1.1 Innovation and the market orientation

A market orientation involves establishing customer needs and finding ways to satisfy them. Very obviously, innovation has a major role to play here. However, what of the kind of innovation that addresses no currently established need? Equally obviously, strategic management must take cognisance of such developments and investigate them carefully to see if they have the capacity to generate entirely new categories of demand. The Sony Walkman is the classic example of technical innovation of this type, but there are non-technological and service industry examples too. For example, before Starbucks, few people realised they needed a cup of coffee to take to work with them.

2.1.2 Innovation and control

One of the sources of innovation is increased delegation. In itself delegation has great value - morale and performance are improved, top management is freed for strategic planning and decisions are made by those closest to the problem concerned and therefore most informed about it. Most importantly, the organisation benefits from the imagination and thinking of its high flyers.

To encourage innovation the objective for management should be to create a more outward-looking organisation. People should be encouraged to use their initiative to look for new products, markets, processes, designs and ways to improve productivity.

Innovation thrives best in an organisation when it is supported by its culture.

- Ensure management and staff know what innovation is and how it happens
- Ensure that senior managers welcome, and are seen to welcome, changes for the better
- Stimulate and motivate management and staff to think and act innovatively
- Understand people in the organisation and their needs
- Recognise and encourage potential 'entrepreneurs'

2.2 Models of innovation

2.2.1 Small organisations and innovation

Research suggests that the following factors are crucial to the success of innovative small organisations.

1 **Need orientation**. Lacking resources, successful small entrepreneurs soon find that it pays to approach potential customers early, test their solutions in the users' hands, learn from their reactions and adapt their designs rapidly.

2 **Experts and fanatics**. Commitment allows the entrepreneur to persevere despite the frustrations, ambiguities and setbacks that always accompany major innovations.

3 **Long time horizons**. Time horizons for radical innovations make them essentially 'irrational' from a present-value viewpoint – delays between invention and commercial production/success can range from three to 25 years.

4 **Low early costs**. Innovators incur as few overheads as possible, their limited resources going directly into their projects. They borrow whatever they can and invent cheap equipment or processes, often improving on what is available in the marketplace.

5 **Multiple approaches**. Committed entrepreneurs will tolerate the chaos of random advances in technology, adopting solutions where they can be found, unencumbered by formal plans that would limit the range of their imaginations.

6 **Flexibility and quickness**. Undeterred by committees, the need for board approvals and other bureaucratic delays, the inventor/entrepreneur can experiment, recycle and try again, with little time lost. They quickly adjust their entry strategies to market feedback.

7   **Incentives**. Tangible personal rewards are foreseen if success is achieved and the prospect of these rewards (which may not be principally of a monetary nature) is a powerful driver.

2.2.2 Large organisations and innovation

Within large organisations, by contrast, the following barriers to innovation and creativity may typically be encountered.

1   **Top management isolation**. Financially-focused top managers are likely to perceive technological innovation as more problematic than, say, acquisitions or organic growth: although these options are just as risky, they may appear more familiar.

2   **Intolerance of fanatics**. Big companies often view entrepreneurial fanatics as embarrassments or trouble-makers.

3   **Short time horizons**. The perceived corporate need to report a continuous stream of upward-moving, quarterly profits conflicts with the long time-spans that major innovations normally require.

4   **Accounting practices**. A project in a big company can quickly become an exposed political target and its potential net present value may sink unacceptably. Also there is a tendency to apply false logic to sunk costs: it is important to remember that costs incurred in the past are not relevant to decisions taken in the present about the future. It is, thus, equally erroneous to cancel a project on the grounds that its forecast revenues do not offer an adequate return on its total costs, as it is to persist with one on the grounds that a large amount has already been spent.

5   **Excessive rationalism**. Managers in large organisations often seek orderly advance through early market research studies or systematic project planning.

6   **Excessive bureaucracy**. Bureaucratic structures require many approvals that cause delays; the interactive feedback that fosters innovation is lost, important time windows can be missed and real costs and risks rise for the corporation.

7   **Inappropriate incentives**. When control systems neither penalise opportunities missed nor reward risks taken, the results are predictable.

Successful large organisations have developed techniques that emulate or improve on the approaches used in small, fleet-of-foot companies.

1   **Atmosphere and vision**. Continuous innovation occurs largely because top managers appreciate innovation and atmosphere in order to support it. They project clear long-term vision for the organisation that go beyond simple economic measures.

2   **Orientation to the market**. Within innovative organisations, managers focus primarily on seeking to anticipate and solve customers' emerging problems.

3   **Small, flat hierarchies**. Development teams in large organisations normally include only six to seven key people; operating divisions and total technical units are kept below 400 people.

4   **Multiple approaches**. Where possible, several prototype programmes are encouraged to proceed in parallel. Such redundancy helps the organisation to cope with uncertainties in development, motivates people through competition and improves the amount and quality of information available for making final choices on scale-ups or new-product/service introductions.

5   **Development shoot-outs**. The most difficult problem in the management of competing projects lies in re-integrating the members of the losing team. For the innovative system to work continuously, managers must create a climate that honours high-quality performance whether a project wins or loses, reinvolves people quickly in their technical specialities or in other projects and accepts rotation among tasks and groups.

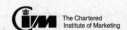

6   **Skunkworks**. This is the name given the system in which small teams of engineers, technicians, designers and model makers are placed together with no intervening organisational or physical barriers, to develop a new product from idea to commercial prototype stage. This approach eliminates bureaucratic controls; allows fast, unfettered communications; permits rapid turnaround times for experiments; and instils a high level of group identity and commitment.

7   **Interactive learning**. Recognising that the random, chaotic nature of technological change cuts across organisational and even institutional lines, the big company innovators tap into multiple sources of technology from outside as well as to their customers' capabilities.

THE REAL WORLD

With the complexities of balancing intellectual property management and the size and structure of research divisions, companies are looking outside of the boundaries of the firm for efficiency and value.

An example of a specific corporate strategy often found in discussions of open innovation is Procter & Gamble's 'Connect + Develop' strategy, by which Procter & Gamble (P&G) is shifting the source of innovation for new products from their internal research department and traditional suppliers to outside external sources (for example, scientists, engineers, universities and other companies, who could all have the know-how and technical expertise to contribute to new product development.)

In 2000, P&G, like many mature organisations, had recognised that its innovation costs were rising faster than sales growth. Therefore, the CEO at the time, challenged the company to spending increasing amounts on R&D, for diminishing returns, and to reinvent the company's innovation business model. Put simply the company's existing 'invent-it-yourself' approach was not capable of sustaining sales growth.

The CEO's challenge prompted P&G to recognise the potential opportunities for innovation which existed outside the company, and it sought to make use of them through its Connect+ Develop programme.

The CEO set the business a target of acquiring 50% of its innovations from *outside* the company.

P&G now practises 'open innovation' which is a means of accessing externally developed intellectual property and, at the same time, allowing its internally developed assets and know-how to be used by others. Through Connect+Develop, P&G actively seeks to collaborate with external partners to generate and develop new product ideas.

By identifying promising ideas from scientists, researches and engineers outside the company, P&G could then apply its R&D, manufacturing, marketing and purchasing capabilities to them to create better products, faster and more cheaply than it could otherwise have done.

And this attempt to 'outsource' ideas appears to be working. P&G's website reports that more than half of the new product initiatives at P&G now involves significant collaboration with partners outside the company, including individual inventors, small companies, multi-nationals and even P&G's competitors.

www.pg.com/connect_develop/

2.3 Managing innovation

2.3.1 Identifying those innovations likely to succeed

Arguably, the new product development process can start with looking at how an innovation can benefit the customer. One way of doing so is by looking at customer benefits, or' buyer utility'.

Table 7.1   **Potential benefits from innovation**

Item	Comment
Customer productivity	Does the innovation save time and effort?
Simplicity	Does the innovation reduce the complexity a customer faces?
Convenience	Does innovation reduce the inconvenience the customer experiences? (eg speedier or automated check-ins)
Risk	Does the innovation reduce risk?
Fun image	Can the innovation be enjoyed?
Environmental friendliness	Is it responsible?

New products should only be taken to advanced development if there is evidence of:

- **Adequate demand**
- Compatibility with existing **marketing ability**
- Compatibility with existing **production ability**

The stages of new product (or service) development are as outlined in Figure 7.1, below.

Figure 7.1   New product development

The mortality rate of new products is very high. To reduce the risk of failure new product ideas must be screened. Only the best will make it to the next development stage.

2.3.2 Organising for innovation

Companies can be organised and run in a way that stimulates innovation, however, this depends in large part on practical measures.

An innovation strategy calls for a management policy of encouraging to innovative ideas which requires positive action as detailed below.

Promote financial backing to innovation, by spending on R&D and market research and risking capital on new ideas.

Give employees the opportunity to work in an environment where the exchange of ideas for innovation can take place. Management style and organisation structure can help here. Management can actively encourage

The Chartered
Institute of Marketing

employees and customers to put forward new ideas. Participation by subordinates in development decisions might encourage employees to become more involved with development projects and committed to their success. Development teams can be set up and an organisation built up on project team-work.

Where appropriate, direct recruitment policy towards appointing employees with the necessary skills for undertaking innovative work. Employees should be trained and kept up-to-date.

Certain managers should be made responsible for obtaining information from outside the organisation about innovative ideas, and for communicating this information throughout the organisation.

Strategic planning should result in targets being set for innovation, and successful achievements by employees should, if possible, be rewarded.

▶ **Exam tip**

Think about (a) why a company would wish to introduce new products and (b) the stages of the product development sequence. Do not forget that NPD can apply to a new service, such as a new route for an airline. Think about the stages that are involved – and be able to apply them to a specific product or market.

2.4 'Big ideas'

Aaker & McLoughlin (2007) suggests that innovation can lead do growth in a number of ways, as the following diagram illustrates:

Figure 7.2   Growth strategies

Source: Aaker & McLoughlin (2007)

THE REAL WORLD

Aaker & McLoughlin (2007, p273) refer to Hamel's theory that 'the real payoff results from development of revolutionary strategies that break out of industry norms or operations' such as Dell, Ikea and Ryanair: 'Ryanair, one of Europe's most controversial companies, provided services at exceptionally low fares and challenged what Ryanair calls the "establishment" within the airline industry, similar to its American counterpart, Southwest Airlines.'

---

3 Relationship marketing

'All organisations depend on establishing and developing relationships. In short, they must develop relationships with other organisations ... and ... with customers. Indeed, this latter relationship provides the fundamental basis of all marketing activity.' Drummond *et al* (2008) p231

In recent times emphasis has increased on building and maintaining good long-term **relationships** with customers. This is because such relationships are more profitable than constantly searching for new customers owing to repeat purchasing, ease of service and so on.

The **customer** is central to the marketing orientation, but so far we have not considered this important concept in detail. Customers make up one of the groups of stakeholders whose interests management should address. The **stakeholder concept** suggests a **wider concern** than the traditional marketing approach of supplying goods and services which satisfy immediate needs. The supplier-customer relationship extends beyond the basic transaction. The customer needs to remain satisfied with his purchase and positive about his supplier long after the transaction has taken place. If his satisfaction is muted or grudging, future purchases may be reluctant or non-existent and he may advise others of his discontent. Customer tolerance in the UK is fairly high, but should not be taken for granted.

In deciding strategic direction and formulating marketing strategy, any company needs to address issues of customer care, because of:

- **Legal** constraints

- Industry **codes of conduct**

- The recognition that keeping existing customers happy is cheaper than acquiring new ones

- The **value chain**. Customer care is part of after-sales service and offers an opportunity for differentiation. It is also a valuable source of information.

Not all customers are the same. Some appear for a single cash transaction and are never seen again. Others make frequent, regular purchases in large volumes, using credit facilities and building up a major relationship. Yet another type of customer purchases infrequently but in transactions of high value, as for instance in property markets. This variation will exist to a greater or lesser extent in all industries, though each will have a smaller typical range of behaviour. However, even within a single business, customers will vary significantly in the frequency and volume of their purchases, their reasons for buying, their sensitivity to price changes, their reaction to promotion and their overall attitude to the supplier and the product. **Segmentation** of the customer base can have a major impact on profitability, perhaps by simply tailoring promotion to suit the most attractive group of customers.

Many businesses sell to intermediaries rather than to the end consumer. Some sell to both categories; they have to recognise that **the intermediary is just as much a customer as the eventual consumer**. Examples are manufacturers who maintain their own sales organisation but appoint agents in geographically remote areas and companies who combine autonomous operations with franchising. While it is reasonable to give the highest priority to the needs of the ultimate consumer and insist on some control over the activities of the intermediary, it must be recognised that he will only perform well if his own needs are addressed. For instance, a selling agent who has invested heavily in stock after being given exclusive rights in an area should be consulted before further demands are made on his cash flow by the launch of a new product.

3.1 Customer retention

Variation in customer behaviour was mentioned above. The most important aspect of this variation is whether or not the customer comes back for more. Customers should be seen as potentially providing a lifetime of purchases so that **the turnover from a single individual over time might be very large indeed**. It is widely accepted that there is a non-linear relationship between customer retention and profitability in that **a fairly small amount of repeat purchasing generates significant profit**. This is because it is far more expensive in promotion and overhead costs to convert a non-buyer into an occasional buyer than to turn an occasional buyer into a frequent buyer. The repeat buyer does not have to be persuaded to give the product a try or be tempted by special deals; he needs less attention from sales staff and already has his credit account set up. New customers usually have to be won from competitors.

The process of retaining customers for a lifetime is an important one and one in which integrated marketing communications has an important role to play. Instead of one-way communication aimed solely at gaining a sale it is necessary to develop an effective two-way communication process to turn a **prospect into a lifetime advocate**. This is shown in the following ladder of customer loyalty.

Figure 7.3 Ladder of customer loyalty

Based on Christopher *et al* (2007)

The purpose of relationship marketing is to establish, maintain and enhance relationships with customers and other parties so that the objectives of both parties involved are met.

1   Because **service and industrial companies** have direct, regular and often multiple contacts with their customers (for example, the regular hotel guest who interacts with reception), the importance of 'part-time' marketers is increased. Customer contact with all employees is vital.

2   **Trust and keeping promises**. To have an ongoing relationship, both parties need to trust each other and keep the promises they make. Marketing moves from one-off potentially manipulative exchanges towards co-operative relationships built on financial, social and structural benefits.

3   **Network of exchange partners**. Customer relationships are important but so too are the relationships which organisations have with other parties such as suppliers, distributors, professional bodies, banks and trade associations.

3.2 Customers as assets

You might already be familiar with the concept of the customer as a **current asset** in financial terms – except in cash businesses eg, a customer is a debtor. **Goodwill** – or a company's reputation – is also considered an asset.

However, it will sometimes help you in evaluating strategic marketing decisions and persuading sceptical management accountants of your case if you consider the customer base as an **asset worth investing in**. After all, if you are looking for repeat business, you will expect future benefits from customers.

Today's highly competitive business environment means that customers are only retained if they are **very satisfied** with their purchasing experience. **Any lesser degree of satisfaction is likely to result in the loss of the customer**. Companies must be active in monitoring customer satisfaction **because very few will actually complain. They will simply depart**. Businesses which use intermediaries must be particularly active, since research shows that even when complaints are made, the principals hear about only a very small proportion of them.

The most satisfactory way to retain customers is to offer them products which they perceive as providing **superior benefits** at any given price point. However, there are specific techniques which can increase customer retention. **Loyalty schemes** such as frequent flyer programmes, augment the product in the customer's eyes. The **club concept**, as used by Sainsbury and Tesco, offers small discounts on repeated purchases. The principal benefit of both these types of scheme, however, is the enhanced **knowledge of the customer** which they provide. Initial registration provides name, address and post code. Subsequent use of the loyalty card allows a detailed purchasing profile to be built up for individual customers. This enables highly targeted promotion and cross-selling later.

Research indicates that **the single largest reason why customers abandon a supplier is poor performance by front-line staff**. Any scheme for customer retention must address the need for careful selection and training of these staff. It is also a vital factor in **relationship marketing**.

THE REAL WORLD

Customer retention

High levels of customer retention, stemming from achieving customer loyalty, can help create competitive advantage.

Citroen UK's fleet marketing manager recognise the need to record and manage information customers and prospective customers because, as he pointed out, 'With a proper database in place, and regularly updated records, we… [can] undertake more effective prospect generation and customer mailing programmes in building a more loyal client base.'

Citroen use a continuously evolving customer relationship management (CRM) system to support the company's sales and marketing efforts. The primary goal for the fleet sales team remains getting sales people in front of customers as much as possible, enabling them to get on with the job of selling. This is essential in a tough fleet market, which currently accounts for around 50% of the total UK automotive sales and which is at least as competitive as the retail market.

However, the CRM system's ability to support the planning process is particularly valuable, as generating sales in the fleet market involves a much longer and more complex sales cycle than the retail market.

Citroen also recognise the importance of the CRM system in improving the client's experience of the company. The CRM system enables better-targeted promotional campaigns and ensures that for each interaction, client-facing staff are armed with a complete up-dated client contact history. Citroen have found that customers respond positively to this, viewing the company as professional and well-informed, thereby giving customers greater confidence in it. As a result Citroen has a greater likelihood of converting prospects into sales and increasing retention rates through improved customer loyalty.

Citroen UK has also established a network of business centres which aims to support the firm's presence in the fleet market by offering more dedicated sales and after-sales services. The company has recognised the importance of providing its business customers with the highest levels of service. And this positive approach to customer service and relationship management appears to be working. Between 2009-2010 Citroen enjoyed a 17% growth in fleet market share across cars and commercial vehicles.

Sources: www.business.co.uk, Citroen's business network completed, 30 June 2010.

www.cxo.eu.com, Citroen UK - Fleet Sales

3.3 Relationship marketing

There is a move away from 'transactions' to **relationship marketing**. Firms aim to build loyalty, especially where switching costs are high and a lost customer is probably lost for a long time.

Much has been written in recent years on **relationship marketing**. Gummesson (2002) suggests it is a 'paradigm shift' requiring a **dramatic change** in marketing thinking and behaviour, not an add-on to traditional marketing.' He suggests that the core of marketing should no longer be the 4Ps, but 30Rs, which reflect the large number of complex relationships involved in business. Kotler (2001) argues that marketing can make promises but only the whole organisation can deliver satisfaction.

Relationship marketing is thus as much about **attitudes and assumptions** as it is about techniques. The marketing function's task is to inculcate habits of behaviour at all levels and in all departments that will enhance and strengthen the alliance. It must be remembered, however, that the effort involved in long-term relationship building is more appropriate in some markets than in others. Where customers are purchasing intermittently and **switching costs are low**, there is always a chance of business. This tends to be the pattern in **commodity markets**. Here, it is reasonable to take a **transactions approach** to marketing and treat each sale as unique.

As stated earlier, **relationship marketing approach** is more appropriate where **switching costs are high** and a lost customer is thus probably lost for a long time. Switching costs are raised by such factors as the need for training on systems, the need for a large common installed base, high capital cost and the incorporation of purchased items into the customer's own designs.

The conceptual or philosophic nature of relationship marketing leads to a simple principle, that of **enhancing satisfaction by precision in meeting the needs of individual customers**. This depends on extensive **two-way communication** to establish and record the customer's characteristics and preferences and build a long-term relationship. Adcock et al (2001) mention three important practical methods which contribute to this end:

- Building a customer database
- Developing customer-oriented service systems
- Extra direct contacts with customers

3.3.1 Databases

Modern **computer database systems** have enabled the rapid acquisition and retrieval of the individual customer's details, needs and preferences. Using this technology, relationship marketing enables telephone sales staff to greet the customer by name, know what he purchased last time, avoid taking his full delivery address, know what his credit status is and what he is likely to want. It enables new products to be developed that are precisely tailored to the customer's needs and new procedures to be established which enhance his satisfaction. It is the successor to **mass marketing**, which attempted to be customer-led but which could only supply a one-size-fits-all product. The end result of a relationship marketing approach is a mutually satisfactory relationship which continues indefinitely.

THE REAL WORLD

Supermarket loyalty cards

A number of supermarkets and other retailers now have customer loyalty cards – for example, Tesco's Clubcard.

If a supermarket customer scans their loyalty card when they pay for their shopping, they earn 'points' on their card which in due course can be converted into vouchers or money off coupons.

However, linking the customer's purchases to their loyalty card also enables the supermarket to create a record of the items the customer has bought. The purchasing behaviour of customers can be used to create a profile of what kind of people the cardholders are.

Data mining techniques could be applied to customers' purchasing information to identify patterns in items which were purchased together, what types of item were omitted from different shopping baskets, and how the make-up of customers' baskets varied by different types of customer.

The supermarket can then target its promotions to take advantage of individual customers' purchasing patterns; for example, by offering customers promotional coupons to buy more of particular product lines which it knows they have purchased in the past.

www.tesco.com/clubcard

3.3.2 Customer care

Relationship marketing extends the principles of **customer care**. Customer care is about providing a product which is augmented by high quality of service, so that the customer is impressed during his transaction with the company. This can be done in ignorance of any detail of the customer other than those implicit in the immediate transaction. The customer is anonymous. **Relationship marketing is about having the customer come back for further transactions by ending the anonymity**.

It is inevitable that **problems** will arise. A positive way of dealing with errors must be designed into the customer relationship. Front line sales people cannot usually deal with the causes of mistakes as they **are built into the products**, **systems and organisation structure**. It is, therefore, necessary for management to promote vertical and horizontal interaction in order to spur changes to eliminate the **sources** of mistakes.

It is inevitable that there will be multiple contacts between customer and supplier organisations. Each contact is an opportunity to enhance or to prejudice the relationship, so staff throughout the supplier organisation must be aware of their marketing responsibilities. Two-way communication should be encouraged so that the relationship can grow and deepen. There is a link here to the database mentioned above: extra contacts provide more information. Confidential information must, of course, be treated with due respect.

THE REAL WORLD

Customer loyalty

The problem with profitable customers is retaining them, because they will attract the attention of your competitors. Building customer relationships may be the answer to both types of problem.

Relationship marketing is grounded in the idea of establishing a learning relationship with customers. At the lower end, building a relationship can create cross-selling opportunities that may make the overall relationship profitable. For example, some retail banks have tried selling credit cards to less profitable customers. With valuable customers, customer relationship management may make them more loyal and willing to invest additional funds. In banking, these high-end relationships are often managed through private bankers, whose goals are not only to increase customer satisfaction and retention, but also to cross-sell and bring in investment.

In determining which customers are worth the cost of long-term relationships, it is useful to consider their lifetime value. This depends on:

- Current profitability computed at the customer level
- The propensity of those customers to stay loyal
- Expected revenues and costs of servicing such customers over the lifetime of the relationship

Building relationships makes most sense for customers whose lifetime value to the company is the highest. Thus, building relationships should focus on customers who are currently the most profitable, likely to be the most profitable in the future, or likely to remain with the company for the foreseeable future and have acceptable levels of profitability.

The goal of relationship management is to increase customer satisfaction and to minimise any problems. By engaging in 'smarter' relationships, a company can learn customers' preferences and develop trust. Every contact point with the customer can be seen as a chance to record information and learn preferences. Complaints and errors must be recorded, not just fixed and forgotten. Contact with customers in every medium, whether over the internet, through a call centre, or through personal contact, is recorded and centralised.

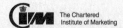
The Chartered Institute of Marketing

Many companies are beginning to achieve this goal by using customer relationship management (CRM) software. Data, once collected and centralised, can be used to customise service. In addition, the database can be analysed to detect patterns that can suggest better ways to serve customers in general. A key aspect of this dialogue is to learn and record preferences. There are two ways to determine customers' preferences: transparently and collaboratively.

Discovering preferences transparently means that the marketer learns the customers' needs without actually involving them. For example, the Ritz Carlton Hotel makes a point of observing the choices that guests make and recording them. If a guest requests extra pillows, then extra pillows will be provided every time that person visits. At upmarket retailers, personal shoppers will record customers' preferences in sizes, styles, brands, colours and price ranges and notify them when new merchandise appears or help them choose accessories.

3.3.3 Differences between transactional and relationship marketing

Table 7.2   Transactional vs relationship marketing

Transactional	Relationship
Importance of single sale	Importance of customer relation
Importance of product features	Importance of customer benefits
Short time scale	Longer time scale
Less emphasis on service	High customer service
Quality is concern of production	Quality is concern of all
Competitive commitment	High customer commitment
Persuasive communication	Regular communication

Adapted from Adcock *et al* (2001)

The most important issue in customer retention is focusing marketing effort on activities that promote a strong relationship rather than a single transaction.

3.3.4 The relationship marketing mix

By now you are familiar with the 4Ps of the basic marketing mix. Relationship marketing is highly dependent upon a fifth P: **people**. The features of the basic 4Ps must support the commitment to developing mutually beneficial customer relationships. The **behaviour of the people** involved in the customer relationship is even more important, because relationship marketing success depends on their motivation to achieve it. In turn, that motivation depends to a great extent upon the leadership exercised by marketing managers. It is not enough to expect self-motivation because *all* staff are involved, not just those with a sales role.

3.3.5 Implementing relationship marketing programmes

Kotler (2001) suggests five steps, suitable for business-to-business or service markets.

Step 1   Identify **key customers**

Step 2   Assign a **relationship manager** to each

Step 3   Develop clear **job descriptions**

Step 4   Appoint a manager to supervise the relationship managers

Step 5   Develop long-term plans for developing **relationships**

3.3.6 Sustaining the relationship

1   Offer **superior customer value** by personalising the interaction, involving two-way communication. This is essential for service industries such as life assurance. Hotels have systems that remember guests' preferences.

2   Be trustworthy and **reliable**, for example by offering a replacement.

3   **Tighten the connection**. Once the relationship is established, it must be nurtured to make it harder for the customer to defect.

4   **Co-ordinating capabilities**. The more successful the relationship, the greater the risk of imitation.

Kotler's approach is suitable for business-to-business markets or personal services such as financial advice. Some firms, however, have sought through data mining techniques to get a long-term view of the customer.

Loyalty cards are designed to reward customers for repeat purchase. They:

- Collect information about customer purchasing habits, enabling targeted marketing communication

- Reward customers for repeat purchase, to encourage sales volumes

Loyalty schemes vary in the benefit they offer.

- Recent UK research indicates that owners of 'loyalty' cards spend more, but they are not necessarily loyal.

- Furthermore, most customers still shop around and have one or more loyalty cards.

- **Loyalty cards may prove to be an expensive failure.**

3.3.7 Key accounts

So far we have considered the retention of customers as an unquestionably desirable objective. **However, for many businesses a degree of discretion will be advisable**. 'Key' does not mean large. A customer's **potential** is very important. The definition of a key account depends on the circumstances. Key account management is about managing the future.

Customers can be assessed for desirability according to such criteria as the profitability of their accounts; the prestige they confer; the amount of non-value adding administrative work they generate; the cost of the selling effort they absorb; the rate of growth of their accounts and, for industrial customers, of the turnover of their own businesses; their willingness to adopt new products; and their credit history. Such analyses will almost certainly conform to a Pareto distribution and show, for instance that 80% of profit comes from 20% of the customers, while a different 20% generate most of the credit control or administrative problems. Some businesses will be very aggressive about getting rid of their problem customers, but a more positive technique would be to concentrate effort on the most desirable ones. These are the **key accounts** and the company's relationship with them can be built up by appointing **key account managers**.

Key account management is often seen as a high level selling task, but should in fact be a business wide team effort about relationships and customer retention. It can be seen as a form of co-operation with the customer's supply chain management function. The key account manager's role is to integrate the efforts of the various parts of the organisation in order to deliver an enhanced service. This idea has long been used by advertising agencies and was successfully introduced into aerospace manufacturing over 40 years ago. It will be the key account manager's role to maintain communication with the customer, note any developments in his circumstances, deal with any problems arising in the relationship and develop the long-term business relationship.

The Chartered Institute of Marketing

The key account relationship may progress through several stages.

1   At first, there may be a typical **adversarial sales-purchasing relationship** with emphasis on price, delivery and so on. Attempts to widen contact with the customer organisation will be seen as a threat by its purchasing staff.

2   Later, the sales staff may be able to foster **a mutual desire to increase understanding** by wider contacts. Trust may increase.

3   A **mature partnership stage** may be reached in which there are contacts at all levels and information is shared. The key account manager becomes responsible for integrating the partnership business processes and contributing to the customer's supply chain management. High 'vendor ratings', stable quality, continuous improvement and fair pricing are taken for granted.

4 Branding

'An important strategic option is to build brand equity ... Brands with high brand equity provide their owners with competitive and financial benefits.' Aaker & McLoughlin (2007) p181

4.1 What is a brand?

Much of the marketing mix activity goes to the development of **brands**, which are what the customers identify. Brands embody a set of expectations about the product. A brand image exists in the customer's mind.

> ▶ **Key term**
>
> A **brand** is a collection of attributes which strongly influence purchase.
>
> 'A name, term, sign, symbol or design or combination of them, intended to identify the goods or services of one seller or group of sellers and to differentiate them from those of competitors.' (Kotler, 2001)

Branding and a firm's reputation are linked. The important thing to remember is that a brand is something **customers** value: it exists in the customer's mind. A brand is the link between a company's marketing activities and the customer's perception.

THE REAL WORLD

What's in a Name?

In suburban Philadelphia, not too many miles from Wharton's campus, is a retail establishment called Ed's Beer Store. It's a wonderfully prosaic name. Customers know what they can buy there, and if they have a complaint, they know whom to talk to.

But what about companies with names like Agere, Agilent or Altria? Or Diageo, Monday and Verizon? Or Accenture, Cingular and Protiviti?

Except for Monday, which may be a strange thing to call a company but it is nonetheless a real word, all these names are fabricated. What's more, none of them, even Monday, tells potential customers anything about the businesses they are in. Plus, they sound so contrived that you might conclude they will do nothing but elicit snickering and confusion in the market place.

According to marketing professors at Wharton, however, that is not necessarily the case. They say peculiar names, by themselves, may mean nothing to begin with. But if backed by a successful branding campaign, they will come to signify whatever the companies want them to mean.

Website: http://www.knowledge.wharton.upenn.edu

4.1.1 What makes up a brand?

Doyle & Stern (2006) suggest that key elements of a brand are:

- Effective product
- Distinctive identity
- Added values

} supported by {

Visible: Symbol, advertising, presentation (eg packaging)

Invisible: assets and competences, strong R&D, supply chain, effective selling, costs

4.1.2 Benefits of branding

Table 7.3 Benefits of branding

Beneficiary	Benefit of branding
Customers	<ul><li>Branding makes it easier to choose between competing products, if brands offer different benefits. Brands help consumers cope with information overload</li><li>Brands can support aspirations and self image</li><li>Branding can confer membership of reference groups</li></ul>
Marketers	<ul><li>Enables extra value to be added to the product</li><li>Creates an impression in the consumer's mind; encourages re-purchase</li><li>Differentiates the product, especially if competing products are similar</li><li>Reduces the importance of price</li><li>Encourages a pull strategy</li><li>Other products/services can exploit the brand image (eg *Virgin*)</li></ul>

Shareholders	<ul><li>A brand is an intangible asset; even though it is not on the financial statements, a strong brand promises to generate future cash inflows and profits. This is called **brand equity**.</li><li>Brands build market share, which can generate high profits through:
	  – Higher volume
	  – Higher value (higher prices)
	  – Higher control over distributors</li></ul>

Evolution of brands. Brands have evolved over time, to the extent that they satisfy customer needs.

- **Classic brands** (post World War II) were linked to a single goal (eg cleaner clothes).

- **Contemporary brands** meet functional needs but give associated benefits (eg Volvo and safety).

- **Post-modern brands**? Consumers use brands to attain a broad array of goals, as a result of 'time famine'.

Some marketers suggest that brands have an emotional content. Certainly, this might be the case for fashion items (eg trainers) where they confer status.

4.2 Brand strategies

There are several basic branding strategies: company, umbrella, range and individual product.

4.2.1 Different types of brand strategy

1   **Company brand**. The company name is the most prominent feature of the branding (eg Mercedes).

2   **The company brand combined with an individual brand name** (eg Kellogg's: Corn Flakes, Rice Krispies). This option both legitimises (because of the company name) and individualises (the individual product name). It allows **new names to be introduced quickly and relatively cheaply**. Sometimes known as **umbrella branding**, firms might use this approach as a short-term way to save money.

3   **Range brand**. Firms group types of product under different brands.

4 **Individual name**. Each product has a unique name. This is the option chosen by Procter & Gamble for example, who even have different brand names within the same product line, eg Bold, Tide. The main advantage of individual product branding is that an unsuccessful brand does not adversely affect the firm's other products, nor the firm's reputation generally.

4.2.2 Choice of brand strategy

1 **Company and/or umbrella brand name**

Advantages	Disadvantages
▪ Cheap (only one marketing effort)	▪ Not ideal for segmentation
▪ Easy to launch new products under umbrella brand	▪ Harder to obtain distinct identity
	▪ Risk that failure in one area can damage the brand
▪ Good for internal marketing	▪ Variable quality

For example, Virgin is a company brand name, supported by advertising, PR and the celebrity status of Richard Branson.

(a) Service industries use umbrella marketing as customer benefits can cross product categories. Marks & Spencer diversified from clothes, to food and to financial services. Tesco and Asda have followed suit.

(b) Communication media are more diffuse and fragmented.

(c) One brand is supported by integrated marketing communications.

(d) Umbrella branding supports **database marketing** across the whole product range.

(e) Distributor/retailer brands are umbrella brands in their own right, so **brand owners** have to follow suit.

2 **Range brands** offer some of the advantages of an umbrella brand with more precise targeting.

3 **Individual brand** name

Advantages	Disadvantages
▪ Ideal for precise segmentation	▪ Expensive
▪ Crowds out competition by offering more choice	▪ Risky
▪ Damage limitation to company's reputation	

4.3 Brand equity

The added value conferred by a brand is largely subjective. In blind testing many consumers cannot tell the difference between different products; however, they will exhibit a preference for a strong brand name when shown it. Apart from the quality and functionality of the product, brand equity is built on suggestion rather than substance.

> ▸ **Key term**
>
> **Brand equity** is the asset the marketer builds to ensure continuity of satisfaction for the customer and profit for the supplier.

Most consumer buying decisions, therefore, **do not depend on the functionality of the product**.

- (Products are bought for **emotional reasons**. For example, most sports trainers are fashion products.

- Branding reduces the need for the intellectually challenging process of rational choice.

4.3.1 Sources of brand equity

Table 7.4   Sources of brand equity

Source	Comment
Experience	Customer's actual usage of a brand can give positive or negative associations.
User associations	Brands get an image from the type of people using them; brands might be associated with particular personalities.
Appearance	Design appeals to people's aesthetic sensibilities.
Manufacturer's name	The company reputation may support the brand.
Marketing communication	Building the brand by establishing its values is a major reason why marketing communication of all kinds is undertaken.

The Chartered Institute of Marketing

The global economic downturn has put retailers under increasing pressure and nowhere has this been more evident than in department stores. Virtually every major department store has been experimenting with initiatives to try to attract more customers and find some light at the end of what has become a very dark tunnel.

In May 2011 the US department store Macy's announced it was going to open a new store outside Chicago. However, the significant point about this was that the store is going to be located in a discount/outlet mall – a new type of location for Macy's.

Yet while the store's location is in a discount mall, Macy's say that their store will not be a discount store. They intend to sell a full range of regularly priced goods that customers would find in any other Macy's location. Macy's view the opening as an opportunity to close a gap in their store coverage rather than a reflection of any change in the company's brand strategy.

Nonetheless, some critics have questioned the logic of the move suggesting that the decision to locate next to discount retailers shifts Macy's brand (even if only slightly) towards becoming a discount brand in consumers' minds.

Summarised from: Stephens, D (2011) Note to Macy's – You Are the Company You Keep, www.retailwire.com, 8 June 2011

4.3.2 Brand identity

▸ **Key terms**

Brand identity: the message sent out by the brand through its product form, name, visual signs, advertising. This is not the same as **brand image** which is how the target market perceives the brand.

Apple has created a brand identity that no other company in the technology industry seems able to match. Apple's products have become synonymous with high-quality, high-end devices which are full of high-tech 'cool'.

In the computing market, Apple's aluminium-based Macs are the industry's beauty queens, compared to the less glamorous Dell and HP products. And in the smartphone and tablet market, Apple's design philosophy has been the benchmark that all other companies have been trying to mimic.

In 2011, BrandIndex, an organisation which measures consumer attitudes towards companies, found that Apple's perception is exceptionally high. It earned a score of 76 out of a possible 100.

However, although Apple's sleek designs often convey a sense that their products offer higher quality and value than their competitors, this perception is not always justified. Although consumers might feel that Apple is delivering the best quality and value, in terms of product specifications and price Dell laptops or HP notebooks actually offer much better value for money.

The same can even be said for Apple's mobile products. For example, the iPhone 4S may be nice, but it doesn't have the quad-core processor found in the HTC One X.

Yet although informed consumers know they can buy cheaper products from Apple's competitors, and get more powerful components in them, the intangibles keep them coming back for iPhones and Macs.

So it seems Apple doesn't need to be the highest of the 'high end' to be successful. Just being Apple seems to be working for it. .

Based on: Reisinger, D. (2012) The unspoken truth about Apple, 30 July 2012,

http://tech.fortune.cnn.com/2012/07/30/the-unspoken-truth-about-apple/

4.3.3 Three aspects to a brand

Table 7.5   Aspects of a brand

Aspect	Comment
Core	Fundamental, unchanging aspect of a brand. (eg Cider is an alcoholic drink made from apples.)
Style	This is the brand's culture, personality, the identity it conveys and so on. Compare the: - Rustic personality of Scrumpy Jack - Almost club-oriented personality of Diamond White
Themes	These are how the brand communicates through physical appearance of the product.

Clearly, the **themes** are more easy to change than the **style**, which is more easy to change than the core.

▶ **Exam tip**

One of the issues an organisation might face is the need to reposition itself, possibly in response to negative connotations associated with its brand. In this context, it will be important to think how the aspects of the brand will need to change to support the repositioning. If an organisation cannot change the aspects successfully, will it be able to reposition the brand successfully?

4.4 How to build brands

Brand building is a logical process that can proceed gradually, step-by-step towards a position of strength.

The process for building the brand is similar to that of building a product (core product, an expected product, an augmented product and a potential product). However, a product is, in some respects, purely functional, whereas a brand offers more.

4.4.1 A step approach to designing brands

Step 1   **Have a quality product** – but remember quality means **fitness for use** not the **maximum specification**. Functionality is only a starting point.

Step 2   **Build the basic brand**. These are the marketing mix criteria.

- They should support product performance
- They should differentiate the brand
- They should be consistent with positioning
- The basic brand delivers the core product in an attractive way

Step 3   **Augmentations** include extra services, guarantees and so on. (Expensive guarantees provide evidence that the firm takes quality seriously.)

Step 4   **Reaching its potential**, so that customers will not easily accept substitutes.

Step 5   Maintain **brand value** by using the marketing mix to persuade customers to buy again.

Step 6   **Build brand loyalty**. Customers who buy again and are loyal are valuable because:

- Revenue from them is more predictable
- Existing customers are cheaper than new customers

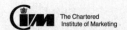
The Chartered Institute of Marketing

Step 7   **Know where to stop in developing the brand**. (For example, an alcohol-free alcopop would be pointless.)

Brands that **reach their potential** have five key characteristics.

- A quality product underpinning the brand
- Being first to market, giving early-mover advantages
- Unique positioning concept: in other words they are precisely positioned
- Strong communications underpinning the brand
- Time and consistency

4.4.2 The brand planning process

Brand strategy is one of the steps in the brand planning process just as marketing strategy is one step in the marketing planning process. Arnold (1993) offers a five-stage brand planning process.

Table 7.6   Brand planning process

Stage	Description
Market analysis	An overview of trends in the macro- and micro-environment and so includes customer and competitor analysis and the identification of any PEST factors which may affect our brand.
Brand situation analysis	Analysis of the brand's personality and individual attributes. This represents the internal audit and questions such as, 'Is advertising projecting the right image?', 'Is the packaging too aggressive?', 'Does the product need updating?' need asking. This is a fundamental evaluation of the brand's character.
Targeting future positions	This is the core of brand strategy. Any brand strategy could incorporate what has been learnt in Steps 1 and 2 into a view of how the market will evolve and what strategic response is most appropriate. Brand strategy can be considered under three headings. - Target markets - Brand positions - Brand scope
Testing new offers	Once the strategy has been decided the next step is to develop individual elements of the marketing mix and test the brand concept for clarity, credibility and competitiveness with the target market.
Planning and evaluating performance	The setting of the brand budget, establishing the type of support activity needed and measurement of results against objectives. Information on tracking of performance feeds into step (1) of the brand management process.

4.5 Brand extension

A brand can be used on a wide range of products and services if its values are appropriate.

> **Key terms**
>
> **Brand extension** uses a brand name successfully established in one market or channel to enter other. It is often termed **brand stretching** when the markets are very different.

4.5.1 Examples of brand extension

- Retailers such as Tesco launching themselves as Internet Service Providers

- Arm & Hammer leveraged its brand equity from basic baking soda into oral care toothpaste and laundry care categories.

- As saw in the previous Chapter, Lucozade extended its brand into the sports drink market.

- One of the greatest exponents of brand extension is Richard Branson. He has extended the Virgin brand, originally based on pop music, to cover mobile phones, trains, airlines, financial services, and even space flights for space tourists (with Virgin Galactic).

4.5.2 Conditions for brand extension

- The **core values** of the brand must be **relevant to the new market**. EasyJet has transferred to car rental and internet cafes.

- The new market area must not affect the core values of the brand by association. Failure in one activity can adversely affect brand equity.

4.5.3 Advantages of brand extension

Table 7.7   Advantages of brand extension

Advantage	Comment
Cheap	It is less costly to extend a brand then to establish a new one from scratch.
Customer-perception	Customer expectations of the brand have been built up, so this lower risk for the customer encourages 'trial'.
Less risky	Failure rate of completely new brands.

4.5.4 Disadvantages of brand extension

Table 7.8   Disadvantages of brand extension

Disadvantage	Comment
Segments	The brand personality may not carry over successfully to the new segment. The brand values may not be relevant to the new market.
Strength	The brand needs to be strong already.
Perception	The brand still needs a differential advantage over competitors.
Over-dilution	Excessive extensions can dilute the values of the brand.

THE REAL WORLD

While brand extension can be the way to get the best financial returns out of a strong brand, sometimes there is a danger that brands extend too far, too fast.

One brand where this may be the case is Ugg Boots. For a while, these fur-lined boots from Australia seemed to be the must have women's accessory. However, now you can buy pretty much anything, from sandals to men's shoes.

Many of the new items seem a long way removed from the brand's origins as a boot made with sheepskin. And they don't appear to have any apparent connection with surfing either – the boots were often worn by surfers to keep their feet warm, and it was this sport which helped propel the brand to international fame.

Therefore, despite the celebrity endorsements which boosted Ugg's brand visibility in the early 2000s there is a danger than Ugg could go from 'iconic' to 'diluted' in the space of a decade.

Summarised from an article in *Brand Strategy insider*, 18 April 2012 by Nigel Hollis: 'Brand Extension: Friend and Foe of Strong Brands' www.brandingstrategyinsider.com

---

4.6 Revitalising and repositioning

At times, the performance of a brand will falter and managers will attempt to rectify the situation by enhancing sales volume and improving profits in other ways.

The Chartered
Institute of Marketing

Revitalisation means increasing the sales volume through:

- New markets (eg overseas)
- New segments (eg personal computers are being sold for family, as opposed to business, use)
- Increased usage (encouraging people to eat breakfast cereals as a snack during the day)

Repositioning is more fundamental, in that it is a **competitive strategy** aimed to change position to increase market share.

Table 7.9 Bases of repositioning

Type of position	Comment
Real	Relates to actual product features and design
Psychological	Change the buyer's beliefs about the brand
Competitive	Alter beliefs about competing brands
Change emphasis	The emphasis in the advertising can change over time

4.6.1 Success criteria for branding

Beneficial qualities of a brand name

- Suggest **benefits**, eg Schweppes' Slimline tonic
- Suggest qualities such as **action** or **colour** (eg easyJet, with an orange colour)
- Be **easy to pronounce**, recognise and remember
- Be **acceptable in all markets**, both linguistically and culturally
- Be **distinctive**
- Be **meaningful**

THE REAL WORLD

Global Brands

The brand consultancy, Interbrand, produces a annual report of the 'Best Global Brands' in which it ranks the brand strength of global companies.

According to Interbrand, the top ten brands in 2011 (and their brand value) were:

1	Coca Cola	$71,861m
2	IBM	$69,905m
3	Microsoft	$59,087m
4	Google	$55,317m
5	GE	$42,808m
6	McDonald's	$35,593m
7	Intel	$35,217m
8	Apple	$33,492m
9	Disney	$29,018m
10	Hewlett-Packard	$28,479m

Interbrand have found that successful brands perform strongly across a set of 10 factors:

Internal factors

Clarity – What the brand stands for internally, in terms of its values, positioning and proposition. Also, clarity about target audiences and customer insights.

Commitment – An internal commitment within an organisation to brand, a belief in the importance of brand, and investment in it.

Responsiveness – The ability to respond to market changes, challenges and opportunities. In this respect, brand leaders should have a desire and ability to evolve and renew the brand.

Protection – How secure the brand is across a number of dimensions: for example, legal protection, proprietary ingredients or design.

External (customer-related) factors

Relevance – Having a good fit with customer/consumer needs and desires, across all relevant demographics and markets

Authenticity – The brand has a defined heritage and a well-grounded value set. It can deliver against the high expectations which customers have of it.

Differentiation – The degree to which customers/consumers perceive the brand to have a differentiated positioning, distinctive from its competitors

Consistency – The degree to which a brand is experienced without fail across all touchpoints or formats

Presence – The degree to which a brand has a presence in society, and is talked bout positively by consumers, customers and opinion formers in both traditional and social media

Understanding – The brand is not only recognised by customers, but they also know about its distinctive qualities and characteristics (and/or the qualities and characteristics of the company which owns the brand).

www.interbrand.com

4.7 Brands in the global market place

Brands, like most aspects of marketing practice, require a decision about standardisation or adaptation when taken into the global marketplace.

The most successful examples of worldwide branding occur where the brand has become **synonymous with the generic product** (eg Sellotape, Aspirin).

4.7.1 Global or local brand?

The key differences between a standardised global brand approach and an approach based upon identifying and exploiting local marketing opportunities are as described below.

1   **Standardised global brand approach**

    (a)   A standardised product offering to market segments which have exactly similar needs across cultures

    (b)   A common approach to the marketing mix and one that is as nearly standardised as may be, given language differences

2   **Local marketing opportunities**

    (a)   A recognition that the resources of the company may be adapted to fulfil marketing opportunities in different ways, taking into account local needs and preferences but on a global basis

    (b)   A willingness to sub-optimise the benefits of having a single global brand (eg advertising synergy) in order to optimise the benefits of meeting specific needs more closely

The Chartered Institute of Marketing

It is possible to move from a local brand to a global brand approach as demonstrated by the Mars Corporation with their Snickers brand.

In the UK market, the biggest confectionery market in Europe, Mars had decided to use the brand name Marathon for the chocolate bar known as Snickers in the US and elsewhere around the world. Reportedly, this was done to avoid confusion with the word knickers. There was a very distinctive brand identity in the UK to the extent that the company would sponsor the London Marathon (1984 – 1988) and other sporting events to tie in with the brand name.

Competition from Nestlé in Europe persuaded the company that they needed to take up the potential benefits of a standardised global brand approach rather than merely relying on a global marketing approach. They, therefore, changed the name to Snickers in the UK market in 1990 at very considerable cost of advertising support.

There were rumours in 2008 that Mars was bringing back the name Marathon after it re-registered the UK trademark amid a wave of nostalgia for 1980s chocolate bars. However, the name has so far remained as Snickers.

For the international company marketing products which can be branded, there are two further policy decisions to be made.

- The problem of deciding if and how to protect the company's brands
- Whether there should be one global brand or different national brands for a product

The major argument in favour of a single global brand is the economies of scale that it produces, both in production and promotion. But whether a global brand is the best policy (or even possible) depends on a number of factors, which address the two basic policy decisions above.

4.7.2 Legal considerations

1   Legal constraints may limit the possibilities for a global brand, for instance, where the brand name has already been registered in a foreign country.

2   Protection of the brand name will often be needed, but internationally is hard to achieve.

   (a)   In some countries registration is difficult
   (b)   Brand imitation and piracy are rife in certain parts of the world

   There are many examples of imitation in international branding, with products such as cigarettes, and denim jeans.

3   Worse still is the problem of piracy where a well known brand name is counterfeited. It is illegal in most parts of the world but in many countries there is little if any enforcement of the law. (Levis is one of the most pirated brand names.) Piracy is also a problem for intellectual property.

ACTIVITY 7.2

Even with trademark protection the impact of a market leader's branding may be weakened by consumers who perceive the brand name as a generic term. Can you think of some examples?

4.7.3 Cultural aspects

Even if a firm has no legal difficulties with branding globally, there may be cultural problems, eg unpronounceable names or names with other meanings, for example Maxwell House is Maxwell Kaffee in Germany, Legal in France and Monky in Spain. But sometimes a minor spelling change is all that is needed, such as Wrigley Speermint in Germany.

4.7.4 Other considerations

Many other influences affect the global branding decision.

1   Differences between the firm's major brand and its secondary brands. The major brand is more likely to be branded globally than secondary brands.

2   The importance of brand to the product sale. Where price, for example, is a more important factor, then it may not be worth the heavy expenditure needed to establish and maintain a global brand in each country; a series of national brands may be more effective.

3   The problem of how to brand a product arising from acquisition or joint venture. Should the multinational company keep the name it has acquired?

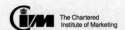

- Critically evaluate the nature of innovation and new product development (NPD) in marketing and the related factors impacting upon marketing decisions, including ongoing innovation management within an organisation

- Assess the relevance to an organisation of mergers, acquisitions and strategic alliances in growing, expanding and maximising business potential

- Critically evaluate a range of growth strategies for an organisation

- Critically evaluate the concept of relationship marketing (CRM) as a means of achieving growth and profitability within an organisation

- Critically evaluate the development of an organisation's brand and its contribution towards increasing the organisation's value and brand equity

FURTHER READING

De Jong, J. & Vermeulen, P. A. M. (2003) Organizing successful new service development: a literature review. *Journal of Management Decision.* Vol 41 (9), pp 844 – 858.

Hooley, G., Nicoulaud, B. & Piercy, N. (2011), *Marketing Strategy and Competitive Positioning,* 5rd edition, Pearson, Harlow.

Kim, C. (2005). *Blue Ocean Strategy.* Boston: Harvard Business School Press.

Piercy, N. (2009) *Market-led strategic change: transforming the process of going to market*, 4th edition, Elsevier, Oxford.

REFERENCES

Aaker, D. & McLoughlin, D. (2007) *Strategic Market Management.* John Wiley, Chichester.

Aaker, D. & McLoughlin, D. (2010) *Strategic Market Management: Global Perspectives.* John Wiley, Chichester.

Adcock, D., Bradfield, R., Halborg, & A. Ross, C. (2001) *Marketing: Principles and Practice.* 4th edition. FT Prentice Hall, Harlow.

Arnold, D. (1993) *The Handbook of Brand Management.* Perseus Books, US.

Christopher, M., Payne, A & Ballantyne, D. (2007) *Relationship Marketing: Creating Stakeholder Value*, Butterworth-Heinemann, Oxford.

Doyle P. & Stern P. (2006) *Marketing management and strategy.* 4th edition. FT Prentice Hall, Harlow.

Drummond, G. Ensor, J. & Ashford, R. (2008) *Strategic Marketing Planning and Control.* 3rd edition. Elsevier, Oxford.

Grönroos, C. (2000) *Service Management and Marketing.* Wiley, Chichester.

Gummesson, E. (2002) *Total Relationship Marketing: Rethinking Marketing Management.* 2nd edition. Butterworth Heinemann, Oxford.

Hamel, G. (1996) 'Strategy as revolution'. *Harvard Business Review.* July-August, pp69-81.

Hooley, G., Nicoulaud, B. & Piercy, N (2011) *Marketing Strategy and Competitive Positioning.* 5th edition. Pearson, Harlow.

Jeannet, J-P. & Hennessey, H. (2004) *Global Marketing Strategies.* 6th edition. Houghton Mifflin (Academic).

Johnson, G., Scholes, K. & Whittington, R (2011) *Exploring Strategy*, 9th edition. Pearson, Harlow.

Kotler, P. (2001) *Kotler on Marketing.* Free Press, New York.

Ohmae, K. (1999) *The Borderless World: Power and Strategy in the Interlinked Economy*. Harper Business, London.

Tidd, J & Bessant, J (2009) *Managing Innovation: Integrating Technological, Market and Organisational Change*, 4th edition. Wiley, Chichester.

QUICK QUIZ

1   What constitutes a brand?

2   Who benefits from branding?

3   Identify two strategies for NPD.

4   What is relationship marketing?

5   What are some of the environmental factors stimulating the need for alliances?

6   List some purposes of acquisitions.

7   What is the biggest problem with relying upon organic growth?

8   Outline the process of new product development.

9   If a significant growth strategy is 'expanding the horizon', what is a 'big idea'?

10   What is repositioning?

11   Give some of the differences between transactional and relationship marketing.

12   What is brand equity?

Activity 7.1

1   They are collaborations between two or more competing companies of similar strength, generally from industrialised countries.

2   The relative contributions by the companies are balanced.

3   The motivation for the alliance is generally broadly strategic or competitive, rather than purely for market access or economies of scale.

4   The relationships are reciprocal and provide the opportunity for learning.

5   They have a strategic and global focus, and seek to enhance global competitiveness via gaining access to a whole series of resources and skills.

Activity 7.2

The classic example in the UK is Hoover, which is now a generic term for any vacuum cleaner and is even used as a verb meaning 'to clean with a vacuum cleaner'. Words you may be surprised to know were once brand names include nylon, aspirin, cellophane and escalator: all have lost trade mark legal status. Kleenex and Xerox almost went the same way.

QUICK QUIZ ANSWERS

1   A branded product has a distinctive identity and added values that exist in the consumer's mind

2   All parties to the transaction: the customers and the management and owners of the supplying company

3   Leader and follower

4   The management of the company's marketing relationships

5   Scarce resources
    Increased competition
    Higher customer expectations
    Pressures from strong distributors
    Internationalisation of markets
    Changing markets and technologies
    Turbulent and unpredictable markets

6   Marketing advantages
    Production advantages
    Finance and management
    Risk-spreading
    Independence
    Overcome barriers to entry

7   It takes a very long time

8   Stage 1

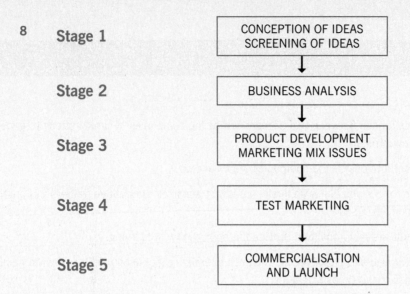

Stage 1 — CONCEPTION OF IDEAS / SCREENING OF IDEAS

Stage 2 — BUSINESS ANALYSIS

Stage 3 — PRODUCT DEVELOPMENT / MARKETING MIX ISSUES

Stage 4 — TEST MARKETING

Stage 5 — COMMERCIALISATION AND LAUNCH

9   A 'breakthrough'

10   Brand repositioning is a competitive strategy aimed at changing position to increase market share.

11
Transaction	Relationship
Importance of single sale	Importance of customer relation
Importance of product features	Importance of customer benefits
Short time scale	Longer time scale
Less emphasis on service	High customer service
Quality is concern of production	Quality is concern of all
Competitive commitment	High customer commitment
Persuasive communication	Regular communication

12   Brand equity is the asset the marketer builds to ensure continuity of satisfaction for the customer and profit for the supplier.

CHAPTER 8

International marketing strategy

Introduction

This chapter deals with the complexities faced in competing internationally. These topics are relevant to all commercial organisations, including those that might feel they are not active internationally. This is because all companies are likely to have suppliers, customers or competitors who are themselves involved in international business operations.

In Section 1, we offer an overview of some of the issues a firm faces when competing overseas. A huge variety of factors have to be dealt with.

In Section 2 we examine specific issues related to new countries and markets. For example, the importance of new technology is without doubt – but technology is influential in different ways, depending on the economic development of each market. Cultural issues also feature very significantly in the difficulties facing firms seeking to do international business.

Topic list

Marketing internationally   ①

Understanding international markets   ②

Standardisation versus customisation   ③

2.2.2	Critically evaluate the appropriateness of developing an international marketing strategy for an organisation investing in international markets:
	▪ Access to low cost materials and labour
	▪ Economies of scale
	▪ Avoiding or bypassing trade barriers
	▪ Access to national/regional incentives eg DFID/Government funding, gateways to strategic markets
2.2.3	Critically evaluate a range of issues that impact on an organisation when entering new countries and markets and consider how they may be managed to achieve the organisation's objectives:
	▪ Extent of global coverage
	▪ Sequence of countries and timing of entry
	▪ Value proposition for global markets
	▪ Standardisation versus customisation
3.1.2	Assess an organisation's readiness for developing a global strategy including:
	▪ Strategic importance of the market
	▪ Position of competitors internationally
	▪ Cost effectiveness
	▪ Barriers to trade

1 Marketing internationally

'Businesses are increasingly able, or indeed compelled, to compete on a world scale.' Drummond *et al* (2008)

1.1 Globalisation

Globalisation of business has a number of aspects and can mean many things, however, it has attracted a great deal of criticism but it can facilitate:

- Relaxation of trade barriers for goods and services
- Free flow of investment capital
- International co-operation and standardisation
- Growth of international business organisations

For companies and marketers, globalisation offers the opportunity to enter new markets. Sound marketing principles still apply but there is no doubt that global marketing is more complex (and risky) than marketing at home.

Conversely, globalisation offers increased competitors to domestic producers.

Key issues for marketers

- Characteristics of overseas markets
- Can the same segmentation and positioning strategies be adopted?
- Is there a global market, or equivalent segments within each country market?
- Impact of culture and regulation on resourcing, distribution, advertising and promotion
- Management and structure of overseas operations

The Chartered
Institute of Marketing

Manchester United

Manchester United is building its own branded social network and media outlet, with the aim of targeting its international base of around 350 million supporters.

The club is working with an integrated marketing services agency – SapientNitro – to design an build a digital platform which will be rolled out over 2012-2013 and will then provide a network for Manchester United fans worldwide.

The club has identified a worldwide target audience of more than 500 million fans, after research agency TNS estimated a potential global audience of 660 million people with an allegiance to the club.

The club's new digital platform will host multimedia content (including behind-the-scenes clips, and video content from the players) and will offer advertising and sponsorship opportunities for brands. It will also sell items such as club merchandise through an e-commerce function.

However, the main driver behind the platform is to increase engagement with the club's fan and tap into Asian markets, where Manchester United already has a strong following, and where smartphone usage is increasingly rapidly.

Interestingly, though, as at July 2012, Manchester United's Facebook page had only attracted nearly 27 million fans (out of more than 900 million Facebook users) so some critics have wondered how Manchester United plans to get 500 million fans to sign up for its new platform.

Based on: Shearman, S (2011) Manchester United to unveil global social-media network, *Marketing*, 1 November 2011, www.marketingmagazine.co.uk

1.2 Should the strategy be global?

▶ **Key terms**

A **global strategy** is representative of 'a worldwide perspective in which the interrelationship between country markets are drawn on to create synergies, economies of scale, strategic flexibility and opportunities to leverage insights, programmes, and production economies'. (Aaker & McLoughlin, 2007)

In contrast, a **multinational strategy** is one in which separate strategies are developed for a series of country markets, and implemented autonomously.

Table 8.1 Motivations for a global strategy

Obtain scale economies	Product, marketing, operations
Create global associations	A global presence symbolises strength
Access low cost labour and materials	Such access can be a source of competitive advantage, but flexibility is needed. See also the 'Marketing at Work' example below, on the dangers
Access to investment incentives	Countries use these to attract investment in targeted/depressed areas
Cross subsidisation	A global strategy allows resources generated in one area to back up efforts in another
Dodge trade barriers	Strategic location of assembly plant can help gain access to markets and foster goodwill
Access to strategically important markets	Important because of size of market resources, trends and developments, and technology

Aaker & McLoughlin (2007, p209) give the following indicators that a company strategy needs to be a global one.

- Its major competitors have a presence in several countries

- Standardisation provides opportunities for scale economies

- Costs can be reduced, and effectiveness increased, by locating value-adding activities in different countries

- The company can use sales volumes and profits from one market to help invest and gain position in another

- A global name is available

- The brand's positioning and advertising will work across countries

- Local markets do not necessarily require a local operation

The following issues need to be addressed:

- Should the firm become global by entering new countries?
- What countries, and in what sequence?
- Should the product/service be standardised?
- Should the brand/marketing activities be standardised?
- How do you manage a global brand?
- Should strategic alliances be used to enter new countries?

ACTIVITY 8.1

Give reasons why a company might want to implement its global strategy on a gradual, country-by-country basis.

Why might a 'full frontal' assault on several countries at once have its advantages?

1.3 Hostility to globalisation

A number of pressure groups have emerged, linked in their hostility to global capitalism. Thanks, possibly, to better communications and the Internet, they are able to co-ordinate their activities on a worldwide scale. Indeed, the anti-globalisation brigade has spawned its own anti-marketing literature. Naomi Klein's book, No Logo (2001), is a key text on the anti-capitalist reading list. In particular she attacks **brands**. Perhaps marketers need to go back to fundamentals as to what brands actually promise.

Globalisation is blamed for environmental degradation and global inequality, standardisation and the destruction of local cultures – all under the control of multinational firms which, it is said, are greedy, exploitative and are not democratically accountable.

THE REAL WORLD

Research published by the charity 'War on Want' (July 2011) highlighted that 85% of the garment workers in Bangladeshi factories which supply garments for Nike, Puma and Adidas are women, and, if the sewing machine operators meet their monthly production targets their salaries start at 3,860 taka (approximately £32 per month).

War on Want's report argues that these wages fall far short of the level which could be considered a living wage – that is, enough to allow a worker to provide her family with basic human necessities such as food, shelter, clothing, water, health, education and transport.

The Chartered
Institute of Marketing

Trade unionist in Bangladesh have calculated that the living wage for a single worker is at least 5,000 taka (approximately £42) per month, while the women interviewed in the research project estimated that the average monthly household expenditure for a family of four is around 8,900 taka per month.

According to Bangladeshi law, workers are supposed to work eight-hour shifts. However, garment workers are forced to work extra hours on a daily basis in order to meet the unrealistic production targets set by factory owners. Their wages are dependent on meeting production targets, but any extra hours worked to meet the targets are not considered overtime and are therefore unpaid. In their report, War on Want claim that 32% of the 998 women workers they interviewed work more than 100 overtime every month.

They also point out that only 37% of the workers they interviewed had received letters of appointment from their employers, while only 68% had factory identity cards despite both being legal requirements which serve as evidence of employment. This evidence of employment also forms the legal framework which enables workers to claim their basic labour rights such as the right to receive a wage, plus payment for overtime.

Based on: War on Want (2011) *Stitched Up: Women workers in the Bangladeshi garment sector*. July 2011.

2 Understanding international markets

2.1 PEST factors

PEST factors are all key issues in a firm's **domestic** environment. The same factors apply when we are discussing a firm's international exposure – they just become more complex.

An organisation is subject to the following international influences.

1   In times of increasing free trade, firms can expect **incoming competition**. That said, the possibility of competing abroad is also available.

2   A firm can **attract investment** from overseas institutions. Competing firms from overseas can receive investments from domestic institutions. For example, non-UK banks paid large sums to acquire UK stock brokers and investment firms.

3   The **barrier** between the domestic and international environment is relatively **permeable**.

4   **Political factors** and **legal factors** include the following.

    (a)   **Political conditions** in individual foreign markets (eg package tour firms and the Middle East after terrorist shootings of tourists) or sources of supply (eg risk of nationalisation)

    (b)   **Relationships between governments** (eg trade disputes in relation to perceived 'dumping' or other abuses of international trade rules)

    (c)   Activities of **supranational** institutions (eg EU regulations on packaging / recycling)

    (d)   **Laws and regulations** (eg EU emission standards for exhaust emissions from new cars sold in EU member states)

5   **Economic factors**

    (a)   The overall level of **economic activity**
    (b)   The relative levels of **inflation** in the domestic and overseas market
    (c)   The **exchange rate**
    (d)   The **relative prosperity** of individual overseas markets
    (e)   **Economic growth** in newly industrialised countries
    (f)   A shift towards **market economies**

The environment of international trade may be analysed in the same way as the domestic environment, though it has its own special features, including international political relationships, supranational institutions, a variety of currencies and a wider range of social and economic influences.

6   **Social and cultural factors**

   (a)   The **cultures and practices** of customers and consumers in individual markets
   (b)   The **media and distribution** systems in overseas markets
   (c)   The differences of **ways of doing business**
   (d)   The degree to which **national** cultural differences matter
   (e)   The degree to which a firm can use its own **national culture as a selling point**

7   **Technological factors**

   (a)   The degree to which a firm can **imitate** the technology of its competitors
   (b)   A firm's access to domestic and overseas **patents**
   (c)   **Intellectual property** protection
   (d)   **Technology transfer** requirements
   (e)   The relative **cost** of technology compared to labour
   (f)   The **competence of potential service contractors** in the target country

---

▶ Exam tip

In almost any question in this syllabus, PEST (or PESTEL) factors can be brought in, but be very careful to make them relevant to the context of the question.

When deciding which country to enter, there are several initial questions to be asked:

- Is the market attractive in terms of size and growth?
- How intense is the competition?
- Can the firm add value?
- Do operational or cultural barriers exist?
- Can a critical mass be achieved?

Aaker & McLoughlin (2007) describe four kinds of 'distance' between countries.

- **Geographic** (affecting distance, access, borders, climate)
- **Administrative** (government policies, taxes, politics, exchange rates, trade barriers)
- **Cultural** (language, religions, social norms)
- **Economic** (income levels, infrastructure, costs)

2.2 The political and legal framework

At some time, most companies engaged in international marketing suffer because of the political or legal structure of a country.

2.2.1 Political risk

Political factors offer extra risks to the exporter, in terms of the stability of the country, the attitude of the government to trade generally and to the company in particular.

The **level of risk** involved will depend on several factors.

- The attitudes of the country's **government**
- The **product** being traded
- The **company** wishing to trade

▶ Key term

Political risk is the possibility of turbulence (eg civil war, revolution, changes in government policy) in the political environment.

The Chartered
Institute of Marketing

2.2.2 Government

The development of plans for international marketing will depend on the following factors.

1 **The stability of the government**. Rapid changes or political unrest make it difficult to estimate reactions to an importer or a foreign business.

2 **International relations**. The government's attitude to the firm's home government or country may affect trading relations.

3 The **ideology** of the government and its **role in the economy** will affect the way in which the company may be allowed to trade, and this might be embodied in legislation.

4 **Informal relations** between government officials and businesses are important in some countries. Cultivation of the right political contacts may be essential for decisions to be made in your favour.

THE REAL WORLD

In December 2010, the oil and gas companies Royal Dutch Shell (Shell) and Gazprom formed a strategic alliance for three years, following a dispute in 2006 in which Shell was forced – under pressure from the Russian government – to cede control of the giant Sakhalin-2 oil and gas project to the Russian company.

However, Prime Minister Vladimir Putin then invited Shell to participate in the nearby Sakhalin-3 and Sakhalin-4 oil and gas project during a meeting with the company's CEO in June 2009.

This partnership will assist these two power houses to deepen co-operation in Russia, and to work together in other countries. However, the agreement also signals Gazprom's recognition that it needs foreign allies to help globalise its gas business and expand further into oil.

Alexander Medvedev, Gazprom's deputy chief executive, said. "We are happy to invite foreign partners to develop our upstream reserves, but only if we get access to first-class projects somewhere else in the world."

Based on extracts from: Shiryaevskaya, A. (2011) Shell said to offer Gazprom assets to expand LNG Plant, *Bloomberg*, 8 February 2011, www.bloomberg.com

---

2.2.3 The product

The nature of the goods or services being offered may affect the **degree of interest which a government takes** in a particular trading deal. Generally the more important the goods to the economy or the government, the more interest will be taken.

2.2.4 The company wishing to trade

The previous relations of the company (and its home country) with the host country can affect the risk to the company. **Factors influencing the company's acceptability** include the:

- Relations between the company's home government and the overseas government
- Size of company
- Past relations and reputation of the company in dealing with foreign governments
- Degree of local employment and autonomy of operations generated by the activity

2.2.5 Expropriation and other dangers

Political risk is still relevant with regard to overseas investment, especially in large infrastructure projects overseas. History contains dismal tales of investment projects that went wrong, and were **expropriated** (nationalised) by the local government.

- **Suspicion** of foreign ownership is still rife, especially when prices are raised.

- Opposition politicians can appeal to **nationalism** by claiming the government sold out to foreigners.

- Governments might want to **renegotiate** a deal to get a better bargain, at a later date, thereby affecting return on investment.

In addition to expropriation, there are other dangers.

- Restrictions on **profit repatriation** (eg for currency reasons)
- **Cronyism** and **corruption** leading to unfair favouring of some companies over others
- Arbitrary changes in **taxation**
- **Pressure group** activity

There are many sources of data. The Economist Intelligence Unit offers assessment of risk. Management consultants can also be contacted. Companies should ask the following six questions (according to Jeannet & Hennessey, 2004).

1   How stable is the host country's political system?

2   How strong is the host government's commitment to specific rules of the game, such as ownership or contractual rights, given its ideology and power position?

3   How long is the government likely to remain in power?

4   If the present government is succeeded, how would the specific rules of the game change?

5   What would be the effects of any expected changes in the specific rules of the game?

6   In light of those effects, what decisions and actions should be taken now?

2.2.6 Coping with political risk

The approach taken depends on the **degree of risk** and the **level of involvement**.

Figure 8.1   **Strategies for coping with political risk**

Level of Involvement

	Low	High
High	• Keep low profile • Communicate via third parties • High level contracts • Short-term deals • Export credit insurance	• Contingency plans • Disinvest? • Act for stability?
Low	No need to worry	No need to worry – but monitor for increasing riskiness

(Left axis label: **Level of risk**)

Measures to **reduce political risk**:

- Use **local partners** with good contacts

- **Vertical integration** of activities over a number of different countries

- **Local borrowing** (although not a good idea in high inflation countries)

- **Leasing** rather than outright purchase of facilities in overseas markets

- Take out **insurance**

2.3 Legal factors

Legal factors in individual markets include product regulations and control over the marketing mix generally. Human resource usage is also determined by legal factors.

In international markets we are interested in legislation which may affect a firm's trade with a particular country.

- Domestic legal system

The Chartered
Institute of Marketing

- Structure of company law
- Local laws

Legal implications extend far beyond the marketing mix. Each country may legislate on issue, and these may affect the marketer to a greater or lesser degree. Here are some examples.

- **Export and import controls** for political, environmental, or health and safety reasons. Such controls may not be overt but instead take the form of bureaucratic procedures designed to discourage international trade or protect home producers.

- **Law of ownership**. Especially in developing countries, there may be legislation requiring local majority ownership of a firm or its subsidiary in that country.

- **Acceptance of international trademark, copyright and patent conventions**. Not all countries recognise such international conventions.

2.4 Protectionism in international trade

Although trade has benefits, many countries have sought to limit its effects in order to **protect** local producers. In the long-term this serves to harm economic welfare as resources are not allocated where they are most productive.

> ▶ **Key term**
>
> **Protectionism** is the discouraging of imports by raising tariff barriers, imposing quotas etc in order to favour local producers.

Some governments seek to prevent the influence of international trade by making it harder to import from overseas.

- **Tariffs**
- Import **quotas and embargoes**

- **Subsidies** for domestic producers
- Exchange **controls**
- Exchange rate policy
- Non-tariff **barriers**

2.4.1 Tariffs

A **tariff** is a **tax on imports**. The government **raises revenue** and domestic producers may expand sales, but **consumers** pay higher prices if they buy imported goods. They may have to buy domestic goods of a lesser quality.

2.4.2 Import quotas

Import quotas are **restrictions** on the quantity of product allowed to be imported into a country. The restrictions can be imposed by **import licences** (in which case the government gets additional revenue) or simply by granting the right to import only to certain producers.

2.4.3 Minimum local content rules

Related to quotas is a requirement that, to avoid tariffs or other restrictions, products should be made **in** the country or region in which they are sold. In the EU the product must be of a specified **minimum local content** (80% in the EU) to qualify as being 'home' or 'EU-made'. This is one of the reasons Japanese and Korean manufacturers have set up factories in Europe.

2.4.4 Minimum prices and anti-dumping action

Dumping is the sale of a product in an overseas market at a price lower than charged in the domestic market. **Anti-dumping measures** include establishing quotas, minimum prices or extra excise duties.

2.4.5 Embargoes

An embargo on imports from one particular country is a **total ban**, a zero quota. An embargo may have a political motive, and may deprive consumers at home of the supply of an important product.

2.4.6 Subsidies for domestic producers

An enormous range of government **subsidies** and assistance for exporters is offered, such as **export credit guarantees** (insurance against bad debts for overseas sales), financial help and assistance from government departments in promoting and selling products. The effect of these grants is to make unit production costs lower. These may give the domestic producer a **cost advantage** over foreign producers in export as well as domestic markets.

2.4.7 Exchange controls and exchange rate policy

Many countries have **exchange control regulations** designed to make it difficult for importers to obtain the currency they need to buy foreign goods.

If a government allows its currency to depreciate, imports will become more expensive. Importers may cut their profit margins and keep prices at their original levels for a while, but sooner or later prices of imports will rise. A policy of exchange rate depreciation in this context is referred to as a **competitive devaluation**.

2.4.8 Unofficial non-tariff barriers

Some countries are accused of having **unofficial barriers to trade**, perpetrated by government. Here are some examples.

- **Quality and inspection procedures** for imported products, adding to time and cost for the companies selling them.
- **Packaging and labelling** requirements may be rigorous, **safety and performance** standards difficult to satisfy and **documentation procedures** very laborious.
- Standards which are much easier for domestic manufacturers to adhere to.
- Restrictions over **physical distribution**.
- Toleration of **anti-competitive practices** at home.

ACTIVITY 8.2

Why might a US car manufacturer support protectionist policies, despite the effects of restraining trade, and a Swedish manufacturer choose to oppose protectionist measures?

2.5 Economic structure and development

Economic factors include the overall level of growth and stage of development, frequently measured by GDP. The balance of payments is an influence on government policy.

Economic factors affect the demand for, and the ability to acquire, goods and services. Even in **lesser developed countries** (see below) there often exists a wealthy elite who provide a significant demand for sophisticated consumer goods.

Countries generally have larger agricultural sectors in the early stages of economic development (for example India and Africa). As the economy develops, the manufacturing sector increases.

Selected figures (2011) for contributions to GDP by industry sector:

Country	Agricultural (%)	Industrial (%)	Services (%)
United Kingdom	0.7	21.4	77.8
United States	1.2	22.1	76.7
China	10.1	46.8	43.1
India	18.1	26.3	55.6
Ghana	28.3	21.0	50.7
Malawi	30.3	16.7	53.0
Sierra Leone	51.5	22.0	28.5
World average	6.1	31.1	62.9

Source: CIA, The World Factbook, www.cia.gov

2.5.1 Level of economic development

GDP on a **per capita** basis, suitably adjusted for purchasing power, is probably the **best single indicator of economic development**.

A danger in using GDP is that it considers only the **average**. The **distribution of wealth** is critical in poor countries, where a market may exist amongst above average sections of the population.

2.5.2 Classification of economic development

Generally each country can be classified under one of five headings.

> ▶ **Key terms**
>
> **Lesser developed country (LDC)**. Relies heavily on primary industries (mining, agriculture, forestry, fishing) with low GDP per capita, and poorly developed infrastructure.
>
> **Early developed country (EDC)**. Largely primary industry based, but with developing secondary (manufacturing) industrial sector. Low but growing GDP, developing infrastructure.
>
> **Semi-developed country (SDC)**. Significant secondary sector still growing. Rising affluence and education with the emergence of a 'middle class'. Developed infrastructure.
>
> **Fully developed country (FDC)**. Primary sector accounts for little of the economy. Secondary sector still dominates, but major growth in tertiary (service) sector. Sophisticated infrastructure.

2.5.3 Measuring levels of economic development

Measures that may be used by the international marketer include the following.

- **GDP** per head

- **Source of GDP** (primary, secondary or tertiary sector based economy)

- **Living standards** (ownership of key durables may be used as a surrogate measure)

- **Energy** availability and usage

- **Education** levels

2.5.4 Identifying market size

The economic worth of a consumer market is based on some general factors.

- The **number of people** in the market
- Their **desire to own** the goods
- Their **ability to purchase** the goods

Thus in measuring a market, the marketer will obtain information on the following, although they are often crude measures.

- **Population**.
  Its size, growth and age structure, household composition, urban v rural distribution. Household size and spatial distribution affect demand for many consumer goods.

- **Income**.
  GDP per head is a crude measure of wealth and account should also be taken of distribution of GDP among various social groups, and their purchasing power.

- **Consumption patterns**.
  The ownership of various goods and the consumption of consumables are indicators of potential demand.

- **Debt and inflation**.
  A high level of debt in a country may indicate import controls (or their possible introduction) or weak currency and currency controls. Inflation may affect purchasing power. In either case ability to pay will be reduced.

- **Physical environment**.
  Physical distance, climate and topography will affect demand in various ways. The availability of natural resources can directly affect demand for equipment and so on to exploit these resources.

- **Foreign trade**.
  The trade relations of a country will affect the attitude towards foreign goods. Factors include economic relations (for example, a member of same economic group such as the EU) and balance of trade.

THE REAL WORLD

Novartis, China

In November 2009, the Swiss pharmaceutical giant Novartis, announced plans to invest $1.25 billion over five years in a pair of research and development centres in China. $250 million will be invested in a new R&D centre in Changshi (near Shanghai) while $1 billion will be spent adding 1,000 new researchers to an existing centre in Shanghai.

The investment will make Shanghai one of Novartis' top three global research bases, alongside Basel (in Switzerland) and Cambridge, Massachusetts.

Novartis' investment in Shanghai reflects its plan to tap into one of the world's fastest growing health-care markets. Speaking after the investment, Novartis' Chairman and CEO, Daniel Vasella, said that the rate at which sales have been growing in China mean that it will be among the company's top three markets in five to seven years.

Earlier in 2009, the Chinese government had outlined plans for a massive expansion of its health-care coverage. In April, the State Council announced China would spend $124 billion over the next three years to widen insurance coverage to include many more of China's millions of rural residents, as well as building thousands of community health-care centres to provide a range of basic services, including access to drugs and vaccinations.

Commentators also noted that it no coincidence that Novartis' in China came at the same time that health care reform was being debated in the US, with a view to reducing American spending on pharmaceutical drugs.

Mr Vasella highlighted the contrasting circumstances the US and China. ' The US is overly indebted, has invested a high percentage in health care, and has an ageing population, so its health bill will increase. So a counter movement will be cost containment… [But] China has a dynamically growing economy, and they have lots of money and no debt. And they you have the willingness of the government to cover many more of its citizens. There will be growth.'

Summarised from: Roberts, D. (2009) Novartis unveils $1.25 billion China investment, *Bloomberg Businessweek*, 3 November 2009, www.businessweek.com

---

The Chartered Institute of Marketing

2.6 Regional trading groups

Regional trading blocs promote trade between countries in groups. The environment of world trade is becoming freer, globally, with the influence of the World Trade Organisation.

Currently, a number of **regional trading arrangements** exist, as well as global trading arrangements. These regional trading groups take three forms.

- Free trade areas
- Customs unions
- Common markets

2.6.1 Free trade areas

Members in these arrangements agree to lower barriers to trade amongst themselves. They enable free movement of **goods** and **services**, but not always the factors of production.

2.6.2 Customs unions

Customs unions provide the advantages of free trade areas and agree a common policy on tariff and non-tariff barriers to **external countries**. Internally they attempt to harmonise tariffs, taxes and duties amongst members.

2.6.3 Economic unions/common markets

In effect the members become one for economic purposes. There is free movement of the factors of production. The EU has economic union as an aim, although not all members, including the UK, necessarily see this goal as desirable. The EU has a 'rich' market of over 300 million people and could provide a counterweight to countries such as the USA and Japan.

Figure 8.2   **Types of trade associations**

The major regional trade organisations are as follows.

- North American Free Trade Agreement (**NAFTA**) – US, Canada and Mexico.

- European Free Trade Association (**EFTA**) – Norway, Switzerland, Iceland, Liechtenstein.

- European Union (**EU**) – Ireland, United Kingdom, France, Germany, Italy, Spain, Portugal, Finland, Sweden, Denmark, Luxembourg, Belgium, Netherlands, Austria, Greece, Bulgaria, Cyprus, Czech Republic, Estonia, Hungary, Latvia, Lithuania, Malta, Poland, Romania, Slovakia, Slovenia.

- Asian Free Trade Area (**AFTA**; a trade bloc agreement by the Association of Southeast Asian Nations (ASEAN)) – Brunei, Cambodia, Indonesia, Laos, Malaysia, Myanmar, Philippines, Singapore, Thailand, Vietnam.

- Asia-Pacific Economic Co-operation (**APEC**) – Australia, Brunei, Malaysia, Singapore, Thailand, New Zealand, Papua New Guinea, Indonesia, Philippines, Taiwan, Hong Kong, Japan, South Korea, China, Canada, US, Mexico, Chile.

- **Mercosur** – Brazil, Argentina, Paraguay, Uruguay and Venezuela (Associate members: Bolivia, Chile, Columbia, Ecuador, Peru).

- Southern African Development Community (**SADC**); Angola, Botswana, Congo, Lesotho, Malawi, Mozambique, Mauritius, Namibia, Seychelles, South Africa, Swaziland, Tanzania, Zambia, Zimbabwe.

- West African Economic and Monetary Union (**UEMOA**) – Ivory Cost, Burkina Faso, Nigeria, Togo, Senegal, Benin, Mali, Cape Verde, Gambia, Ghana, Guinea-Bissau, Liberia and Sierra Leone.

- South Asian Association for Regional Co-operation (**SAARC**) – India, Pakistan, Sri Lanka, Bangladesh, Maldives, Bhutan, Nepal and Afghanistan.

- **Andean Pact** – Venezuela, Ecuador, Peru and Bolivia.

- Union of South American Nations (**UNASUR**) – integrates the two existing customs unions of Mercosur and the Andean Community.

THE REAL WORLD

Mercosur

Venezuela joined Mercosure in 2012, but growing protectionism within the bloc's leading economies, coupled with political posturing, have reduced the effectiveness of the bloc.

When Argentina and Brazil teamed up with Paraguay and Uruguay to form the customs union in 1995, they hope to boost regional trade and investment by forming a bigger market along the lines of the European Union.

Since 1995, trade within Mercosur has quadrupled - to $51 billion in 2011 - but with economic growth slowing and Argentina and Brazil locked in a series of trade disputes over everything from cars to olives, analysts expect it to fall this year.

"Argentina is seen as hostile to foreign capital, Paraguay is fragile and unstable, Uruguay has an open economy but it's very small, and Brazil continues to draw investment. Mercosur, as a whole, does not," said Jose Botafogo Goncalves, a former Brazilian diplomat and representative to the bloc.

The decision to allow Venezuela to join Mercosur has stirred further controversy within the group and fueled criticism that it has become little more than a political club for left-leaning leaders who harbor ambitions of Latin American unity.

Free Trade?

When Mercosur was first established, the only products that were not part of the 'free trade' rules were automobiles and sugar. All other goods were supposed to be traded freely within the bloc or gradually stripped of duties.

This goal was largely being met until Argentina expanded the use of non-automatic import licenses in 2011 and imposed a new system to pre-approve nearly all purchases abroad in February 2012.

In May 2012, Brazil and Argentina got Mercosur's approval to raise import tariffs on up to 200 products of their own choosing (thereby further diluting the objectives of a common tariff) on the grounds that each nation must protect its industry as economies get hit by fallout from Europe's debt crisis.

In an effort to try to safeguard its own trade surplus, Argentina has used the non-automatic licenses and new approvals system to block imports, affecting goods such as farm machinery and textiles from Brazil and shoes and food products from Uruguay.

This represents a clear violation of Mercosur principles, but the response from within Mercosur has been muted grumbling and a raft of reprisals by Brazil's government, which like Argentina is under pressure to revive flagging local industry.

Brazil has sporadically restricted the entry of some Argentine goods, including fruit, olive oil and cookies.

The decision by Argentina and Brazil to virtually abandon the common external tariff - the backbone of Mercosur – allows individual members to raise tariffs as high as 35 percent, compared with current levels of about 10 percent to 12 percent.

The Chartered Institute of Marketing

The tension between Mercosur's two heavyweights (Brazil and Argentina) have also proved a headache for the bloc's smaller members. All three of Uruguay's car assembly plants - run by Chery Socma, Nordex SA and Effa Motors - have threatened to close and have laid off hundreds of employees since October 2011, when import restrictions in Argentina and Brazil began taking a toll on their shipments.

Based on: Nejamkis, G. (2012) Venezuela joins trade bloc big on politics, protectionism, *Reuters*, 30 July 2012, www.news.yahoo.com

2.6.4 Regional trading agreements and the global market

Regional trading blocs only extend the benefits of free trade to their members. They may distort **global** trading patterns.

There is a widely held idea that the industrial world is falling into **three trading blocs**, each led by a lead country. (This is called the 'Triad' theory.)

- The EU (led by Germany)
- The Americas (led by the USA) and particularly NAFTA
- The Far East and Pacific Rim (led by Japan)

Trading within the blocs would be relatively **liberalised** but there would be **barriers to competition** from outside. The blocs would trade with each other, but this would be more restricted. Countries would have to try to attach themselves to one of the blocs.

Non-bloc countries were not seen as terribly important. Given that some non-bloc countries (eg India and China) are likely to be some of the world's largest and fastest growing markets, suggestions to restrict trade to bloc countries are short-sighted. The Chinese economy, for example is growing at over 10% per annum.

The theory of trading blocs does not provide a complete analysis of world trade.

- The bloc theory works better for some industries than others.

    - The EU and US have had extensive programmes to protect agriculture, to the outrage of more efficient producers (such as the Cairns Group representing Australia and some other countries).

    - Even in sensitive industries aerospace, there is free trade.

- The bloc theory does not really take **investment flows** into account.

- The bloc theory does not account for all **trade** flows. The US is Japan's most significant **individual** export market, although East Asia as a region has overtaken the US as a market for Japanese's goods.

- The **World Trade Organisation** (WTO) regulates world trade.

- **Knowledge-based industries** (which many writers believe are the motors of future economic growth) are hard to evaluate and control. **Technology** might make ideas as to trading blocs obsolete.

- All trading blocs have extensive economic interactions with **third world countries**. They will have a growing relationship with countries in the former Soviet Union which have recently entered the global market.

A significant effect of regional trade blocs has been the rush to qualify for **local status** by multinational firms. This has been achieved by the multinationals setting up within one or more member states. Thus France, Germany and the UK have seen considerable inward investment from US and Japanese firms.

2.7 Social issues

Social factors include overall global population growth, and the disparity between the ageing and stable (in numbers) populations of the developed world, with the young and growing populations of lesser developed countries. In individual markets, **culture** can be a determining factor of marketing success.

The higher rate of population growth in **less-developed countries** compared with developed countries has arisen due to a continuing high birth rate and a declining death rate although some populations are being threatened by the HIV virus (for example, in South Africa). Social changes (eg attitudes to large families) have not accompanied medical advances imported from developed societies. People are living longer.

Growing populations

- Require fast economic growth just to maintain living standards
- Result in overcrowding on land and/or cities and a decline in the quality of life
- Require more resources for capital investment
- Stimulate investment (as the market size is increasing)
- Lead to enhanced labour mobility

Falling populations

- Require more productive techniques to maintain output
- Make some scale economies harder to achieve
- Put a greater burden on a decreasing number of young people
- Exhibit changing consumption patterns

2.7.1 Buying patterns

Buying behaviour is an important aspect of marketing. Many factors influence the buying decisions of individuals and households. Demography and the **class structure** (the distribution of wealth and power in a society) are relevant in that they can be both **behavioural determinants** and **inhibitors**.

- **Behavioural determinants** encourage people to buy a product or service. The individual's personality, culture, social class, and the importance of the purchase decision (eg a necessity such as food or water, or a luxury) can predispose a person to purchase something.

- **Inhibitors** are factors, such as the individual's income, which will make the person less likely to purchase something.

Socio-economic status can be related to buying patterns in a number of ways, both in the amount people have to spend and what they spend it on. It affects both the quantity of goods and services supplied, and the proportion of their income that households spend on goods and services.

THE REAL WORLD

Global retail expansion

The 2012 Global Retail Development Index (GRDI) produced by A.T. Kearney's Global Consumer Institute revealed that Brazil is the most attractive market for retail investment for the second year in a row.

The GRDI is a ranking of the top 30 developing countries for global retail expansion. Brazil benefits from a growing middle class economy, high consumption rates, a large, urban population, and reduced political and financial risk. In addition, Brazil's relatively young population and high per capita spending in the apparel and luxury sectors make this country a top destination for specialty retailers.

However, the 2012 GRDI also highlighted that while the world's largest developing markets – particularly the BRIC nations of Brazil, Russia, India, and China – still tempt the largest global retailers, and show no signs of slowing down as a source of growth, many smaller, untapped markets are now providing new growth opportunities.

New countries in the 2012 Index include several "small gems" such as Georgia (ranked 6th), Oman (8th), Mongolia (9th) and Azerbaijan (17th). These countries are showing progress as attractive destinations for global retailers, particularly specialty and luxury players. Although they are relatively small in terms of their total retail market size, they have strong fundamentals that appeal to retailers targeting a concentration of wealth and seeking to be first movers in fast-growing markets.

Overall, the 2012 study highlighted that developing countries are positioning themselves as value global retail markets for luxury brands looking to expand in these areas. Luxury goods sales in the US and Europe are not growing as fast as these markets. However, the study also highlights that luxury is not restricted to large countries, and there is enough wealth in small countries like Azerbaijan and Mongolia to justify the entry of a luxury brand.

See the 2012 GRDI Report at: www.grdi.atkearney.com

The Chartered Institute of Marketing

2.8 Technology

Technology creates new products and industries, and enhances productivity and growth. It also influences the marketing mix.

The history of the past 200 years has been one of enormous economic growth. Many countries are able to support populations which in the early 19th century would have been inconceivable.

Material advances have promoted a large complex of economic, social, political and cultural changes. These changes have included the following.

- **Industrialisation** (eg movement of labour and resources from agriculture to industry) which has been a feature of many overseas markets.

- **Modernisation** (urbanisation, reduction in death rates, centralising government and so forth).

2.8.1 Technological development and the marketing mix: a cautionary perspective

Technology, or investment in it, in the narrow sense, cannot on its own promote economic growth. The first use of steam power was discovered, not in 18th century England, but almost 2,000 years before: there was, however, no 'use' for it. Societies with large pools of slave labour had little need for 'labour-saving' inventions.

Modern apparatus and techniques have had very uneven success in 'modernising' underdeveloped countries.

1.   The **environmental consequences** of introducing western technology to underdeveloped countries have been ill thought out.

2.   The **economic consequences** have not been as beneficial as might at first be supposed. The prestigious new production technologies have not worked optimally or even satisfactorily. The problems are two-fold.

   (a)   **Technological dependency** leading to a heavy foreign currency payments burden. The country has to import **spare parts**, and even raw materials, to run machinery. It might have to pay for **expatriate technicians**. This is expensive, and so the costs of the technology might be greater than anticipated, thus reducing any economic benefit.

   (b)   The inappropriateness of Western technology. **Climatic** conditions can affect performance. **Infrastructural** deficiencies such as naturally poor roads affect, for example, the 'good design' of a car. The **labour/capital** mix means that in poor countries, with surplus labour, labour intensive industries rather than labour saving capital equipment might be a better use of resources.

ACTIVITY 8.3

The Republic of Rukwa is a largely agricultural society. For foreign exchange, it is dependent on the exports of kwat. Kwat is a grain which can only be grown in Rukwa's climate. It is, however, widely in demand in Western markets as a 'health' food. Kwat is grown by peasant farmers on small plots of land on banks of the River Ru. At present, the harvested Kwat is transported by ox-drawn barges down the River Ru to Port Ruk for export. The process is slow, owing to bottlenecks on the river. The government is thinking of several alternatives to ease this situation. Rukwa has no other natural resources.

1   Build a high speed road, and use foreign loans to buy lorries and four-wheel drive vehicles for farmers.
2   Build a railway, with imported steel and engines.
3   Widen the River Ru at key points, and purchase outboard motors for the barges.

What do you think is right or wrong with all these alternatives?

The relevance of this to international marketers is as follows.

1 **How do you define customer needs?** Elite groups sometimes 'need' products which are not economically beneficial for society.

2 To what extent do you apply the societal marketing concept to overseas markets?

3 The marketing mix may presuppose a level of **technological development** which is in fact non-existent for large parts of the population.

2.8.2 Level of technological development

The level of technological development in a country is important in the marketing of many products.

- **Understanding how the product is used**: Many products are technically sophisticated and require a level of **technological awareness** that may not be widely available. Technologically aware cultures recognise switches and buttons and instructions almost instinctively.

- **The provision of support services for the product**: Many products require maintenance and spare parts which may be unavailable outside the most technologically advanced economies. The classic solution is known as the **'backward invention'** in which the product is simplified to either the level of support available or, ultimately, the point at which the owner can support the product himself.

- **The existence of an appropriate distribution network**: Certain products require an **infrastructure for their distribution** and use. Thus a TV requires both electricity and a TV transmission service. Telephones require a carrier network. Distribution of medicines and foodstuffs require careful handling and temperature conditions in transit, necessitating specialised and sophisticated transport.

- **Communication with the customer**

ACTIVITY 8.4

A firm has developed a drug which can cure Alzheimer's disease. What factors do you think would distinguish its export marketing efforts to a country in the EU from its export marketing efforts to a country in the Third World?

2.8.3 The internet and globalisation

The internet should also be a force for globalisation, and it increases the 'globalisation potential' of individual industries (Yip, 2000).

Clearly, internet usage varies significantly around the world, with developing economies lagging behind the industrialised world to a large degree. It is important to recognise this difference in coverage around the world, but the internet does still have the potential to increase global commonality in customer needs, to create new global standards, strength the presence of already popular brands, and help develop new ones.

The Chartered Institute of Marketing

Table 8.2   World internet usage by region

Region	Internet usage (%) (2011)	Internet usage (%) (2010)
Africa	13.5	10.9
Asia	26.2	21.5
Europe	61.3	58.4
Middle East	35.6	29.8
North America	78.6	77.4
Latin America	39.5	34.5
Oceania Australia	67.5	61.3
Total	**32.7**	**28.7**

Source: *www.internetworldstats.com*

Yip (2000) highlights several ways in which the internet helps drive globalisation:

1. **The Internet makes it easier to become a global customer**, sourcing products from anywhere in the world. This is probably most relevant to the business-to-business (B2B) market. The web has facilitated the operation of global production and supply networks. For example, Intel accepts more than 95% of its orders through the internet. The emergence of online buying portals suggests the possible efficiencies to be gained from global supply chain management.

2. **The Internet has facilitated the opening up of global distribution channels**, both for traditional 'bricks and mortar' companies as well as those that are entirely web-based. The online retailer Amazon.com is a frequently (perhaps too frequently) cited example of a web-based company. Such distribution channels do however ultimately depend upon physical delivery of goods to the customer by traditional carriers, regardless of how they were ordered, so it is possible that this driver of globalisation is, currently at least, overstated.

3. **The Internet supports global marketing**, both via the ability to reach customers anywhere in the world, and the adoption of global brand names. Electronic media provide opportunities to sell into markets which may not previously have been accessible. The internet makes it possible to sell to a country without having a local sales team there.

   However, a possible downside of the internet for any business hoping to charge different prices to different markets for the same product is that price comparison is made easier. The Internet promotes **price transparency**.

3 Standardisation versus customisation

Entry into foreign markets mandates decisions about whether or not to adopt the marketing mix to local conditions. The choice is between standardising the product in all markets to reap the advantages of scale economies in manufacture and, on the other hand, adaptation which gives the advantages of flexible response to local market conditions.

Haier

Haier is a leading Chinese manufacturer of 'white goods' (fridges, washing machines etc).

It was founded in Qingdao in 1984, and first established in China. By 1991 it had become the market leader there. Then, from a strong domestic based it expanded internationally. It is now the world's 4th largest 'white goods' manufacturer, and the world's No 1 major appliances brand. In 2011 it had a market share of 7.8% of the 'Major Appliances' market.

Haier now views itself as 'a global brand with local operations'.

Haier has established 29 manufacturing bases and 16 industrial parks in Europe, North America, Asia, the Middle East and Africa to enable it to localise its production within various markets. And with 8 research and development centres in the US, Germany, China, Japan and Korea, Haier aims to bring its products in line with the wide variety of consumer needs.

In China, Haier's four leading product categories – refrigerators, refrigerating cabinets, air conditioners, and washing machines – have over 30% market share. In international markets, Haier products are available in 12 of the top 15 chain stores in Europe and 10 leading chain stores in the USA. Haier is approaching its goal of being 'local' in American and European markets via localised design, manufacturing and sales processes.

Haier, Japan

In February 2012, Haier announced that it planned to establish its Asian headquarters in Osaka, and two R&D centres in Tokyo and Kyoto, a development which establishes Japan as an overseas market which combines all of the three key elements for the business – R&D, manufacturing and marketing.

At the same time, Haier officially unveiled its second brand in Japan – AQUA. In 2011, Haier purchased SANYO's washing machine and refrigerator businesses in Japan, as well as its washing machine, refrigerator and consumer electrical appliance businesses in Indonesia, Malaysia, the Philippines and Vietnam.

Haier expects its sales in Japan to reach 50 billion yen in 2012, including an estimated 35 million yen from AQUA. However, the company emphasised that its move into Japan is not based only on a desire to increase market share. Its Executive Vice President Liang Haishan said 'What is the most important for us is to better understand Japanese consumers, and provide high-quality appliances to meet the demands of their lives through our localized operations, technology innovation, and resource consideration.'

www.haier.com

Complete global standardisation would greatly increase the profitability of a company's products and simplify the task of the international marketing manager. The extent to which standardisation is possible is controversial in marketing. Much of the decision-making in an international marketing manager's role is concerned with taking a view on the necessity, or lack of it, of adapting the product, price and communications to individual markets.

3.1 Marketing communications and the product

The question of whether or not to adapt the product is often considered in conjunction with the **promotion/communication** issue. This gives us four possible product and communication strategies.

Table 8.3   Standardisation vs adaptation

	Product standardised	Product adapted
Communications standardised	This is the obvious strategy for the occasional exporter but also for some major international companies seeking economies of scale. Marketing costs can be considerable. Even so, language may be an insuperable barrier. Many perfumes and cosmetics are marketed in this way. Cosmetic firms often adopt a named actor/actress to be their 'face' on all their advertising.	This strategy is relevant where the product satisfies the same need (or solves the same problem) in many markets but conditions of use vary. Car manufacturers need different tyres and temperature control systems in Saudi Arabia compared to those needed, say, in Germany.
Communications adapted	This strategy is used where a product meets different needs in different countries. Take bicycles for example. The product is the same, but communications can suggest different uses (eg recreation, commuting).	Both product and communications adapted: this is the most expensive strategy but enables full exploitation.

(Source: *Keegan*, 2009)

3.2 Factors encouraging standardisation

- Economies of scale
    - Production
    - Marketing/communications
    - Research and development
    - Stock holding

- Easier management and control.

- Homogeneity of markets, in other words world markets available without adaptation (eg denim jeans).

- Cultural insensitivity, eg industrial components and agricultural products.

- Consumer mobility means that standardisation is expected in certain products.
    - Camera film
    - Hotel chains

- Where 'made in' image is important to a product's perceived value (eg France for perfume, Sheffield for stainless steel).

- For a firm selling a small proportion of its output overseas, the incremental adaptation costs may exceed the incremental sales value.

- Products that are positioned at the high end of the spectrum in terms of price, prestige and scarcity are more likely to have a standardised mix.

Adaptation may be mandatory or discretionary.

Mandatory product modification normally involves either adaptation to comply with government requirements or unavoidable technical changes. An example of the former would be enhanced safety requirements, while the requirements imposed by different climatic conditions would be an example of the latter.

Discretionary modification is called for only to make the product more appealing in different markets. It results from differing customer needs, preferences and tastes. These differences become apparent from market research and analysis; and intermediary and customer feedback.

- Levels of customer purchasing power. Low incomes may make a cheap version of the product more attractive in some less developed economies.

- Levels of education and technical sophistication. Ease of use may be a crucial factor in decision-making.

- Standards of maintenance and repair facilities. Simpler, more robust versions may be needed.

- 'Culture-bound' products such as clothing, food and home decoration are more likely to have an adapted marketing mix.

These strategies can be exercised at global and national level, depending on the type of product. Not all products are suitable for standardisation.

THE REAL WORLD

Cadbury's chocolate

Before Cadbury was acquired by Kraft (in 2010) the UK company was also having talks with fellow confectioner Hershey.

However, the prospect of Cadbury – the UK's chocolate-maker in chief – being taken over by an American company was causing concern among some chocolate-lovers.

Whilst there is a degree of patriotism behind this response, for many loyal British chocoholics the word 'Herschey' sets alarm bells ringing.

To many people, Herschey's chocolate has a more bitter, less creamy taste than its British equivalent, and seems to have a grittier texture.

But this all comes down to what 'chocolate' actually is.

In the UK, chocolate must contain at least 20% cocoa solids. In the US, however, cocoa solids need only make up 10%.

A Cadbury Dairy Milk bar contains 23% cocoa solids, whereas a Hershey bar contains just 11%.

Interestingly, much of Europe would scoff at either definition. The preference in continental Europe is for richer, darker chocolate, with a significantly higher cocoa solid count. Many European chocolatiers make chocolate with over 40% cocoa solids, creating a product which is significantly different from the chocolate bars which British consumers buy from their local newsagents for a morning snack.

Abridged from: Purser, E (2009) The great transatlantic chocolate divide, *BBC online*, 15 December 2009, bbc.co.uk

---

3.3 Global brand management

Global brands were first discussed in the previous chapter in the context of branding and growth strategies. A global, standardised brand may be sought after by many companies, but it is unlikely to work in the following circumstances:

- Different market share positions in different countries will necessitate different positioning
- Different brand images in different countries will mitigate against a standardised strategy
- Names and symbols may not be appropriate everywhere
- Customers will have different motivations in different cultures
- A competitor may have already occupied the chosen position with their own product

Successful global brand management depends upon excellent cross-country communications, common planning systems across the various business branches and an organisation structure that supports the operation of a "global brand team" with the necessary authority to manage the brand fully.

ACTIVITY 8.5

"The key to a standardised brand is to find a position that will work in all markets."

Give three examples of true worldwide brands, and note their positions.

The Chartered Institute of Marketing

3.4 International competitive strategy

Standard strategic models may be applied to international business, but must be applied in a suitable way.

As we have already established, competitive strategies are the strategies an organisation will pursue for competitive advantage. They determine how you compete. Competitive advantage is anything which gives one organisation an edge over its rivals in the products it sells or the services it offers. This is equally applicable to global strategic decisions.

Porter's generic strategies may be applied in global operations, but they must be managed in a way that takes account of the international business environment.

- **Cost leadership** means being the lowest cost producer in the industry as a whole.
- **Differentiation** is the offer of a product or service which is unique or in some way different from other products.
- **Focus** involves a restriction of activities to a segment through:
  - Providing goods and or services at lower cost to that segment (a cost-focus)
  - Providing a differentiated product or service for that segment (differentiation-focus)

Cost leadership and differentiation are industry-wide strategies. Focus involves market segmentation, but involves pursuing, within the segment only, a strategy of cost leadership or differentiation.

Although there is a risk with any of the generic strategies, Porter argues that a firm must pursue one of them. A stuck-in-the-middle strategy is almost certain to make only low profits, he says. Recent research has indicated that this is too simplistic. Being the lowest cost producer does not mean you have to compete on price.

It is, of course, fairly easy to see how such competitive strategy decisions can be taken in a large domestic market, such as the US, where many economies of scale are readily available. But international marketing involves recognising differences between country markets, the barriers to entry caused by national and cultural borders, and the global market.

It is hard to achieve overall **cost leadership**. In terms of international and global marketing it perhaps only applies to a few companies, and even they might face restrictions on market entry.

- Only a few companies are available to take advantage of global sourcing and the economies this offers.
- Cost leadership is a dangerous strategy, as companies from developing countries might, for a short time, benefit from those countries' comparative advantages in lower labour costs. (Generally speaking higher productivity in advanced economies neutralises many of the gains from cheap labour. Thus, the NAFTA agreement has not led to a collapse in US employment. US workers are far more productive than Mexican ones.)
- Domestic producers might have substantial cost advantages owing to their proximity to the local markets.
- A firm's ability to compete as the lowest cost producer in certain markets will be hampered.
  - Tariffs raise the price of your goods in relation to competitors (eg producers of Scotch whisky trying to export to Japan)
  - Exchange fluctuations can render your efficiently-made products more expensive than a those of local producers
- Many of the costs of goods can be increased by factors outside management control, such as intricacies of the distribution system.

Clearly, then, a strategy of **differentiation** or **focus** can be more realistic.

- Products can be differentiated for the international market, while keeping the same brand name (eg coffee).
- The fact that, despite trade liberalisation, there are real differences between markets might suggest that focus is appropriate. Use national boundaries as a means of segmentation, or, as has been suggested,

concentrate on those consumers in the international market who share characteristics across national segments.

Models such as the Ansoff matrix, described in earlier chapters, can also be applied to international strategies, although its application might be more complex than in the single domestic market.

How can it be applied to international marketing strategy? Unfortunately the categories tend to shift.

- It is easy to suggest what the new market might be: another country.

- What, however, do we mean by 'new product'? Is the product new to the company? Has it only been developed? Is the company still on a learning curve in its domestic market? In this case there might be a choice.

  - Introduce the new product simultaneously in domestic and overseas markets.

  - Have a continuing rolling programme.

    Year 1: the domestic market is dealt with first
    Year 2: existing overseas markets are serviced
    Year 3: genuinely new overseas markets are addressed

  By year 3, the decision to introduce new products into new markets has effectively become one of market development, on the grounds that product has already been on sale at home and in existing overseas markets.

- It would appear unlikely that a company would set up abroad in a completely unfamiliar market with a completely new product, when there are easy opportunities to minimise the risk.

▶ **Exam tip**

The Ansoff matrix can be applied equally to a company looking for new international development or to an established global player. Many strategic developments are concerned with building on where the organisation currently sits in the global market, via current products and competences and stretching them to improve competitive position.

Note that other strategic models such as the BCG matrix may also be applied to global operations.

The Chartered
Institute of Marketing

CHAPTER ROUNDUP

- Critically evaluate the appropriateness of developing an international marketing strategy for an organisation investing in international markets
- Critically evaluate a range of issues that impact on an organisation when entering new countries and markets and consider how they may be managed to achieve the organisation's objectives
- Assess an organisation's readiness for developing a global strategy

FURTHER READING

Jordan, R.O. (1988) " Going global: how to join the second major revolution in advertising", *Journal of Services Marketing*, Volume: 2, Issue: 2, pp. 65 - 70

Quinn, T. & Fally, J-M, (2010), Retail Global Expansion – The journey starts at home, Deloitte, Online publication, www.deloitte.com

REFERENCES

Aaker, D. & McLoughlin, D. (2007) *Strategic Market Management*. John Wiley, Chichester.

Ansoff, H.I. (1988) *Corporate Strategy*. 2nd revised edition. Penguin Books, NY.

Drummond, G. Ensor, J. & Ashford, R. (2008) *Strategic Marketing Planning and Control*. 3rd edition. Elsevier, Oxford.

Jeannet, J-P. & Hennessey, H. (2004) *Global Marketing Strategy*. 6th edition. Houghton Mifflin (Academic), London.

Keegan, W. (2009) *Global Marketing Management*.8th edition. New Jersey: Prentice Hall.

Klein, N. (2001) *No Logo*. Flamingo, London.

Porter, M.E. (2004) *Competitive Strategy: Techniques for Analysing Industries and Competitors*. Free Press, NY.

Yip, G. (2000) Global strategy in the Internet era, *Business Strategy Review*, Vol. 11, Issue 4, pp. 1-14.

QUICK QUIZ

1 On what factors does the level of political risk depend?

2 Draw up a checklist for companies to consider when dealing with the political environment.

3 List some protectionist measures.

4 What is meant by LDC, EDC, SDC?

5 How do you measure economic development?

6 Contrast a global and a multinational strategy.

7   What questions should be asked when deciding upon which country market to enter?

8   What is 'administrative' distance?

9   What is the DFID?

10   What is an 'inhibitor' in the context of buyer behaviour?

11   How might a marketer measure the level of technological development in a target country?

12   What is a 'differentiation' strategy?

ACTIVITY DEBRIEFS

Activity 8.1

A 'gradual' strategy has the advantage of reduced initial commitment, which can be tested and improved as a regional presence is built up.

A 'full frontal' strategy can bring economies of scale and 'first mover' advantages.

Activity 8.2

Protectionism is about the relative benefits and drawbacks to countries of restraining trade. For commercial organisations, however, protectionism has some short-run advantages. The USA is the largest market for automobiles. US car manufacturers produce overseas for foreign markets, generally speaking, as opposed to exporting from the US itself. Free trade in motor vehicles automatically means a great deal of competition at home (particularly from Japan).

A closed market would allow them to raise prices. On the other hand, Swedish car manufacturers, such as Volvo, depend on successful exports since the home market is too small to support them. The benefits of protection would be exceeded by the disadvantages.

Activity 8.3

There is often no right answer, but here are some ideas.

- Will the foreign exchange earnings from Kwat justify the infrastructural investment at all? After all, the government will have to use the foreign exchange earnings to pay interest on loans. Option (3) might be the least risky here.

- Does the country have an educational and technical infrastructure to support the technology? Road vehicles need spare parts and trained service personnel. Spare parts might be an additional drain on foreign exchange. Again option (3) might be the least risky.

Activity 8.4

You could write a long, in-depth answer here, but as a guide we have offered a few preliminary ideas:

Western countries

- Attitudes to elderly.
- Distribution: over the counter? Prescribed by doctors?
- Current health care of elderly.
- Demographic trends: is the age structure of the country becoming more heavily weighted towards older people?
- Drug testing and certification regime.

The Chartered
Institute of Marketing

Third World country

- Is Alzheimer's seen as a major problem, compared to other medical conditions (eg diseases from poor sanitation)?

- Would the drug be affordable?

- Attitudes to elderly.

- Age structure of the country (fewer old people than in the West).

You will doubtless think of more.

Activity 8.5

Aaker & McLoughlin (2007) pp 212-213 give several examples.

You may have thought of examples such as Disney (family entertainment); Mercedes (high-end); Levi's (American classic).

QUICK QUIZ ANSWERS

1   Government attitudes; the nature of the product; the company involved.

2   - How stable is the country politically?
    - Are the local rules of the game known and enforced?
    - How long is the government likely to be in power?
    - How would a new government change the rules?
    - What would be the effects of expected changes to the rules?
    - What decisions and actions should be taken now?

3   Tariffs; barriers; import quotas and embargoes; domestic subsidies; exchange controls; exchange rate policy.

4   Lesser developed country; early developed country; semi-developed country.

5   Several measures are used including: GDP/head; sector source of GDP; living standards; energy usage; education level.

6   A global strategy is representative of a worldwide perspective which is used to create economies of scale and other advantages through an integrated global approach.

    In contrast, a multinational strategy is one in which separate strategies are developed for a series of country markets, and implemented autonomously.

7   Is the market attractive in terms of size and growth?

    - How intense is the competition?
    - Can the firm add value?
    - Do operational or cultural barriers exist?
    - Can a critical mass be achieved?

8   Differences between countries created by factors such as government policies, taxes, politics, exchange rates and trade barriers.

9   The Department for International Development (DFID), which oversees the application of British aid in needy areas throughout the world.

10 Inhibitors are factors (such as the individual's income) which will make the person less likely to purchase.

11   Level of understanding of how the product is used

  - The provision of support services for the product
  - The existence of an appropriate distribution network
  - Level of communication with the customer

12   **Differentiation** is the offer of a product or service which is unique or in some way different from other products.

CHAPTER 9
Financial assessment of marketing opportunities

Introduction

Those developing marketing strategy should:

- Understand the impact of their decisions on the finances of the business
- Be able to work effectively with the finance professionals in the business
- Be competent in the use of financial techniques necessary in day-to-day management and planning for their own departments

Financial comparisons can aid decision-making.

- **Past comparisons and trends**. Looking back at the organisation's financial history and records can identify similar situations and help draw conclusions and trends from the information.
- **Competitor analysis**. Examining published information of other organisations, such as competitors, for financial indicators may aid decision-making.
- **Forecasting the future** is based in part on financial assumptions.
- **Modelling**. Financial data may be used to model the effect of decisions.

The interpretation of financial data is the therefore a key part of understanding any business, either in a practical application or during your studies. This chapter looks at financial tools that can be used by the marketer, the sources of funds that are available to a business, and the important concepts of shareholder value and economic value.

You will not be required to undertake lengthy and complicated numerical analysis in the exam, but it is worth noting the words of the syllabus guidance for this unit:

'Students will be expected to apply a range of financial and risk models to support their assessments ... ultimately, students should be able to prepare a business case or investment appraisal to support the strategic marketing decision-making process.'

Topic list

Financial tools ① 1

Sources of funds ② 2

Shareholder value analysis ③ 3

Value drivers ④ 4

3.1.1	Critically assess strategic alternatives against pre-determined criteria for an organisation, including:
	▪ Scenario planning – stability versus uncertainty
	▪ Potential for Return on Investment (ROI)
	▪ Opportunity to achieve competitive advantage
	▪ Feasibility, viability and resource
	▪ Capacity and capability to deliver
3.2.1	Utilising a range of financial tools, assess the financial benefits and risks for an organisation when selecting from its strategic options:
	▪ Ratios (INITIAL Financial Descriptors), eg Return on Investment (ROI)
	▪ Investment Appraisal Techniques, eg Payback, Net Present Value (NPV), Discounted Cash Flows (DCF), Internal Rate of Return (IRR)
	▪ Cost of capital and Weighted Average Cost of Capital (WACC)
3.2.2	Critically evaluate the source of funds appropriate to the strategic marketing choice and the long-term sustainability and impact of their utilisation:
	▪ The concept of the cost of capital
	▪ Capital Asset Pricing Model (CAPM)
	▪ Weighted Average Cost of Capital (WACC)
	▪ Optimal capital structure
3.2.3	Assess the impact of the strategic choice upon the shareholder value of organisations in different contexts:
	▪ The concept of shareholder value-added
	▪ Cash flow valuation methods
	▪ Economic value methods
	▪ Financial value drivers
	▪ Timing, sustainability and risk factors in financial valuation
3.2.4	Assess the impact on the economic value of an organisation arising from specific decisions on expenditures/cash flows:
	▪ The concept of economic value added
	▪ Cash flow based valuation methods
	▪ Financial value drivers

1 Financial tools

1.1 Ratios

Large companies have been effectively managed for many years simply by ensuring that the ratios relevant to their businesses were kept within acceptable limits. These are the important lessons to be learned.

- **Ratios** are a useful measure when in comparison with something else: either the company's history, or a competitor or an industry norm.

- **Consistency in calculation** and in the base data is important otherwise we could end up comparing apples and oranges.

The Chartered
Institute of Marketing

- **Return on capital employed** is the product of two other ratios.

  ROCE = profit margin × asset turnover

- **Gearing** is a measure of how funds have been generated to buy assets.

- Proper control of cash is vital to the continued financial strength of any company. Marketing managers should be aware of the **debt collection periods** (also known as the debtor turnover or day sales outstanding) and other tests of liquidity such as stock turnover.

The financial statements provide sources of useful information about the condition of a business. They are in the **public domain** and can be an important feature in a **competitor analysis**. A company which is losing money and has borrowed heavily may behave quite differently in marketing terms than one which has many sources of cash.

The analysis and interpretation of these statements can be carried out by calculating certain ratios and then **using the ratios for comparison**.

1   Comparison between **one year and the next**, for a particular business, is used to identify any trends, or significantly better or worse results.

2   Comparison between **one business and another**, is used to establish which business has performed better, and in what ways. You should be very careful, when comparing two different businesses, to ensure that the accounts have been prepared in a similar way.

Below we identify some typical ratios used.

1.2 Profitability and performance ratios

1.2.1 Profit margin

Profit margin is the ratio of **profit before interest and tax to sales turnover**. For example, in 20X0, ARC's profit margin was 17.6% (hence costs as a percentage of sales were 82.4%). Profit before interest and tax (PBIT), is also known as the **operating profit**. In the accounts of ARC Ltd, the PBIT for 20X1 is £20,640,000 and for 20X0, £9,400,000. The profit margins for the two years are:

$$\textit{20X0} \qquad\qquad \textit{20X1}$$

$$\frac{9,400}{53,470} = 17.6\% \qquad\qquad \frac{20,640}{98,455} = 21\%$$

If the ratio of costs to sales goes down, the profit margin will automatically go up. For example, if the cost: sales ratio changes from 80% to 75%, the profit margin will go up from 20% to 25%. What does this mean?

- A **high margin** indicates costs are controlled and/or sales prices are high.
- A **low margin** can mean **high costs** or **low prices**.

Adidas

Despite the uncertain economic environment, the adidas Group delivered a strong financial performance in the first half of 2012. The Group was able to take advantage of the growth opportunities provided by the year's major sporting events, and Group sales increased by 11%.

The Group's gross margin decreased 0.8 percentage points (from 48.8% to 48.0%) as the increase in input costs offset the positive impact from product price increases.

However, the Group's operating margin was up 0.7 percentage points from 8.4% to 9.1%. This reflects the Group's strong discipline which led to a reduction in operating expenses as a percentage of sales.

The following are extracts from the Half Year Results:

	First half year 2012	First half year 2011
Sales	€7,341 m	€6,337 m
Gross Profit	€3,522 m	€3,093 m
Gross margin	48.0%	48.8%
Operating profit	€665 m	€532 m
Operating margin	9.1%	8.4%

www.adiadas-group.com

1.2.2 Asset turnover

Asset turnover is the ratio of **sales turnover** in a year to the amount of **net assets**, which should equate to the amount invested in the business. In the accounts of ARC Ltd, the asset turnover for 20X1 and 20X0 is:

$$20X0$$
$$\frac{53,470}{9,000} = 5.9 \text{ times}$$

$$20X1$$
$$\frac{98,455}{16,100} = 6.1 \text{ times}$$

This means that for every £1 of assets employed in 20X0, the company generated sales turnover of £5.90 per annum. To utilise assets more efficiently, managers should try to create a higher volume of sales and a higher asset turnover ratio.

1.2.3 Return on capital employed (ROCE)

Return on capital employed (ROCE) is the **amount of profit** as a **percentage** of **capital employed** (net assets). If a company makes a profit of £30,000, we do not know how good or bad the result is until we look at the amount of capital which has been invested to achieve the profit. £30,000 might be a good sized profit for a small firm, but this would not be satisfactory for a 'giant' firm such as Tesco. For this reason, it is helpful to measure performance by relating profits to capital employed. The ROCE of ARC Ltd for 20X1 and 20X1 is:

$$20X0$$
$$\frac{9,400}{9,000} = 104.4\%$$

$$20X1$$
$$\frac{20,640}{16,100} = 128\%$$

The Chartered
Institute of Marketing

You may already have realised that there is a mathematical connection between return on capital employed, profit margin and asset turnover:

$$\frac{\text{Profit}}{\text{Capital employed}} = \frac{\text{Profit}}{\text{Sales}} \times \frac{\text{Sales}}{\text{Capital employed}}$$

ie ROCE   =   Profit margin ×   Asset turnover

This is important. If we accept that ROCE is the single most important measure of business performance, comparing profit with the amount of capital invested, we can go on to say that business performance is dependent on two separate 'subsidiary' factors, each of which contributes to ROCE, **profit margin** and **asset turnover**. We can improve ROCE by increasing profit from the same assets, or by matching the same profit with a lower level of assets.

Example

Company A and Company B both sell electrical goods. Both have £100,000 capital employed (net assets) and both want to achieve a target ROCE of 20%. Company A is a specialist retailer and Company B is a discount warehouse.

- **Specialist Company A** might decide to sell its products at a fairly high price and make a profit margin on sales of 10%. It would require an asset turnover of 2.0 times to achieve a ROCE of 20%. It would, therefore, need annual sales of £200,000.

- **Discount warehouse Company B** might decide to cut its prices so that its profit margin is only 2½%. Provided that it can achieve an asset turnover of eight times a year, attracting more customers with its lower prices, it will **still make a ROCE of 2½% × 8 = 20%**. It would need annual sales of £800,000.

ACTIVITY 9.1

What might be the implications for marketing mix decisions of the two approaches to achieving a target ROCE in the example above?

ACTIVITY 9.2

Suppose that Swings and Roundabouts Ltd achieved the following results in 20X6:

	£
Sales	100,000
Profit	5,000
Capital employed	20,000

The company's management wish to decide whether to raise its selling prices. They think that if they do so, they can raise the profit margin to 10% and by introducing extra capital of £55,000, sales turnover could be increased to £150,000.

You are required to evaluate the decision in terms of effect on ROCE, profit margin and asset turnover.

A single ratio is nearly meaningless. What is important is the movement in that ratio over time and the comparison of that ratio with other companies in a similar business.

1.2.4 Investment ratios

Earnings per share (EPS) shows the return due to the ordinary shareholders. This simply divides profit after tax by the average number of ordinary shares in issue while the profit was generated.

The **price/earnings (P/E) number** (also known as the P/E ratio and the P/E multiple) reflects the investors' view of the **future prospects** of a share. Share prices depend on expectations of future earnings.

$$P/E = \frac{\text{The market price of a share (in pence)}}{\text{Earnings per share}}$$

In effect, the P/E number calculates the payback period for money invested in a share.

Dividend per share is important to investors who seek a regular income from their investment.

Dividend cover is also important, since it indicates the company's ability to pay dividends and still retain some profit for purpose of investment.

$$\text{Dividend cover} = \frac{\text{EPS}}{\text{Dividend per share}}$$

1.3 Gearing

Gearing is a method of comparing how much of the long-term capital of a business is provided by **equity** (ordinary shares and reserves) and how much is provided by long-term **loan capital**.

Why is gearing important?

- If a company's gearing is too high (say over 50%), we might find that it is difficult to raise more loans.

- Loan capital is cheaper, because the interest cost diminishes in real terms if secured on company assets and attracts tax benefits.

- Interest must be paid, whereas the directors of a company can decide not to pay a dividend.

- High gearing might be considered risky for lenders in that the more loan capital a business has, the bigger becomes the size of profit before interest and tax (PBIT) which is necessary to meet demands for interest payments.

1.4 Operational ratios

Operational ratios relate to the **cash cycle** of a business.

1   A business which cannot pay its debts as they fall due is insolvent. **Liquidity** is a critical and urgent issue, which is why working capital is monitored thoroughly. A company facing crises in liquidity has few options.

2   Often external parties, such as banks, will provide extra funds, but in extreme cases **marketing strategies** must be devised to raise as much cash as possible.

Consequently, the finance function will monitor **turnover periods**. These ratios, usually expressed in days, measure how long or how many times the business is exchanging cash over a period of time.

Debtors' (receivables) turnover period, or **debt collection period**: the length of the credit period taken by customers or the time between the sale of an item and the receipt of cash for the sale from the customer.

1   This describes the level of debtors compared with the sales turnover. So the ratio for ARC Ltd is:

	20X0	20X1
$\dfrac{\text{Debtors}}{\text{Sales}}$	$\dfrac{8,900}{53,470} = 17\%$	$\dfrac{27,100}{98,455} = 28\%$

2   This can be expressed in days. By multiplying our ratio by 365 we recognise that the debtors are on average:

20X0   20X1

$$\frac{8,900}{53,470} \times 365 = 61 \text{ days} \qquad \frac{27,100}{98,455} \times 365 = 100 \text{ days}$$

We can, of course, do similar turnover calculations for **stock turnover period**. This is the length of time an item stays in stores before use.

$$\frac{\text{Average finished goods stocks (use closing stock)}}{\text{Total cost of goods sold in the period}} \times 365 \text{ days}$$

20X0   20X1

Stock (inventory) turnover period $\frac{5,000}{40,653} \times 365 = 45 \text{ days} \qquad \frac{15,000}{70,728} \times 365 = 77 \text{ days}$

Similarly, the **creditors' (payables) turnover period**, or period of credit taken from suppliers, is the length of time between the purchase of materials and the payment to suppliers.

$$\frac{\text{Average trade creditors (use closing creditors)}}{\text{Total purchases in the period}*} \times 365 \text{ days}$$

20X0   20X1

Creditors' payment period $\frac{6,000}{40,653} \times 365 = 54 \text{ days} \qquad \frac{10,000}{70,728} \times 365 = 52 \text{ days}$

* Cost of sales can be substituted as an approximation

Again these can be expressed in days or months.

The **importance** of turnover ratios is their impact on **cash requirements**. An increase in the **stock turnover ratio** or in the **debtor turnover ratio** means that more money is being tied up in funding **working capital** and this may not be desirable.

1.5 Liquidity ratios

Liquidity, as we have seen, is an organisation's ability to convert its assets into cash to meet all the demands for payments when they fall due. They are particularly important for **credit control**.

Current liabilities are items which must be paid for in the near future. When payment becomes due, enough cash must be available to make the payment.

Let us see how some ratios apply.

Ratio	*Current ratio* Current assets Current liabilities	*Quick ratio* Current assets less stock Current liabilities
ARC 20X0	$\frac{14,500}{13,000} = 1.1:1$	$\frac{14,500 - 5,000}{13,000} = 0.7:1$
ARC 20X1	$\frac{42,100}{38,400} = 1.1:1$	$\frac{42,100 - 15,000}{38,400} = 0.7:1$

The best way to judge liquidity would be to look at the current ratio at different dates over a period of time. If the trend is towards a **lower current ratio**, we would judge that the **liquidity position is getting steadily worse**.

Calculate liquidity and working capital ratios from these accounts of a manufacturer of products for the construction industry.

	20X3 £m	20X2 £m
Turnover	2,065.0	1,788.7
Cost of sales	1,478.6	1,304.0
Gross profit	586.4	484.7
Current assets		
Stocks	119.0	109.0
Debtors (note 1)	400.9	347.4
Short-term investments	4.2	18.8
Cash at bank and in hand	48.2	48.0
	572.3	523.2
Creditors: amounts falling due within one year		
Loans and overdrafts	49.1	35.3
Corporation taxes	62.0	46.7
Dividend	19.2	14.3
Creditors (note 2)	370.7	324.0
	501.0	420.3
Net current assets	71.3	102.9

Notes

1	Trade debtors (receivables)	329.8	285.4
2	Trade creditors (payables)	236.2	210.8

1.6 Investment appraisal techniques

The best project appraisal method is net present value, but payback period is also useful. Note that all investment appraisal methods depend for their use on having reasonably accurate estimates of the cash flows associated with the proposal, both the immediate cost and the costs and revenues expected in the future. In this context remember that profit is not the same thing as positive cash flow, since profit is affected by non-cash flow items such as depreciation.

We will look first at the payback method.

1.6.1 Payback

▶ **Key term**

Payback is the time it takes the cash inflows from a capital investment project to equal the cash outflows, expressed in years.

Payback is often used as a 'first screening method'. By this, we mean that when a capital investment project is being considered, the first question to ask is: 'How long will it take to pay back its cost?' The organisation might have a target payback, and so it would reject a capital project unless its payback period was less than a certain number of years.

However, a project should not be evaluated on the basis of payback alone. If a project passes the payback test, it ought then to be evaluated with a more sophisticated investment appraisal technique.

Almost as soon as the 'Gorilla' television commercial for Dairy Milk chocolate first aired on August 31, 2007, the questions began. What role did the extraordinary take-up of the gorilla ad on the internet play in Dairy Milk's success? . . .

By 2007, Cadbury's Dairy Milk seemed to be running out of steam. Its sales had flat-lined and were entering a third year of decline, and Dairy Milk appeared to be losing relevance to younger generations. Its advertising model also felt tired.

The solution was to create Glass and a Half Full Productions, a content-led campaign including 'Gorilla', 'Eyebrows' and 'Trucks'. This new direction moved Cadbury Dairy Milk from being a manufacturer of chocolate to 'a producer of joy'.

The campaign generated £5.22 million of incremental sales growth, without any need for range extension. 'Gorilla' was credited with delivering an incremental revenue of £4.88 for every £1 spent.

The campaign also helped to transform decline into growth and to engineer a more profitable business model.

www.ipaeffectivenessawards.co.uk

The reason why payback should not be used on its own to evaluate capital investments should seem fairly obvious if you look at the figures below for two mutually exclusive projects (this means that only one of them can be undertaken).

	Project P £	Project Q £
Capital asset	60,000	60,000
Profits before depreciation (a rough approximation of cash flows)		
Year 1	20,000	50,000
Year 2	30,000	20,000
Year 3	40,000	5,000
Year 4	50,000	5,000
Year 5	60,000	5,000

Project P pays back in year 3 (about one-quarter of the way through year 3). Project Q pays back half-way through year 2. Using payback alone to judge capital investments, project Q would be preferred. However the returns from project P over its life are much higher than the returns from project Q. Project P will earn total profits before depreciation of £140,000 on an investment of £60,000. Project Q will earn total profits before depreciation of only £25,000 on an investment of £60,000.

There are a number of serious drawbacks to the payback method.

- It ignores the timing of cash flows within the payback period, the cash flows after the end of payback period and therefore, the total project return.

- It ignores the time value of money (a concept incorporated into more sophisticated appraisal methods). This means that it does not take account of the fact that £1 today is worth more than £1 in one year's time. An investor who has £1 today can either consume it immediately or alternatively can invest it at the prevailing interest rate, say 10%, to get a return of £1.10 in a year's time.

- Payback is unable to distinguish between projects with the same payback period.

- The choice of any cut-off payback period by an organisation is arbitrary.

- It may lead to excessive investment in short-term projects.

- It takes account of the risk of the timing of cash flows but not the variability of those cash flows.

Advantages of the payback method

In spite of its limitations, the payback method continues to be popular, and the following points can be made in its favour.

- It is simple to calculate and simple to understand. This may be important when management resources are limited. It is similarly helpful in communicating information about minimum requirements to managers responsible for submitting projects.

- It uses cash flows rather than accounting profits.

- It can be used as a screening device as a first stage in eliminating obviously inappropriate projects prior to more detailed evaluation.

- The fact that it tends to bias in favour of short-term projects means that it tends to minimise both financial and business risk.

- It can be used when there is a capital rationing situation to identify those projects which generate additional cash for investment quickly.

1.6.2 Discounted cash flows (DCF)

Discounting is a numerical process that determines the **present value** of a future cash flow.

In the next section we will discuss shareholder value analysis (SVA). This technique depends on the **discounting** of cash flows, both current and in the future. Discounting is a basic tool of financial analysis that is also widely used in other business techniques, so we will start off by showing you how it works.

The **basic principle of compounding** is that if we invest £X now for n years at r% interest per annum, we should obtain £S in n years' time, where $£S = £X(1+r^n)$.

Thus if we invest £10,000 now for four years at 10% interest per annum, we will have a total investment worth $£10,000 \times 1.10^4 = £14,641$ at the end of four years (that is, at Year 4 if it is now Year 0).

> ▶ **Key term**
> The basic principle of **discounting** is that if we wish to have £S in n years' time, we need to invest a certain sum now (Year 0) at an interest rate of r% in order to obtain the required sum of money in the future.

For example, if we wish to have £14,641 in four years' time, how much money would we need to invest now at 10% interest per annum? This is the reverse of the situation described above and, fairly obviously, the answer is £10,000. We can prove this, as explained below.

Using our formula, $S = X(1 + r)^n$

Where: X = the original sum invested
  r = 10%
  n = 4
  S = £14,641

$£14,641 = X(1 + 0.1)^4$

$£14,641 = X \times 1.4641$

Therefore, $X = \dfrac{£14,641}{1.4641} = £10,000$

£10,000 now, with the capacity to earn a return of 10% per annum, is the equivalent in value of £14,641 after four years. We can, therefore, say that £10,000 is the **present value** of £14,641 at Year 4, at an interest rate of 10%.

The discounting formula is:

$$X = S \times \frac{1}{(1+r)^n}$$

Where: S is the sum to be received after n time periods

X is the present value (PV) of that sum

r is the rate of return, expressed as a proportion

n is the number of time periods (usually years)

The rate r is sometimes called the cost of capital.

Example: Discounting

1   Calculate the present value of £60,000 at Year 6, if a return of 15% per annum is obtainable.

2   Calculate the present value of £100,000 at Year 5, if a return of 6% per annum is obtainable.

3   How much would a person need to invest now at 12% to earn £4,000 at Year 2 and £4,000 at Year 3?

Solution

The discounting formula, $X = S \times \frac{1}{(1+r)^n}$ is required.

1   S = £60,000

       n = 6

       r = 0.15

       $PV = 60,000 \times \frac{1}{1.15^6}$

            $= 60,000 \times 0.432$

            $= £25,920$

2   S = £100,000

       n = 5

       r = 0.06

       $PV = 100,000 \times \frac{1}{1.06^5}$

            $= 100,000 \times 0.747$

            $= £74,700$

3   S = £4,000

       n = 2 or 3

       r = 0.12

       $PV = (4,000 \times \frac{1}{1.12^2}) + (4,000 \times \frac{1}{1.12^3})$

            $= 4,000 \times (0.797 + 0.712)$

            $= £6,036$

This calculation can be checked as follows:

	£
Year 0	6,036.00
Interest for the first year (12%)	724.32
	6,760.32
Interest for the second year (12%)	811.24
	7,571.56
Less withdrawal	(4,000.00)
	3,571.56
Interest for the third year (12%)	428.59
	4,000.15
Less withdrawal	(4,000.00)
Rounding error	0.15

ACTIVITY 9.4

What is the present value at 7% interest of £16,000 at Year 12?

Discounted cash flow techniques can be used to evaluate expenditure proposals such as marketing budgets or plans to purchase equipment.

> ▶ **Key terms**
>
> **Discounted cash flow (DCF)** involves the application of discounting arithmetic to the estimated future cash flows (receipts and expenditures) from a project in order to decide whether the project is expected to earn a satisfactory rate of return.
>
> The **net present value (NPV) method** works out the present values of all items of income and expenditure related to an investment at a given rate of return, and then works out a net total. If it is positive, the investment is considered to be acceptable. If it is negative, the investment is considered to be unacceptable.

1.6.3 The net present value (NPV) method

The **net present value** of a project is the sum of the present values of all the future cash flows associated with it.

Example: The net present value of a project

Dog Ltd is considering whether to spend £5,000 on an item of equipment. The excess of income over cash expenditure from the project would be £3,000 in the first year and £4,000 in the second year.

The company will not invest in any project unless it offers a return in excess of 15% per annum.

Required

Assess whether the investment is worthwhile.

Solution

In this example, an outlay of £5,000 now promises a return of £3,000 **during** the first year and £4,000 **during** the second year. It is a convention in DCF, however, that cash flows spread over a year are assumed to occur **at the end of the year**, so that the cash flows of the project are as follows.

	£
Year 0 (now)	(5,000)
Year 1 (at the end of the year)	3,000
Year 2 (at the end of the year)	4,000

The NPV method takes the following approach.

- The project offers £3,000 at Year 1 and £4,000 at Year 2, for an outlay of £5,000 now.

- The company might invest elsewhere to earn a return of 15% per annum.

- If the company did invest at exactly 15% per annum, how much would it need to invest now to earn £3,000 at the end of Year 1 plus £4,000 at the end of Year 2?

- Is it cheaper to invest £5,000 in the project, or to invest elsewhere at 15%, in order to obtain these future cash flows?

If the company did invest elsewhere at 15% per annum, the amount required to earn £3,000 in Year 1 and £4,000 in Year 2 would be as follows.

Year	Cash flow £	Discount factor 15%	Present value £
1	3,000	$\frac{1}{1.15} = 0.870$	2,610
2	4,000	$\frac{1}{(1.15)^2} = 0.756$	3,024
			5,634

The choice is to invest £5,000 in the project, or £5,634 elsewhere at 15%, in order to obtain these future cash flows. We can therefore reach the following conclusion.

- It is cheaper to invest in the project, by £634.

- The project offers a return of over 15% per annum.

The net present value is the difference between the present value of cash inflows from the project (£5,634) and the present value of future cash outflows (in this example, £5,000 × 1/1.15^0 = £5,000).

An NPV statement could be drawn up as follows.

Year	Cash flow £	Discount factor 15%	Present value £
0	(5,000)	1.000	(5,000)
1	3,000	$\frac{1}{1.15} = 0.870$	2,610
2	4,000	$\frac{1}{(1.15)^2} = 0.756$	3,024
Net present value			+634

The project has a **positive net present value, so it is acceptable**.

Notes

(1) $\frac{1}{1.15} = 0.870$

(2) $\frac{1}{(1.15)^2} = 0.756$

ACTIVITY 9.5

A company is wondering whether to spend £18,000 on an item of equipment, in order to obtain cash profits as follows.

Year	£
1	6,000
2	8,000
3	5,000
4	1,000

The company requires a return of 10% per annum.

Required

Use the NPV method to assess whether the project is viable.

Discount tables

Assuming that money earns, say, 10% per annum:

- The PV (present value) of £1 at Year 1 is $£1 \times \dfrac{1}{1.10}$ = £1 × 0.909

- Similarly, the PV of £1 at Year 2 is $£1 \times \dfrac{1}{(1.10)^2}$ = £1 × 0.826

- The PV of £1 at Year 3 is $£1 \times \dfrac{1}{(1.10)^3}$ = £1 × 0.751

Discount tables show the value of $1/(1 + r)^n$ for different values of r and n. Note, however, that in practice NPV calculations will usually be done using a spreadsheet.

Limitations of using the NPV method

There are a number of problems associated with using the NPV method in practice.

1 **The future discount factors** (or interest rates) which are used in calculating NPVs can only be **estimated** and are not known with certainty. Discount rates that are estimated for time periods far into the future are therefore less likely to be accurate, thereby leading to less accurate NPV values.

2 Similarly, NPV calculations make use of estimated **future cash flows**. As with future discount factors, cash flows which are estimated for several years into the future cannot be predicted with any real certainty.

3 When using the NPV method it is common to assume that all cash flows occur **at the end of the year**. However, this assumption is also likely to give rise to less accurate NPV values.

There are a number of computer programs available these days which enable a range of NPVs to be calculated for different circumstances (best-case and worst-case situations and so on). Such programs allow some of the limitations mentioned above to be alleviated.

2 Sources of funds

2.1 The cost of capital

Many groups of companies have a corporate treasury function within the holding company, which controls the use of the group's internally generated funds by means of a central banking system.

The holding company will loan capital to subsidiary operating units and charge out the funds at the corporate **cost of capital**. The target DCF rate of return selected by an organisation might be based on the following:

1 The **weighted average cost of capital (WACC) is the average of the cost of equity and the cost of debt. If the cost of equity for a company is 10% and its cost of debt is 6%, the cost of capital will be 8% (assuming that the amounts of debt and equity are equal).**

2 The **marginal cost of capital** – ie the cost of the extra capital required to finance a specific project

3 The **opportunity cost** of the capital required to finance the project (ie what is lost by not investing somewhere else, such as putting the money into the bank and earning interest on it)

4 A cost of capital that is adjusted to allow for the **risk element** in the particular capital investment

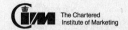

5   A return based upon the **capital asset pricing model (CAPM)**.   This is expressed in the formula below:

$$\bar{r}_a = r_f + \beta_a\left(\bar{r}_m - r_f\right)$$

Where: $\bar{r}_a$ = expected return on the security

$\bar{r}_f$ = risk free rate

β_a = Beta of the security

$\bar{r}_m$ = Expected market return

The general idea behind CAPM is that investors need to be compensated in two ways: for the time value of money, and for risk. The time value of money is represented by the risk-free (r_f) rate in the formula and compensates the investor for placing money in an investment over a period of time. The other half of the formula represents risk, and calculates the amount of compensation the investor needs for taking on that risk. This is calculated by taking a risk measure (beta) that compares the returns of the investment with those of the market over a period of time and to the market premium ($\bar{r}_m - r_f$).

The CAPM says that the expected return of an investment equals the rate on a risk-free investment, plus a risk premium. If this expected return does not meet or beat the required return, then the investment should not be undertaken.

Using the CAPM model and the following assumptions, we can compute the expected return of a project: if the risk-free rate is 3%, the beta (risk measure) of the project is 2 and the expected market return over the period is 10%, the investment will be expected to return 17% (3% + 2 (10% – 3%)).

Calculating an accurate cost of capital is very difficult and the subject of much debate and research by financial management professionals. While the level of loan interest is clearly easily available, it can vary from loan to loan and in the case of overdraft finance may vary from time to time. The cost of share capital is much more difficult to compute since it is really only accessible through an examination of stock market behaviour and that is extremely complex. A further complication is the issue of risk premium. To some extent this is built into the cost of loan and share capital, but where money is allocated internally, management must make up their own minds. All these factors mean that choice of discount rate is very much a matter of judgement and the 'correct' rate may be unknowable to an accuracy of better than plus or minus several percentage points.

2.2 Optimal capital structure

In determining what is the appropriate level of debt to be held by a business, one useful ratio is the debt-to-equity ratio. The higher this ratio is, the larger the interest payment burden and the lower the ability of the business to generate additional funds via debt (or loans) in the future or in an emergency.

The optimal level of debt/equity is influenced by a number of factors (Aaker & McLoughlin 2007).

- The ability to carry added interest payments
- The policy of the firm towards debt
- The return expected on investments
- The debt/equity ratio of competitors

3 Shareholder value analysis

Shareholder value analysis may be used to measure corporate (and hence management) performance in terms of benefit created for shareholders. **Economic value added** is a simple measure but backward looking. The cash flow approach is a better method for assessing future prospects.

Shareholder value analysis (SVA) is a method of approaching the problem of business control by focusing on the **creation of value for shareholders**. Independent financial analysts measure the **value offered by a**

company's shares by considering the **market value** of all the shares in existence (the **market capitalisation**), in the light of the **company's prospects** for generating both cash and capital growth in the future. If the current market capitalisation is less than the estimate of actual value, then the shares are undervalued. Investment is necessary to produce either assets that grow in value or actual cash surpluses, so the process of shareholder value analysis is essentially one of estimating the likely effectiveness of the company's **current investment decisions**. It is thus both a system for judging the worth of current investment proposals and for judging the performance of the managers who are responsible for the company's performance.

In the past, marketing managers have tended to pursue purely **marketing objectives**, such as sales growth, market share, customer satisfaction and brand recognition. None of these marketing objectives *necessarily* translates into increased shareholder value, and as a result, marketing has suffered from a lack of perceived relevance to true business value. An emphasis on profitability as a measure of success has led to a certain amount of **short-termism** in strategic management, with an emphasis on **containing and reducing current costs** in order to boost current profits. Unfortunately, this approach tends to underestimate the longer-term effect of such action and can lead to corporate decline. Investment in **intangible assets** such as brands can make a positive contribution to long-term shareholder value.

3.1 Computing value

According to Doyle (2008), the extent of a company's success may be measured in two ways. The first is by using the concept of **economic profit** (trademarked by Stern, Stewart and Company as **Economic Value Added**®). The expression economic profit is used to distinguish the measure from accounting profit, which is computed according to the strict rules of accountancy. These feature, in particular, the principle of **prudence**. This makes it impossible for **accounting profit** to recognise spending on pure research, for instance, as an investment in an asset, since there is no guarantee that it will ever produce anything worth having; the same would be true of much marketing spending on building long-term effectiveness.

Economic profit is created when the return on a company's capital employed exceeds the cost of that capital.

Economic profit = NOPAT – (capital employed × cost of capital)

where NOPAT is net operating profit after tax.

However, there are some important differences in the way that NOPAT is calculated, compared with the profit figure that is used for RI. There are three main reasons for adjusting accounting profits to derive NOPAT:

(a)   Costs which would normally be treated as expenses in the financial statements, but which are considered within an EVA calculation as **investments building for the future**, are added back to derive a figure for 'economic profit'. These costs are included instead as assets in the figure for net assets employed; in other words, they are deemed to be investments for the future. Costs treated in this way include items such as **advertising costs**, and **research and development expenditure**.

(b)   **Cash accounting versus accruals**. Investors are primarily interested in cash flows, so accounting adjustments for non-cash items, such as allowances for doubtful debts, is eliminated when calculating NOPAT.

(c)   Investors, who are interested in maximising their wealth, will be interested in the continuing performance of the company. Therefore **one-off, unusual items** of profit or expenditure should be ignored when calculating NOPAT.

Cost of capital

The cost of capital is, effectively, the return that has to be made to providers of capital in the form of interest on loans and dividends on shares. It may be calculated as a **weighted average**, which takes account of both the expectations of shareholders and lenders. (Buying shares generally entails greater risk than making a loan, so

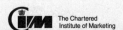

shareholders generally demand higher returns than lenders. This is why a weighted average figure must be used.)

Economic profit is related to capital employed by **return on capital employed** (ROCE). This is a percentage and may thus be compared directly with cost of capital. When ROCE exceeds the cost of capital (r), economic value is created: under these circumstances (ROCE > r), the company is offering a greater return on capital than is available elsewhere.

3.1.1 The cash flow approach

Economic profit is useful for examining the company's **current and past performance**, but is less useful for **assessing future prospects**. Doyle suggests that it is more appropriate to use the second of the methods he discusses, the **cash flow approach** for this purpose. Be aware that both the **economic profit** method and the **cash flow method** should produce the same result when applied to a particular company.

The **cash flow approach** may be used to estimate the degree of economic value a company may be expected to create in the future. It is based on an estimation of likely future **cash flows**, both positive and negative, as indicated in the corporate plans. (A cash flow is simply a sum of money paid or received by the company.) This is easier to compute than future NOPAT, because it is far less complex and depends on far fewer variables.

3.2 Discounting cash flows

Because the SVA technique depends very much on the estimation of future cash flows arising from current investments, it is necessary to use **discounting arithmetic** in order to make the necessary judgements.

3.2.1 Business risk

Some businesses are inherently **riskier** than others: the degree of risk can be measured by the degree of predictability that attaches to its expected cash flows. A low risk business will have steady income from period to period, without any unexpected highs and lows. A high-risk business will have returns that vary wildly and unexpectedly from period to period, though its total long-term return may be as great or greater than the low risk operation. Generally, **investors are risk averse** and, as a result, they demand higher returns from high-risk businesses than from low risk ones. The high-risk business must therefore use a **higher cost of capital** in its shareholder value analysis than the low risk business.

3.3 Value-based management

Value-based management is about maximising shareholder returns by developing competitive advantage in segments where profits can be made.

Doyle (2003), tells us that business success should be measured by shareholder value analysis because of the property rights of shareholders and the 'pressures to oust management that does not deliver competitive returns'. Purely marketing objectives are no longer acceptable to investors or the analysts whose reports they rely on. What Doyle calls **value-based management** is based on three elements.

- A **belief** that maximising shareholder returns is the objective of the firm.

- The **principles**, or strategic foundations of value are first, to target those market segments where profits can be made and second, to develop competitive advantage 'that enables both the customer and the firm to create value'.

- The **processes** 'concern how strategies should be developed, resources allocated and performance measured'.

SVA is particularly appropriate for judging strategic investment decisions and applies the same principles that have long been used for appraising investment in such tangible assets as premises and plant. It is necessary to consider both the **cash costs** of the strategic investment to be made, and the **positive cash flows** that are expected to be produced by it. These may then be discounted to a net present value (NPV) using an appropriate cost of capital, and a judgement made on the basis of the NPV. Any specific marketing proposal, such as an enhanced advertising spend or a new discount structure may be assessed in this way, though it will almost certainly be necessary to take advice from the finance function on the process.

Estimating the value of such investments forms one part of basic shareholder value analysis. Doyle also recommends that when considering the total value of a business, it is also necessary to consider the probable **residual value** of the business. This is the present value of cash flows in the more distant future, outside the normal planning horizon, which Doyle suggests is five years. This assumes no special competitive advantage from current investments and simply uses the cost of capital as an estimate of the rate of return on investment.

3.3.1 Marketing assets

Value-based management means that purely marketing investment proposals will be judged as detailed above. It will be necessary for marketing managers to justify their spending requests in such terms, on the basis that such spending is not a cost burden to be minimised but an investment in intangible assets such as the four that Doyle suggests.

- Marketing knowledge
- Brands
- Customer loyalty
- Strategic relationships with channel partners

The obstacle that lies in the path of this approach to marketing use of SVA is the common perception that marketing spending is merely a cost to be controlled and minimised. The onus is on marketing managers to demonstrate that their budgets do in fact create assets that provide competitive advantage for the business and that the benefits exceed the costs.

---

4 Value drivers

Doyle (2003) suggests that it is possible to identify the factors that are critical to the creation of shareholder value. These he calls **value drivers**; he divides them into three categories.

- Financial
- Marketing
- Organisational

It is important to remember that **the financial drivers should not be targeted directly**: they are objectives, not the components of strategy. The company influences them by the proper management of the **marketing** and **organisational** drivers.

4.1 Financial value drivers

There are four drivers of **financial value**.

- Cash flow volume
- Cash flow timing
- Cash flow risk
- Cash flow sustainability

4.1.1 Cash flow volume

Clearly, the higher that positive cash flows are and the lower negative cash flows are, the greater the potential for creating value.

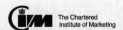

Profitability. In the most simple terms, profit margin is measured by net operating profit after tax (NOPAT). NOPAT can be increased in three ways.

- **Higher prices**. Marketing strategies such as building strong brands can enable the charging of premium prices. A particularly powerful route to higher prices is **innovation**, since desirable new products will normally justify increased prices.

- **Reduced costs**. Cost reduction depends on increased efficiency in all aspects of the business operation.

- **Volume increases**. Other things being equal, volume growth increases the absolute profit margin and may increase the profit rate as well.

Sales growth. If increases in sales volume can be achieved without disproportionate increases in costs or, in particular, excessive discounting, positive cash flows will naturally increase. Increased sales can also bring increased **economies of scale**, which will take the form of reduced costs of all types. Overheads are spread over greater volumes and purchasing discounts reduce the cost of sales.

Investment. Investment provides the resources necessary to do business. These include premises, equipment, stocks, transport and well-trained, experienced staff. However, ill-advised investment can destroy value faster than profitable investment can create it, so any proposal for investment must be judged on its potential for generating acceptable returns. The **net present value** (NPV) approach is the investment appraisal method best suited to the shareholder value principle, in that any project that has a NPV greater than zero provides a return greater than the cost of capital used in the discounting arithmetic.

4.1.2 Cash flow timing

The further into the future a cash flow occurs, the lower its present value. If positive cash flows can be achieved in the near future and negative ones delayed, the company benefits. This is why companies and individuals put off paying their bills for as long as possible. Buying on credit and selling for cash is another approach.

Doyle gives five examples of ways that marketing managers can accelerate cash flows.

- **Faster new product development** processes, including the use of cross-functional teams and conducting projects concurrently rather than consecutively.

- **Accelerated market penetration** through pre-marketing campaigns, early trial promotions and word-of-mouth campaigns using early adopters.

- **Network effects**: that is, achieving market status as the industry standard. This is a self-reinforcing, feedback effect in which success leads to even greater success. Aggressive marketing measures to build the installed base are required.

- **Strategic alliances** speed market penetration, normally by providing extra distribution effort.

- **Exploiting brand assets**: new products launched under a suitable, established brand are likely to be more successful than others.

4.1.3 Cash flow risk

The higher the degree of **risk** associated with future cash flows, the greater the proportion of them that will not actually come to pass. High risk can produce low returns as easily as high ones. Apart from this overall averaging effect, there is the disadvantage associated with **infrequent large cash flows**: failure of such a cash flow to occur can have catastrophic consequences. Risk is also associated with timing: the further into the future that a cash flow is expected to occur, the greater the risk associated with it, since there is a greater likelihood of **changed conditions** affecting its eventual value and even whether or not it actually occurs.

Doyle suggests that the most effective marketing route to reduced cash flow risk is 'to increase customer satisfaction, loyalty and retention' by deploying such techniques as loyalty programmes and measures to increase satisfaction. Building **good channel relationships** also helps, both by building an element of loyalty based on good service and by sharing information on demand patterns to smooth stock fluctuations.

4.1.4 Cash flow sustainability

A single positive cash flow is useful. A positive cash flow that is repeated at regular intervals is much more useful. Quite apart from the extra cash involved, sustainable cash flows make it easier to plan for the future. Positive cash flows derive from the creation of competitive advantage and a sustainable advantage will lead to sustainable cash flows.

There are many **threats to sustainable profits**, including aggressive competition from copies and substitutes and, particularly in B2B markets, the bargaining power of customers. Part of the role of marketing management is to counter such threats using techniques, such as those outlined above, in connection with reducing risk.

Sustainable advantage also offers a benefit in the form of **enhanced options** for future development. Just as financial options to buy and sell securities and currency have their own value, so a strategy that creates **real options** for future activity has a value over and above any immediate competitive advantage it may offer. A simple example is the development of a completely new product for a given market that can also be made viable in other markets at low incremental cost. Richard Branson's ability to use his brand Virgin with almost any consumer product is another example. There are network effects here too, in that as more and more dissimilar Virgin products become available, the brand's suitability for use with even more types of product grows.

4.2 Marketing value drivers

Doyle analyses four **marketing value drivers**. The first, choice of markets, is only applicable to the large, diversified organisation, but the remaining three apply to all companies.

4.2.1 Choice of markets

A large organisation operating a number of strategic business units (SBUs) must apply a continuing **portfolio analysis** to them. You will be familiar with such portfolio analysis tools as the BCG matrix and the GE business screen from your earlier studies, but you may only have considered their use at **the product level**. Nevertheless, it is both feasible and proper to apply the concept at **the SBU level** in order to determine priorities for investment and policies for exploitation. Doyle suggests a very simple, one-dimensional classification of SBUs.

- **Today's businesses** generate the bulk of current profits and cash, but probably have only modest growth potential. If successful, they attract modest investment for incremental developments; if performing badly they are put right rapidly or sold off.

- **Tomorrow's businesses** have high potential and require major investment.

- **Options for growth** are the seeds of more distant businesses; such as research projects, market trials and stakes in new, small businesses that are a long way from success. Recognising the worth of such ventures is a difficult task; in the world of venture capital, it is recognised that many good ideas will come to nothing in the end.

A large company needs a suitable mix of the three types of SBU each with its own appropriate strategic objectives, though there may be opportunities for **synergy**, such as the use of common brand names. SBUs that do not fit into one of the categories should be divested.

4.2.2 Target markets

Most customers are not worth selling to. The loyal, long-term customer that pays full price and requires little special service attention is the ideal – but very few fall into this category. Nevertheless, it is appropriate to target this class of customer specifically rather than simply to aim for a large customer base. Desirable customers display four important characteristics.

- They are **strategic** in that their needs match the company's core capabilities.
- They are **significant** in terms of their size or potential for growth.
- They are **profitable**.
- They are **loyal**.

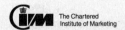

4.2.3 Differential advantage

For other than convenience purchases, customers must have a reason for buying from a particular supplier. **Differential advantage** is created when target customers decide to buy and to remain loyal. Doyle proposes four types of customer, each of which is suited by a particular strategic approach to creating differential advantage.

A strategy of **product leadership** is based on innovation and speed to market. It is the differential advantage that enables a company to sell to **customers who want the latest, most fashionable products**. A good example is Sony, with its continuing development of well-designed, expensive customer electronics.

Operational excellence is needed to offer a combination of **customer convenience** and the **lowest prices**. Wal-Mart and Toyota are good examples of this approach.

Brand superiority is based on careful marketing research and strong and consistent marketing communication. This approach works with customers who identify with the **brand's values** or seek the **reassurance** that brands provide.

A growing segment is made up of customers seeking customised solutions to their specific wants. The appropriate strategy here is **customer intimacy**. This approach is becoming more feasible as information technology developments improve the ability of companies to store and access details of customer habits, needs and preferences.

Note that concentration on one particular strategy does not mean that the others can be neglected. A level of **threshold competence** must be achieved in all four, with one being established as the field of **core competence**.

4.2.4 Marketing mix

Marketing mix decisions derive from, and should support, policies established for the other three marketing value drivers. For example, the chosen market segment will have characteristics and usage patterns that govern decisions about promotion and distribution, while differential advantage derived from brand superiority will lead to, and be supported by, a policy of premium pricing.

4.3 Organisational value drivers

Organisational capabilities and culture will have great influence on success and failure. The McKinsey 7S model illustrates the interplay of the factors involved.

Doyle declares that 'in most situations organisational capabilities and culture are more important than strategy', and goes on to make several comparisons between pairs of companies that use similar strategies in the same industries but with markedly differing degrees of success. The differences arise from the extent to which the companies involved are able to develop and deploy appropriate **core competences** and this in turn is highly conditional upon the **culture** of the organisation and the **attitudes** of the people working in it.

An important variable is **organisational structure**. In the days of mass marketing, a vertically organised hierarchical form was appropriate for achieving economies of scale and expertise. Companies now seeking to cut overheads, achieve fast response to changing markets and competition and exploit the advantages of a mass customisation approach need something better. Increasingly, advances in IT are producing organisations based on **networks**.

- **Internal networks** take the form of horizontally-oriented, cross-functional teams with responsibility for processes that deliver customer satisfactions. Communication flows freely, making the best use of resources whatever their functional label. This style of working reduces costs, speeds response and improves motivation.

- **External networks** are created when companies withdraw from activities that are not fundamental to their specific value-creating strategy and **concentrate on their core competences**. They buy in the services they no longer perform for themselves, using the core competences of other companies to support their own. This type of organisation arises under the pressure of new technologies, new markets and new processes that make it difficult for any organisation to do everything well.

CHAPTER ROUNDUP

- Utilising a range of financial tools, assess the financial benefits and risks for an organisation when selecting from its strategic options

- Critically evaluate the source of funds appropriate to the strategic marketing choice and the long-term sustainability and impact of their utilisation

- Assess the impact of the strategic choice upon the shareholder value of organisations in different contexts

- Assess the impact on the economic value of an organisation arising from specific decisions on expenditures/cash flows

- Critically assess strategic alternatives against pre-determined criteria for an organisation

FURTHER READING

King, S., & Ockels, C. (2011). *Intuit 2020 Report: The Future of Financial Services*. Retrieved June 29, 2012 from http://www.banking2020.com/2011/04/11/intuit-2020-report-the-future-of-the-financial-services-industry/Marketing Management: PwC Estonia 14

REFERENCES

Aaker, D. & McLoughlin, D. (2007) *Strategic Market Management*. John Wiley, Chichester.

Doyle, P. (2008) *Value-Based Marketing: Marketing Strategies for Corporate Growth and Shareholder Value*. 2nd edition. John Wiley & Sons, Chichester.

Doyle, P. (2003) *Strategy as Marketing*. In Cummings, S. & Wilson, D. (eds) *Images of Marketing*. Blackwell Publishing Ltd, London.

QUICK QUIZ

1   How is liquidity defined?

2   How can ratios be used?

3   If I expect to receive a payment of £10.50 in six months' time and I can earn 10% by putting money on deposit, what is the payment worth today?

4   A marketing project costing £10,000 is assessed as having a net present value of £147. Should the project go ahead?

5   What, in the context of SVA, are value drivers?

6   In simple terms, what is the formula for EVA?

7   Define ROCE.

8   Why is gearing important?

9   What is the WACC of a company?

10 'The CAPM says that the expected return of an investment equals the rate on a
.... investment, plus a .... premium.' Fill in the
blanks.

11 What is 'economic profit'?

12 What are Doyle's three value drivers?

13 How can cash flow risk be reduced?

14 What factors will influence the optimal capital structure for a company?

15 'The further into the future a cash flow occurs, the .... its present value.' Fill in
the blank.

ACTIVITY DEBRIEFS

Activity 9.1

1 Company A – low volume of sales, but high margin on each unit sold. To justify the high profit margin,
the firm might have to differentiate its offer in some way, for example, by superior service or another
differentiating factor, or by effective segmentation.

2 Company B – high volume, low margin. This might be similar to the 'Every Day Low Pricing' policy
adopted by B&Q. Its explicit aim was to increase sales volume by lowering prices. It is unlikely that A or
B would sell exactly the same product/service. Of course, they might sell the same equipment, but
augmentation to the product might be made.

Furthermore, Company A and Company B may have little option but to pursue their different strategies,
because of the characteristics of the industry and their existing position within it. This is relevant to strategic
group analysis.

Activity 9.2

Is the increased profit figure necessarily a good thing?

(a) At present, ratios are:

Profit margin	5%
Asset turnover	5 times
ROCE (5/20)	25%

(b) With the proposed changes, the profit would be 10% × £150,000 = £15,000, and the asset turnover
would be:

$$\frac{£150,000}{£75,000} = 2 \text{ times} , \text{ so that the ratios might be:}$$

Profit margin × Asset turnover = ROCE

$$10\% \times 2 \text{ times} = 20\% \text{ ie } \frac{15,000}{75,000}$$

(c) In spite of increasing the profit margin and raising the total volume of sales, the extra assets required
(£55,000) only raise total profits by £(15,000 – 5,000) = £10,000. The return on capital employed
falls from 25% to 20% because of the sharp fall in asset turnover from 5 times to 2 times. In other
words, the new investment is not used efficiently.

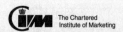

(d)   This does not mean that the management of the company would not raise its prices. However, the financial analysis has provided them with another piece of the decision-making jigsaw. It may be that this is a weakness because the owners of the business, although very happy with the increased profitability, may not be happy with the reduced ROCE. The management must judge which aspect is most acceptable.

Activity 9.3

	20X3	20X2
Current ratio	$\dfrac{572.3}{501.0} = 1.14$	$\dfrac{523.2}{420.3} = 1.24$
Quick ratio	$\dfrac{453.3}{501.0} = 0.90$	$\dfrac{414.2}{420.3} = 0.99$
Debtors payment period	$\dfrac{329.8 \times 365}{2,065.0} = 58$ days	$\dfrac{285.4 \times 365}{1,788.7} = 58$ days
Stock turnover period	$\dfrac{119.0 \times 365}{1,478.6} = 29$ days	$\dfrac{109.0 \times 365}{1,304.0} = 31$ days
Creditors turnover period	$\dfrac{236.2 \times 365}{1,478.6} = 58$ days	$\dfrac{210.8 \times 365}{1,304.0} = 59$ days

Activity 9.4

$$\boxed{£7,104}$$

Working

Using the discounting formula, $X = S \times \dfrac{1}{(1 + r)^n}$

Where: S = £16,000
      n = 12
      r = 0.07
      X = PV

$PV = £16,000 \times \dfrac{1}{1.07^{12}} = £7,104$

Activity 9.5

Year	Cash flow £	Discount factor 10%	Present value £
0		1.000	(18,000)
1	6,000	$\dfrac{1}{1.10} = 0.909$	5,454
2	8,000	$\dfrac{1}{1.10^2} = 0.826$	6,608
3	5,000	$\dfrac{1}{1.10^3} = 0.751$	3,755
4	1,000	$\dfrac{1}{1.10^4} = 0.683$	683
Net present value			(1,500)

The NPV is negative. We can therefore draw the following conclusions.

- It is cheaper to invest elsewhere at 10% than to invest in the project.
- The project would earn a return of less than 10%.
- The project is not viable (since the PV of the costs is greater than the PV of the benefits).

1   Liquid assets can be converted quickly into cash. Liquidity is an organisation's ability to convert its assets into cash to meet all the demands for payments when they fall due.

2   Generally, ratios are used for making comparisons. The same ratio can be compared year on year to see if progress is being made and different ratios can be compared to give clues to problem solutions.

3   £10

4   Yes, in theory. Any NPV greater than zero means that wealth is being increased. However, a more robust NPV might be required to allow for the uncertainty of future cash flows.

5   The factors having significant impact on shareholder value. Management attention is focused upon them.

6   Profit minus a charge for the use of capital.

7   Return on capital employed (ROCE) is the amount of profit as a percentage of capital employed (net assets).

8   (a)   If a company's gearing is too high (say over 50%), it might become difficult to raise more loans.

      (b)   Loan capital is cheaper, because the interest cost diminishes in real terms if secured on company assets and it attracts tax benefits.

      (c)   Interest must be paid, whereas the directors of a company can decide not to pay a dividend.

      (d)   High gearing might be considered risky for lenders in that the more loan capital a business has, the larger the interest payments.

9   The weighted average cost of capital (WACC) is the average of the cost of equity and the cost of debt.

10   Risk free; risk.

11   Economic profit is created when the return on a company's capital employed exceeds the cost of that capital.

12   ■   Financial
      ■   Marketing
      ■   Organisational

13   Doyle suggests that increasing customer satisfaction, loyalty and retention by deploying such techniques as loyalty programmes and measures to increase satisfaction will reduce the risk. Building good channel relationships also helps, by building an element of loyalty based on good service and by using information on demand patterns to smooth fluctuations in demand.

14   ■   The ability to carry added interest payments
      ■   The policy of the firm towards debt
      ■   The return expected on investments
      ■   The debt/equity ratio of competitors

15   Lower

The Chartered
Institute of Marketing

CHAPTER 10

Corporate and reputational risk

Introduction

Some businesses are inherently riskier than others: the degree of risk can be measured by the degree of predictability that attaches to its expected cash flows. A low risk business will have steady income from period to period, without any unexpected highs and lows. A high-risk business will have returns that vary wildly and unexpectedly from period to period, though its total long-term return may be as great or greater than the low risk operation. Generally, investors are risk averse and, as a result, they demand higher returns from high-risk businesses than from low risk ones. The high-risk business must therefore use a higher cost of capital in its shareholder value analysis than the low risk business.

Topic list

3.3.1	Utilising a range of risk analysis tools, assess the strategic risks facing an organisation in the selection of strategic alternatives leading to strategic choice:
	▪ Risk of strategic uncertainty
	▪ Risk of diverting from core business, vision and core competencies
	▪ Risk of changing technology and capability
	▪ Risk of reputation visibility and vulnerability
	▪ Financial risk, including shareholder value, investment, liability and loss
3.3.2	Assess the potential for organisational constraints to limit an organisation's success in using any given strategic choice:
	▪ Regulation
	▪ Structure and competencies
	▪ Capital and investment capability
	▪ Stakeholder/shareholder engagement and involvement
	▪ Competitor activity
3.3.3	Assess the risk to an organisation of hostile or declining markets and recommend mitigation strategies, including:
	▪ Milk, harvest, divest, liquidate, consolidate
	▪ Review margins and develop stronger cost structures
	▪ Reduce potential for proliferation of the product and/or brand
	▪ Manage share-shifting
	▪ Focus on customer
3.3.4	Recommend a range of mitigation strategies designed to reduce risks, so as to enhance an organisation's selection of a strategic option:
	▪ Scenario planning
	▪ Forecasting
	▪ Changing approach/direction
	▪ Avoidance strategies
3.4.1	Critically analyse the impact of the priority decisions on an organisation:
	▪ Strategic vision and direction
	▪ The organisation's value proposition
	▪ The key success factors
	▪ Assets and competencies
	▪ Positioning, segmentation and targeting
	▪ Distribution
	▪ Branding
	▪ Investment
	▪ Innovation
	▪ Manufacturing
	▪ Increased opportunities and threats

The Chartered Institute of Marketing

1 Strategic risks

'The conventional wisdom that the strategist should seek out growth areas often overlooks a substantial set of associated risks.' Aaker & McLoughlin (2010 p74)

Figure 10.1   Risks of high growth markets

Based on Aaker & McLoughlin (2007)

Risk must be managed and to do this, it must be quantified and its implications considered.

As Figure 10.1 illustrates, there are a number of risks associated with markets high growth markets:

- If the market growth attracts a large number of new entrants into the market, the number of competitors may become greater than the market can support

- Competitors entering the market may do so with a noticeably superior product to existing firms (enabling it to differentiate itself from existing products), or new entrants may have a cost advantage over existing firms (enabling it to pursue a cost leadership strategy successfully)

- Technology may change, meaning that a firm's product inferior to competitors' offerings

- Although the market continues to grow, the level of growth may not meet expectations - which again may lead to over-crowding in the market. This is likely to lead to price wars, and could see a shake-out in the market, as some competitors decide to leave.

- Price instability may result – either from overcapacity, or from retailers using promotional offers to attract customers

- Key success factors (KSFs) might change, and an organisation may not be able to adapt its offering to meet the new requirements. Aaker & McLoughlin (2010) highlight that many product markets have experienced shift over time from a focus on product technology, to a focus on process technology and low-cost production as the product becomes more standardised. A firm which may might be capable of achieving competitive advantages through its product technology may not have the resources, competencies and culture to develop the process technology-based advantages that the evolving market demands.

- The company's resources might not be sufficient to maintain a high growth rate (for example, it may not have sufficient finances to be able to invest in new production equipment)

- Adequate distribution networks and channels may not be available. Many distribution channels can only support a small number of brands. For example, retailers will only have shelf space for a small number of electrical appliances. Therefore, some competitors will not be able to get their products stocked, even though they may be attractive products.

This last points also highlights the potential bargaining power of distributors (retailers), particularly as market growth begins to slow. They could use this power to extract price or promotion concessions from manufacturers. These concessions could be particularly beneficial in helping the distributors to sustain their margins, particularly if the distributors, in turn, are facing increased competitive pressure (eg on price) to retain customers.

1.1 Assessing risk and uncertainties

> ▶ **Key term**
>
> **Strategic uncertainties** focus on specific unknown factors that will impact a strategic decision. For example, for a holiday firm thinking of extending its market from budget to luxury accommodation and tours to more unusual destinations, a key strategic uncertainty might be 'What is the likely future demand for luxury travel to certain countries?'

The impact of strategic uncertainties was discussed in Chapter 1 in the context of the external environment.

In Chapter 1 we also highlighted the environmental context (macroenvironment and microenvironment) in which organisations operate, and the opportunities and threats which the environment presents also create uncertainties for an organisation.

These factors (which could be assessed through PEST analysis, or SWOT analysis, for example) include:

- New developments in technology, including the growth of the internet and e-commerce
- The emergence of new market opportunities
- The internationalisation of markets
- Economic growth/decline
- The emergence of new and/or aggressive competitors
- The emergence of substitute products
- The emergence of new distribution channels
- Increased legislative demands

Therefore within their strategic analysis organisations need to be asking:

- What changes are taking place in the environment?
- How will those changes affect the organisation, its activities and how/where it competes?
- What resources does the organisation have to deal with the changes?

In this context, Gilligan & Wilson (2009) highlight the importance of an external **marketing audit** in helping to identify the opportunities and threats facing an organisation. However, Gilligan & Wilson also note that it is important that the audit does not simply lead to a list of opportunities and threats being identified, but also that they are sorted according to their significance for an organisation.

Figure 10.2:   Responding to opportunities and threats

Probability of occurence

Low ——————————————————————▶ High

Significance to the organisation	High ↑ / ↓ Low	Develop a scenario plan	Think about possible contingency plans	Analyse and plan in detail
		Review periodically	Monitor on an ongoing but general basis	Monitor closely and plan
		Monitor in very general terms	Review periodically	Monitor and review

Based on Gilligan & Wilson, (2009)

The Chartered Institute of Marketing

1.2 Analysing strategic opportunities

It is also important to remember that the logic driving many companies' strategies is that they are looking for ways to create and capture value, either by launching new, innovative products and/or by entering new markets, or even by acquiring other companies.

However, any such strategic choices also lead to strategic risk. This risk arises as a result of an organisation committing to a specific way of creating value in a particular marketplace. However, this commitment could then be undermined by different sets of circumstances which the organisation may not be able to control. The commitments may have seemed entirely reasonable when they were, but there is simply no guarantee that they will be successful. For example, Mini-disc may have seemed like a potentially successful new product when they were launched, but they never captured market share anywhere except Japan and they have subsequently been superceded by MP3 players.

This also highlights that the opportunities or threats which an organisation identifies should not be viewed as 'absolutes.' For example, an opportunity which might initially seem very promising might become less so when examined against an organisation's resources, its culture, the expectations of its shareholders, or the feasibility of actually implementing it.

Therefore it could be useful to rank opportunities according to the probability of them being successful, and their attractiveness:

Figure 10.3:   The opportunity matrix

<table>
<tr><td></td><td colspan="2">Probability of success</td></tr>
<tr><td></td><td>High</td><td>Low</td></tr>
<tr><td>Low (Attractiveness of opportunity)</td><td>1</td><td>2</td></tr>
<tr><td>High (Attractiveness of opportunity)</td><td>3</td><td>4</td></tr>
</table>

Based on Gilligan & Wilson, (2009)

Cell 1 consists of the opportunities offering the greatest scope for an organisation, so it should focus primarily on any opportunities it identifies in this cell.

The probability of success could be influenced by a number of factors, but perhaps the most important ones are the extent to which the organisation's strengths and its distinctive capabilities match the key success requirements for operating effectively in the target market, *and* exceed those of its competitors.

1.2.1 Factors influencing strategic risk

Factors that determine the level of strategic risks a business will face include:

- The types of industries/markets within which the business operates
- The state of the economy
- The actions of competitors and the possibility of mergers and acquisitions
- The stage in a product's life cycle, higher risks in the introductory and declining stages
- The dependence upon inputs with fluctuating prices, eg wheat, oil etc

- The level of operating gearing – the proportion of fixed costs to total costs
- The flexibility of production processes to adapt to different specifications or products
- The organisation's research and development capacity and ability to innovate
- The significance of new technology

There may be little management can do about some of these risks, they are inherent in business activity. However, strategies such as **diversification** can contribute substantially to the reduction of many business risks.

1.3 Types of risk

- **Physical risk**, such as fire, earthquakes, computer failure.
- **Economic risk**. The strategy might be based on assumptions as to the economy which might turn out to be wrong.

- **Financial risk** relates to the type of financial arrangement in the decision, and the quality of the cash flows. The potential for erosion of shareholder value (see below).

- **Business risk**. These risks relate to commercial and industry factors. In other words, there is the possibility that the strategy will fail because of new technology, competitors, customer reaction, operational failures. Diverting from the core business carries with it another type of business risk, ie that the business does not have the resources or expertise to carry out the strategy

  Two particularly important risks within business risk are:

  Competitor risk – the threats to cash flows arising from the actions of competitors. For example, the risk that a competitor introduces a new product which offers customers' greater value than your product; or the risk that competitors reduce the price of their product so that it becomes more attractive to customers because it is cheaper than yours.

  Product risk – the risk that revenues from products falls; for example, due to a change in customer tastes or trends. However, product risk also includes the risk of producing a poor quality product which could lead to a reduction in customer satisfaction, with any decline in customer loyalty and future sales which might result from this. (For example, this is the issue which faced Toyota in 2010, when they had to recall millions of cars due to potential problems with faulty accelerator pedals).

- **Political or country risk** includes nationalisation, sanctions, civil war and political instability, if these have an impact on the business.

- **Exchange risk**. Changes in exchange rates affect the value of a transaction in a foreign currency.

- **Information risk**. The data may not be reliable.

Another issue an organisation needs to consider is the potential dilemma between risk and innovation. Organisations need to develop new ideas and translate them into new products or services if they are to remain competitive. However, at the same time organisations need stable and efficient day-to-day operations in order to accomplish their routine tasks effectively. The process of introducing new ideas and process might disrupt day-to-day tasks in the short term, but if an organisation avoids introducing any new ideas this is likely to damage its competitiveness in the longer term.

Any of the factors arising from the different types of risk we have mentioned could also contribute to:

- **Reputation risk**. Reputation risk is any risk to an organisation's reputation which is likely to destroy shareholder value. In effect, reputational risk is the risk of negative perceptions about an organisation from any of its key stakeholders. And, as such, it is likely to arise from other kinds of risk. For example, it might result from an ill-conceived business plan (business risk), or as a result of a funding crisis (financial risk).

The Chartered
Institute of Marketing

Reputation risk is likely to lead to negative publicity for an organisation, but could also lead to loss of revenue and profits; loss of customers, suppliers or distributors; or loss of employees and difficulty in recruiting new talent.

1.4 Risk appraisal in strategy evaluation

Some strategies are inherently more risky than others.

We can see this by looking at the different strategic options suggested by the Ansoff matrix.

Market penetration is the lowest risk option of the four, because it involves targeting market segments a firm already understands, using products or services it already knows.

Product development (developing new products to serve existing markets) carries more risk that market penetration because it involves a new product; so there will be uncertainty about how that product will be perceived by the organisation's existing customers. There could also be a risk that there will be a degree of cannibalisation between the new product and the organisation's existing products; in other words, rather than gaining additional revenue by introducing the new product, customers will switch from the existing product to the new product.

Market development (selling existing products in new markets or new market segments) is likely to carry more risk than either product development or market penetration. Before an organisation enters a new market, it will need to undertake an environmental analysis in order to understand the new market: to assess how attractive the market is, and whether the organisation's product has the necessary attributes to be successful in it.

In a product development strategy, there is likely to be some uncertainty as to how well existing products, without any modifications, will satisfy the requirements of customers in different market segments, which it does not currently serve.

Diversification is probably the riskiest of the four alternatives identified, because involves both new products and new markets. Conversely, though, because it utilises new products and new markets, the potential returns from diversification could be higher than those from the other alternative approaches.

Producing new products is likely to require an increase in resources used, and a reasonable amount of investment. Therefore, an organisation will have to consider how feasible such an approach is before committing to it.

Equally, an organisation will need to analyse the microenvironment (including customers, competitors, and distributors) in its target market or market segment before deciding to enter it.

1.4.1 Reliability of data

One of the problems arising when evaluating alternative strategies is the reliability of the data used. Since the figures are compiled on estimates of the future, there must be considerable uncertainty about the final accuracy of the figures. Business planners frequently use the following:

- **Operational research** techniques to measure the degree of uncertainty involved
- **Probability theory** to express the likelihood of a forecast result occurring

1.4.2 Risk and evaluating strategies

1   If an individual strategy involves an **unacceptable amount of risk** it should be eliminated from further consideration in the planning process.

2   However, the risk of an **individual strategy** should also be considered in the context of the **overall 'portfolio' of investment strategies** and products adopted by the company.

Risk can be quantified in statistical terms. In decision trees, a variety of possible outcomes are developed. Each is given an **expected value (EV)**, based on probabilities. The EVs at each decision point are then aggregated to produce an EV for the decision as a whole. However, the EVs do not deal in the relative riskiness of each project.

1   Project A might offer **profits** of £1,000,000 and **losses** of £500,000. If the probability of each is 50:50, the EV is (£1,000,000 × 50%) – (£500,000 × 50%) = £250,000.

2   Project B offers a 75% probability of a £300,000 profit and a 25% probability of a loss of £100,000. The EV is thus £200,000 ie (£300,000 × 0.75%) – (£100,000 × 25%)

Project A would be favoured, on a basis of EV **alone**, which is £250,000. There is a much higher prospect of **large** profits or **large** losses compared to project B. However, A is much more **risky** as the spread of outcomes is diverse.

ACTIVITY 10.1

The daily sales of Product T may be as follows.

Units	Probability
1,000	0.2
2,000	0.3
3,000	0.4
4,000	0.1
	1.0

Required

Calculate the expected daily sales.

Sensitivity analysis involves asking 'what if?' questions. By changing the value of different variables in the model, a number of different **scenarios** for the future will be produced. Price rises can be altered to 10% from 5%, demand for a product can be reduced from 100,000 to 80,000, the introduction of new processing equipment can be deferred by six months, on the revised assumption that there will be delays, and so on. Sensitivity analysis can be formalised by identifying **key variables** in the model and then changing the value of each, perhaps in progressive steps. For example, prices might be increased in steps by 5%, 7½%, 10%, 12½% and 15% and the effect on demand, profits and cash flows under each of these assumptions can be tested.

Sensitivity analysis would show which were the **key variables**.

Example

A company is producing a new product and a key variable is time to market. If it launches on time, it will sell 1,000 units at £10 each. If it is a month late, demand will fall by 50%. Each unit costs £5 to make. The company has learned that a material supplier has gone out of business. It can get the material for the same price, at the expense of being a month late, or it can pay £1 per unit more for the material and keep to the original deadline.

	Original plan £	Month delay £	Pay more for material £
Revenue	10,000	5,000	10,000
Cost	5,000	2,500	6,000
Profit	5,000	2,000	4,000

In this example we can see that profits are more sensitive to **demand** than to costs, so the firm would pay more for the new material.

A firm has a choice.

- Apply the most stringent controls to the most critical variables
- Alter the plans so that the most critical variables are no longer as critical
- When different planning options are available, choose a lower-risk plan

2 Organisational constraints

'Consideration of organisational components [structure, systems, people and culture] can help a business identify actual and potential implementation problems, as well as determine how its organisation would adapt to a new strategy.' Aaker & McLoughlin (2007, p322)

The internal organisation of a company – its structure, systems, people and culture – can be an important source of both strengths and weaknesses. However, internal organisation could also affect the feasibility of some strategies; and in order to be successful there needs to be a 'fit' between the strategy and the elements of an organisation (Aaker & McLoughlin, 2010). If the strategy does not fit well with the internal elements, it may be expensive – or even impossible – to make the strategy work.

Financial resources and constraints

Another important decision companies have to make is whether or not to invest in particular products, business units or markets, or whether they should withdraw cash from particular areas (to help finance other areas). And a fundamental consideration underlying such decisions will be the level of financial resources they have available to invest; or whether they can obtain the finance they need, by either debt or equity financing.

2.1 Organisational strengths and weaknesses

When considering potential internal constraints which could affect a strategic decision, it is important to remember that one of the key assessments which should underpin any strategic decision is an assessment of organisational strengths and weaknesses.

Gilligan & Wilson (2009, p 270) identify a number of factors (weaknesses) which could make an organisation vulnerable to the actions of competitors. However, these factors could equally be seen as constraints which could limit the organisation's success:

Marketing factors

- Strengths are predominantly in declining market sectors
- Little presence in growing and/or high margin markets
- Low market share
- Distribution weaknesses
- Weak segmentation of the market
- Unclear and/or unsustainable positioning
- Weak reputation and/or poorly-defined image

Financial factors

- Cash flow problems
- Under-funding (and lack of investment resources)
- Low margins
- High-cost operations and/or distribution

Market- and performance-related factors

- Slow growth in market or limited scope for growth
- Overdependence on one market

- Overdependence on a small number of customers (or even on a single customer)

Product-related factors

- Outdated products and a failure to innovate
- Product weaknesses (eg inferior designs to rival products; quality issues)
- Weak or non-existent selling propositions

Managerial factors

- Over-confidence, or unjustified confidence in the organisation's ability to succeed
- Managerial arrogance, and a belief that the organisation has an automatic right to retain its place in the market
- Short-term orientation (eg focus on short-term profits, rather than on future investment)
- Poor management of staff
- Failure to prioritise and focus on what is important
- Competitive arrogance, and failure to see (or acknowledge) competitive threats
- Managerial predictability and strict adherence to well-tried formulae (rather than being prepared to try anything new)

Bureaucratic structures

- Product or service obsolescence/weaknesses
- Fixation with annual budgets and short term financial performance (rather than considering the longer term or non-financial aspects of performance; eg quality, or customer service)

▶ **Exam tip**

Chapter 4 is specifically devoted to organisational capability. Note that the syllabus lists the following organisational constraints:

- **Regulation** – legal influences on a business should be familiar to you from your studies of PEST factors

- **Structure and competencies** – see Chapter 3 on the internal marketing environment, which includes organisational performance.

- **Capital and investment capability** – see Chapter 9 on financial assessment of marketing opportunities

- **Stakeholder/shareholder** engagement and involvement – see Chapter 5 for a discussion of stakeholder analysis and relationships

- **Competitor activity** – Chapter 1 discusses the competitive environment

---

2.2 Strategic issues analysis

In Chapter 1 we introduced the idea of the marketing audit, and one of the key elements of the marketing audit is strategic issues analysis.

Strategic issues analysis examines the suitability of marketing objectives and segmentation based on the light of changes in the market place (Jobber, 2010, p. 44).

As a result of the analysis, competitive advantages and core competences on which marketing objectives and segmentation are based may need to be reassessed, and positioning in the market critically reviewed.

However, Jobber (2010) also highlights that one of the dangers a company faces is moving away from its core competences into areas where its skills and capabilities do not provide a competitive advantage. Jobber cites the example of the toy brick maker Lego, which tried (unsuccessfully) to diversity into the manufacture of clothing, bags and accessories – areas which required very different skills to making and marketing toy bricks. This diversification led to Lego over-complicating its product portfolio and overstretching its brand. So its solution was to re-focus on its core brick-based product range, and focus back on its key target group – boys aged between five and nine years old.

The Chartered Institute of Marketing

2.2.1 Portfolio analysis

Another element of strategic issues analysis is portfolio analysis, which can be carried out using the BCG matrix, General Electric business screen (Market Attractiveness - Competitive Position model), or the Shell Directional Policy Matrix – models which we discussed in Chapter 3 earlier.

These models illustrate that building sales and market share is not the only strategy objective for a product or a business unit. For example, in some cases, harvesting (where sales and market share are allowed to fall, but profit margins are maximised) may be more appropriate. However, portfolio models, in conjunction with life cycle models, highlight that a firm should try to have a balanced portfolio in order to maintain a sustainable competitive advantage over its rivals.

3 Hostile and declining markets

'A declining market involves a fall in demand, often caused by an external event such as the creation of a competing technology, a change in customer needs or tastes, or a shift in government policy.' Aaker & McLoughlin (2007) p296

Markets decline because of **environmental factors**. However, some market can be revitalised. In others, a firm has to choose whether it wants to stay in the market or withdraw.

Many of the portfolio models assume that markets are growing. However, this is certainly not the case in many markets, but firms within them still have to develop strategies to survive.

The **GE Business Screen** model could be useful for highlighting the possible options (growth, survival or divestment) an organisation should consider, based on attractiveness of a market and the organisation's position in it.

Figure 10.4:   GE Business Screen and strategic options

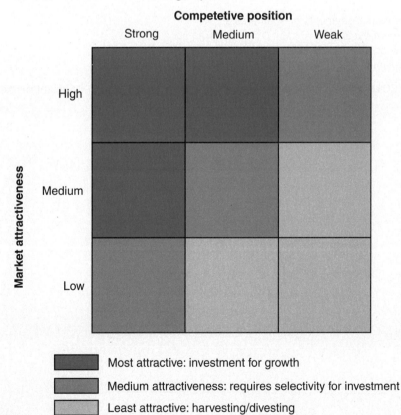

Most attractive: investment for growth

Medium attractiveness: requires selectivity for investment

Least attractive: harvesting/divesting

Equally, the **product life cycle** concept could be useful for highlighting potential marketing objectives and strategies for products in the mature or decline stages of their life cycle.

3.1 Declining markets

3.1.1 Why do markets decline?

- Obsolete technology
- Change in customer needs or customer tastes and trends, leading to a fall in demand

Strategic alternatives include:

- Revitalising the market
- Becoming a profitable survivor
- Milk (harvest) or divest (withdraw)

3.1.2 Revitalising the market

Some products (or markets) go into decline not because they are inherently unpopular but because they have suffered from a lack of investment. Ironically, the conventional strategy applications for the decline stage (eg low marketing expenditures and little promotion) could have contributed to the decline in sales and profits.

Jobber (2010) suggests the cinema market in the UK was a good example of this. Long periods of under-investment had led to cinemas becoming dull and unexciting places by the 1980s, offering a limited choice of films as their owners employed a classic 'harvest' strategy. However, one company saw this as a marketing opportunity and Showcase Cinemas was launched (in 1986) offering a wide choice of films in modern purpose-built premises near large conurbations. This changed the experience of going to the cinema, resulting in a revitalisation of the industry and a growth in cinema attendances and profits.

Possible ways to revitalise the market include:

- Identifying new market segments or submarkets
- Introducing new products
- Introducing new applications of existing products
- Changing the market

Aaker & McLoughlin (2010) offer the following summary of routes to revitalising a stagnant market:

Figure 10.5   Revitalising a stagnant market

Aaker & McLoughlin (2010)

When Tim Richards decided to leave his job as a high-flying executive at Warner Brothers in 1998 to create a UK cinema business, there were those who had their doubts.

After all, cinema attendance at that time was stagnating and, after a period of aggressive expansion, even Warner Brothers had ceased the development of new circuits. This, plus the rise and proliferation of new forms of home entertainment such as video games and DVDs, appeared almost to sound the death knell for the industry.

Yet Vue Entertainment has grown from strength to strength. From a garage-based start-up operating one cinema, it operated 68 multiplex cinemas across the UK by 2010, and accounted for more than 20% of the market, when it was sold to the private equity firm Doughty Hanson in a deal which valued the business at about £450m. In turn, the deal with Doughty paved the way for Richards and Alan McNair (his deputy chief executive) to expand the chain further.

However, the deal Doughty also showed that the cinema market itself had become an attractive investment proposition, due to the growing popularity of 3D films which is set to boost the UK cinema market over the coming years.

Nonetheless, Vue's success had come as no surprise to Mr Richards . . .

'No matter how big TVs get. No matter how sophisticated surround sound systems get, people are always going to want to get out and see a movie . . .

'We are inherently social beings who enjoy a laugh collectively. We enjoy being scared and frightened together. There will always be a demand for that. You just have to give spectators a really good reason to go back to the theatres.'

In particular, Mr Richards wanted to break away from the 'nightclub feel' of UK cinemas in the 1990s, which he felt alienated a very large segment of the cinema going audience.

'We wanted to make cinemas more accessible and accommodating to a broader group of people, especially greying baby boomers,' he says. 'These are the people with higher disposable income and more leisure time, yet their needs are not being catered to . . .

'We invested fairly heavily to give the cinemas a new and more upmarket look,' he says. 'It's no longer the horrible old flea pit or the loud flashing discotheque that made families and older people stop going to the cinemas so many years ago'

This move to reposition cinemas appears to have been taken up by all the major cinema operators in the UK. Vue and Odeon now offer premium seating options within their cinemas. However, Cineworld has taken the shift one stage further, and in 2011 opened a new 'premium cinema experience' called The Screening Rooms, in Cheltenham.

The Screening Rooms were housed in a conversion from an existing Cineworld site. They target the over 45 cinema-goer, and under 18s are only allowed in with a parent. Positioned as a deluxe experience, they offer a 'boutique style bar and at seat service' with ticket prices ranging from £8 to £19 depending on the time of day.

Sourced from: Kwan Yuk Pan, Reel Sense of achievement, *Financial Times,* 14 November 2006

Goff, S & Arnold, M (2010) Doughty Hanson buys Vue cinemas, Financial Times, 7 November 2010, www.ft.com

Johnson, B. (2011) Cineworld unveils marketing for deluxe brand, Marketing Week, 7 July 2011, www.marketingweek.co.uk

3.1.3 Becoming a profitable survivor

In such a situation, a firm decides to become the sole survivor in a declining market. A strong survivor can be profitable because of the lack of competition facing it. However, in order to achieve such a position, a firm may have to incur losses while competitors drop out. Moreover, if the firm fears that it could take a long time for competitors to drop out, it may have to accelerate their exit from the market. The cornerstone in a 'sole survivor' strategy is to encourage competitors to exit the market (Aaker & McLoughlin, 2010).

Possible ways (Aaker & McLoughin, (2010); Jobber, (2010)) an organisation could try to encourage competitors to exit the market are through:

- Making clear its commitment to be the surviving leader in the industry

- Further reducing the attractiveness of the market to the competitor, for example by introducing price cuts or by increasing its promotional expenditure

- Introducing new products and covering new market segments, thereby making it more difficult for competitors to find a profitable niche in the market

- Reducing the barriers which may be preventing competitors from exiting the market; for example, by agreeing to take over their long-term contracts (for example, for supplying spare parts or maintenance agreements) in exchange for the competitor dropping out of the market.

However, the ultimate way for an organisation to remove a competitor is by acquiring that competitor or its product lines which compete in the market in question. (A firm might be able to make such acquisitions quite cheaply due to the markets being relatively unattractive.)

This approach has the added advantage that the organisation knows that the competitor can no longer be taken over by another organisation (which could potentially be pursuing a similar strategy to itself.)

Once the survivor has established itself as the sole supplier in the market, it can enjoy the benefits of a monopoly, and so can raise prices and resume profitable operations.

3.1.4 Milk, harvest and withdraw

A milking (or harvesting) strategy aims to generate cash flow by reducing investment and operating expenses, even if doing so leads to a reduction in sales and market share. The underlying assumptions here are that funds can be better employed elsewhere; the business being 'milked' is not central to a company (either financially or through synergies with other parts of the company) and that 'milking' is feasible because sales will decline relatively slowly (Aaker & McLoughlin, 2010).

Milking strategies are likely to involve minimal promotional expenditure; using premium pricing where possible; reducing product variability and controlling costs rigidly.

The aim of such a strategy is to 'milk' the business and extract maximum revenue from it over a short period, despite the potential loss of longer-term future sales. In effect, a company pursuing a milking strategy will rely on the short-term loyalty of customers to cushion the effect of declining sales.

Profits can still be made under a milking strategy. However employees and customers may fear the lack of commitment and go elsewhere. Nonetheless, a milking or harvesting strategy could be reversed, as the firm still has a market presence.

Conditions favouring a **harvesting** (milking**) strategy** (Aaker & McLoughlin, 2010):

- The decline rate is pronounced and is unlikely to change. However , some pockets of demand still exist and the decline rate is not too steep
- There is enough customer loyalty to generate some profits during the 'milking' stage
- The price level is stable and still profitable (for efficient firms)
- The business is not central to the current strategic direction , therefore the risk of losing strategic position overall is low
- There are sufficient resources to ensure that the milking strategy can be successfully managed

By contrast, the following conditions would suggest that an **exit decision** would be the most appropriate:

- The decline is rapid and accelerating
- Price pressures are extreme (through competition and lack of brand loyalty)
- Business position is weak against competitors
- Strategic direction has changed, and the role of the business is superfluous
- Exit barriers can be overcome

3.2 Hostile environments

Aaker and McLoughlin (2010) write on the conditions for hostile markets to exist. These include overcapacity, low margins, intense competition and management in turmoil. They continue to remark that most industries are hostile or likely to become so.

These characteristics of overcapacity, low margins and intense competition could also be seen as characteristic of industries or products which are in the mature stages of their life cycles, moving into the decline phase.

> ▶ **Key term**
> **Hostility** arises from a decline in demand and/or competitive expansion.

One approach is to describe a six-phase cycle for hostile markets.

Phase 1: **Margin pressure**. Overcapacity leads to predatory pricing, benefiting large customers

Phase 2: **Share shift**. Each year, up to 5% of market share will shift under price pressure, and is difficult to regain

Phase 3: **Product proliferation**. Firms create excess value by adding new lines

Phase 4: **Self-defeating cost reduction**. Firms cut costs but, in doing so, weaken themselves

Phase 5:   **Shakeout**. Closures, mergers

Phase 6:   **Rescue**. Some markets recover with fewer companies competing

3.2.1 Winning in hostile markets

- Focus on **large customers**, to benefit from economies of scale
- **Differentiate on intangible factors** such as reliability and relationships
- Offer a broad **array of products** at a variety of prices
- Turn price into a commodity by **removing price from the customer's buying criteria**
- **Control cost** structures

3.3 Wear-out and renewal

> ▸ **Key term**
>
> **Strategic wear-out** occurs when firms continue with old strategies that are no longer viable.

Strategic and tactical **wear-out** is the problem that any organisation will face if it retains its current strategies and tactics without any review or consideration of changed circumstances.

The following factors give rise to wear-out.

- Market changes
    - Customer requirements
    - Distribution requirements
- Competitor innovations
- Internal factors

- Poor cost control
- Lack of consistent investment
- Ill-advised tinkering with successful strategies

Some organisations still continue to pursue marketing programmes long after their effectiveness has diminished. Many reasons can be put forward to explain this.

1 **Fear of change**. Most people are afraid of change, preferring to stay in their own comfort zone.

2 **Change is becoming harder to forecast**. Many organisations opt to stay with what is familiar.

3 **'If it ain't broke, don't fix it!'** Market leaders, having developed a successful strategy, are understandably reluctant to change it.

4 **Change too late**. The need for change often only becomes apparent when the gap between what a company is doing and what it should be doing increases to a point at which performance suffers in an obvious way.

5 **Failure to learn**. Companies fail because managers' **theory of the business** no longer works. A theory of the business contains the assumptions (about markets, technology etc) that shape any organisation's behaviour.

6 **The wrong customers**. Keeping too close to existing customers, rather than thinking about future customers, can also result in strategic wearout: 'an industry's leaders are rarely in the forefront of commercialising new technologies that do not initially meet the functional demands of mainstream customers'.

7 **New technologies** are developed and take industry leaders unawares.

8 **Failure to look**. Some organisations do not have environmental monitoring and strategic review procedures embedded within their marketing planning systems.

Four interlinked avenues of action are required to overcome the danger of strategic wear-out.

1 **Regular and detailed reviews** of each of the significant elements of the external environment
2 **Identification** of the ways these elements are changing
3 **Evaluation** of the implications of these changes on the organisation
4 **Internal audit** to establish the appropriateness of actions both currently and for the future

In order to avoid strategic wear-out a multi-functional perspective is required. A combination of strategic, organisational and cultural change is required. Companies are likely to be unsuccessful in maintaining change unless five demanding criteria are met.

- **Coherence** of direction, actions and timing
- **Environmental** assessment of competitors, customers and regulatory climate
- **Leading** change by creating the correct climate
- **Linking** strategic with operational change (communication and reward systems)
- Treating **people as assets** and investments rather than costs

---

▶ **Exam tip**

A past examination question at this level was based on a manufacturing company suffering from strategic wear-out. The requirement was to say how the firm should reassess its capabilities and use them to exploit a new opportunity. The value chain is the obvious model to use when answering this question.

This illustrates an important point about examinations at this level: it is easy to think of each exam as a separate and distinct entity, but this is not the case. You must be prepared to treat the entire level as an integrated whole and, as in this example, be prepared to apply knowledge you have gained from studying for a particular paper to the other exams if appropriate.

4 Impact analysis

An important objective of external analysis is to rank the strategic uncertainties which an organisation faces in order to decide how they should be managed over time. (Aaker & McLoughlin, 2010.)

As we identified in Chapter 1, impact analysis can be used to help assess the relative importance of different strategic uncertainties. Aaker & McLoughlin identify the two key variables which need to be assessed in impact analysis are the potential **impact** of the uncertainty and the **immediacy** of it.

In more general terms, the importance of the impact analysis matrix is that highlights the importance of ranking potential risks, based on the **likelihood** of them occurring, and the potential **effects** they could have on an organisation.

Risks (or threats) which fall into the top right hand quadrant of the matrix are both serious and have a high probability of occurring. Because of this, organisations need to analyse and developments in relation to them very carefully and develop a strategy to deal with them.

Figure 10.6:   Impact analysis

	Immediacy	
	Low	**High**
High	Monitor, analyse and consider contingent strategies	Analyse in detail and develop a strategy
Low	Monitor	Monitor and analyse

(Impact — vertical axis label)

Based on Aaker & McLoughlin (2010)

▶ **Exam tip**

Aaker & McLoughlin (2010, p. 93) give the example of a beer firm thinking about the future prospects of the microbrewery market. It has a proposed entry into the microbrewery market, but it already has an imported beer positioned in the same area.

An impact analysis based upon the syllabus criteria could look like this:

1   **Strategic vision and direction** – is a microbrewery compatible with the beer firm's existing position?

2   **Value proposition** – the company might adopt a position along the lines of 'quality beers for discerning customers'

3   **Key success factors** – quality, availability, innovation.

4   **Assets and competencies** – can they run the new business?

5   **Positioning, segmentation and targeting** – this is a niche market, requiring specialist expertise to deliver to demanding and expert customers.

6   **Distribution** – dependent upon pubs and retailers; packaging considerations (bottles, cans etc)

7   **Branding** – should the company use its existing brand, or design a new one?

8   **Investment** – resources may be overstretched. What is the payback?

9   **Innovation and manufacturing** – developing the capability and capacity to deliver the new product.

10   **Increased opportunities and threats** – this is a new market, with other players already established; does the company have the resources to support market growth?

CHAPTER ROUNDUP

- Utilising a range of risk analysis tools, assess the strategic risks facing an organisation in the selection of strategic alternatives leading to strategic choice

- Assess the potential for organisational constraints to limit an organisation's success in using any given strategic choice

- Assess the risk to an organisation of hostile or declining markets and recommend mitigation strategies

- Recommend a range of mitigation strategies designed to reduce risks, so as to enhance an organisation's selection of a strategic option

- Critically analyse the impact of the priority decisions on an organisation

FURTHER READING

Mazzarol, T., Sweeney, J.C. & Soutar, G.N. (2007) Conceptualising word-of-mouth activity, triggers and conditions: an exploratory study, *European Journal of Marketing*, 41, 11/12, pp. 1475-1494.

Ries, A & Ries, L. (2002) *The Fall of Advertising and the Rise of PR*. Harper, New York.

REFERENCES

Aaker, D. & McLoughlin, D. (2007) *Strategic Market Management.* John Wiley, Chichester.

Aaker, D. & McLoughlin, D. (2010) *Strategic Market Management: Global Perspectives.* John Wiley, Chichester.

Gilligan, C. & Wilson, R. (2009) Strategic Marketing Planning, (2nd edition), Butterworth-Heinemann, Oxford.

Jobber, D. (2010) Principles and Practice of Marketing, (6th edition), McGraw-Hill, Maidenhead.

QUICK QUIZ

1   What are the three risks in high growth markets as identified by Aaker and McLoughlin?

2   What is 'business risk'?

3   What are the potential organisational constraints identified by the syllabus?

4   What is the application of probability theory to risk appraisal?

5   Why do markets decline?

6   How does a company become a profitable survivor?

7   How does a company win in a hostile market?

8   Why would a company 'milk' a market, rather than exit?

Activity 10.1

The EV of daily sales may be calculated by multiplying each possible outcome (volume of daily sales) by the probability that this outcome will occur.

Units	Probability	Expected value Units
1,000	0.2	200
2,000	0.3	600
3,000	0.4	1,200
4,000	0.1	400
		EV of daily sales 2,400

In the long run the expected value should be approximately the actual average, if the event occurs many times over. In the example above, we do not expect sales on any one day to equal 2,400 units, but over a large number of days, average sales should equal 2,400 units a day

QUICK QUIZ ANSWERS

1   Competitive risk, market changes and company limitations.

2   Business risk relates to commercial and industry factors: the possibility that the strategy will fail because of new technology, competitors, customer reaction or operational failures. Diverting from the core business carries with it another type of business risk, ie that the business does not have the resources or expertise to carry out the strategy.

3
- Regulation
- Structure and competences
- Capital and investment capability
- Stakeholder/shareholder engagement and involvement
- Competitor activity

4   Probability theory can be used to assess the likelihood of a forecast event occurring, and this will help to assess the level of risk

5
- Obsolete technology
- Change in customer needs, leading to fall in demand
- Alternative satisfactions

6
- Make a visible commitment to the market, as a signal to other competitors.
- Encourage competitors to leave by aggressive competition or by making it easier for them to quit.
- Purchase the competitor's capacity, close it down and carry on in a smaller niche.

7
- Focus on large customers, to benefit from economies of scale
- Differentiate on intangible factors such as reliability and relationships
- Offer a broad array of products at a variety of prices
- Turn price into a commodity by removing price from the customer's buying criteria
- Control cost structures

The Chartered
Institute of Marketing

8   ■   The decline rate is pronounced and 'set in', but some demand still exists to ensure that the decline rate is not too steep.

■   The price level is stable and still profitable.

■   There is enough customer loyalty to generate some profits during the 'milking' mode.

■   The business is not central to the current strategic direction.

■   There are resources to ensure that the milking strategy can be successfully managed.

When less favourable conditions exist (eg prices are under pressure, or the decline rate is steep, or there has been a change in strategic direction) then an exit strategy may be preferred.

Analysis and Decision

The Chartered
Institute of Marketing

Index

The Chartered
Institute of Marketing

The Chartered
Institute of Marketing

The Chartered
Institute of Marketing

The Chartered
Institute of Marketing

The Chartered
Institute of Marketing

The Chartered
Institute of Marketing

The Chartered
Institute of Marketing

The Chartered
Institute of Marketing

Review form

Please help us to ensure that the CIM learning materials we produce remain as accurate and user-friendly as possible. We cannot promise to answer every submission we receive, but we do promise that it will be read and taken into account when we update this Study Text.

Name: _____   Address: _____

_____

_____

1. How have you used this Text?
(Tick one box only)

☐ Self study (book only)

☐ On a course: college_____

☐ Other _____

3. Why did you decide to purchase this Text?
(Tick one box only)

☐ Have used companion Assessment workbook

☐ Have used BPP Texts in the past

☐ Recommendation by friend/colleague

☐ Recommendation by a lecturer at college

☐ Saw advertising in journals

☐ Saw information on BPP website

☐ Other _____

2. During the past six months do you recall seeing/receiving any of the following?
(Tick as many boxes as are relevant)

☐ Our advertisement in *The Marketer*

☐ Our brochure with a letter through the post

☐ Our website www.bpp.com

4. Which (if any) aspects of our advertising do you find useful?
(Tick as many boxes as are relevant)

☐ Prices and publication dates of new editions

☐ Information on product content

☐ Facility to order books off-the-page

☐ None of the above

5. Have you used the companion Assessment Workbook?   Yes ☐   No ☐

6. Have you used the companion Passcards?   Yes ☐   No ☐

7. Your ratings, comments and suggestions would be appreciated on the following areas.

	Very useful	Useful	Not useful
Introductory section (How to use this text, study checklist, etc)	☐	☐	☐
Chapter introductions	☐	☐	☐
Syllabus learning outcomes	☐	☐	☐
Activities	☐	☐	☐
The Real World examples	☐	☐	☐
Quick quizzes	☐	☐	
Quality of explanations			
Index	☐	☐	☐
Structure and presentation	☐	☐	☐

	Excellent	Good	Adequate	Poor
Overall opinion of this Text	☐	☐	☐	☐

8. Do you intend to continue using BPP CIM products?   ☐ Yes   ☐ No

On the reverse of this page is space for you to write your comments about our Study Text. We welcome your feedback.

Please return to: CIM Publishing Manager, BPP Learning Media, FREEPOST, London, W12 8BR.

TELL US WHAT YOU THINK

Please note any further comments and suggestions/errors below. For example, was the text accurate, readable, concise, user-friendly and comprehensive?